SOVIETISTAN

SOVIETISTAN

TRAVELS IN TURKMENISTAN, KAZAKHSTAN, TAJIKISTAN, KYRGYZSTAN, AND UZBEKISTAN

ERIKA FATLAND

Translated by Kari Dickson

PEGASUS BOOKS
NEW YORK LONDON

Sovietistan

Pegasus Books, Ltd.
148 West 37th Street, 13th Floor
New York, NY 10018

First Pegasus Books paperback edition July 2021
First Pegasus Books hardcover edition January 2020

ISBN: 978-1-64313-769-8

10 9 8 7 6 5 4 3

Printed in the United States of America
Distributed by Simon & Schuster
www.pegasusbooks.com

"... the collapse of Russian rule in Central Asia has tossed the area back into a melting pot of History. Almost anything could happen there now, and only a brave or foolish man would predict its future."

Peter Hopkirk

The Great Game. On Secret Service in High Asia, 2006

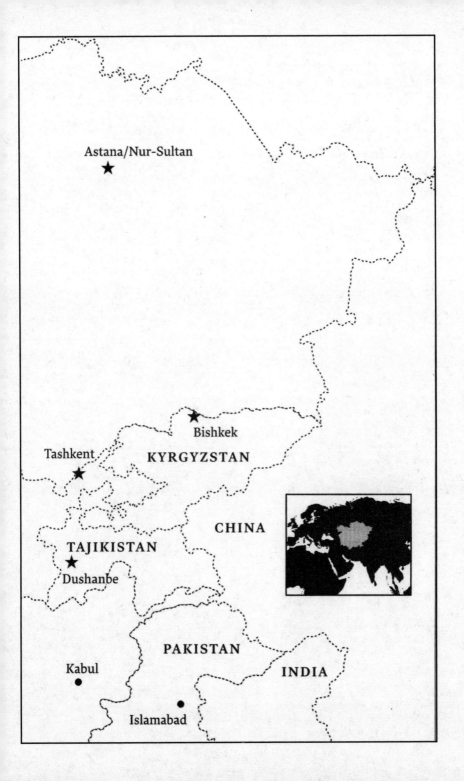

Astana/Nur-Sultan
★

Bishkek
★
KYRGYZSTAN

Tashkent
★

TAJIKISTAN
Dushanbe
★

CHINA

PAKISTAN

Kabul
●

INDIA

Islamabad
●

NAMES

Central Asian names, both personal and place names, are often confusing for western readers. Not only do they sound unfamiliar to us, but many of them have reached our own language via Russian, which was the dominant language of the Soviet Union. The names and spellings have thus been further complicated by Russian transcription rules. Another issue is that, since the dissolution of the Soviet Union, many places have been given new names, for example, Krasnovodsk in Turkmenistan is now called Turkmenbashi, and the capital of Kyrgyzstan, Bishkek, was formally known as Frunze.

With very few exceptions, I have used the new place names in this book. One exception is Semipalatinsk in Kazakhstan, which is now called Semey. I have written about historical events that took place here when the town was called Semipalatinsk, so I have chosen to use the Russian name.

CONTENTS

UZBEKISTAN

LIST OF ILLUSTRATIONS

TURKMENISTAN

1. Rush hour in Ashgabat. "Long Live Neutral Turkmenistan!" is the message to all motorists.
2. Ruhnama, "The Book of the Soul", still has pride of place in central Ashgabat, but no longer opens up in the evening.
3. The Turkmen Horse Beauty Contest. The audience holds its breath.
4. The president prepares for the special horse owners' race. So far, so good.
5. It is no longer known why this fort outside Merv's city walls is called Kyz Kala, the Maiden's Castle.

KAZAKHSTAN

6. The Bayterek Tower in the futuristic centre of Astana.
7. Traditional Kazakh wrestling. On horseback, of course.
8. Point Zero. The Soviet Union carried out 456 nuclear tests at Polygon.

TAJIKISTAN

9. Dushanbe: the world's tallest flagpole (the presidential palace to the left is included to give a sense of scale).
10. Nisor on her way up the last slope to her new home in the Yagnob Valley. She has never been alone with Mirzo, her groom, before.
11. By the Kyrgyz border. The journey's highest point.

THE DOOR TO HELL

I am lost. The flames in the crater have erased the stars and then drained all the shadows of light. The fiery tongues hiss and spit; there are thousands of them. Some are as big as a horse, others no bigger than raindrops. A gentle heat strokes my cheeks; there is a sweet, sickly odour. Stones loosen from the edge and tumble into the flames without a sound. I step back onto firmer ground. The desert night is cold, without fragrance.

The burning crater was created by accident in 1971. Soviet geologists believed that the area was rich in gas and so started to bore-test. And they did indeed find gas, a vast reservoir. Plans were immediately drawn up for large-scale extraction. But then one day the ground opened under the rig, like a great grin, some sixty metres long and twenty metres deep. Foul-smelling methane gas poured out from the crater. All drilling was put on hold, the engineers and geologists packed their bags and struck camp. In order to reduce any risk to the local population, who, several kilometres away, had to hold their noses because of the nauseating smell of methane, it was decided that the gas should be burned off. The geologists estimated that this would take a matter of days or weeks.

Eleven thousand and six hundred days later, more than three decades, in other words, the crater is still burning furiously. The locals used to call it the "Door to Hell". But there are no locals anymore. The village was evacuated by Turkmenistan's first president, who did not want tourists visiting the crater to see the miserable conditions there, so all 350 inhabitants were moved elsewhere.

The first president is no longer there, either. He died two years after the village was cleared. His successor, the dentist, has decided that the crater should be filled in, but, as yet, no-one has lifted a single spade to fill in the Door to Hell, and the methane gas is still escaping from its apparently inexhaustible underground reserve through thousands of tiny holes.

I am swallowed by the dark. All I see are dancing flames and billowing, transparent gas that lies like a lid over the crater. I have no idea where I am. Gradually I start to pick out stones, ridges, stars. Tyre tracks! I follow the tracks for a hundred metres, two hundred metres, three hundred metres; gingerly I feel my way forwards.

From a distance the gas crater is almost beautiful: thousands of flames that melt together to become an oblong, orange fire. I walk slowly on, following the tracks, and stumble across another set of tyre tracks, and then some more, which criss-cross each other: fresh, deep and damp tracks, and dry, worn, dusty ones. There is little help to be had from the stars which now fill the heavens like fireflies. I am no Marco Polo, I am a twenty-first century traveller and can only navigate using the G.P.S. on my mobile. But my iPhone lies dead in the pocket of my trousers, so is no help at all. And even if I did have a full battery and reception, I would still be utterly lost. There are no street names in the desert, no point by which to orient oneself.

Two beams of light cut through the night. A vehicle comes hurtling towards me; the noise of the engine is almost brutal. Inside the dark windows I catch a glimpse of peaked caps, uniforms. Have they spotted me? In a wave of paranoia, I think that they are after me. I entered the country, one of the most closed in the world, on false pretences. Even though I have weighed my words and not told anyone why I am here, they must have long ago guessed. No student would come here on a guided tour, alone. A gentle push and I could disappear for ever through the Door to Hell, engulfed and burned to a cinder.

The headlights blind me, and then they are gone, as fast as they came.

I do the only sensible thing. I choose the highest ridge that I can see and scramble to the top in the grey darkness. From up here, the Door to Hell looks like a glowing mouth. The desert stretches away from the crater in all directions, like a melancholy patchwork cover. For a brief moment it feels as if I am the only person on the planet. An oddly uplifting thought.

Then I spot a bonfire, our little bonfire, and head straight towards it.

TURKMENISTAN

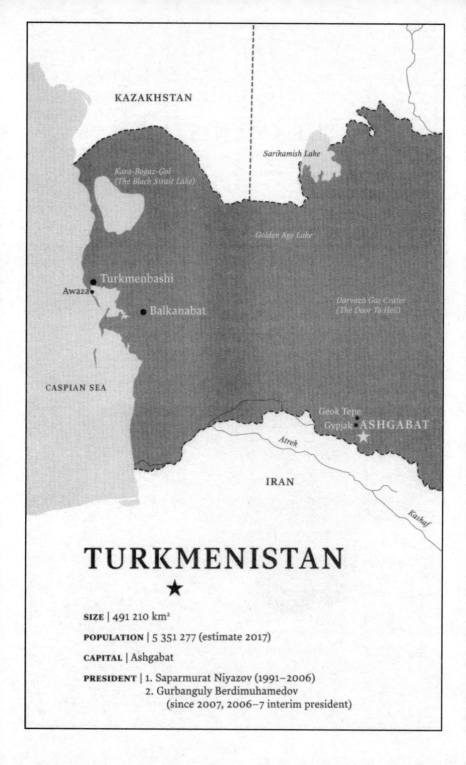

TURKMENISTAN

★

SIZE | 491 210 km²

POPULATION | 5 351 277 (estimate 2017)

CAPITAL | Ashgabat

PRESIDENT | 1. Saparmurat Niyazov (1991–2006)
2. Gurbanguly Berdimuhamedov
(since 2007, 2006–7 interim president)

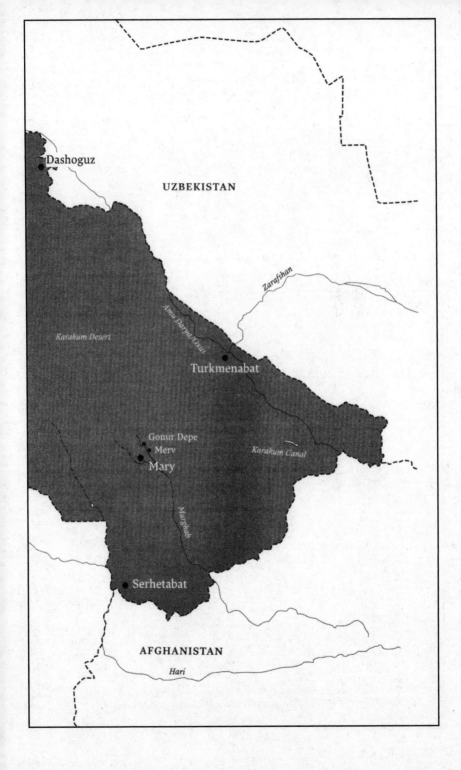

THE UNDERGROUND PEOPLE

Gate 504. It had to be wrong. All the other gates were 200-and-something: 206. 211. 242. Was I in the wrong terminal? Or worse – the wrong airport?

East meets West at Atatürk Airport in Istanbul. The travellers are a glorious gallimaufry of pilgrims on their way to Mecca, sunburned Swedes with bags full of duty-free Absolut Vodka, businessmen in mass-produced suits, white-clad sheiks with black-clad wives weighed down by exclusive European designer bags. No airline in the world flies to as many countries as Turkish Airlines and, as a rule, anyone going to a lesser known capital with an unfamiliar name can expect to change planes here. Turkish Airlines flies to Chisinau, Djibouti, Ouagadougou and Usinsk. And to Ashgabat, which was my destination.

Eventually I spotted the elusive number at the end of a long corridor. 504. As I made my way towards the gate, which seemed to move further away the closer I got, the crowds of people thinned. Until finally I was alone, at the furthest end of the terminal, in an out-of-the-way corner of Atatürk Airport to which only a handful have been. The corridor ended in a wide staircase. I descended into a world of colourful headscarves, brown sheepskin hats, sandals and kaftans. I was the one who stood out in my waterproof jacket and trainers.

A dark-haired man with narrow eyes hurried towards me. In his hands he had a package the size of a cushion, meticulously sealed with brown tape. Could I possibly carry it for him? I pretended not to understand Russian. "Sorry, sorry," I mumbled, moving quickly on. What kind of a man could not carry his own luggage? A couple of middle-aged women in long, purple cotton dresses with large matching scarves wrapped round their heads came to his defence: was it so much to ask? Could I not just help him? I shook my head, *Sorry, sorry*. There was no way I was going to help a Turkmen man, a complete stranger to me, with his suspect package. All my alarm bells were ringing.

I had gone no more than five or six metres when I was stopped again. A willowy young woman in her twenties in a long red dress took me by the arm. Could I please help her with her luggage? Just a little?

"*Nyet!*" I said, forcefully, and pulled myself free.

Once I was in the actual waiting area, I understood: almost every one of the passengers had far too much hand luggage, and the airline staff guarded the entrance to the gate armed with bathroom scales and fierce faces. But as soon as the passengers were through they pulled off even more packages that they had taped to their bodies.

There was apparently no limit to what these women had managed to hide under their long dresses. Laughing, they unburdened themselves, without seeming to care that the flight attendants could see them. They were through now.

However, the main mystery remained unsolved: why on earth did they all have so much hand luggage? One of the flight attendants behind the counter must have noticed my puzzled expression, as she gave me a knowing nod and indicated that I should come closer.

"They're business women," she explained. "They come to Istanbul at least once a month to buy things which they then sell at a profit at the market in Ashgabat. Nearly everything that is sold in Turkmenistan is made in Turkey."

"Why don't they pack it all in suitcases?" I said. "Are they scared their luggage will get lost on the way?"

The attendant laughed.

"They've got suitcases as well, believe me!"

Boarding was a lengthy process. Passengers with excess hand luggage, and that was most of them, had to seal their cheap plastic bags with tape and put them in the hold along with the normal luggage. Inside the plane there was chaos. The women sat down on whatever seat they fancied, to loud protests from the white-bearded men in kaftans. Every time a passenger complained, twenty others, men and women, would join the discussion.

"Please call for the cabin crew if there is any disagreement regarding seat reservations," one of the flight attendants instructed over the P.A., but no-one bothered to call them. Squeezed as I was between kaftans and cotton dresses, I had no choice but to follow the interrupted flow down the aisle. A flight attendant pressed her way through the sea of bodies, rolling her eyes.

There was already a middle-aged matriarch in a purple dress sitting in seat 17F, my seat.

"There must have been a mistake," I said in Russian. "This is my seat."

"You wouldn't want to split up three sisters, would you?" the woman replied, nodding at the two matrons in the seats beside her. They were more or less identical to her. All three sat there glaring at me.

I got out my boarding card, pointed at the number and then at the seat.

"This is my seat," I said again.

"You wouldn't want to split up three sisters, would you?" the matriarch repeated.

"Where am I going to sit then? This is my seat."

"You could sit there." She pointed to an empty seat in front of us. When I opened my mouth to protest again, she gave me a look that said: *You wouldn't want to split up three sisters, would you?*

"It's not a window seat," I muttered, but obediently sat down in the seat she had pointed to. It was true, I did not want to separate three sisters. But more than that, I did not want to sit for four hours, alone, beside two of them. When the rightful occupant of the seat I had been assigned to showed up, I passed him on to the three sisters behind me. The man immediately abandoned any attempt to negotiate and carried on to see if he could find another seat further back. When the plane started to taxi down the runway, there were still four hapless men wandering up and down the aisle, looking for a seat.

Normally I fall asleep as soon as the wheels leave the tarmac, but on this flight I did not even manage to close my eyes. The man sitting next to me smelled like an old brewery and was constantly smacking his lips in his sleep. And the tall woman by the window tapped impatiently on the T.V. screen in front of her. She could not find anything that interested her, but she refused to give up and kept pressing with increased frustration.

To pass the time, I leafed through the neat little Turkmen dictionary I had taken with me. For the other four countries I was going to visit, there were extensive Teach Yourself language courses, complete with text books, work books and D.V.D.s, and in a moment of optimism I had bought them all. But this modest pamphlet that was half dictionary, half survival guide, was all I had found for Turkmenistan. The second part included useful phrases, such as *Are you married? No, I'm a widow(er). I don't understand, please speak more slowly.* The author gradually introduced situations and problems that might arise when travelling in the country: *The flight is delayed by how many hours? Does the lift work? Please slow down!* The section on hotels gave grounds for concern: *The toilet is blocked. The water is turned off. There is a power cut. The gas has been turned off. It is not possible to open/close the window. The air conditioning is not working.* From such general, but often not especially dangerous problems, the author then moved on to cover a number of more alarming situations that one might encounter, from *Stop thief!* and *Call an ambulance!* to more critical phrases: *I did not do it!* and *I did not know it was wrong!* And finally a short but vital chapter on the theme of checkpoints. I taught myself *Don't shoot!* and *Where is the nearest international border?* Then put the book away.

The woman in the window seat had given up trying to find anything to watch on the screen and was now snoring, her mouth wide open. So there I sat, and looked out at the red-streaked evening sky. Over the next eight months, I would visit five of the newest countries in the world: Turkmenistan, Kazakhstan, Tajikistan, Kyrgyzstan and Uzbekistan. When the Soviet Union was dissolved in 1991, these countries became independent states for the first time in their history. And we have heard very little from them since. Even though they cover an area of four million square kilometres and have a combined population of more than 65 million people, most of us know next to nothing about the region. It is something of a paradox that the person who has done most to make it "known" in the West is British comedian Sacha Baron Cohen. His film "Borat: Cultural Learnings of America for Make Benefit Glorious Nation of Kazakhstan" was a huge hit in Europe and the U.S.A. Cohen decided that Borat should come from Kazakhstan for the very reason that virtually no-one had even heard of the country. Thus he would have complete artistic freedom. The parts of the film that are supposed to be set in Borat's village in Kazakhstan were not filmed in Kazakhstan at all, but in Romania. "Borat" was the first non-pornographic film to be banned in Russia, following the dissolution of the U.S.S.R. The authorities in Kazakhstan threatened to sue the film company, but realised in the end that this would only further damage the country's reputation. The fact that a ridiculous film has become our most important reference point speaks volumes about our ignorance of the region: Kazakhstan is the ninth largest country in the world, and yet for many years after the premiere of the film, it was simply called "Borat's home country", even by some serious news media.

As a rule, the post-Soviet states in Central Asia are lumped together whenever they are mentioned, as Turkistan, as the region was known in the 1800s, or simply the Stans, or the comedy-inspired Farawayistan. The suffix "stan" comes from Persian and means "place" or "land". Turkmenistan therefore means "land of the Turkmen people". Despite this common suffix, the five Stans are remarkably dissimilar: Turkmenistan is more than eighty per cent desert, whereas more than ninety per cent of Tajikistan is mountains. Kazakhstan has become so wealthy – thanks to oil, gas and minerals – that it recently put in a bid to host the Winter Olympics. Turkmenistan, too, has vast oil and gas reserves, whereas Tajikistan is poor as a church mouse. In many towns and villages in Tajikistan, inhabitants have electricity for only a few hours each day in winter. The regimes in Turkmenistan and Uzbekistan are so authoritarian and corrupt that they are comparable with the dictatorship in North Korea: there is no free press and the president is omnipotent. In Kyrgyzstan, on the other hand, the people have deposed two presidents.

Although the five countries are in many ways very different, they share the same origin and fate: for almost seventy years, from 1922 to 1991, they were part of the Soviet Union, a gigantic social experiment without parallel in history. The Bolsheviks abolished private ownership and other individual rights. Their goal was a communist,

classless society, and they stopped at nothing to achieve this. Every
area of society underwent radical change. The economy was steered
by ambitious five-year plans, farming was collective, and heavy
industry was developed from more or less nothing. The Soviet
Union was a staggeringly detailed system. The individual was
subservient to the common good: entire peoples were exiled, and
millions were classified as "enemies of the people" because of their
religious, intellectual or financial background. They were either
executed or sent to labour camps in remote parts of the empire
where the chances of survival were slim.

There was widespread suffering, and the social experiment was
a catastrophe in terms of the environment. But not everything
was bad in the Soviet Union. The Bolsheviks prioritised schools and
education, and almost succeeded in eradicating illiteracy in parts
of the Union where it had previously been widespread, such as
Central Asia. They invested in road systems and infrastructure,
and made sure that all Soviet citizens had access to healthcare, as
well as ballet, opera and other welfare and cultural benefits. If you
spoke Russian, you could be understood everywhere, from Karelia
in the west to the Mongolian steppes in the east, and, wherever you
went, the red Communist flag fluttered on the flagpoles. From the
ports on the Baltic to the shores of the Pacific, society was organised
according to the same ideological model, with the Russian ruling
class in all positions of power. At its peak, the Soviet Union covered
one sixth of the surface of the earth, and was home to more than
a hundred ethnic groups.

As I was growing up, the end of the Soviet Union was in sight.
When I was in my second year at primary school, the vast Union
started to come undone at the seams and then quickly fell apart. The
world map changed in autumn 1991: the fifteen republics that had
together constituted the Soviet Union, also known as the Union of

Soviet Socialist Republics, broke out of the Union to become independent states, more or less overnight. In the course of a few months, Eastern Europe acquired six new countries: Estonia, Latvia, Lithuania, Belarus, Ukraine and Moldova. Central Asia got five new countries: Kazakhstan, Kyrgyzstan, Uzbekistan, Tajikistan and Turkmenistan. And three new countries emerged in the Caucasus region: Georgia, Azerbaijan and Armenia.[1]

On December 26, 1991, the Soviet Union was formally dissolved. However, the old map continued to be used in our classrooms for as long as I was at school. At regular intervals, the teacher would unroll it and point to the new countries, which were not marked by any borders. For years, we dealt with this vast superpower's fictitious border, which no longer existed, and the invisible but very real borders of these new countries. I remember I was fascinated by both its size and physical proximity. The Soviet Union, a name which like Yugoslavia and the Second World War was already dusty with history, had been our closest neighbour.

My first meeting with the former Soviet Union was in the company of a large group of Finnish pensioners. I spent my final year of school in Helsinki, and had bought a ticket for a cheap bus tour to St Petersburg. As soon as we got to border control, the change in atmosphere was tangible: armed soldiers came onto the bus five times to check our passports and visas. When we stopped for lunch at Vyborg, several of the pensioners burst into tears.

"This used to be such a beautiful town," one woman said.

In the inter-war period, Viipuri, as the town is called in Finnish,

---

1 However, Chechnya and the other republics north of the Caucasus mountains remained a part of Russia. These areas had not had the status of full Soviet republics in the U.S.S.R., but were *autonomous* Soviet socialist republics, in other words, federal subjects of the Russian Soviet Republic. There were 44 such autonomous Soviet republics, none of which gained independence in 1991.

was the second largest city in Finland. Then, after the Second World War, the Finns had to cede this part of Karelia to the Soviet Union. Signs of decline were visible everywhere: the paint was peeling from the buildings, the pavements were full of holes, and the people looked grim and serious, dressed in dark, sombre clothes.

Our accommodation in St Petersburg was in a concrete block. With its broad streets, tired trolley buses, pastel-coloured classic buildings and rude ticket sellers, there was something both poignant and hostile about the city; it was hideous and beautiful, repulsive and alluring. I thought: I am never coming here again, but no sooner was I back in Helsinki than I had bought some Russian textbooks. Over the next few years, I learned vocabulary and case declension, struggled with perfective and imperfective aspects, practised soft and hard consonants in front of the mirror. There were more trips to St Petersburg and Moscow, but also to the peripheries of the former Soviet Union, to North Caucasus, Ukraine and Moldova, and to the breakaway republics of Abkhazia and Transnistria. Everywhere from the mountains of Ossetia to the palm trees of the Crimea, from sleepy Chisinau to the traffic jams of Moscow, there were traces of the Soviet Union. It had left its mark on the buildings and the people, and places looked the same, no matter how many hundreds of kilometres lay in between.

While opinions on Putin and modern day Russia ranged from profound admiration to impotence and loathing, I met the same nostalgia for the Soviet era everywhere. Practically everyone who was old enough to remember the Soviet Union longed for the good old days. This surprised me, initially, as we had been taught about the labour camps and deportations, the constant surveillance and the hopelessly inefficient financial system and environmental catastrophes. No-one had told us about the flights that were so cheap they were as good as free, or about subsidised stays in sanatoriums on the coast for worn-out workers and free nurseries and schooling for all, not to mention all the good news. Until Gorbachev came to power, the newspapers and news broadcasts were full of good news and positive stories. According to the state media, everything was going swimmingly in the Soviet Union: there was no crime, there were never any accidents, and for every year that passed they achieved ever greater heights.

The more I travelled in Russia and the former Soviet Union, the more curious I became about the empire's peripheries. Many of the ethnic groups who had been colonised by Russia in the nineteenth century, and subsequently become subjects of the Soviet Union, were very different from the Russians in terms of their appearance, language, lifestyle, culture and religion.

This was particularly true of the people in Central Asia. When the Russians arrived, most of the people in the northernmost regions, today's Kazakhstan, Kyrgyzstan and Turkmenistan, were nomads. There were no countries as such and society was loosely organised according to clan affiliation. The people in the south, in the areas that are now Uzbekistan and Tajikistan, were settled, but had been isolated from the world for centuries, so society had stagnated in many areas. The feudal khanates in Khiva and Kokand, as well as the Bukhara emirate, which now are all part of Uzbekistan, were therefore easy spoils for the Russian soldiers. Both the nomadic tribes and Central Asians were predominantly Muslim. In the streets of Samarkand and Bukhara, women traditionally covered themselves up, and polygamy was widespread, as it was among the nomads. In the eleventh century, cities like Bukhara and Samarkand had been important scientific and cultural centres, but by the time the Russians arrived this intellectual golden age was long gone: very few people in Central Asia could read a hundred years ago, and the few schools that existed focused mainly on religious studies.

Through the ages, many different peoples – the Persians, the Greeks, the Mongols, the Arabs and the Turks – have conquered Central Asia.[2] These frequent invasions were the price that Central Asia had to pay for its position between East and West. But it was precisely this position that enabled many of the towns and cities to flourish in connection with the silk trade between Asia and Europe more than a thousand years ago.

To date, no foreign power has intervened in the daily lives of the Central Asian people so systematically, or to the same extent, as the Soviet authorities. Under the tsars, the Russians were primarily interested in financial gain, so they introduced cotton plantations and controlled the Central Asian markets, but tended not to get involved in the lives of the locals. The Emir of Bukhara was even allowed to remain on the throne, so long as he did what the Russians said. The Soviet authorities, however, had a more ambitious agenda: they were going to create a utopia. In the space of a few years, the people of Central Asia underwent a managed transition from a traditional, clan-based society to hardcore socialism. Everything from the alphabet to the position of women in society had to change, by force if necessary. While these drastic changes took place, Central Asia in effect disappeared from the world map. During the Soviet regime, large parts of the region were hermetically sealed to outsiders.

What marks have the years of Soviet rule left on these countries, on the people who live there, and on the towns and landscapes? Has any of the original culture, from pre-Soviet days, survived? And

2 Definitions of Central Asia vary: Afghanistan is often included, and sometimes also parts of Russia and China. However, the countries that I write about in this book, Turkmenistan, Kazakhstan, Tajikistan, Kyrgyzstan and Uzbekistan, are always included in modern definitions of Central Asia. Unless otherwise stated, these are the countries I am referring to when I talk about Central Asia.

most importantly, how have Turkmenistan, Kazakhstan, Tajikistan, Kyrgzystan and Uzbekistan fared in the years since the fall of the Soviet Union?

I had boarded the plane to Ashgabat with these questions in my notebook. The decision to start my travels in Turkmenistan was based on the fact that it was the least certain card. Only a few thousand tourists visit the country each year, and the visa requirements are strict. Foreign journalists are almost never allowed into the country, and the few that are accredited are followed all the time. I had said in my visa application that I was a student, which was not actually a lie, as I was still registered at the University of Oslo. After months of exchanging e-mails with the travel agency, I was told two weeks before I was due to leave that my invitation had been confirmed. Finally I could order plane tickets and start to prepare for my trip.

For every two hours that we flew through the night, the clocks went forward one hour. When the plane started its descent, the sun was glowing red in the east. As soon as the tyres hit the ground, all the passengers undid their seatbelts. The cabin crew had given up and made no attempt to reason with the kaftan-clad men who staggered around in the aisle gathering up their hand luggage. Through the oval plastic window I caught a glimpse of the new airport terminal, all white marble, gleaming in the morning sun.

Never had I felt so far from home.

THE MARBLE CITY

The marble blinded me. Apartment blocks rose up like a forest blanketed in snow, tall and elegant but devoid of character. No matter where I turned, there was more of the same: shining, white marble. I snapped photographs wildly through the window of the car, like a Japanese tourist on speed, at speed. Most of the pictures were useless.

The road between the lines of apartment blocks was worthy of an oil-rich state: eight lanes wide, and illuminated by white, specially designed lights. And the cars, which could actually be counted on the fingers of one hand, were spotlessly clean. Mercedes was the preferred manufacturer. There was not a pedestrian to be seen on the broad pavements, only the occasional policeman equipped with a red flashing baton, which they used to flag down every second car, presumably out of sheer boredom.

It was as though everything in the city belonged to the future, even the bus stops, which were air-conditioned. But the future people were missing. The contrast to the chaos on the airplane was striking: the expensive marble buildings were nothing more than empty shells, the streets were deserted. The only sign of life was by the side of the road. An army of bent women in orange vests, their faces covered to protect them from the sun, was working furiously to keep the city clean. They looked like guerrilla soldiers as they cut, raked, swept and dug.

"Ashgabat has become a very beautiful city, *thanks-to-our-president*,"

my driver, Aslan, commented. He was in his thirties, wan, and the
father of young children. The last four words were spoken quickly,
an automatic response, in the way that Muslims follow any mention
of the Prophet with "peace be with him", or we trot out politenesses
such as "you're welcome" and "lovely to see you again". I was to
discover that there were many variations of this presidential hom-
age, invariably spoken with the same gravity.

Ashgabat was built to stun visitors. "Look what we have
achieved!" the marble buildings seemed to shout. "Look at us, look
at us!" The world media may not always have followed closely what
goes on in this small desert nation in Central Asia, but the *Guinness
Book of Records* has been familiar with its eccentricities for some
time. In 2013, the capital's inhabitants celebrated yet another record: Ashgabat is now officially the city with the most marble-clad
buildings per square kilometre in the world. It is said that the marble
quarries in Carrara in Italy are being emptied by the Turkmens'
insatiable appetite for the white stuff. Ashgabat's inhabitants could
already boast that they lived in the city with the greatest number
of fountain pools in the world, and that despite the fact that more
than eighty per cent of Turkmenistan is desert. Beyond the eight-
lane boulevards, barren sand dunes stretch away in every direction,
but within the white marble walls, water flows and cascades in
abundance. Everywhere you go, there is the sound of burbling, running water. Ashgabat is also home to the world's biggest enclosed
Ferris wheel, an astonishing 47.6-metre high glass construction
with closed cabins that slowly revolve. The Turkmenistan Broadcasting Centre's tower is 211 metres high and incorporates the
world's largest architectural star. For a while, the world's highest
flag pole also stood in Ashgabat, but this record has since been
overtaken by other ex-Soviet republics.

The luxury apartment blocks are clad in somewhat inferior

marble, though marble all the same, while only the best and most expensive Italian marble is used for prestige buildings such as the presidential palaces, the various ministries and the most important mosques. These were all designed and constructed by foreign companies, primarily French and Turkish, and engineers have gone to some lengths to give each ministry a unique feature. The Ministry of Foreign Affairs is topped by a blue globe, the Ministry of Education is shaped like a half-open book. The faculty of dentistry looks like a tooth (with input from the current president, no doubt, who is a dentist by profession). The Ministry of Communications is also shaped like a book, but this time a wholly open book. At the top of the right-hand page a gold profile of the First President shines like an illuminated letter.

The two presidents are ever-present in Turkmenistan. Every town still has a statue of Saparmurat Niyazov, known as Turkmenbashi, the country's first president from the dissolution of the Soviet Union until his death in 2006. The capital is full of them, and they are identical: an upright bureaucrat in a suit and tie, with resolute, visionary features. His successor, Gurbanguly Berdimuhamedov, best known as the New President, has chosen a more modern approach: a portrait photograph. His enormous, fatherly face hangs everywhere in the city. He is smiling in all the pictures, a thin, mysterious, Mona Lisa smile. I first saw his portrait at passport control in the airport, and then again at the city gates, and then again in the hotel reception, where an entire wall was dedicated to him. You are never alone in Turkmenistan. No matter how deserted the streets may be, the presidents see you.

I hung out of the car window and clicked until my index finger was tender and numb, caught half a globe, gold domes, deserted eight-lane boulevards. Aslan was kind enough to slow down, but not to stop. Whenever there were a lot of police around, he asked me to hide the camera. For some obscure security reason, it is forbidden to take photographs of strategic buildings, such as the presidential palace and lavish government buildings. It is also illegal to photograph administrative buildings, of which there were many. I could, on the other hand, take as many pictures as I liked of the memorials and monuments. Every milestone of the independent nation was honoured with grand statues and fountains: the fifth anniversary, the tenth anniversary, the fifteenth anniversary and twentieth anniversary had all left their mark on the cityscape. The Independence Monument symbolised secession in 1991, whereas the Monument to the Constitution celebrates Turkmenistan's young constitution. The nation clearly had a lot to prove and a huge city to fill. The Soviet authorities in Moscow never saw Ashgabat as a priority. The Russians established a garrison town here as early as 1881, and gradually a modern city emerged in the desert. In 1948, the entire town was flattened by a powerful earthquake. Hundreds of thousands of people lost their lives. The Soviet authorities rebuilt the city, but without much enthusiasm. They built the usual grey concrete apartment blocks, brought in parts for the obligatory amusement park with dodgem cars and a Ferris wheel, tidied the way for a couple of green parks and reopened the regional museum with the inevitable displays of stuffed animals and pottery fragments. The Soviet town planner would not recognise his own town today.

"And this is the Olympic village," Aslan explained, as we drove past yet another row of marble mastodons. Enormous posters of skaters and medal ceremonies had been put up on the white walls. "The swimming pool is finished already, *thanks-to-our-president's-foresight*. And so is the ice rink, and the accommodation where all the athletes will stay."

"I didn't know that Turkmenistan was going to host the Olympics," I said.

Aslan gave me a wounded look.

"We're hosting the Asian Indoor and Martial Arts Games in 2017,"[3] he informed me.

I had no idea that Asia had its own Olympics, but chose not to say anything. It was not even lunchtime, and already my head was spinning. I would normally plan my own travel, but here I was slave to the travel agency's Itinerary. With the exception of those who pass through the country on a short transit visa, tourists who want to visit Turkmenistan have to leave all travel arrangements to a state-authorised travel agency. The agency is then responsible for these foreigners for every second they are in the country, and they are seldom left alone. Since the First President's death, the rules have relaxed a little and it is now possible for tourists to walk around Ashgabat on their own. But the police force is so big that they are under surveillance all the same. For the next three weeks, at least one representative from the agency was to accompany me at all times, except for at night. Three weeks is the maximum any tourist can stay in the country.

Aslan turned onto a huge, empty square. One end was dominated by a palace, with an elaborate entrance, adorned with Greek pillars and a blue onion dome that reached into the sky. Visitors were greeted by two gold winged horses atop the pillars.

"Is this the presidential palace?" I was suitably impressed.

"No, are you crazy? *Our-Good-President* lives outside town, in a gated community. This is the National Museum of History, which

3   The Asian Indoor and Martial Art Games took place in Ashgabat in September 2017. All forty-five member countries of the Olympic Council of Asia participated, as did seventeen Oceania National Olympic Committee countries, who were participating for the first time. These are not to be confused with the Asian Games, also organised by the Olympic Council of Asia, and held every four years, most recently in 2018 in Indonesia.

was opened by the First President in 1998." Aslan sorted out my
entrance ticket and sent me in through the sliding doors. An attendant switched on the light as I stepped into the hall. The interior
was brown and Soviet-style, in sharp contrast to the baroque exterior. Women in long dresses were standing along the walls, talking
quietly to each other. My guide, Aina, was in her early twenties
and dressed in the student uniform: a red, ankle-length dress with
an embroidered collar and front, with her smooth, black hair in
two plaits, as was the tradition for young Turkmen women. She
shook my hand firmly and ordered me into the lift.

"Does the museum get many visitors?" I said, for the sake of
conversation more than anything.

"Yes," Aina replied, without a hint of irony.

"But not today?"

"No," she said, just as earnestly.

Aina was a machine. Equipped with a pointer, she guided me
efficiently through Turkmenistan's 5,000-year history. She rattled
off the dates and foreign-sounding names in a monotonous voice.
Several times, I had to ask her to repeat when such-and-such a town
was established and when this-or-that empire existed. Aina started
all her answers with an exasperated "*As I said ...*"

As she marched me past pottery fragments, gold jewellery and
decorated drinking horns, it dawned on me just how little I knew
about this part of the world. There were flourishing cultures and
cities here long before the Romans became the Romans. Great
dynasties like the Medes, the Achaemenids, the Parthians, the
Sasanians and the Seljuks, and mighty provinces such as Margiana
and Khwarazm ... As the country is so exposed, caught between
East and West, with nothing more than inhospitable desert to
protect it, there have been very many invasions and power shifts
over the centuries, which further complicates the picture.

"Were they not Buddhists in the east then?" I said, confused, when Aina started to tell me about Islamic pottery in eastern Turkmenistan.

"As I said, that was before the Islamic invasion in the eighth century."

According to the Itinerary, I was free to do as I wished in the afternoon. I used the time to wander around the broad, empty streets wearing light summer shoes. It was early April and gentle as a summer's day in Norway. Turkmen summers are anything but gentle: the temperature frequently pushes fifty degrees. No wonder, then, that they have invested in air-conditioned bus shelters.

Poker-faced policemen followed me with their eyes. Every now and then a flock of students ran by, girls in red dresses, boys in suits and ties, and then I was alone again. The New President gazed down at me with gentle, inscrutable eyes from the walls of buildings. I briefly felt I had been transported back fifty or sixty years to the heyday of the Soviet Union, when it was Stalin who had watched his good comrades on the street. The artists of the time had a particular knack for capturing whatever good qualities the dictator had: despite Stalin's harsh nature, paranoid personality and absolute hold on power, they always managed to make him look kind and sensitive, almost paternal. The photographer behind the portraits of the New President clearly shared this talent. The man in the enormous, framed photographs had round, generous cheeks, but did not look fat or overweight. On the contrary, he exuded good health as he looked out over the streets with his caring eyes and mysterious smile.

The shopping centres, with their luxurious facades covered in gold, marble and neon lights, would not have been out of place on the fashionable shopping streets of Dubai, but appearances can deceive. Inside, they were like any other poorly equipped bazaar, with dimly lit halls and shelves of cheap Turkish clothes and cosmetics. There were only three A.T.M.s in the entire country that accepted foreign cards, and one of them had been given prime position in the lavish lobby of the Sofitel Oguzkent Hotel. As an experiment, I put my card in and tried to withdraw fifty dollars. *Connection failed*, the message flashed at me.

Once darkness fell, the city became a festival of light. Every single marble slab was carefully illuminated, and the fountains and water channels continually changed colour. No corner was left in the dark.

"Ashgabat is even more beautiful at night," Aslan said. He had come to take me to one of the best restaurants, where, from the top floor, you could see the whole city. To begin with, I had the entire outdoor terrace to myself, but it soon started to fill up with very well-dressed guests. The men wore tailored Italian suits, the women body-hugging, glittering creations. There were no ankle-length dresses, long plaits or head scarves here. The waiters came out with drinks and juices that were as colourful as the illuminated waterways. The loudspeakers pumped out music. It was eight o'clock and the party was in full swing.

But as I finished my last spoonful of dessert, the party was over and people were getting ready to leave. The Turkmen capital closes at 11 p.m. on weekdays and weekends. Bars or restaurants that stay open beyond that risk being closed down and receiving a hefty fine.

Back at the hotel, I went into the bathroom to get ready for bed. There was an ashtray by the basin. It had not been possible to get a no-smoking room, and the sour smell of stale smoke was pervasive. When the first president, Turkmenbashi, had to stop smoking after a heart operation in 1997, he introduced a ban on smoking in public places. Smoking is now only allowed indoors in Ashgabat.

I undressed quickly, suddenly feeling insecure. The guidebook had warned that all rooms for foreigners were bugged. Perhaps they had installed cameras as well? I looked behind the two paintings of flowers, checked the drawers and inspected the telephone, T.V. and fridge, but found nothing. Yet I could not shake the feeling that someone was watching me. I lay under the thin top sheet and felt the springs in the mattress pressing into my back. As I closed my eyes, a forest of marble towers swayed around me, all decorated with the president's boyish smile and inscrutable brown eyes.

DICTATORSTAN

An unjust ruler is like a farmer
who plants corn and expects wheat.

RUHNAMA

A few farmers are digging in the fields. They are wearing simple, dirty cotton clothes and behind them an enormous dome glitters gold like a rising sun. There are no cars on the wide, newly asphalted road. A tall marble arch welcomes us to Gypjak, the First President's birthplace.

Saparmurat Niyazov, better known as Turkmenbashi, a man who is recognised the world over as one of the most bizarre dictators ever, was born on February 19, 1949 in Gypjak, then a modest village on the outskirts of Ashgabat. His father died during the Second World War, purportedly fighting valiantly against the Germans. His mother died in the powerful earthquake that levelled Ashgabat in 1948, leaving the eight-year-old Saparmurat an orphan, a fate he shared with many others at the time. Victory over the Nazis had come at a cost for the Soviet Union: between twenty and thirty million people had lost their lives in the fighting and thousands of towns and villages lay in ruins. Any joy at the return of peace was overshadowed by food shortages and disease. People were dying in droves, and hundreds of thousands of children grew up on the streets.

As an adult, Saparmurat milked these sorrowful circumstances for all they were worth, but he was one of the lucky ones. He never had to live on the streets. The authorities placed him in a children's home and took care of him. He was there only for a short while before one of his uncles took him in. He was sent to the best schools in Ashgabat, then went on to study at the prestigious Polytechnic Institute in Leningrad and graduated in electrical engineering. While the years in Leningrad did not in any way make him a serious scholar, there were few Turkmens at the time who could boast a similar background, so the door to politics was wide open for the orphan Saparmurat.

He rose swiftly through the ranks, and in 1985, after very many career politicians in Turkmenistan lost their positions following a corruption scandal, Niyazov was appointed First Secretary of the Communist Party of Turkmenistan. He made a name for himself as one of the least reform-friendly leaders in the Soviet Union, and was a strong opponent of Gorbachev's perestroika movement. Niyazov wanted to maintain a powerful union, a desire that was evidently shared by the Turkmen people: in a referendum in March 1991, 99.8 per cent of the population voted to remain a part of the Soviet Union, if the figures are to be believed.

Life in the Soviet Republic of Turkmenistan, one of the poorest in the empire, was not a bed of roses, but the lives of the majority did slowly improve under Soviet rule. Children went to school, and both young and old had access to healthcare. Roads, railways and domestic flights linked the country with the rest of the Union. Given this background, it is not hard to understand why Niyazov was a quiet supporter of the attempted coup against Gorbachev in August 1991 by those who opposed his reforms. When the coup failed, it became clear to most that the days of the Soviet Union were numbered. Niyazov was forced to change tack, and, on October 27, Turkmenistan declared itself an independent, sovereign state following a second referendum. According to the Turkmen authorities, 94 per cent were now in favour of Turkmenistan leaving the Soviet Union.

At the same time that Turkmenistan declared its independence, the Supreme Soviet in Ashgabat voted on who should be appointed president. Niyazov was elected with a 98.3 per cent majority. In the first few months of his presidency, he made some cosmetic changes. The Communist Party of Turkmenistan changed its name to the Democratic Party of Turkmenistan. Other parties were not as yet permitted, so Turkmenistan continued to be a one-party state. Most politicians who had held important posts during the Soviet era were given similar positions in the new, independent Turkmenistan.

The first worrying signs started to appear in December of the same year. A new law regarding "the President's honour and dignity" allowed the dismissal of anyone who expressed views that did not accord with those of the President. A long-term "stability programme" was also launched: ten years of stability would lead Turkmenistan safely into the twenty-first century, which was heralded as a future utopia: *Altyn Asyr*, the Golden Age.

The propaganda machine, which was already well oiled when it came to personality cults after seventy years of Soviet rule, was set in motion to reinforce the image of Niyazov as the country's uniting father. And in 1992, the state publishing house published several books that praised him extravagantly. Just as Iosif Vissarionovich Dzhugashvili became Stalin, the Steel Man, in 1993 Saparmurat Niyazov officially became Turkmenbashi, Leader of the Turkmen. Schools, streets, villages, mosques, factories, airports, vodka brands, perfume and even the old Russian garrison town of Krasnovodsk on the Caspian Sea were now renamed Turkmenbashi. When a meteorite landed in the Turkmen desert, there was no doubt who the celestial body should be named after. An official slogan, which is strikingly similar to that of the Nazis, was adopted to great excitement: "One people, one mother country, one Turkmenbashi."

The statues of Lenin and Marx were removed from villages and towns and replaced with gold statues of Turkmenbashi dressed in a suit and tie. The few tourists who visited the country were only allowed to photograph these bizarre, mass-produced statues on the condition that they took a full-figure picture – as only full-figure photographs of Turkmenbashi were permitted. When Turkmenistan got its own currency, the manat, in 1993, there was a portrait of Turkmenbashi on all the notes. All the three state television channels had a profile of the president in gold in the top right-hand corner of the screen. Turkmenbashi's face was everywhere, even on vodka bottles, and that, apparently, was how things would be for ever more: in 1999, he was declared President for Life. Two years later, he added *beyik*, "the great", to his title. The orphaned eight year old had grown up to become President Saparmurat Turkmenbashi the Great.

In terms of foreign policy, Turkmenbashi, who initially had not been in favour of independence, made a point of distancing the country from former Soviet states. As early as 1993, he decided to get rid of the Cyrillic alphabet, which had been in use for more than fifty years, and to replace it with a specially adapted version of the Latin alphabet. It took time to roll out the school curriculum in the new alphabet, so for some years Turkmen schoolchildren were without textbooks. Teachers and bureaucrats were given no instruction in the new alphabet, with the result that many adults still have problems reading and writing their own language. Turkmenistan was also the only former Soviet republic to introduce visas for nationals from Russia and other post-Soviet states. The current entry requirements are some of the most stringent in the world, and no foreign nationals can visit the country without a visa.

In 1995, Turkmenistan was recognised as a neutral country by the U.N., and Turkmenbashi saw this as one of his greatest political feats. Any documents referring to Turkmenistan now had to say "the independent, neutral Turkmenistan". In order to mark the occasion, Turkmenbashi built a 75-metre tower in the heart of the capital. On top of the tower, which he named the Arch of Neutrality, there was a twelve-metre gold statue of himself in a suit and something akin to a Superman cape. The statue was illuminated at night and rotated by day, so he was always facing the sun. The Arch of Neutrality was the tallest structure in Ashgabat and became the symbol of the city. In the evening, people thronged there to admire the panorama from the top of the tower. But for Turkmenbashi, the country's neutral status was primarily a practical, political manoeuvre: he could now decline to take part in any agreements, or simply take a passive stance, and did not need to cooperate with the other Soviet states. At the same time, he could continue to trade with questionable neighbours such as the clerical elite in Iran and the Taliban in Afghanistan.

It would appear that when the initial decade of stability was over and Turkmenistan moved into the Golden Age, Turkmenbashi started to see himself as a divine being. He claimed he was a prophet, descended from Alexander the Great and the Prophet Mohammed. Then one day at the start of the century, shortly after the Golden Age had begun, the country's citizens awoke to a wonder: overnight the president's youthful mane of hair had been miraculously restored. There was not a single grey hair to be seen in any of the framed portraits that hung at the front of every classroom throughout the land, or the gigantic posters that were plastered on every empty wall in the towns. Not long after this miracle, the president introduced a new law banning long hair and beards for men. Anyone travelling to the country who was unaware of the new ban risked having their hair cut and their beards shaved at the border.

Turkmenbashi also had marked views on the appearance of his countrywomen. He had already decided that schoolgirls and female students should wear ankle-length dresses and traditional skullcaps, based roughly on the traditional Turkmen dress, if not altogether historically correct. This now extended to what women should look like on television: he declared that anchorwomen should no longer wear make-up. Why would Turkmen women need make-up? They were naturally beautiful! He also banned the circus and opera, for not being sufficiently Turkmen.

The president became increasingly concerned with what *was* Turkmen and with Turkmen culture. In September 2001, Turkmenbashi's long-awaited masterpiece, *Ruhnama, The Book of the Soul*, was published. It comprised a number of personal talks by the president, which all began with phrases such as "Dear Turkmens!" and "My dearly beloved Turkmen people!" It also included pages of the original manuscript in the president's handwriting, with some words scored out and some added, to demonstrate that the president had indeed written the book himself.

The two volumes were an attempt to summarise Turkmenistan's history and to provide a kind of manual of Turkmen customs and culture, interwoven with lyrical descriptions: "Since I was five years old, I have thanked God hundreds of thousands of times for the fact that I have inherited, in both body and soul, the honour, nobility, patience, reverential spirit and sense of purpose of my parents. My character has been strengthened rather than weakened by good times and bad. This source will never run dry for my Turkmen people, my holy country, my motherland, for the past and present, for future generations." According to Turkmenbashi, the purpose of writing *Ruhnama* was "to reopen the dwindling spring of national pride by cleaning out all the grass and stone, so it can flow freely once more" and to create "the first, fundamental reference work for Turkmenistan. It is the essence of the Turkmen mind, Turkmen customs and traditions, intentions, actions and ideals."

As dictators often do, Turkmenbashi included a rather curious rewriting of history in the *Ruhnama*. He traced the Turkmen people back five thousand years, to Noah no less. According to more reliable sources, Turkmen tribes have lived in the country for less than a thousand years, having come there from Eastern Siberia with other Turkic tribes. There is barely a mention of tribal feuds or external influences in either of the president's two volumes, and the colonisation by Russia in the 1800s and seventy years of Soviet rule are described as "a yoke of slavery" that prevented the Turkmens from entering a new golden age – the previous golden age being under the leadership of the mythical Oguz Khan, during the Seljuk empire in the eleventh century. The truth is that a united Turkmen nation did not exist when the Russians arrived in the 1800s, only loosely connected tribes who were often in conflict with one other. Concepts such as the Turkmen culture and nationality, the country's borders, even the Turkmen alphabet, stem from the Soviet era. Turkmenbashi, who was educated in Leningrad and rose to power under Gorbachev, was a product of the Soviet heritage he now denied.

The launch of *Ruhnama* would put the marketing departments of any publisher to shame. On the day, Turkmenbashi unveiled a new, spectacular monument in Ashgabat: an enormous copy of *Ruhnama* that opened at a given time each evening, to the accompaniment of solemn music. Over the loudspeakers, a sonorous male voice then declaimed several lines of verse from the masterpiece before the covers of the book slowly closed again. In order to ensure that *Ruhnama* was read, Turkmenbashi introduced the book into the curriculum for primary schools and universities. Children in class one had to learn to read with the help of *Ruhnama*, and it was the only reference book used in Turkmen history lessons. Thus, Turkmen schoolchildren learn that both the wheel and the robot were invented by Turkmens.

All other subjects were steeped in *Ruhnama*. Even maths classes were based on studies of *The Book of the Soul*. Not even that was enough for the President for Life, however, and in 2004 he decided that all humanities and science subjects should be removed from secondary and higher education, as they were "obscure and out of touch with reality". They were to be replaced by more suitable subjects, such as "Political independence under Saparmurat Turkmenbashi the Great", "Saparmurat Turkmenbashi's literary heritage" and "*Ruhnama* as a spiritual guide for the Turkmen people".

It was not only pupils and students who were forced to read *Ruhnama*: exams on *Ruhnama* were introduced as an obligatory part of the driving test. Imams were ordered to preach the *Ruhnama* in mosques – those who refused were imprisoned. All foreign companies wanting to do business in Turkmenistan had to ensure that *The Book of the Soul* was translated into their respective language. In 2005, the first volume was fired into space in a Russian rocket. "The book has won millions of hearts here on earth, and now will conquer space," one Turkmen newspaper said.

Despite the book's global and potential universal reach, *Ruhnama* was still not enough to satisfy Turkmenbashi's need to leave a mark. His ambition was to mould the country in his image, including the language. In 2002, he decided to change the names of the days and the months. He claimed that the old names, which were borrowed from Russian, were "un-Turkmen". The first month of the year was named after him, *Turkmenbashi*. February was changed to *Baydak*, which means "flag", as the Turkmen flag was celebrated on 19 February, Turkmenbashi's birthday. April was renamed *Gurbansoltan*, the name of Turkmenbashi's mother. He also changed the name for bread from *chorek* to the rather more unwieldy *Gurbansoltan Edzhe*, his mother's full name. September, the month when *Ruhnama* was launched, naturally became *Ruhnama*, while December was changed to *Bitaraplyk*, which means "neutrality". The names given to the days of the week were more prosaic. Monday was renamed "The First Day", Thursday became "Day of Justice" and Sunday "Day of Rest". All street names in Ashgabat, with the exception of some of the main boulevards (which were allowed to keep the name Turkmenbashi), were replaced by numbers.

In the years that followed, the dictator continued to tighten his grip. All Internet cafés in the country were closed, which in effect meant the Internet was no longer available to ordinary people. In 2003, a new law was introduced that declared anyone who questioned the president's policies was a traitor, following on from the law of 1991 pertaining to "the President's honour and dignity". Ballet was also banned, in addition to circus and opera, and as the president could not stand the smell of dogs they too were banned from Ashgabat. It was also forbidden to play recorded music on TV or at major events – the music had to be live, without any lip synching.

Power corrupts and absolute power corrupts absolutely, the British historian Lord Acton told us. Few examples better illustrate this than Turkmenbashi's life. How did the orphaned Saparmurat Niyazov become Turkmenbashi, the dictator who banned the circus and dogs, and put all opponents in jail? One explanation lies within the Soviet system, which was corrupt, authoritarian and had a well-tested tradition of cults of personality. Turkmenbashi grew up in this system, it was all he knew. When the Soviet Union dissolved, there was no Moscow to keep him in check. He could do as he wished. The other politicians were used to obeying the First Secretary, and continued to obey him when he changed his name to Turkmenbashi. They had no choice: whoever dared oppose the president soon found themselves under lock and key. For every year that passed, Turkmenbashi became more of a megalomaniac and his ideas grew ever wilder, yet, no matter where he turned, he was met with deep bows and subservience. He wanted no opposition, and he never encountered it. He had absolute power.

Even though, after independence, Turkmenistan could keep all profits from its gas and oil exports, there was not enough money to pay for all the marble in Ashgabat or Turkmenbashi's other pharaonic whims. After 1991, little or nothing was done to maintain the educational institutions or the health service. The vaccine programme collapsed, and health centres were eventually left with no equipment and no medicine. The welfare system that the Soviet authorities had built up from scratch was now left to crumble at its foundations. In order to camouflage this disaster, doctors were banned from making diagnoses such as Aids or tuberculosis. Teachers, for their part, were not allowed to give poor grades, and obligatory education was reduced from ten years to nine. This was a tactic that Turkmenbashi had learned during the Soviet era. He honed it to perfection: if reality did not live up to expectations, all you had to do was fix the facade and cook the books, and the problem was solved!

To save money, ten thousand teachers were made redundant. After all, Turkmenbashi said, they were not particularly useful. In 2005, it was decided that all district hospitals would be closed down. Some hundred thousand health workers were made redundant and replaced by soldiers. If people needed medical help, they were advised to go to the hospitals in bigger towns and cities. But Turkmenistan is big and the infrastructure is poor, so many were left with no healthcare provision. The then minister of health, Gurbanguly Berdimuhamedov, who is now the president, was given the task of implementing the reform. Turkmenbashi decided at the same time that newly qualified doctors no longer needed to take the Hippocratic Oath but instead should swear allegiance to him, Turkmenbashi the Great. Then he decided to close any libraries outside

Ashgabat, as he believed that the Qur'an and *Ruhnama* gave people more than enough to read. Why would they need any other books? People in rural areas were not able to read properly anyway, he argued, and in the same breath made a snap decision to cut obligatory education by a further two years. The Golden Age had begun.

This seems not to have solved the financial problems, as just before he died Turkmenbashi introduced another great reform. This time it was pensioners who were affected. A new law was passed whereby only those who were able to show that they had worked for at least twenty years and did not have grown-up children qualified for a pension. In order to receive a full pension, it was necessary to prove that you had worked for at least thirty-eight years. More than one hundred thousand people, nearly a third of all pensioners, lost their pensions as a result of the new ruling. A further two hundred thousand had their pensions cut by at least a fifth. The law was introduced retroactively, so those who did not meet the new criteria had to pay back any excess they might have received in the two previous years.

But it was not only the country's finances that were failing, so too was Turkmenbashi's health. In 1997 he underwent heart surgery in Germany. The operation was kept secret. Only in 2006 did Turkmenbashi choose to tell the people about this. He could, however, assure his "dearly beloved Turkmen people" that the German doctors had confirmed that he was now completely healthy again, and he even claimed that they had promised he would live to at least eighty. A few months later, just before Christmas 2006, Turkmenbashi had a massive heart attack and died at the age of sixty-six. The official date of his death is 21 December, but his opponents living abroad believe the president died a few days earlier. The regime needed those days to reflect before sharing the news with the people.

Turkmenbashi had ruled the country for twenty-one years and as an autocrat for fifteen. Why had the Turkmen people tolerated his misrule and eccentricities for so long?

The simple answer is that they had no choice. The Turkmen legal system is one of the most impenetrable in the world; arbitrary imprisonment is common and torture is deemed to be a normal interrogation technique. The security police and the president's personal security service are both extensive, and people are legally obliged to report any spoken or unspoken criticism of the authorities they encounter, as is the case in North Korea. Most people are therefore reluctant to talk about politics at all. In addition to receiving long prison sentences, critics also risk being incarcerated in psychiatric institutions, and drugged with pills, as happened in the Soviet era. The threshold for punishment is so low that nearly all the country's top politicians and senior management have served a prison sentence at some point.

Another answer is the carrot. In 1992, as one of the pillars of his stability programme, Niyazov passed a motion that all essential goods and services such as electricity, gas, petrol and salt should be free. Bread would be heavily subsidised so that everyone could afford it. No-one needed to pay tax. Wages were low, it is true, and unemployment at close to 60 per cent, but at least people could drive their cars as much as they liked – if they still had one, that is.

We turn into an empty car park. Sunbeams dance on the golden dome. The already striking building has gilded minarets and gates, and Greek marble pillars on every side. It is remarkably similar to the presidential palace in Ashgabat, except that the dome is bigger. The paved square in front of the mosque is newly washed and sparkling clean. Once again, I am the only visitor.

"Turkmenbashi built the mosque in honour of his mother, who

was killed by an earthquake here in 1948," Aslan tells me. "It is the fourth largest mosque in the world and it took a French engineering company two years to build it."

It is unusual for it to take so long to finish a building in Turkmenistan. Until recently, it was the biggest mosque in Central Asia, but it has now been surpassed by the new mosque in Astana, the capital of Kazakhstan. Our steps echo as we cross the empty square. There used to be a big gold statue of Turkmenbashi here before, but it was removed after his death.

"Isn't it a bit excessive to build such a big mosque in such a small village?" I ask.

"Not at all, the mosque is for the surrounding villages as well," Aslan says.

A serious young attendant follows us into the holy building. As we wander around on the star-shaped carpet, he reels off a number of facts:

The minarets are ninety-one metres high, in honour of the year that Turkmenistan gained its independence.

The carpet we are standing on is handmade and weighs more than a ton.

The mosque can hold ten thousand worshippers.

The complex includes an underground car park with room for a hundred buses and four hundred cars.

The golden dome has a diameter of fifty metres, and is said to be the largest in the world.

He neglects to mention that the dome turned green only a few years after the mosque was completed. But now it sparkles and shines once again. Nor does he mention that the inscriptions on the minarets are not quotes from the Qur'an, but rather slogans praising the president and *Ruhnama*. "*Ruhnama* is the holy book; the Qur'an is Allah's book" it says on one of the pillars. On the inside

of the dome there are carved phrases praising Turkmenbashi, leader
of the Turkmen people.

I wonder if anyone ever comes here to pray.

The mausoleum next to the Turkmenbashi mosque seems modest
by comparison, to the extent that a marble building crowned by a
gold dome can be called modest. Two guards stand by the entrance.
A soldier orders us to leave all our belongings outside before we
are allowed to enter the dimly lit room.

A marble balustrade stands between us and Turkmenbashi's
grave, which is in the crypt below. His resting place, a black marble
sarcophagus on a white marble star, is surrounded by those of family
members who died either during the Second World War or in the
earthquake. On a table by the wall lies a copy of the Qur'an. To my
surprise, there is not a copy of *Ruhnama* beside it, even though Turkmenbashi had proclaimed that the two books should sit side by
side in every mosque in the country. In death, he clearly preferred
the one book after all.

Aslan stands in silence beside me, looking down at the grave,
gripped by the solemnity. Before we go out into the sun again, he
quickly wipes away a tear.

—m—

For me, one of the best indicators of how a country is doing is its
bookshops. The selection of books on the shelves often says more
about the country's inhabitants and politicians than all the exhib-
itions in all the national museums. Mira's bookshop in Ashgabat
was said to be the best in Turkmenistan. But it was more like a
local council library with such obscure opening times that no-one
ever went there. Tattered copies of Russian classics lay in big boxes
lined up against the walls, all published by Soviet publishers. Gogol.

Volume two of Dostoevsky's *The Idiot*. A couple of Chekhov plays. A textbook on algorithms.

I was the only customer. A pattern seemed to be emerging.

The new books were kept in glass display cases in prime position behind the counter. Deluxe editions with glossy covers and four-colour printing. All the books had a picture of Gurbanguly Berdimuhamedov, the New President, on the front. Gurbanguly on a horse, Gurbanguly at his desk, Gurbanguly in the Turkmen desert, Gurbanguly in action on the tennis court. Most of the books were also written by him and were arranged according to topic, from sport and health to medicine and political vision.

"I would like to buy a book about Gurbanguly Berdimuhamedov, but I don't have much room in my suitcase," I explained. "Do you have any normal-sized books?"

The rotund bookseller began to trawl the shelves, obviously unsure where books were kept. Eventually she found a book that was just a little larger than a normal hardback novel. It was even in English: *The Grandchild Realising his Grandfather's Dream*. On the cover was a photograph of the New President surrounded by a flock of smiling children with Turkmen flags in their hands.

"I would also like a book about the First President," I said.

The bookseller seemed surprised. "I'll see what we've got," she mumbled and disappeared in among the shelves again. I had time to study all the postcards while she looked. Eventually she came back and said apologetically that they had no books about him left.

"Not even *Ruhnama*?"

After another hunt, she appeared behind the counter with a pink book in her hand: "Unfortunately we only have the Russian edition, and only the second volume."

Ruhnama was clearly no longer the ABC for a driving licence.

*

I had to see the miracle with my own eyes, so asked Aslan to drive to the Ruhnama monument. He said that it was no longer usual to take tourists there, but in the end agreed. It was in the centre, after all, only a short distance from Mira's bookshop.

The pink book was almost as big as a house. It stood in the middle of a large, open square, surrounded by beautiful fountains, over-looked by marble apartment blocks. Powerful spotlights ensured that the book was never in the dark. There was a carefully arranged stage that did not appear to be used anymore. Again, I was the only visitor. The square around the enormous pink book was deserted and forlorn. And not a single light was to be seen in the marble apartments. They looked uninhabited.

"I don't understand why you're so interested in *Ruhnama*," Aslan said, shaking his head. "It's just a normal history book."

"When does it open in the evening?"

"I think there's a technical fault. It doesn't open anymore."

We drove on in silence. All the white marble did not seem as impressive now. There was something monotonous about it, colour-less. A female weed fighter was attacking the beds by the side of the road.

"Is the New President popular?" I asked innocently, knowing full well that it was part of his job to offer words of praise for the president.

"He is most excellent!" The answer was heartfelt. "Electricity, gas and salt, all free. Do you know of any other country where gas and electricity are free?"

"No," I said. "Who do you like best, the First President or the New President?"

Aslan appeared to reflect on my question.

"The first was perhaps even better, because petrol was free then as well. Now we have to pay a little. But before, we didn't have the

Internet, which we do now. You see, it's hard to compare. Both have their good points."

"A lot of the websites are blocked," I said. "YouTube and Facebook, for example. And what about Twitter?"

"That's to protect the young people. Lots of girls post naked pictures of themselves on Facebook. They're young and don't think about the consequences. Our Good President is only trying to prevent them from ruining their lives and the honour of their families."

"It's not possible to post naked photographs on Facebook."

"Isn't it?" Aslan looked at me, dumbfounded. "But then why has Our Good President blocked Facebook?"

In the period immediately after the inauguration of the New President, human rights campaigners and dissidents nurtured a hope that Turkmenistan was on the brink of a sorely needed democratisation process. One of the first things that Gurbanguly Berdimuhamedov did was to overturn some of Turkmenistan's most unpopular laws. The months and days reverted to their old names, and pensioners were once more given their pensions. Obligatory schooling was increased again to ten years. The ban on ballet, opera and the circus was also lifted.

But this hope was extinguished as soon as it had been ignited. *Ruhnama* is no long part of the school curriculum, but now pupils have to read instead *The Grandchild Realising His Grandfather's Dream*, which I had bought in English translation at Mira's bookshop, as well as *The Bird of Happiness*, which is about the New President's background and childhood. Gurbanguly Berdimuhamedov's father was a policeman in a small town, and his former office has now been made into a museum. The unit where he worked has been named after him. Since 2008, university students have not been able to take *Ruhnama* Studies, but are now offered Berdimuhamedov Studies.

Gurbanguly Berdimuhamedov has followed a fascinating career

path. He was born in 1957 and grew up as an only son with seven sisters. He qualified as a dentist at twenty-two, and a few years later completed his education with a Ph.D. in Odontology. He worked as a dentist for fifteen years, before being appointed minister of health in 1997. Then, in 2001, he was appointed additionally as deputy chairman of the cabinet of ministers, the second most powerful position in the country. Turkmenbashi was also the prime minister. When Turkmenbashi died in 2006, Gurbanguly Berdimu-hamedov became president. The speaker of parliament, the person who according to the law should assume the presidential duties after the death of a president, was imprisoned on the same day that Berdimuhamedov took office.

No-one can explain why Berdimuhamedov, Turkmenbashi's dentist, took over as president. He was one of the few ministers who survived the crises of Turkmenbashi's reign without ever being sacked or put in prison. There has long been a rumour that Ber-dimuhamedov is in fact Turkmenbashi's illegitimate son, and many have pointed out the striking physical resemblance between the two. If true, Berdimuhamedov must have been conceived when Turkmenbashi was seventeen. A more credible explanation is that Berdimuhamedov managed to become and remain one of Turkmen-bashi's trusted confidants, and that he was skilful when positioning himself in the power hierarchy. If documents leaked from American diplomats are to be believed, he is otherwise not especially intelli-gent: Berdimuhamedov "does not like people who are smarter than he is. Since he's not a very bright guy, he is suspicious of a lot of people."[i]

Since coming to power Berdimuhamedov has not only contin-ued to keep an iron grip on the country, he has refined his hold. The media has as little freedom as it had under Turkmenbashi, and Turkmenistan has kept its bottom ranking in Reporters without

Borders' World Press Freedom Index, alongside Eritrea and North Korea. Even small errors are harshly punished – for example, the cockroach incident in 2008. During the nine o'clock news one February evening, a brown cockroach scuttled across the studio table without anyone in the studio noticing. The programme was then shown again later the same night, cockroach and all. When the Ministry of Culture staff came to work the next morning, all hell broke loose. As expected, the cockroach's cameo appearance was not well received by the president, and on his orders thirty employees of the state T.V. channel were fired.

In 2010, the dentist adopted the name *Arkadag*, The Protector. Two years later, the first statue of him appeared in the capital. In contrast to Turkmenbashi's gold statues, it was made from white marble.

Yet again, we turned into an empty car park. We were in the middle of nowhere, somewhere between the town and mountains. The Museum of Neutrality, a three-legged arch that towered in front of us, looked more like a futuristic space rocket than anything else. There is a lift that goes to the top of the tower from one of the feet. On top, there is a twelve-metre gold statue of Turkmenbashi, the same one that had been on the top of the Arch of Neutrality in the centre of Ashgabat. The original Arch of Neutrality was taken down in 2010, and this new monument was built outside the centre. To compensate for its less central location, the new monument is ninety-five metres high, a full twenty metres taller than its predecessor. However, the gold statue of Turkmenbashi no longer turns with the sun.

"Lots of foreigners think we just moved the Arch of Neutrality," Aslan said, with an amused chuckle. "Of course we didn't. Our Good President ordered a whole new monument. Obviously."

"Why did the old one have to be pulled down?"

"For security reasons," he said earnestly. "People could see into the presidential palace from the top. And obviously that wasn't on."

It is also possible that Berdimuhamedov was simply tired of the view from his office being blocked by an enormous tower with a gold statue of his predecessor on top.

From the panorama windows in the body of the tower we could look out over the whole of Ashgabat. When we were driving along the broad boulevards between the marble apartment blocks the city had felt enormous. But from here I could see that it was not so big after all. A few clusters of marble apartment blocks, and straight, empty roads. And all around the centre of the city, the barren desert stretched in every direction, as far as the eye could see, until it disappeared into a haze.

DESERT FLOWER

For the first time on my travels, I am without language. In Ashgabat, everyone spoke Russian; this is a different world, another Turkmenistan – here they cannot even understand the simplest phrases. I try hello: *privet!* The children smile at me and shake their heads. Their clothes are torn and dirty, none of them have shoes. *Kak vas zovut?* what are you called? The eyes that meet mine show no comprehension. I dig out my slim dictionary and look up how to say hello, but there must be something wrong with my pronunciation, because they still do not understand. In a final attempt, I show them the page and point to the words. They look at the letters, full of curiosity, then shake their heads again: they are clearly illiterate. Instead, they grab hold of my arm and lead me behind the mud-brick houses to a fenced enclosure. There are three camels inside, each tied to a stake. The animals look at us with no curiosity as they munch on the hay in their odd, crooked mouths. The hair hangs from their bellies in clumps. And there is a strong smell of dung and urine.

A young woman comes towards us. She is wearing a wide, flowery dress and her long hair is partially covered by a scarf. Her face is round and brown as a nut. *Privet!* I try again. She covers her mouth with a corner of her scarf and shakes her head. Giggling, she sits down on a pail beside one of the camels and starts to pull its teats. The children point at my camera impatiently, and I obediently start to take pictures. They laugh when they see themselves on the small display screen. They pose again, in front of the camel, straighten their dirty clothes and smile disarmingly.

We are only a few hours from Ashgabat, but we could as well be on the other side of the world. This small village comprises ten or twelve families, as many as the well can support. The simple, flat-roof houses are made from mud bricks. They are sparsely furnished. A brand new solar panel ensures that they have a little electricity in the evening, but only enough to watch a couple of hours of T.V. after the sun has gone down. A small, open shack behind the camel enclosure serves as the only toilet in the village. The excrement out in the fields is proof that most people prefer to answer nature's call under the open sky.

Once the woman has finished milking the camel, she takes me by the arm and leads me into one of the low houses. Her house. There are two chests up against one of the walls, some big cushions, thin mats and a cloth on the stone floor. The walls are bare, except for a machine-woven brown hanging and a couple of photographs: one of her parents and a wedding picture of her and her husband in Ashgabat. She is wearing traditional Turkmen bridal garb, with a bride's thick, embroidered veil in white, gold and red. Her face is hidden behind the lace and long, thin tassels. Her husband is a bit shorter than she is, and stares sombrely at the camera. Ashgabat's futuristic marble buildings rise up behind them.

I sit on one of the large cushions. The young woman comes in with a piece of dry bread and a pot of tea. She stands and watches as I pull off a piece of bread and take a sip of tea. I look up at her and smile, she smiles back. I nod and smile. She nods and smiles again. "Tastes good," I say in English and Russian, and what I believe is Turkish. My hostess smiles and shakes her head. I shrug and smile. She smiles back, and points at the bread and tea. I take another piece of the dry bread and wash it down with tea. She smiles. I smile.

How long do I have to stay sitting here to avoid being seen as rude? Ten minutes? Fifteen? Fortunately, my guide, Murat, comes to my rescue. He is a good-natured man, with kind eyes and weathered skin. Even though he is the oldest of my guides, he is in many ways the most youthful. He smiles and laughs a lot, and is one of the few who dare to criticise the regime.

"You're supposed to rest your back against that," he whispers and points to the cushion I am sitting on. I quickly slip down onto the mat.

The woman is called Peach Blossom and, according to Murat, is the same age as me. She was married when she was eighteen and has five children.

"Then she certainly has enough to keep her busy."

Murat translates. Peach Blossom nods eagerly.

"I work from five in the morning until late at night," she says. "There's always something to do. Bake the bread. Get water from the well. Milk the camels. Wash the clothes. Wash the house. I never have time to sit down. What about you – how old are you, are you married, do you have children?"

Murat answers her questions for me. Yes, she is married. No, she does not have children. Peach Blossom's hostess-smile changes to one of sympathy.

"You still have time," Murat translates, and says something to Peach Blossom. She disappears out and after a while returns with two pots full of a white, lumpy mass.

"*Chal!*" Murat says reverently, and lifts the wooden spoon to his mouth. "This is better than in town. Fresher. We Turkmen can never get enough *chal*, it's our favourite thing."

The drink smells very yeasty. I lift a spoon to my mouth and swallow. The taste is indescribable.

"Delicious, isn't it?" Murat watches me with bated breath. "People in the villages drink it all the time. That's why they're never ill."

I take another spoonful, and then one more. It tastes of yeast and old milk, with a rancid, bitter top note. The taste sticks in my throat and comes up again in reflux. I drink yet another spoonful. The methodology courses in social anthropology have drummed into me that if you do not eat the local food, all is lost. I hold my breath and take one more mouthful.

"I knew you'd like it," Murat says happily, and sends Peach Blossom out for more. "Making *chal* is a long process, almost an art. And these villagers are masters at it. They mix half and half fresh camel milk and water, and let it stand a while. Then they add a *chal* culture and leave it to mature at room temperature. They drink a little every day and add some fresh camel milk."

"How long does the mixture stand?"

"Oh, that depends. But usually a year, sometimes longer."

I have to get away from the free-flowing soured camel's milk, but where should I go? In a moment of inspiration, I ask to see the village school. Peach Blossom takes me to a simple building at the end of the village. With a small key, she opens the door to the spartan classroom. There are eight or nine worn desks in the room. Posters of the Turkmen alphabet hang on the walls, illustrated with colourful figures. Above the blackboard is a framed portrait of the New President.

"Is it a holiday today?"

Peach Blossom shakes her head and embarks on a long explanation.

"The teacher is ill," Murat translates.

As Peach Blossom locks the door behind us, I feel the soured camel milk taking effect and have to run over to the improvised toilet shack. I get there only just in time.

During the night, I will have ample opportunity to study the corrugated metal walls of the toilet shack. In the light from my head torch, they look as if they are alive and rippling.

―⁓―

"The Karakum Desert is at its most beautiful and welcoming in April," Murat tells me. The landscape we are driving through is flat and monotonous, and yet, at the same time, constantly changing, which strangely enough only amplifies the monotony. It is as though time is standing still. As though we are standing still.

I had never imagined the desert could be like this. The Sahara is a sea of brown, umoving waves, enormous and timeless, but the Karakum Desert is full of colours. The sandy ground is covered in a delicate layer of grass. Scrubby bushes and small, twisted trees grow up the sandy hills; in their shadows, white and yellow flowers bloom. In the middle of the day, the sun in the cloudless sky is warm, but the evenings are cool and the nights just above freezing. No matter how many of the travel agency's dirty military sleeping bags Murat gives me, I am still cold and lie in the tent longing for the camels' morning bellow.

"The sun will soon burn off any sign of life, and the landscape will be brown and colourless again," Murat says. "It's beautiful here then as well, but in a more brutal way."

The Karakum Desert covers more than seventy per cent of the territory of Turkmenistan. *Karakum* means black sand, and in the olden days the name was enough to strike fear in the hearts of most merchants and explorers. The Karakum Desert was reckoned to be one of the most dangerous parts of the Silk Road: in winter, the caravans risked heavy snow and violent storms, and the summers were also harsh. The wild tribes that lived in the desert were not always friendly. Many of them profited from plundering the caravans and selling the travellers at the slave market in Khiva.

The colours gradually disappear and everything turns brown. The bushes are stripped of any green, and there are no leaves on the trees.

"We're getting closer to people," Murat remarks.

There are more and more tyre tracks, criss-crossing each other to create a chaotic pattern. From the top of a hill, a shallow valley suddenly opens out. The square mud houses below almost blend in with the ground. If it had not been for the solid cars parked outside some of the houses, we could well have been in the Middle Ages. The village probably looked much the same back then. We know from travellers of that time that this village, Damla, has been here for over a thousand years, protected from marauding hordes by its isolated location. Not even Genghis Khan's feared horsemen found their way here.

We stop at the head of the valley, where the first family lives. Two young, giggling daughters meet us and show us into the yurt, the round, carefully made tents of Central Asia, which they have built beside the small mud house. The smoke vent in the middle of the roof lets in streaks of daylight. The floor and walls are covered in red carpets, and there are lots of cords and tassels to make the circular interior cosy, almost like a cabin. We sit down on the soft, colourful mats, and I, now in the know, lean my upper body against the big cushions. The sisters start to chop onions and tomatoes in the small kitchen area by the entrance, the women's domain. They are both thin and lanky, with narrow, squinting eyes and fine lines on their faces. They glance at us from their pots when they think we are not looking. I find myself feeling sorry for them because they are obviously not married yet, but then I find out that they are only nineteen and twenty-one years old. The younger is called Ogulnar and is a walking prayer: *nar* means pomegranate, and *ogul* means son. The parents, who already had two daughters but no sons, hoped that God would hear their offering, a pomegranate for a son. And God listened. The mother bore three more children, and each of them a son.

The sisters' soup is piping hot and tastes of sun and green apples. The eldest has started to wash up outside. Ogulnar stands in the entrance and looks at us. A shy smile reveals that she is missing a front tooth. In her hands, she holds a big, thick notebook.

"Come and read for us!" Murat urges her. She stays standing where she is, hesitant. Murat encourages her again, and again. Only then does she come and sit down with us. She starts to read. Her eyes half-closed, she recites from the neatly written verses in the notebook. Her voice is surprisingly strong. The strange sounds find each other on each exhalation and link together; it is as though she is singing without a melody. "Oh Karakum!" is the only thing I understand, and yet I feel that I understand it all. Praise for the desert, for her country, for the sky and sand and everything that surrounds her. Afterwards, Murat translates as best he can:

> Oh, Karakum, oh black sand, which is
> forever changing and always the same!
> Oh, Karakum, which has given me life
> and gives me all that I need!
> Oh, Karakum, oh my desert,
> what would I do without you?
> I never tire of looking at you,
> you always have something new to teach me.
> Your plants, which heal,
> water that quenches thirst,
> my village, which is here for me,
> which has fostered me;

there is always someone here I can ask,
always someone who will help me.
Oh, Karakum, I will never leave you!
Oh, my village, you will always be my home.

Everything except the content vanishes in Murat's spontaneous translation – and mine – but it is as close as I can get to Ogulnar's poetry. She continues to read, from another page, from another book. I have no idea how many such books she has, all closely written in neat letters, full of praise for the small, big world she lives in. Her parents do not understand how they came to have such a daughter. She has gone to the village school like all the other children, and has barely read a book, let alone poetry, because they have none. But from the time that she learned to understand the mystery of letters, Ogulnar has written. It comes over her all of a sudden, she becomes distant and strange, and the family then know that shortly she will run from the boiling pots and goats with udders full of milk to fill another page in one of the thick notebooks.

—ɯ—

I spent days and days like this, in a jeep bumping along shallow, uneven tracks in the sand, through a flat, unchanging landscape. This is the real Turkmenistan. More than half the Turkmen population live in small settlements and villages in the desert, and they live from hand to mouth. To these poor farmers, the white marble buildings, shining cars and groomed people of Ashgabat must seem like Disneyland, a mirage.

There are no reliable statistics for unemployment in Turkmenistan. In 2004, the last year for which there is an estimate, the *C.I.A. Factbook* puts unemployment at around sixty per cent. The same

year, the National Institute for Statistics and Information of Turkmenistan stated that unemployment was unchanged at 2.6 per cent.
Around half the labour force is employed in the agriculture sector,
which accounts for a mere seven per cent of the country's gross
domestic product. Most Turkmen farmers, like the families of Peach
Blossom and Ogulnar, live from what the ground, camels and goats
can give them, and are not really part of the country's gas-driven
economy. These poor farmers live and die in their villages, detached
and cut off from the rest of the state, which is centred around the
towns, gas works and the political elite's marbled luxury lifestyle.

And yet it was here, among these poor people, who own nothing
more than a few cooking utensils, a couple of camels and a flock
of goats, that I was given the warmest welcome. These people
must have been just as isolated and cut off during the Soviet era,
because even after generations of Soviet domination and socialist
schooling, scarcely any of them knew so much as a single word of
Russian. Even though we had no shared language, I was welcomed
like a long-lost daughter wherever I went. With bright smiles, they
waved me into their yurts and simple mud houses, and shared what
little they had: a cup of tea, a bowl of soured camel milk, a piece
of dry bread.

I, however, spent most of the time behind closed doors, in the
passenger seat of the travel agency's Land Cruiser. The desert is truly
a deserted place. We could drive for hours, sometimes a whole day,
without seeing anyone. One morning was pretty much like the next.
The days rolled into each other. The monotony was occasionally
broken by well-fed desert rats with insolent eyes that darted across
the tracks with a hair-breadth's margin, and golden eagles that sailed
and glided on air currents on the horizon. Sometimes we drove past
a plain, dilapidated caravan, belonging to a lone desert nomad, and
occasionally we spotted a cluster of tents somewhere in the haze.

Petrol is cheap in Turkmenistan and domestic flights are as good as free. The travel agency had therefore not bothered to work out the most (transport) efficient itinerary, but had me criss-crossing the country, from one end to the other. During these long journeys, the drivers and guides were my only companions. Some of them were with me for days, others just sat behind the wheel for a few hours before they were relieved by the next driver at a crossroads or in one of the towns we passed through. These emissaries from the travel agency were the only real contact I had with the dictatorship's subjects. They were my key. They *had* to be my key, because I had no-one else. The eyes of power were omnipresent in the towns. Even though I had the impression I could walk about freely in Ashgabat, I could not strike up a conversation with anyone about anything other than the most banal things: ordering a coffee or haggling for a carpet. A Turkmen who criticises the regime is putting his or her life at risk; simply having contact with a foreigner gives rise to suspicion. Outside the major towns and cities, I was dependent on my guides and drivers to act as interpreters. The rural population spoke only Turkmen.

Deep in the desolate Yangykala Canyons, I dared to ask one of the drivers a politically sensitive question. We were hundreds of kilometres from the nearest settlement and we were totally alone. The majestic silence was broken only by the odd gust of wind. The landscape rolled away below us in frozen waves. The red, green and white formations went on and on and on, eroded over millions of years.

The eighteen-year-old driver looked at me, aghast. He could hardly have been more horrified if I had asked if he had slept with his mother.

"It's not allowed even to *think* critical thoughts about the president," he said gravely. Then he started to tell me about gas, which is free, about electricity, which is free, about water, which is also free, about salt, which is free, and about petrol, which is *almost* free. To support his argument, he pulled up the sleeve of his sweater and showed me a black plastic watch. The dentist president gives me a Mona Lisa smile from under the second hand.

"Everyone in my class was given one of these watches when *The Good President* came to inspect our school," he told me. "He works night and day to improve living standards for his people. No, no-one can criticise *him*! If I was going to criticise anyone, it would be myself."

"Why would you criticise yourself?"

"Because I don't work hard enough. Each one of us has a responsibility to play our part and to help our country develop."

His answer was both childishly naive and unyielding, presumably not too dissimilar to how the Communists expressed themselves in the days of the Soviet Union. I should not have been surprised. The driver was born into it, he had never experienced anything else. Every day, throughout his life, he had absorbed propaganda about how wonderful the president was and how benign the regime was, it had been drummed into him. No wonder that his belief was strong.

What is more, his arguments were not unfounded. One of the reasons that the regime in North Korea is faltering is that the state cannot provide its people with basic provisions. It is hard to believe you live in the best country in the world when you go to bed hungry, night after night. Everyone in Turkmenistan has access to free goods such as gas and salt, and subsidised petrol, so the people, even the poorest, feel that the state cares about them. And most important of all: no-one need go to bed hungry.

—⁊⁊—

I was supposed to travel the final stretch through the desert without a guide, to the ruins of the oasis town of Dehistan and then on to the modern oil refinery town of Balkanabat. I wanted to save money and thought I would manage fine with only a driver. However, the travel agency sent Maksat with me all the same and gave various reasons for doing so. We had to drive through a nature reserve and there might be a problem at the checkpoints if I was travelling without a guide. It would be boring for me to travel all that way on my own with only the driver. The driver was not familiar with the route, so needed someone to help him follow the right tracks.

"Ah, so that's what they said," Maksat said when I explained what the head of the travel agency had told me. He was about my age, and taller than most Turkmens, with broad shoulders and a chiselled, masculine face. His hair was black and short, his lips thin and sensitive, and, from a flattering angle, he looked a bit like Tom Cruise. Until he smiled, and flashed his gold teeth.

"So why are you here?"

"Ah, so that's what they said," he repeated, and narrowed his eyes.

Maksat was nice enough, but he knew nothing about ruins. When we got to Dehistan, he wandered around the mounds of earth, showing no interest in them whatsoever, and read to me from the guidebook: "Dehistan was the largest and most important town in Western Turkmenistan from the tenth to the fourteenth century. Parts of the minaret were built by the architect Abu Bini Ziyard in 1004. Of the mosque of Muhammad Khorezmshah, only the eighteen-metre portal remains. The town covered an area of more than two hundred hectares and was protected by a double wall. The town was abandoned in the fifteenth century."

The preferred building material of the time was dried clay, so all that remained of the walls and most other buildings were some overgrown mounds and other lumps and bulges in the terrain. I wandered around in the sand and tried to imagine how it had looked a thousand years ago, when everything was contained within the town walls.

"Are you nearly finished?" Maksat said. We had been there only five minutes.

"No." After all, it had taken us eight hours to drive there.

After another five minutes: "Are you done now?"

"No."

"Is it O.K. if I wait in the car?"

"Of course."

When we were driving, however, Maksat talked incessantly. About spies, in particular.

"A quarter of all my tourists have been spies," he confided in me.

"How do you know?"

"Well, it's not that difficult to tell. You just need to know the signs."

"Such as?"

He did not answer straight away. "Spies never look you in the eye and wear sunglasses all the time, indoors too. Their shoes are always well polished. They take pictures of people, not ruins. They pretend not to understand Russian."

"I take pictures of people."

"You're not a spy."

"How do you know that?"

"Your shoes."

I did not get a chance to ask Maksat what he thought about the president, as he pipped me to the post.

"Dictatorships are good," he declared out of the blue. We were talking about eagles. "We're in a transition phase right now, so we need a strong leader. There are five major tribes in Turkmenistan, and lots of smaller ones. Had-it-not-been-for-our-president they would all be at war with each other. Thanks-to-our-president there is peace and prosperity in our country."

"But is it really necessary to have pictures of him everywhere?"

"Our Good President has such an ordinary appearance that it could be anyone on the photographs. His face represents the people in general."

In the evening, Maksat got out a bottle of vodka that he said was for all three of us. When he had drunk most of it himself, he started to talk about President Putin.

"He's a good man. He has *understood*."

"Understood what?"

"That homosexuality is unnatural. It should not be allowed. Then everything will go to the dogs, but you Europeans don't seem to understand. Fortunately, homosexuals are kept under control in Turkmenistan."

—⁊⁊⁊—

Not all the travel agency's representatives were as loyal. Some of the older guides and drivers were less impressed by the president's propaganda machine. Bekdurdy was one of them. He was only going to drive me a few hundred kilometres, then another driver would take over at some crossroads. But in the space of the short time we had together, Bekdurdy told me the story of his son, who had been born with a serious hearing defect. The Turkmen doctors could not help him and recommended that the parents pray to God. Russian doctors, on the other hand, could fix the boy's hearing with an operation that was seen as routine in most western countries.

"The clinic in St Petersburg wanted to give me a free medical visa, but in the end I had to pay for an expensive tourist visa. As Turkmenistan has a functioning health system, in theory, it shouldn't be necessary for us to leave the country for medical treatment. To do so is seen as an indirect criticism, and everyone with a medical visa is stopped at the airport."

So, like most Turkmens in similar situations, Bekdurdy and his son applied for a tourist visa. As his son's disability was invisible, they left the country without any problems. Turkmens who are visibly ill are routinely stopped at the airport and denied the right to travel, even if they are going "on holiday".

The operation in St Petersburg was a success. When they returned to Turkmenistan, his son could hear again. Presumably the Turkmen doctors wrote in his journal that his parents' prayers had been answered.

"They're just lying to us," Bekdurdy said, bitterly. "They're not telling the truth. They say that everything is fine here, but just look around. Look at the roads, they're full of holes, they're falling apart. Look at our houses, they're draughty and there are power cuts all the time. No-one has any money. No-one is free."

—∽—

When Murat, the oldest of my guides, started to talk about Turkmenbashi, we got stuck.

"He was stark raving mad, and got madder and madder. He didn't realise that people were laughing at him behind his back. People named schools and villages after him because they knew they would be given money."

He spoke in a hushed voice, as he always did when he talked about the president and the authorities, even though we were utterly alone in the middle of the enormous black desert. We had driven and driven, halfway across the country, from the border with Uzbekistan far into the desert. There were no roads, only narrow tyre tracks in the sand. Whoever was unlucky enough to run out of petrol here, or get stuck in the sand, risked having to wait days or even weeks before being found.

"Turkmenbashi thought he was loved, but most of the people hated him. They cursed him silently and wished he were dead. Lots of people believe that's why he died so early."

The wheels spun in the sand and the car turned here and there without moving. Murat muttered something in Turkmen and managed to reverse a few metres. Then he put his foot on the accelerator, but halfway up the slope, the tyres started to spin again and we were stuck.

"Everything will be fine, don't you worry," Murat assured me. He got out of the car and found a set of sand ladders that he put in front of the tyres. Then he tried to accelerate again. The wheels spun in the sand, and the car did not budge.

"Luckily, the New President is better than the old one," Murat said, as he let the car roll back once more. "Not only has he given the old names back to the days and months, but he also belongs to the Soviet generation. He copies Putin in every way he can, and is supposed to be so sporty and athletic. I wonder when someone's going to tell the emperor that he's not wearing any clothes..."

This time we nearly got to the top of the slope before the car slid to the side and the sand piled up in front of the wheels.

"My hope is that the new generation, who have studied abroad and seen the world, will bring change," Murat said, and put the car into reverse. "This is all going to be fine, don't you worry. The problem with the current regime is that they won't listen to criticism. They're terrified of change. My hope is with the young. They're the future."

On the fourth attempt we made it. The front wheels struggled over the edge and the back wheels followed. The desert in front of us was flat and unpredictable. Murat tried to hide his relief.

THE DICTATOR'S FALL

A week before the great day, the usual video clips of glimpses from the president's working day that were shown on the big screens in Ashgabat were replaced with horses. The newspapers were full of articles about horses and all the T.V. programmes were about horses.

Three days before the great day, I read an interview in Turkmenistan's largest Russian paper that astounded me. In the interview, a certain E. Fatland expressed her admiration for the unique qualities of the Turkmen horse. She also enthused about what a fantastic country Turkmenistan was and all the wonderful hospitable people who lived there. The article was illustrated with a photograph of me on horseback in the desert. At the start of my stay I had gone for a ride in the desert, arranged by the travel agency, but I had not been informed that a photograph from this trip might end up in the newspaper. Nor had I ever spoken to the journalist.

The day before the great day, there was to be a huge beauty contest for horses. The bus that was to take us to the hippodrome left at six in the morning. Men in freshly pressed suits and women in red dresses squeezed onto the bus. The guides from the travel agency had also dressed up. I felt rather shabby in my practical travelling clothes, but it was too late to do anything about it; we were already late in departing. The bus driver ferried us safely through police blocks and checkpoints until we were far from the centre of town. For the last few kilometres, the road was lined with students holding white plastic flowers.

Half Ashgabat was there to see the contest for the most beautiful Turkmen horse. Outside the hippodrome, there were queues of parked white buses. A sea of black plaits and red dresses flowed from the car park towards the entrance. There were yet more students with flowers and flags by the roadside. They must have been standing there for a long time. They waved their small flags diligently, without a hint of a smile. Outside the brand new hippodrome, built in white marble, of course, the dancers had started their performance. I stopped to take a photograph, but was briskly waved on by an authoritative man in a suit: "Hurry, hurry!"

Students and civil servants are duty-bound to be present at events like this. The Turkmen horse beauty contest and National Horse Day on the following day are among the most important events of the year. There are between forty and fifty public events every month; everything from the opening of a new sports academy to the opening of a bridge, no matter how small, was celebrated. And while Turkmenbashi's birthday is no longer celebrated, February 18, the day the dentist was inaugurated as president, is now marked with pomp and circumstance.

There is a clear hierarchy on the grandstand. The front rows are reserved for old men with long beards and blue kaftans. Behind them the matronly older women wearing flowery headscarves and blue waistcoats. The students in red dresses sat to the right, and the boys in suits sat to the left. We foreigners, who were dressed in all kinds of colours, were given our own row towards the back. We filled barely half the available seats.

At seven o'clock the doors closed. All the important seats were taken. There was still no sign of any activity on the track, but, thanks to some enormous screens, we could watch the dancers waving their arms in the square outside. A young journalist from the state channel was going around interviewing V.I.P. guests. The journalist clearly knew that we would be waiting a while, as the guests were given as much time as they liked. The screens had to be filled, regardless of whether there was anything new, and an increasingly desperate looking journalist interviewed one old man after another. Soon she had spoken to all the guests of honour. As she and the cameraman passed our row of unsuitably dressed foreigners, their eyes lit up. Before I knew what was happening, I was standing in front of the camera and hearing myself say: "Good morning, Turkmenistan!"

I do not recall much from my three minutes of fame, except that I was terrified I would forget to congratulate the president on the celebrations. I had been clearly instructed to remember this. Apart from that I could say whatever I liked, as long as I smiled. Everything I said would be dubbed into Turkmen in anyway.

The sun was beating down from a blue sky, but we were sitting under the roof. The Italian lady beside me was so cold in the northerly wind that her teeth were chattering. I stamped my feet and checked the time. Nearly eight o'clock. And still no sign of activity on the track. The journalist was interviewing one of the honourable guests for a second time. The young female students in front of us were chattering away, apparently oblivious to the cold. They were experienced spectators, and had fruit and nuts with them, which they generously shared with us and each other. I looked at my watch again. Five past eight. The Italian lady let out a heartfelt sigh.

At ten past eight, a groom led a horse into the arena. Behind him, another groom, and then more followed. Nine horses were lined up by the fence, and there they stood. To liven up the atmosphere, the manager of the travel agency suggested a game: which of the horses did *we* think was most beautiful? I chose number eight, with its shining, golden coat.

People in Turkmenistan have two great passions: carpets and

horses. Unlike their neighbours to the north in Kazakhstan, the Turkmens do not eat horse meat. They have an almost religious attitude to horses, the *akhal teke* race, in particular. This Turkmen horse breed is thought to be one of the oldest in the world and has a reputation for endurance. The horses are not especially big, but they are slim and well proportioned, with shiny, metallic coats. As some of the horses have a distinctive gold colour, they are also known as the golden horses. In 1956, Queen Elizabeth was given an *akhal teke* horse by Nikita Khrushchev, and the story goes that no matter how hard the queen's grooms tried to wash the gold polish from the horse's coat, it only got shinier. They thought that the Russians had painted the horse to impress them.

The breed almost died out during Stalin's rule. In an attempt to subdue the Turkmens, the Soviet regime banned private horse breeding and required farmers to slaughter their horses for meat. At one point, there were only 1,250 *ahal teke* horses left in the entire Soviet Union. So, in 1935, a group of riders set off on the journey of more than four thousand kilometres from Ashgabat to Moscow, in order to demonstrate to the authorities the unique quality of the breed. They rode day and night for eighty-four days, and the record soon became part of the history of the Turkmen Soviet Socialist Republic. The Turkmens slowly won support for their demands to stop the slaughter. During the Olympic Games in Rome in 1960, an *ahal teke* horse won the gold medal in dressage, and this heralded brighter times for the Turkmen breed. Today, it plays an important role in the Turkmen nation-building project. Every single town boasts a new hippodrome, and Turkmenistan is probably the only country in the world to have a special minister of horses.

At 9.30 a.m., when we had been waiting for three hours, the audience stood up as one and started patiently to clap. Everyone's eyes were on the centre of the course, where a figure dressed in a green jacket and traditional sheepskin hat nodded and smiled at the audience. The man in the green jacket was none other than Our Good President. I tried to read the impassive faces around me. Were they happy? Did they care at all? A booming man's voice drowned out the applause. With great enthusiasm and passion, he presented each horse as though it were the last hoofed creature on earth. Each one was paraded in front of the president, who nodded and smiled.

"Those horses are gifts to the president," Murat whispered, cynically. "The competition hasn't even begun."

The Italian lady put her head in her hands and groaned.

When the golden horse was presented, the president declared spontaneously that he wanted to take a ride. After the president's decision had been announced over the loudspeakers, it felt as though the applause would never end.

Then the president disappeared without any explanation. Perhaps he went to have breakfast, or to make an important telephone call. Or maybe he needed to lie down for a while. Whatever the reason, he was gone for some time. And while he was away, it was as though time slipped into another dimension, a non-time, and we all fell into a kind of trance. The sun was now high in the sky, but we were still in the shade. I tried to feel if my toes were still there. The Italian lady's eyes were black.

It was as though the audience had developed an ability to pre-empt the president's movements, because everyone stood up and started to clap well before he came into view. He strode into the stadium, nodding and smiling in every direction. With very masculine movements, he pulled off his green jacket, and, like a god in pure white, mounted the golden horse. He rode around in small circles for a couple of minutes, and, with the help of the groom, persuaded the horse to rear gently. The president was plainly encouraged by

THE DICTATOR'S FALL 88

all the jubilation, because when the ninth and final horse was presented, he decided to have a ride on that one too. This time, he wanted to do more than just ride round in small circles. He decided to go round the whole track. Every time the president switched pace from a trot to a gallop, the audience applauded enthusiastically, but most of the time he progressed at a majestic pace. The audience stayed on its feet and followed him until he was no more than a small dot on the other side of the hippodrome. The students in front of me were shivering now, but the president looked warm and happy as he sauntered along in the sun.

"It's always like this," Murat muttered so quietly that only I could hear. "It's a one-man show. No-one really wants to be here."

When the president finally withdrew to his box again, to yet another round of applause, the actual competition could finally begin. Half-wild beauties were led out onto the track, first unsaddled, so that their muscles and shining coats were shown at their best in the sun, then dressed up with ornate bridles, silk blankets and decorated saddles. The pompous voice on the loudspeaker introduced each horse in detail, and with every new contestant the enthusiasm and pitch increased, until eventually the voice took on North Korean dimensions. When all the horses had been presented, there was another pause and more waiting while the international jury deliberated and made their final decision. Minutes turned, it seemed, to hours. Perhaps the international jury were having a passionate debate. Maybe they were sitting there, drinking hot tea, chatting in the warm, cosy jury room. Maybe they were even eating a lavish lunch.

We had ample time to speculate about what they might be up to. The poor journalist had run out of guests of honour and was sending us desperate looks again. This time it was the Italian lady who was asked to speak. "Dear Turkmenistan," she started.

"Congratulations on this great day!" The journalist coughed discreetly. "But most of all I would like to thank the president for this fabulous event. Congratulations. I would also like to congratulate the Turkmen people . . ."

Around midday, a tremulous voice announced over the loudspeakers that the jury had reached their decision. A black, nervy horse was paraded back and forth to deafening applause and jubilation. The prize for the proud owner was a white sports car. The audience clapped wildly. Their enthusiasm felt genuine this time, possibly because the event was nearly over. Finally we were free. People jumped to their feet and headed towards the exits.

Outside, the flower girls were still standing there with glazed expressions. The dancers were still dancing in circles and lines, but now with stiff arm movements and strained smiles.

I squinted up at the sun and regained feeling in my toes.

Later on that evening, Murat phoned. He was very apologetic, but I could sense that he was relieved. There was a new group coming, he explained, and he had to go and meet a French couple at the airport and show them around town. Which meant that he, *unfortunately*, could not accompany me to the Horse Day celebrations the following day, as was set out in the Itinerary.

"As I said, I'm terribly sorry, but you'll be fine on your own, won't you? Just follow the other foreigners."

No doubt he later regretted that he had not been there.

When I came down to the hotel lobby just before six the following morning, rather pleased with myself for my discipline and punctuality, the young driver was already waiting for me.

"Why are you so late? Everyone left about two hours ago. The town was full of people and buses."

"Can we not just drive there ourselves?"

"Are you mad? There are police and roadblocks everywhere. Only buses are allowed in."

Luckily, we managed to catch up with and stop one of the last buses, which was full of people dressed in their finest, photographers and camera crews. Then off we set. After half an hour, the bus stopped outside a hippodrome that was even bigger and more ostentatious than that of the day before. Everything was bigger and better. There were guards and attendants everywhere, and the flower girls were lined up side by side along the road. I tried to count the number of buses, but had to give up.

Unlike the hippodrome from the day before, however, there was no roof. The morning sun had already warmed the plastic seats. I was placed between a row of men in expensive suits and a contingent of chattering French women, presumably the wives of the engineers employed by Bouygues, the French construction company behind the most prestigious buildings in Ashgabat.

A host of women handed out programmes with the start times for each race. They had a plan! A timeframe! The first race was due to start at 8.30 a.m., and all seven races would be over by eleven. There was a photograph of every horse and jockey, as well as the names of all the trainers and owners. The owner, in most cases, was the president of Turkmenistan or some other public body.

I had learned my lesson the day before, and was now prepared for the cold. It was easy enough to take off the extra layers on top, but my woolly long johns would be more of a problem. It was not yet eight, and already I could feel the sweat pooling in the small of my back. Another hour passed before anything happened on the tracks. Neither the horses nor the jockeys who took their positions at the start line bore any resemblance to those in the programme. The riders were dressed in traditional Turkmen clothes with sheepskin hats, the whole works. They were all presented *in extenso*, in

Turkmen. When the last jockey came into the stadium, the audience immediately stood up and clapped so loudly and for so long that I realised that it was none other than the president himself. Dressed in a red jacket and white hat, he mounted the waiting horse, number three. His entourage moved across to the other participants who were lined up on the other side of the track.

"It's a special race for the horse owners," the Russian sitting next to me whispered. He must have noticed how bewildered I was. "The first prize is eleven million dollars."

Despite the huge prize money, there was little evidence of excitement when the starting pistol was fired and the horses galloped off. By the first bend, one of the horses had already pulled ahead. The other riders discreetly held their horses back as they galloped towards the final straight. By the time they were a hundred metres from the finish line, the president was leading by about a length and a half. The crowd cheered wildly, but as the president crossed the finishing line, he shifted slightly in the saddle. This small movement caused the horse, which was still galloping at top speed, to lose its balance, stumble and fall. The president was thrown forward and landed on his back in the sand. The horse got up and trotted off, but the president did not move. The applause faltered. The horses right behind miraculously managed to swerve and avoid trampling the fallen jockey. When all the horses had galloped past and the dust had settled again, a legion of broad-shouldered men in dark suits stormed onto the track. They formed a ring around the president, but none of them seemed to know what to do, so they just stood there, surrounding the head of state.

The audience remained standing as well. The whole hippodrome held its breath. No-one said a word.

A couple of minutes passed before a small ambulance drove onto the track, blue light flashing. The bodyguards picked up the president's lifeless body and bundled him rather unceremoniously into the back. The ambulance then drove slowly out of the hippodrome, as if there was all the time in the world. Once it had disappeared, people sat back down, uncertain what to do. No-one spoke. The faces around me were inscrutable, closed, impossible to read. What were they thinking? Were they afraid? Were they secretly rejoicing?

The broad-shouldered security men stayed out on the track. Some of them paced back and forth, others turned in small circles, or just stood there, straight-backed, their hands by their sides. It was obvious that they had no idea what to do. Was their leader dead? Was the country without a president? The big screens showed clips of the dancers outside, moving in formation. The loudspeakers crackled, but still nothing was said.

I have no idea how long we sat like that. Maybe ten minutes, maybe half an hour. It was as though we were in a vacuum. No-one smiled, no-one cried. Had I just witnessed the death of a dictator? Was there a heated discussion going on at this very moment about who would succeed the dentist president?

The loudspeakers crackled again and a voice said something in Turkmen. The dancers vanished from the screen and were replaced by the final moments of the race, when the president galloped towards the finishing line, the clear winner. The clip of him triumphantly crossing the finishing line was shown over and over again, in slow motion. Applause spread through the stands.

Suddenly the bodyguards were busy. A couple of them fixed the part of a fence that had fallen, others started to kick sand into the depression where the president had fallen. The atmosphere on the stands eased. People ate sweets and chatted.

With no explanation, the audience rose abruptly to its feet. It was nearly half-past ten and everyone turned to look at the presidential stand. Through a window, we caught a glimpse of a figure in white. He waved. A cheer went up, followed by enthusiastic applause, but the people's faces remained impassive. Were they happy? Disappointed?

The figure moved away from the window, and a short while afterwards he walked out onto the track. His movements were as stiff as his smile. He lifted his hand in majestic greeting, then disappeared indoors again.

As if at the wave of a wand, the system clicked back into place. It was quickly decided that what had happened had in fact not happened. Once the normal races were underway, the men in suits moved around the stands with lists, picking out the tourists, one by one. We were told to take our cameras and follow the guards over to the main building, where we were forced to delete any photographs documenting the president's fall.

By the time the races were finally over, the sun was directly overhead and my woolly long johns were soaked with sweat. The president tottered out onto the podium to accept his eleven million dollar prize. In a drowsy voice, drugged with painkillers, no doubt, he gave a long thank-you speech. Even though I did not understand the language, I knew that he was heaping praise on the Turkmen horses. Before he withdrew, no doubt to sleep off the medicine, a groom appeared with the unfortunate winning horse, number three. The president gave him a conciliatory pat on the neck, and even kissed him on the muzzle. Cameras flashed. The audience cheered.

Horses clearly get away with more than people do in Turkmenistan.

I was later told that foreign journalists were kept in a separate room during the races. The photographers were forced to let a representative from the Ministry of Culture and Broadcasting look through their memory cards. And young female students in long red dresses made sure that no-one squirrelled away their card. Someone must have managed, however, as the following day an embarrassing clip was posted on YouTube.

Thanks-to-the-President's-vision, YouTube is fortunately blocked in Turkmenistan.

THE FINAL EXPEDITION

History is like a *matryoshka*, or Russian nesting doll. One doll opens to reveal another hidden inside; some are identical, others are painted in different colours and patterns. Layer upon layer, the colours fade and the materials disintegrate. Was this once a doll? And what about that splinter of wood? Finally we get to a doll that cannot be opened but sounds hollow when we shake it. We realise there must be more dolls inside. We may not even be halfway yet. But we can go no further. Not this time.

How many layers will we manage to uncover? We want to go back past Turkmenbashi and his gold statues, past Stalin and the Soviet Union, even further back, to before Russia's annexation of Turkmenistan, to a time before national borders. What traces of the past have survived to the present day?

Before ships and airplanes became the main means of transport for people and goods from one part of the world to another, Central Asia was the link between East and West. Caravans laden with silk, paper, ceramics, pepper and other exotic goods made their way from India and China via Central Asia to the aristocracy of the Roman empire. Central Asia, with its powerful rulers, great scientists and well-organised cities was not just a place of transit, however, it was also a conveyor of civilisation. People in the desert started to live together behind protective walls very early on. In the first century CE, the Greek historian and geographer Strabo described Central Asia as a "land of a thousand cities".

The ruins of the once renowned metropolis of Merv in eastern Turkmenistan cover such a large area that it is easiest to get around them by car. Merv was part of Alexander the Great's empire in the fourth century BCE, but was at its most powerful more than a millennium later, in the twelfth century. Even though little survives today, Merv is still deemed to be one of the best-preserved oasis towns on the Silk Road. Travel companies describe the ruins as one of the high points of any visit to Turkmenistan, and I had been looking forward to it. At first sight, Merv was a disappointment. Most of the structures are nothing more than mounds in the sand, and, in other places, unattractive scaffolding had been erected in anticipation of archaeological digs. The desert people did not build for eternity. Their main building material was clay, which was easy to work with, and efficient, as it provided good insulation against both the heat and cold. But it is not a material that withstands the test of time. Wind and weather wear down the walls and roofs, and if the buildings had not been regularly maintained, they collapsed and soon become part of the ground they once stood on.

Murat and I clambered up onto the remains of the city walls, which are now a slight wave across the landscape. From the top, we looked out over the light brown, flat earth that stretched to the horizon. Even here in Turkmenistan's largest and most important ruins, we were completely alone. No-one knows for certain what lies hidden beneath the ground within the ruins of these city walls. It may be houses or temples, perhaps even entire palaces. Although there were a number of excavations during the Soviet era, the work is still very much in its earliest phase – many, many more years of painstaking work remain.

Only a few structures stand above the rubble and mounds, such as the high, almost intact outer walls of Kyz Kala fortress, with its enormous round earthen pillars. Kyz Kala means "Maiden's

Castle", but no-one now knows when or why it was given this name.

"Some believe that the daughters of the king and his noblemen were educated here," Murat said. "The fortress was just outside the city walls, so at a safe distance from the sinful temptations of the town. According to legend, a neighbouring fortress, which is nothing more than rubble now, housed only boys. If one of them wanted to marry one of the girls from Kyz Kala, he had to throw an apple from his fortress over to hers. Given the distance between the two fortresses, the custom, if it ever existed, must have made lots of young men very unhappy." Murat laughed. He was full of stories and glowed every time he had a chance to tell one.

"There's another popular legend that there was once a princess in Merv who was loved by all for her beauty and kind, gentle nature," he said. "One day, a famous soothsayer came to the city. He foretold that the princess would die young. The king was of course horrified. In order to protect his daughter from all possible danger, he locked her inside an impregnable fortress outside the city. The princess could not understand what she had done to deserve this, and was sad and lonely in her new home. The king sent her a basket of lovely, ripe grapes to cheer her up. A poisonous snake lay hidden beneath the fruit. When the princess helped herself to the fruit, the snake bit her and she died."

Sleeping Beauty, I thought. Did the familiar old fairytale have its roots here in the desert? We may never know the origins of these stories about Kyz Kala, and whether there is any truth to them or not. The past speaks to us in half-finished sentences, and not always in a language we understand. But what we do know is this:

During the second golden age in the twelfth century, when Ahmad Sanjar was sultan of the Seljuk empire, Merv was one of the largest cities in the world with more than two hundred thousand inhabitants. The city's first golden age had been around 280 BCE, under King Antiochus 1 Soter, who was son of the Sogdian princess, Apama, and King Seleucus I Nicator, one of the generals who served in the army of Alexander the Great. Some say that Alexander the Great himself had previously visited the town, but there is no evidence to support this. The city was definitely called Alexandria for a short period, like so many other towns, before King Antiochus renamed it Antiochia in Margiana. Merv was at the time the capital of Margiana.

In the centuries that followed, Merv was ruled by kings and sultans from various kingdoms and empires. Thanks to its location, the city quickly became a cultural melting pot, with Jews and Buddhists and Nestorian Christians all settling here. They built houses of worship and followed their religions freely, living in peace with local Persians, who generally were Zoroastrians. They all practised tolerance. The caravans filled with silks and other goods from China also brought new fashions with them. Over time, the craftsmen in Merv learned how to produce silk, and by the tenth century, Merv had surpassed China to become the greatest exporter of silk to the West. Most of the city's inhabitants had converted to Islam by then and Merv quickly became one of the most important centres of learning in the Muslim world. The city's twelve libraries and observatory attracted students and scientists from near and far.

Today, the ruins of Merv are surrounded by desert, which was not always the case. In the first century CE, the Roman historian and naturalist Pliny the Elder describes the region as the most fertile in all Asia. A good number of geographers believe that the Amu Darya, known by Europeans as the Oxus, previously flowed into the Caspian Sea to the west, and not into the Aral Sea. If that is correct, the Karakum Desert may well have been a fertile basin a thousand years ago. Only when the Oxus changed course in the

thirteenth or fourteenth century, possibly as the result of an earthquake, did Turkmenistan become a desert.

Irrespective of where the river ran, we know for certain that
inhabitants of Merv had an ample supply of water: a carefully
designed, underground pipe network provided the city with fresh,
cold water from the Murgab river. In the twelfth century, as many
as twelve thousand people were employed in maintaining this
advanced water system. There were ice houses with suitably thick
walls outside the city, so the inhabitants could enjoy a refreshing
ice lolly on hot days. Merv was truly an oasis.

Then, in 1221, Genghis Khan's Mongol hordes came knocking
at the city gates. For a few days they wreaked havoc, killing nearly
all the inhabitants and leaving the city in ruins.

Genghis Khan is a remarkable historical figure. While it is not
certain in which year he was born, it is most likely that it was 1162.
He was the son of Yesügei, who was chief of the Kiyad tribe. His
mother, Hoelun, was abducted from the Olkhunut tribe and forced
to become Yesügei's second wife. When Genghis Khan, or Temüjin,
as he was actually called, was nine or ten, his father Yesügai was
poisoned and died while visiting an enemy tribe. Yesügei's two wives
were thrown out of the Kiyad tribe and had to fend for themselves.
Not much is known about Temüjin's youth, other than that he may
have killed his older half-brother, Begter, following a conflict. He
was then enslaved by a neighbouring tribe and forced to wear a
heavy wooden yoke around his neck and wrists. One day he managed to knock out his guard with the cangue, and escaped. Shortly
after, he married Börte, to whom he had been engaged since he was
nine. But no sooner were they married than Börte was abducted
by the Merkits, possibly as revenge for the abduction of Temüjin's
mother many years before. Temüjin succeeded in gathering an army
of shepherds and nomads, ten thousand strong. They attacked the

Mergids, who were then spread to all winds, and rescued Börte. Over the next few years, Temüjin gathered an even greater army, and many of the tribes nearby simply joined him. His goal was to become the sole ruler of all the Mongol tribes, a goal he achieved in 1206, when he was given the honorary title of Genghis Khan.

Genghis Khan made a number of changes to the Mongol way of life. Among other things, he introduced a law that banned the abduction of women and granted religious freedom to all people in the Mongolian empire. He also had the Uighur alphabet adapted to the Mongolian alphabet, so that it was possible to send written messages. He established an efficient messenger service, with posts all over the empire. With rested horses waiting at every post, the messenger could ride straight on to the next. Thus was the postal system invented. Conscription was introduced for all men who were fit to fight. The army was organised according to the decimal system, with base units of ten that were subordinate to larger units of a hundred, and a thousand, and finally ten thousand men. Genghis Khan based his choice of leaders for these units on their skills and personal merit, rather than kinship. Each soldier had his own horse, and as the Mongols more or less grow up on horseback, they were able to ride for days.

But such a big army needs something to do. Once Genghis Khan had conquered all the neighbouring tribes, including the Tatars, the Tanguts and the Uighurs, he turned his sights south, towards the wealthy dynasties and empires of what today is China. After several years of endeavour, the disciplined Mongolian army succeeded in conquering these people too, even though they initially had no experience whatsoever of capturing fortified towns. On occasion, the Mongols diverted entire water courses in order to force the people behind the town walls to surrender. They learned something new and improved their tactics and techniques from every tribe and people they vanquished. From the Chinese, they learned to use catapults and gunpowder.

Every time the Mongols conquered a town, they took everything of value. Soon all the women on the Mongolian steppes were wearing luxurious silk clothing. The men had modern swords, and the craftsmen they abducted supplied them with new, handmade goods. The problem was that all these craftsmen needed materials and equipment, as well as clothes and food. The Mongols were traditionally nomads and produced nothing of value other than the clothes they wore and the tents they lived in. The nomads' thirst for luxury goods was apparently unquenchable: the richer the Mongols became, the more towns and people they had to conquer in order to maintain their new extravagant lifestyles. It was not until 1217, when Genghis Khan turned fifty, that he seemed to have had his fill. By then he had conquered all Mongolia and two-thirds of what is now China. The Mongols were fabulously wealthy, with a constant flow of taxes from their vassal states in the south.

At that time, the Turkic sultan Muhammad II was the ruler of Khwarazm, an empire that covered the greater part of modern Afghanistan, Iran, Uzbekistan and Turkmenistan, including Merv. Genghis Khan wanted to establish trading links with the Sultan of Khwarazm, in order to gain access to the fine glasswork made by the Islamic craftsmen there.

"My greatest wish is to live in peace with you," he wrote to the sultan. "I will look on you as my son. You are of course aware that I have conquered China and all the tribes to the north. You know that my empire has a surplus of warriors and a silver mine, and that I have no need whatsoever to win more land. It is in our mutual interest to develop trade relations between our two peoples."[ii]

The sultan agreed to enter a trade agreement, and Genghis Khan sent off the first caravan loaded with luxury goods, including white camel hides, Chinese silk and jade. When the caravan reached the north-eastern province of Otrar, in the southern part of what is today Kazakhstan, it was attacked. Only one of the four hundred and fifty merchants in the caravan survived. It is unclear if it was Muhammad II himself who ordered that the caravan be plundered, or if the governor of Otrar had the caravan attacked on his own initiative. Whatever the case, the result was catastrophic. As the Persian historian Juviani remarked, the governor's attack not only wiped out a caravan, but "laid waste a whole world."

Genghis Khan who normally had no tolerance for betrayal and broken promises, took the incident with surprising calm. He sent a small delegation to Sultan Muhammad II and asked him to ensure that the person responsible for the attack was punished. Instead of agreeing to this reasonable request, the sultan had several members of the delegation killed and sent the survivors back to Mongolia with disfigured faces.

Genghis Khan was humiliated – and furious. He gathered his army, now more than 150,000 men, and set off west. The Mongolian army annihilated Otrar, and many of the other towns in Khwarazm. The soldiers plundered every town they conquered. They left rivers of blood in their wake. It is estimated that three-quarters of the people in Samarkand were killed. Kath, which had been the capital of Khwarazm, was destroyed. Urgench, Nishapur and Balkh suffered the same fate.

In 1221, the army reached Merv. The third legend that Murat told me about the Kyz Kala fortress was that forty girls sought refuge in the fortress when the Mongols invaded the city. The terrified girls saw with their own eyes the horror that the Mongols inflicted on the inhabitants of Merv, and, in order to avoid the same unhappy fate, they climbed onto the roof, mustered their courage and jumped to their deaths.

Tolui, Genghis Khan's youngest and most ruthless son, was responsible for this campaign. According to a contemporary account, after the city had surrendered Tolui settled down on a gold chair to watch a mass execution. Men, women and children were separated and divided between the various military units. With the exception of four hundred craftsmen, everyone was beheaded. No-one was spared, not babies, nor old people.

Is it even possible to imagine the panic and screams? The smell of urine and excrement as the dead emptied themselves? The sound of tens of thousands of heads rolling, and the warm, pumping blood that stained the desert sand dark red?

Some days after the massacre, the Mongol soldiers returned to the battleground and killed the few survivors who had managed to crawl back to the ruins of their homes.

In addition to the gigantic human cost, the Mongols destroyed all the bookshops, observatories, libraries and schools. Priceless treasures were lost for ever. They were also careful to destroy the water system in Merv and many of the other oasis towns, and either killed or abducted anyone who knew anything about the construction and maintenance of the system. Thus knowledge that had been acquired over generations was lost. Three years later, swathes of Central Asia lay in dust.

The Mongols continued their campaign west, to Russia and to modern day Poland, and south to the Islamic caliphates in the Middle East. When Genghis Khan died in 1227, his empire was divided up between his descendants, who continued to rule until the empire gradually broke up in the fourteenth and fifteenth centuries.

Trade did flourish under Mongol rule and the so-called *Pax Mongolica*. The Mongols were brutal warriors, but as rulers they were relatively tolerant and did not interfere much with the lives and culture of the people they conquered. There was religious freedom throughout the empire and many Mongols converted to Christianity. Since they were nomads, the Mongols left no buildings of their own behind, but they did finance the construction of churches in China and Buddhist stupas in Persia. Their single most important contribution to the history of the world is perhaps the extensive exchange of ideas and inventions between East and West that the empire facilitated. The Mongols brought German miners to China and Chinese doctors to Baghdad. They paved the way for the modern cannon by combining different inventions such as Chinese gunpowder, Muslim flame-throwers and European bell-founding techniques. Genghis Khan's grandson, Kublai Khan, who ruled the eastern section of the empire, introduced paper money as a universal means of payment.

Central Asia did not derive any benefit from this exchange of ideas and goods. Its towns were so broken and the number of inhabitants so reduced that it took the region generations to rebuild itself. Most of the Mongol trade routes were therefore to the south of the Silk Road, which lay in ruins.

People continued to live in Merv for several centuries, but the city never regained its former status or influence, and the libraries and observatory were not rebuilt. The only thing that has survived to the present day as a reminder of Merv's golden age is the mausoleum of Sultan Ahmed Sanjar from 1157. The walls of the elegant, square building are so thick that they survived not only the Mongols but also centuries of seismic activity. The most impressive thing about the building is the dome: the builders realised that a dome of the size they planned to build would collapse with the first earthquake, if not before. Their solution was to build two domes, one internal and one external. Three hundred years later, in 1436, Filippo Brunelleschi used the same solution for the cathedral in Florence as the architects had in Merv.

Before the Mongol raids, the mausoleum was amongst palaces, mosques and libraries. Today, the mausoleum stands alone, surrounded by grazing camels.

—〰—

Since the dissolution of the Soviet Union, Merv has become once more the financial heart of Turkmenistan. The city was resurrected in modern dress a few kilometres from the ruins, and renamed Mary by Stalin. Mary is the second largest city in Turkmenistan, and the country's gas capital: there are enormous reserves under the desert that surrounds the city. It is not as impressive as Ashgabat, but there is construction going on everywhere. The new regional museum is a magnificent, white marble building with an entire department dedicated to the New President's political and sporting triumphs.

The ruins of a civilisation even older than Merv, the Bronze Age town of Gonur Depe, lie a three-hour drive to the north of Mary.

A dilapidated Soviet road led to the small car park. And stopped. In front of us lay miles and miles of desert. The ticket seller had left for the day, and there were no barriers of any kind. We could just walk straight into the Bronze Age ruins.

A labyrinth of earthen walls unfolded before of us. We could make out large and small houses and, between the buildings, narrow streets. To the trained eye, it was still possible to see the contours of the three walls that defended the town.

"Gonur Depe was discovered by the Greek Soviet archaeologist, Viktor Sarianidi, in the 1970s," Murat told me. "He had noticed there wasn't much growth out here and the ground was full of small mounds, a fairly typical sign that there are ruins beneath. When they started to dig, they discovered what can only have been a large and well-organised town from as far back as four thousand years ago.

The people who lived here had developed a complex irrigation system and had their own water treatment plant. The fire worshipping temples here are the oldest in the world, and traces of ephedrine have also been found, which the Zoroastrian priests used as an ingredient in their ritual drink. Sarianidi believes this is proof that Zoroaster, the founder of Zoroastrianism, came from Gonur Depe."

In the middle of the labyrinth, we come to a large, open space that was possibly once a hall, protected by thick walls. At the end of one of the shorter walls, the ground is raised, just enough to be comfortable to sit on. Could this have been the throne room? Did the ruler hold court here, surrounded by guards?

"Gonur Depe is one of several Bronze Age settlements that Sarianidi has discovered in the area," Murat said. "It was previously thought that there were only three major Bronze Age civilisations in the world, in India, Mesopotamia and Egypt. So a fourth had to be added after Sarianidi's find: the Oxus Civilisation. No-one has done more to uncover Turkmenistan's past than Professor Sarianidi. Nor Afghanistan's," he added. "It was Professor Sarianidi who discovered the famous Scythian grave in northern Afghanistan in 1978. There they found the remains of five women and a man, and as many as 22,000 gold artefacts in the grave!"

The further back in time you go, the more you have to guess. As the people who lived in Gonur Depe did not have a written language, archaeologists have to interpret what little material evidence they left behind: the ruins of mud-brick houses, seeds, small figurines, a few coins, bones.

In the 1990s, a huge grave with the skeletons of more than three thousand people was discovered a few hundred metres to the west of the town walls. None of them had signs of being wounded in battle. This goes some way to proving that life in Gonur Depe must have been unusually peaceful, and yet the town was abandoned after only a few hundred years. The inhabitants packed up and left in a very short space of time. Why? Was it because of an accident or disease? Did they run out of water? Had they chopped down too many trees, and depleted the soil? Where did they go? Archaeologists can only guess.

One of Professor Sarianidi's most mysterious findings is protected from the sun and rain by a tin roof. In a grave, consisting of one large and three small chambers, he found the skeletons of a donkey and three lambs. There was nothing more than a skeleton in the donkey's grave, whereas food remains and small ceramic pots were found in the lambs' graves. One of the lambs had a crown on its head. Was it part of a tomb belonging to a person of power and influence? In which case it is odd that no human grave was found nearby. Were the animals sacrificed to the gods, perhaps in place of human beings? Or did they believe that the animals were divine?

When we got back to the car park, we saw that a light was on in the simple house opposite the ticket office. We popped our heads in through the open door. The room was sparsely furnished, with a simple camp bed, a table and two chairs. A small, rotund man with messy, white hair and a big beard was sitting on one of the chairs. He had his nose in a thick book and did not hear us come in.

"Good afternoon," Murat said in Russian. He suddenly looked awestruck. "I hope we are not disturbing the professor?"

The old man put down his book and looked up. We had stumbled upon Professor Sarianidi in person.

"Good afternoon," he bellowed. "Are you archaeologists?"

Murat and I shook our heads.

"That's a shame, there's still plenty of work to be done here!" He struggled to get up, supporting himself with a stick. He picked up a coin and a small clay statue from the table.

"The people who lived here probably came from Syria originally.

But objects like these indicate that they must also have had contact with India." He held up the statue and the coin. "And things from here have been found in India. Perhaps some of the people who lived here went to India when the water ran out three thousand years ago? If that's what actually happened, that is. But we presume it is. Some people must have gone to Merv, which we assume was founded by the people of Gonur Depe."

He spoke slowly, in a deep, booming voice. The hand holding the stick was shaking and his face had a greyish, almost blue, pallor.

"How many people lived here?" I said.

"Impossible to say, completely impossible! I've come back here every year for forty years now, and there's still so much left to uncover. We have only scratched the surface."

"We've just been to have a look at the animal graves," I said. "Have you discovered anything more about them?"

"I'm afraid I have to disappoint you again," Professor Sarianidi said. "To be frank, it's a mystery to us all. We may never know why they buried the animals in this way, and why one of the lambs was wearing a crown. There's so much more to discover about this part of the world. So, so much more."

He fell into a silent reverie going back thousands of years. We respectfully said our goodbyes and went to pitch our tents by the car park. My last night in the desert. When we left bright and early the next morning, as the birds twittered deliriously in the trees, Sarianidi had been up for hours and was already busy excavating more ruins in the Bronze Age town.

The expedition that spring was to be his last. Some months after I met him, on December 23, 2013, Professor Viktor Sarianidi died in Moscow. He was eighty-four.

THE ERA OF SUPREME HAPPINESS

The Caspian Sea lay bathed in an orange light as the wheels of the Turkmenistan Airlines plane touched down. The waves on the surface glittered like gold. A portrait of Gurbanguly Gerdimuhamedov vibrated behind glass at the front of the cabin as we taxied towards the terminal building. Arkadag, the Protector, was with us, even in the air, perhaps to remind us who we had to thank for the extraordinarily cheap tickets. Domestic flights in Turkmenistan must be the cheapest in the world: a ticket to anywhere in the country costs around twenty pounds.

Seeing the light reflected in the Caspian Sea, it was not hard to understand why the Russians called this town Krasnovodsk, which means "red water". The castle that was built here in 1869 was used as a base for the campaigns against Khiva and the wild Turkmen tribes. The town still has only the tiniest Turkmen population, the smallest in the country, while the majority of inhabitants are Russians from the north and Azerbaijanis from beyond the Caspian Sea.

In 1993, two years after independence, the town was given a new name: Turkmenbashi. It would seem that the president wanted to remind the non-Turkmen inhabitants here who made the decisions. Berdimuhamedov has so far not changed the name given by his predecessor.

I was met outside the grand, marble terminal building by a spritely young boy of twelve or thirteen. He introduced himself as my driver. I trotted after him to a tired elderly Mercedes, in which, fortunately, his father was sitting behind the wheel.

The father and son were solemn and said nothing as we drove through the centre. Low, brown mountains framed the town. The Soviet-style apartment blocks were painted in pastel colours and adorned with satellite dishes. The young women on the pavement wore high heels and short, tight skirts.

As soon as we left the centre, the father and son came to life. They talked and talked, mostly about how hard they worked, that they never had time for a holiday, how they never had time to swim in summer, even though they lived right by the beach, they just worked and worked, without stop, all the time, and very hard. Then, without a pause or any kind of obvious segue, the son started to talk about how wonderful it was to live in Turkmenistan.

"Everything is free," he boasted. "Salt is free, electricity is free, gas and water are free, even petrol is almost free, thanks-to-our-president."

"Why do you work so much then, if everything is free?" I asked.

"Wages are low," the boy said. "We earn max three hundred dollars a month, and seventy-five per cent of that is spent on food. As we earn so little, we always buy on credit, whether it's something big, like a car, or small, like bread and milk. When we get paid, we pay off our loan, then get more credit."

As we drove onto the peninsula where I was to spend my last night in Turkmenistan, the bumpy Soviet road turned into a sumptuous modern avenue. We had seven or eight lanes all to ourselves. A huge sign said WELCOME TO AWAZA INTERNATIONAL TOURISM ZONE! A few dozen slim skyscrapers rose up on the horizon. The peaks of the waves on the inland sea turned pink as the sun went down.

For a moment it felt as if I was in Dubai. But only for a moment.

*

Nothing is more desolate and forlorn than a tourist resort out of season. I had to use the side entrance to get into the Oil Workers' Hotel. The revolving doors were closed. The lobby was decorated in gold leaf and marble. A sleepy receptionist gave me the key to my room. I was the only guest.

"Do you have Internet?" I said, full of hope. After all, there were five promising stars on the shiny facade.

"No, they only have trendy things like that in Ashgabat," the receptionist said, swallowing a yawn.

Other than a security guard who paced around in the garden outside, I did not meet a single person as I wandered between the enormous hotel buildings. Everything was beautifully maintained; the marble sparkled and the grass was cut with military precision. Even the wide, eight-lane avenue was empty, except for the occasional police car that cruised by.

Down at the pier, I met an old, hunchbacked woman with grey, unkempt hair. She was fishing. A modest pile of small fish lay flapping at her feet.

I said hello. She did not answer or look up.

"Good fishing this evening?" I said, more loudly.

The old woman glanced at me fleetingly and grunted in a way that could mean either yes or no. Her eyes were as lacklustre as her fish. I walked on, down to the small hotel beach. It was only a few metres long and full of sharp stones. There was a thin film of oil floating on the surface of the water. To my left, I could see the port, one of the largest in the region, and an oil refinery.

The Awaza tourist resort is one of Gurbanguly Berdimuhamedov's prestigious projects. It was actually Turkmenbashi who came up with the idea, but everyone seems to have forgotten that. No more than a year after Turkmenbashi's death, in 2007, Berdimuhamedov began to realise his predecessor's grand plan. There used to be hundreds of cabins and allotments on the peninsula. They were ruthlessly flattened and erased from the map, so that Bouygues could start work. Already more than thirty skyscrapers reach up into the sky, each one unique in style, but apparently almost identical inside. The resort was built in the firm belief that guests would come once the facilities were there. If the incredibly positive article on Wikipedia is to be believed, the strategy has been a success: "Tourists are attracted by excellent infrastructure. Near the city of Turkmenbashi is situated a modern international airport, it is considered one of the best in Turkmenistan. The roads in the resort are perfect and from year to year the situation is only getting better."

The most striking thing about the visitors here, to date, is their absence. The majority of hotels are empty, even in high season. Very few people from Turkmenistan can afford to pay more than ten pounds a night for a room. And those who can afford it prefer to spend their summer holidays on one of Turkey's long sandy beaches.

To make Awaza more attractive to foreigners, the authorities plan to construct two artificial islands on the Dubai model, and to make Awaza a visa-free zone for some nationalities. But how tempting is it, really, to be shut off in an asphalt and marble resort with Soviet-style service, bad food and no Internet?

As all the restaurants were closed, I went back to the Oil Workers' Hotel. The dining room was done out as if for a wedding. The menu was as thick as a telephone directory, and I was hungry. The kitchen offered twenty different fish dishes and even more meat dishes.

"I would like to have the sturgeon with caviar and a white wine sauce, please," I said.

"I'm afraid we don't have any sturgeon," the waitress said in a small voice.

"Then I'll take the baked salmon with soy, please."

"I'm afraid we don't have salmon," the waitress whispered.

"Ah, what do you have then?"

She took the menu, leafed back and forth, and eventually pointed to a fish dish at the back of the menu.

"I'll have that then, and a glass of white wine, please. As it's my last day in Turkmenistan."

"We don't have wine. You'll have to go to the bar."

"O.K., I'll have a bottle of mineral water then, sparkling."

"We have only still water."

"No bubbles then." I flicked through the huge menu again, not really looking for anything. The dessert menu and wine list were both extensive. "Oh, do you have any ice?"

No-one answered. I was alone in the dining room.

After brushing my teeth, I stood by the panorama window and looked out over the gentle floodlit waves. Three weeks in Absurdistan were over. I was tired to the very tips of my toes. For three weeks I had followed the Itinerary in every detail, travelled far and wide, several times crossed the desert, fallen asleep to camels grunting, flown back and forth across the country, eaten too many poor hotel breakfasts and devoured bowls and bowls of soured camel's milk.

Turkmenistan lies at the bottom of Transparency International's corruption index, at number 168, and the president owns and controls almost everything, from hotels to restaurants and shops. There is only one bank, the national bank, and prices and wages are kept artificially low to suit the closed, Turkmen market. Absolutely everything in Turkmenistan is micro-managed by the state, including the economy. As a tourist in Berdimuhamedov's ideal Turkmen state, one cannot rely on a global neo-liberal language – the language that is used every day without thought in the West does not exist there.

With only five million inhabitants and the world's fourth largest gas reserves, Turkmenistan has all that it needs to be successful. And

yet, so far, the only thing it has excelled in is big words. Turkmenbashi steered his country through the Epoch of Great Revival into
the Golden Age. And Berdimuhamedov, or the Protector, as he is
now called, has in his turn led the country through the Era of Great
Renewal. According to the authorities, the country is approaching
its ultimate goal: in 2012 the state broadcaster (and there are no
other media organisations) announced that Turkmenistan has
entered the Era of Supreme Happiness.

It does not get much better than that.

BORDERLAND

The driver who was going to take me from Turkmenbashi to the small, busy Kazakh border checkpoint confided in me that he was planning to emigrate.

"My wife and children are there already. I'll follow them as soon as my papers are in order."

"To where?"

"To Kazakhstan, of course."

The road was in such a dreadful condition that it was often less painful to drive in the tracks in the sand. We passed closed-down factories and abandoned buildings, ghost towns of empty houses with broken windows and rusty fronts. Almost all the Kazakhs who lived in Turkmenistan during the Soviet era have moved back across the border to Kazakhstan. More than half the Russians have gone back to Russia. For the most part only Turkmens remain.

The journey took four hours. Occasionally we overtook an Iranian or Turkish semi-trailer. Otherwise we had the desert to ourselves. The driver got bored and asked me to guess how old he was. I was kind and said forty-five.

"Thirty-three," he said, offended.

The paranoia I had experienced during those first few days in Ashgabat flared up again. What if they discovered that I had lied on my visa application? What if I was stopped at the border and thrown into one of Turkmenistan's notorious prisons? The nearest Norwegian embassy was hundreds of miles away and Norway's sole representative in the Statoil offices in Ashgabat was unlikely to be much help.

After hours of sand, desert rats and derelict industrial buildings, I caught sight of a golden dome shining through the dust: the Turkmen-Kazakh border. The driver would normally be able to drive to the nearest Kazakh town on the other side, but today, for some reason that no-one could or would share with me, it was not possible. I said goodbye to the driver from the travel agency and entered the building with trepidation. A soldier pointed to a pile of forms. I had not managed to pick one up when the driver came running back, took my passport and filled in the form at top speed. Then he hurried back to the car before I had a chance to thank him.

For the first time on my trip, I was on my own.

I went to the first counter and handed over the form and my passport. The soldier looked at the Turkmen form sceptically.

"Did you fill it in yourself?"

"No," I said. I had no idea what boxes the driver had crossed.

"You have to fill in the form yourself," the soldier informed me. "We have forms in both Russian and English." Then he marched off with my passport and the form that the driver had filled in. I was told to go into the customs control next door. A crowd of soldiers, customs officers and guards were sitting at various counters, toying with their mobiles. It seemed that I was the only person crossing the border that afternoon, so now they gave me their full attention. My suitcase was opened and the contents thoroughly examined, one pair of pants after the other, sock by sock. One of the soldiers went through the photographs on my camera. Another took my mobile. A third checked my iPad.

"Why are you in Turkmenistan?" one of the soldiers said.

"I'm visiting as a tourist."

"Where do you work?"

"The University of Oslo, I'm a student." This was not entirely true, but nor was it a lie.

"What are you studying?"

"Languages."

"How many semesters have you taken?"

"This is my sixth," I lied.

"Why on earth have you got a Kazakh language course with you?" shouted the soldier who was looking through my suitcase. "Why do you need to know the Kazakh language?"

"I couldn't find any Turkmen courses," was my defence.

"But why do you want to learn *Kazakh*?"

When the soldiers had gone through all the photographs, an older man in a blue uniform appeared out of an office. He said something in Turkmen, then disappeared into another office with my mobile and my camera. Another man in a blue uniform started to interrogate me: "Why did you come to Turkmenistan?"

"To see the country. I'm a tourist."

"Where do you work?"

"The University of Oslo. I'm a student."

"What are you studying?"

"Languages."

"How many semesters have you taken?"

"Six."

"What does a kilo of meat cost in Norway?"

"I beg your pardon?"

"What does a kilo of meat cost in your country? Meat is very expensive here."

I made up a price. The border guard perked up. "What about milk? Bread? Cigarettes?"

"Everything is very expensive, very expensive," I said seriously.

Several of the soldiers had crowded around us now. The questions came thick and fast. What about petrol? A flat? A car? A house? A kilo of butter? Eggs? Sugar? Salt? Electricity?

Eventually the older man in blue came back. He solemnly gave me back my mobile and camera.

"Everything was in perfect order," he said. In other words, he had not found any compromising photographs of the president lying lifeless in the sand at the race track.

One more stamp and then I was out in the cool evening air again. In the distance, through the barbed wire fences, I could see the Kazakh border station.

A soldier studied my passport one last time.

Then I was through.

"Do you a have a driver waiting for you at the other side?" one of the soldiers called after me.

"No, I have to find my own way," I said. The wind played with my hair. I felt free.

"It's three hours to the nearest town," the soldier said.

"I know," I replied. "I'll get a taxi."

The soldier laughed. "There are no taxis on the other side. There's *nothing* there!"

KAZAKHSTAN

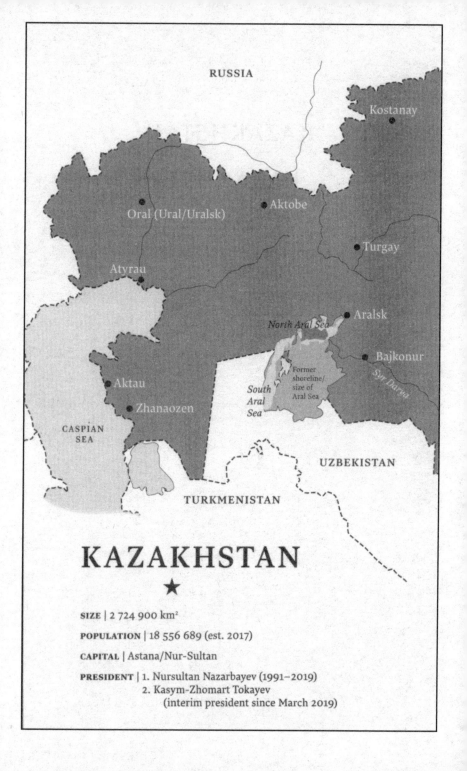

KAZAKHSTAN

★

SIZE | 2 724 900 km²

POPULATION | 18 556 689 (est. 2017)

CAPITAL | Astana/Nur-Sultan

PRESIDENT | 1. Nursultan Nazarbayev (1991–2019)
2. Kasym-Zhomart Tokayev
   (interim president since March 2019)

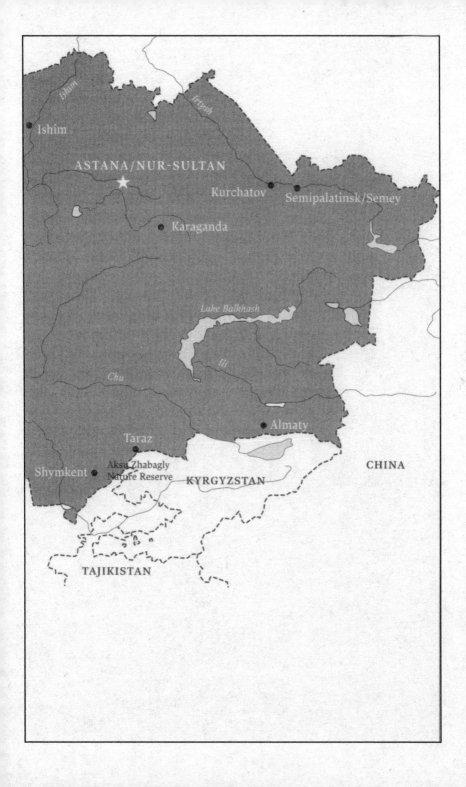

AN OASIS OF SUSHI AND A.T.M.s

The no-man's-land between Turkmenistan and Kazakhstan was wider than it looked. The sun shone down from a clear, blue sky, but there was a touch of winter in the desert air. On the other side of the barbed wire fences, the brown, barren soil stretched out in every direction. Apart from the two border stations, there were no buildings here, no people, only wolves, and mile upon mile of poorly maintained Soviet roads.

About halfway across, a lorry passed me. So I was not, after all, the only person wanting to cross the border that day. The driver stopped and offered me a lift for the last few hundred metres. As soon as I had climbed up into the driver's cab and closed the door, he started to complain.

"They're not normal, that lot," he hissed in Russian, and waved a thick wodge of papers. He was a Kazakh and had to cross the border several times a month. "They do this every bloody time, it takes hours. Before, when we were part of the Soviet Union, no-one thought twice about crossing the border between Kazakhstan and Turkmenistan, no-one stopped you, you just drove through. Now they want to check every single bloody document!"

In the time of the Soviet Union people could, in principle at least, travel freely within the vast empire, from Tallinn in the west to Vladivostok in the east. With independence came border controls. While Europe has gone the opposite way, towards freedom of movement, hundreds of new border checkpoints have been built in Central Asia. Thousands of soldiers, officers and customs officers are employed to protect the borders that were drawn up under Stalin in the 1920s and 1930s. People who previously crossed these invisible lines without thinking about it now have to be prepared for detailed questioning, lengthy form-filling and nitpicking inspections of their luggage before they are allowed to pass through the barbed wire barriers. If they are lucky.

Fortunately it was easier to enter Kazakhstan than it was to leave Turkmenistan. The Kazakh passport control officers were cheerful and efficient, and within minutes all the paperwork was done and my visa stamped and signed according to the rules.

"Are there any taxis here?" I said.

"Taxi? Here?" The young border guard looked at me, incredulous. "Do you know how far it is to the nearest town?"

"Unfortunately, yes, I do."

The guard took off his cap and scratched his head.

"There are some trucks outside," he said. "Perhaps you could hitch a ride part of the way with one of them. Hold on a minute, I'll ask." He disappeared out of the very basic office. And there I stood, passport in hand, visa stamped, ready, but unable to pass Go. Luckily, the guard did not take long.

"Damiar, who works here, is going into Aktau. You can get a lift with him. But first we would like to offer you some lunch."

The border guards ate their meals in the basement. They were served by two matronly women with lacy aprons and white headscarves. The men, about a dozen of them, slurped down the salted meat soup with undisguised pleasure. The tea flowed freely.

"Do you have a king in Norway?" the oldest guard said.

I nodded.

"So he's in charge, then?"

I explained that it was not the king who made the decisions but the politicians.

"But he must decide some things," the grey-haired man objected. "Otherwise, what's the point of being king?"

"He's an important national figurehead," I said. "And people love him."

The man shook his head in disbelief. He seemed to feel sorry for the king. The short-sighted man sitting next to me then leaned over and asked in a conspiratorial whisper: "Do you have many Negros in Norway?"

"Not many," I said.

"That's good," he nodded with approval.

"But we do have quite a lot of Pakistanis," I told him.

"Oh, Pakistanis are not good," he said, and pulled a face. "Nor are the Chinese," he added, but more to himself.

For a long time there was nothing to be heard but the slurping of a dozen men finishing their bowls of soup. I had only walked a few hundred metres, but everything was different. The faces around me did not have the European features of the Turkmens, they were more Mongolian, with narrow eyes, and high, round cheeks. The tone was more relaxed, a little rougher. Even the soup tasted different.

But the green tea was the same. And the roads. Those first hours on the road in Kazakhstan were much like my final hours on the road in Turkmenistan. It was, after all, the same road, built by Soviet engineers long before the checkpoints were built. The Turkmen–Kazakh border was clearly not a priority for either country, and the road surface was such that for the first part of the journey we had to zigzag to avoid the worst potholes. But we had the road to ourselves. On either side of the tarmac, the desert stretched as far as the eye could see, flat and devoid of colour.

"I killed that wolf yesterday," Damiar said, pointing to a furry tail hanging from the rear view mirror.

"Did you shoot it?"

"No, I was driving the car. It tried to get away, but I chased it and hit it in the end. When I get home and show the tail to my neighbours, they'll give me a present or some money. You're always well rewarded if you kill a wolf. There are far too many of them here, they're a pest."

Damiar then seamlessly switched to complaining about the Kazakh president. Those who dared criticise the president on the Turkmen side of the border had done so in hushed voices, no matter how far we were from listening ears. Damiar said what he thought, outright, without my even asking.

"He's been in office far too long, since 1991!" he shouted. "Nazarbayev is frightened to let young people have a say, that's the problem. I don't bother voting in the elections, it's all rigged anyway. The whole system is corrupt. We ordinary folk don't earn anything near enough, scarcely three hundred to four hundred dollars a month. You can't live off that."

"Do you ever accept small gifts from people crossing the border?"

"Of course not!" He grinned. "What do you take me for?"

According to Transparency International's annual overview, Kazakhstan is the least corrupt of the post-Soviet states in Central Asia, but that says more about its neighbours than about Kazakhstan itself. It is still towards the bottom of the list, 140th out of 177 countries, thirteen places behind Russia. Like Turkmenistan, Kazakhstan has major oil and gas reserves, and is without a doubt the strongest economy in Central Asia. For a long time, Kazakhstan was also deemed to be the most democratic republic in the region, but, again, that says more about the neighbouring regimes. President

Nursultan Nazarbayev has been head of state since he was appointed by Gorbachev in 1989, and shows no sign of wanting to step down.[4] With each year that has passed, he has become more and more authoritarian and autocratic, and there is no real political opposition. Freedom of expression is under threat: in the past few years, a good number of independent newspapers and websites have been closed down by the regime. Nevertheless, Kazakhstan feels likes a bastion of liberty compared with Turkmenistan.

Damiar's mobile rings.

"Is that you, sweetheart? – Sorry, darling, but I can't get away this evening. – Yes, I know I promised to come home this evening, but I have to work, there's so much to do here. – See you tomorrow, give my love to the kids!"

He had barely ended the call before his mobile rang again. "Yes, babe, I'm on my way. – No, I didn't call you yesterday. – Yes, I know I promised to call every day, but I didn't have any reception yesterday, you know what it's like. – I'll be there in an hour, beautiful. – No, not before, I won't make it. – Yes, I'll come straight to you."

Damiar gave a dramatic sigh and then winked at me. "Women, eh . . . nothing but trouble."

When we got to Aktau, he parked his car in a residential area full of apartment blocks some way from the centre of town. We had to take a taxi from there. He explained that he did not want his friends to see his car and find out that he was in town already. He wanted "a night off with no hassle". Before he went off to see his girlfriend, who had rung every five minutes for the past hour to make sure he was on his way, he dropped me off by a big shopping centre in the centre of town.

"Just so you don't get the wrong idea, my wife and I have a lot

4 Nursultan Nazarbayev announced his resignation as President of Kazakhstan on 19 March 2019.

of respect for each other," he said in parting. "Perhaps we could meet up for a drink later this evening, when I'm free again, just you and me?"

The shopping centre in Aktau was a revelation, a *fata morgana*, an oasis of western civilisation. Familiar brand names greeted me. The shops were full of people, all in jeans, miniskirts, leather jackets, high heels, trainers. Adele's latest hit was playing over the loudspeakers. And, in a corner, I came across a whole row of A.T.M.s. I put my card in one of them and pressed 30,000 tenge, which was a little more than one hundred pounds. Like magic, the machine started to count the notes.

The restaurant on the ground floor had sushi and pasta on the menu. I ordered both. One of the waiters gave me the WiFi code, and before I could say Open Sesame, all that had been forbidden in Turkmenistan was there. Twitter. Facebook. YouTube. As I gorged on maki rolls and ravioli, I caught up with what friends and acquaintances had been doing on Facebook. One friend had cut her hair. My boyfriend was lonely. An old school friend had had a baby. Spring had sprung in Oslo, judging by all the images of sunglasses and the first outdoor beer. Travelling in the age of Internet, one seldom feels far from home. Even in Turkmenistan, where it is still a fairly new thing, I had occasionally been able to read some of the Norwegian papers online. Here, I was spoilt for choice.

At the same time that your local newspaper is just a click away, the whole world will soon be wearing jeans made in China. Even though the Mongolian features around me were unfamiliar, I no longer felt so far from home. The reference points were known; this was a system I understood.

Back in a culture that resembled that of the West, I could see the peculiarities of Turkmenistan more clearly: the country remains outside the market economy. Even though the authorities have abandoned Communism and the grey concrete apartment blocks have been replaced by gleaming white marble buildings, the economy is still hermetically sealed and as regulated as it was during the Soviet era. Western brand names are rare, and there is no real competition to speak of, let alone *free* competition.

"I want to go to Hotel Chagala," I told the taxi driver.

"What's the address?"

"I couldn't find the street name on the Internet, but it's in the first microdistrict."

"Oh, I'll find it then," the driver assures me. "Apart from the President's Avenue, we don't have street names in Aktau. The city is divided up into microdistricts, and every building and apartment has a number. I live in the eighth microdistrict, building fifty, flat nine. Eight, fifty, nine. Practical, isn't it?"

Any illusion of western culture was dispelled. I was back in the Soviet Union.

We drove through the broad, open streets. On each side were low, functional apartment blocks, painted in bright colours, surrounded by lawns and trees. Aktau is a city built according to Soviet principles. It is hard to identify a centre or heart. Every so often, there are grand brick houses, built in a more American style, which bear witness to the current oil boom: this is one of the richest – and most expensive – cities in Kazakhstan.

Aktau was established in the 1960s, following the discovery of uranium deposits in the vicinity. A few years later it became clear that the area was also rich in oil and metal, and the town started to grow. It was called Shevchenko from 1964 to 1991, after the famous Ukrainian poet who was exiled here by Tsar Nicholas I in the 1840s. At the time, it must have seemed like the end of the world, far from anywhere, with few buildings other than the Russian fortress that stood here.

At regular intervals we drove past large posters of a grey-haired man in a suit, surrounded by smiling children holding balloons.

I pointed at the colourful posters. "Is that the president?"

"Of course," the driver said, casually, without even looking up.

ON THE TRACKS

When I stepped into the train carriage, it was like walking into a furnace, or entering a hermetically sealed box. A long row of men in tracksuits stood leaning against the windows in the narrow corridor. They stared out at the platform, their faces devoid of expression, and there was an overpowering smell of sweat. No-one moved to let me pass and I had to struggle over trainers and bulging bags as I went further into the iron sauna. My back was clammy with sweat.

I eventually found my compartment. My fellow passengers, a young Kazakh family with a baby son, were busy installing themselves with all their bags and carriers and pillows and teddy bears and cured meat and milk bottles and toy cars and everything a family with a small child might need. There was a pyramid of biscuit packets and dried fruit on the small table by the window, and almost every inch of the floor was covered in colourful bags. A man was lying on one of the top bunks, his hands folded on his stomach, eyes closed. He had short, grey hair, a neat moustache and fair, Russian features.

"Hello," I said, and sat down on the edge of the bunk. After a few days of solitude in Aktau, mostly spent lounging around in my hotel room, in a blissful bubble of Internet and cable T.V., finally free of guides, guardians and omnipresent policemen, I had been looking forward to being sociable on the train. Long train journeys normally provide the perfect opportunity to make new friends, as there is nothing to do other than sleep, eat and talk.

. The young father was unable to hide his irritation when he looked at me and said: "That's your reservation," pointing at the other top bunk.

The bunk to which I was banished had a mattress, white sheets, a pillow and woollen blankets. I rolled out the mattress and started to struggle with the sheets. This was not very easy with the floor filled with plastic bags. The young mother exchanged glances with her husband, but neither of them said anything. Or did anything. In the end, the man in the bunk opposite mine could stand it no longer. He got up onto his knees and grabbed the sheet, then very efficiently had my bed made within thirty seconds, without having got out of his own. When he had finished, he gave me a curt nod and lay down again, his hands folded over his stomach. I thanked him effusively. He grunted in acknowledgment, without opening his eyes. A few minutes later he was snoring loudly. I clambered into my berth and managed to wriggle down. It was so cramped that I could not sit up without banging my head on the ceiling, and the berth was just too short for me to stretch out my legs. The mattress was hard and lumpy, but the sheet covering it was stretched tight, without so much as a crease. The air in the compartment was as stale as in a coffin.

The train pulled away from the platform with a jolt. A stream of fresh air found its way in through the half-open window. The young father leaped up and crossed to the window, closed it and pulled the curtains shut. Then he closed and locked the compartment door. I protested a little, but the father responded by pointing at his young son who was busy pressing the buttons on his mother's mobile.

"Draughts are not good for babies," he said tersely.

A stuffy twilight descended over the small compartment. The train rattled along. My feet bumped against the compartment wall. The lumps in the mattress rubbed against my spine. The Russian in the berth opposite was snoring like a bear, undisturbed by the two year old who squealed every time his mother's mobile made a sound, which was rather often.

I could feel the sweat on my brow. I gasped for air as it sank in that this was how I would spend the next thirty-six hours. Two whole days and one and a half nights. On the map, Aral looked relatively close to Aktau, but then all distances in Kazakhstan are immense. I had estimated about twelve to fourteen hours by train when I went to the ticket office. What I did not know was that the line between the two cities was not straight, that it first went north before slowly curving south again towards Aral, and then continuing on to Almaty.

My only reason for going to Aral was that I wanted to see with my own eyes the consequences of one of the greatest man-made catastrophes. Aral had been built on the shores of the Aral Sea and was an important fishing port until the 1960s, when the sea began slowly to shrink. The fish factory had been closed for decades and today the city is surrounded by sand and desert. The sound of breaking waves is no more than a distant memory. What happens when an inland sea disappears?

Below me, the young couple were feeding their son biscuits and fizzy drinks. To make this even more entertaining, the mother had produced a toy with buttons that made different siren noises depending on which button he pushed. Fire engines. Police cars. Ambulances. The boy shrieked with delight every time a siren sounded. When the police sirens went off for the sixth time, the Russian in the berth opposite mine suddenly woke up, rummaged around in his bag and pulled out a bottle of something brown. He took a couple of slugs, then lay down under the blanket and retreated into his own world again.

Why do we travel? Why do we put ourselves through all the discomfort that moving across great distances and staying in faraway, foreign lands usually entails? My theory is that nature has equipped us with deceitful, flawed memories. That is why we forever set off on new adventures. Once we are home again, the discomfort transforms itself into amusing anecdotes, or is forgotten. Memory is not linear, it is more like a diagram full of points – high points – and the rest is empty. Memory is also abstract. Seen from the future, past discomfort seems almost unreal, like a dream.

I lasted an hour. My legs were stiff when I clambered down, put on my shoes and wrenched open the door. The air in the corridor was blissfully cool. I stood for a long time by the dusty half-open window and filled my lungs with fresh air, again and again. I greedily drank in the steppe air. The landscape outside was so monotonous that we could almost have been standing still. Not a tree or hill in sight, just flat, scrubby dry grass, which blended into the blue, cloudless sky on the horizon.

I stood like this for an hour, maybe two. The train snaked through the desert and steppe at forty or fifty kilometres an hour. Kazakhstan covers an area of 2,724,900 square kilometres, which is bigger than Western Europe. It is the ninth largest country in the world, and the largest one without a coast. And there, by the dusty train window, I started to realise just how big 2,724,900 square kilometres is. Kazakhstan is more than twice the size of the four other Central Asian countries combined. The Kazakh Soviet Socialist Republic, today's Kazakhstan, accounted for twelve per cent of the total area of the Soviet Union, which was a staggering 22,402,200 square metres. By comparison, Russia is currently 17,075,200 square kilometres. In other words, Kazakhstan alone accounts for more than half the territory lost by Russia in the breakup of the Soviet Union.

The other passengers had closed the doors to their compartments. I had the corridor to myself. I spotted the occasional eagle soaring up under the clouds, but apart from that the desert was desolate, with no sign of life. Here and there a tuft of grass or a dry bush stuck out of the stony sand, tiny variations in the vast, light-brown landscape. Kazakhstan's modest population does not tally with its enormous size; the country is barren and sparsely populated. More than three-quarters of it is desert or semi-arid. There are around seventeen million inhabitants in Kazakhstan, which means on average fewer than six people per square kilometre. Only eleven other countries in the world have a lower population density. Perhaps, I speculated, that was why the other passengers were all burrowed away in their compartments. They were not used to being in such close proximity to other people and so did what they could to maintain the illusion of relative isolation.

It was dark in the compartment when I went back. The two year old was sleeping like an angel on his mother's stomach. The father lay watching them, his eyes half-open. I crept up into my berth and closed my eyes. I lay there for a long time listening to the rhythm of the train. My body absorbed it: *tatam-tatam, tatam-tatam.* Eventually I fell into a light sleep.

Later on in the evening the compartment came to life, and I went out into the corridor again to get some air. The short-haired gentleman followed, stood beside me by the dusty window, a little too close for comfort, and started to tell me about his life.

"Before I retired, I was a colonel in the army," he said. His Russian was perfect. "I served for seven years in Afghanistan and one year in Chechnya. You can't imagine the things I saw there . . . Afghanistan was terrible too, but do you know what the worst thing was?"

I shook my head.

"How meaningless it all was. What were we doing there? It was the same in both Afghanistan and Chechnya. Neither war made sense." He stared out at the desert that had turned golden in the setting sun.

"My name's Alexander, by the way." He held out his hand. His eyes were unfocused, but his handshake was firm and steady.

"Why did you fight in Chechnya?" I said. "That was after independence, in Kazakhstan, that is. Surely, as a Kazakh citizen, you had nothing to do with the war in Chechnya?"

"It was my job," he said simply. "And I'm Russian, even though I was born and brought up in Kazakhstan. I didn't feel I could say no. But after a year I did, all the same. Fighting your own people like that . . ." He shook his head.

"It must be hard to adjust from being a serving officer in a war to being a pensioner in peaceful Kazakhstan."

He gave a dry laugh. "I've never worked as hard as I do now. I have five jobs to make ends meet."

A cluster of whitewashed houses appeared outside. The train slowed down.

"What is your favourite fruit?" Alexander looked at me intently.

"Apples," I said. "Don't apples originally come from Kazakhstan?"

"That's what they say," he said and shrugged. "But then they say a lot of things."

A few minutes later the train came to a halt. Alexander hopped down onto the platform, and I followed. The air was cool and fresh. It was late in the evening, but the platform was teeming. Mature women with flowery headscarves and long skirts sat on low, folding stools, their colourful wares spread out in front of them on small cloths. The women sold everything a traveller might want: home-made pancakes, fruit, piroshki, soup, dried fish, juice, vodka, newspapers, toilet paper, soap . . . The range of big and small goods on offer seemed to be limitless. The smells, the tastes, the sudden activity: as if by magic, all the compartment doors opened and the whole train stirred to life. And there on the platform, the hot food from the steaming pots tasted better than anything the best of restaurants could offer.

Alexander returned with two plastic carriers full of green apples. He inspected the contents of both bags, and selected one of the biggest apples, which he then gave to me.

"Thank you so much, you really didn't need to."

"Eat it!" he commanded.

"I've just brushed my teeth, so I think I'll save . . ."

"Eat!" the retired colonel said.

I obediently took a bite of the apple. It was sweet and juicy.

"Well, do you like it?" He gave me a pointed look.

I nodded, my mouth full of apple.

"Good. These are for you." He handed me the two carrier bags. I protested a little, saying that I would never manage to eat all the apples, but he would not listen.

A night calm fell over the train. The air in the compartment was still stuffy and clammy, but fortunately it was no longer so warm. When I turned off my reading light, it was pitch black. I lay there for a while listening to the soporific sounds of the train. *Tatam-tatam. Tatam-tatam*. My thoughts became looser and looser. Then I fell asleep.

I was deep in a dream when I was woken by something fumbling at my back. I sat up like a shot, found my mobile and pressed the screen. The sharp light almost blinded me, but I did see the colonel's white, sinewy hand on my mattress. He lay without moving in the berth opposite, with his eyes closed. For once he was not snoring. When I pushed the hand away, it disappeared into the dark with no resistance.

I turned on my side and closed my eyes again, but sleep eluded me. I could not help thinking of what the colonel's hand might have done in Afghanistan and Chechnya.

The following day the colonel said nothing at all. He lay in his berth with his eyes closed and did not even get up to take a swig from his bottle. Later in the afternoon, the train stopped at a station that was so small there was not even a sign. He took the bags of apples and his suitcase and left the compartment without so much as a goodbye.

There was no need to despair, if, for some reason, you did not manage to buy things on the platform: hawkers passed through the train at intervals, laden with watches, smoked fish, mobiles, newspapers and whatever else they thought a traveller might fancy. Their calls could be heard from far away. The young parents had not shown any interest in their wares, and as a rule did not get out when the train stopped at stations. But then they had enough with them to last for weeks. However, not long after the colonel had left us, one of these hawkers did catch their attention. The slender woman was selling plastic toys in neon colours. With a big smile, she demonstrated the acoustic features of all her toys. The father gave her his full attention, and eventually bought three things from her. The two year old was overjoyed when these miracles were presented to him.

The only things I could do in this inferno were read and sleep, to the accompaniment of cheap Chinese sound effects. But I had taken only one book with me, *The Silent Steppe. The Memoir of a Kazakh Nomad under Stalin* by Mukhamet Shayakhmetov. So I read slowly to make it last.

The author, who was born in 1922, was one of the last to experience the traditional Kazakh nomadic lifestyle:

The Kazakh nomads could not imagine an existence without their livestock: they knew of no other kind and believed that to be left without their animals would mean certain death. The pattern of our year was dictated by the needs of our herds and flocks. In order to provide enough grazing for them, we

were always on the move between pastures, following routes
established by our forefathers.

Most Kazakhs lived in yurts, the characteristic round tents of
Central Asia, and families lived together with other relatives in an *aul*
or herding community. Only in winter, when the snow lay thick
on the steppe, did they live in houses. The economy was based on
bartering, and the better-off families with lots of animals were
morally obliged to help and support less privileged relatives. In
other words, with their nomadic customs and traditions they were
closer to the communist ideals of equality and solidarity than the
Bolsheviks ever were.

The biggest changes took place in 1929, the year that Stalin, in
characteristic dictator style, had called "the Year of Great Change".
As very few of the nomads had willingly participated in the merging
of farms to build collectives, the Soviet authorities started to confiscate goods and animals from the richest nomads, who were then
branded "kulaks". The Russian word *kulak* means fist, and the Soviet
authorities used it as a derogatory term for rich farmers. As he
owned more than three hundred and fifty sheep, Mukhamet
Shayakhmetov's uncle was classified as a kulak and had his entire
flock – and everything he owned – confiscated. But that was not all.
According to the authorities' calculations, his now very poor uncle
still owed tax. He was not in a position to pay the draconian taxes
imposed on him, so he was sentenced to two years in prison.

Despite all the confiscations and arrests, collectivisation was
slow. Very few Kazakhs wanted to give up their free, nomadic lifestyle in order to farm the land, like the Russians. The authorities'
response was to step up the number of arrests. They had, in time,
arrested so many kulaks that the prisons were full. In order to
increase capacity, they turned some of the rich farmers' houses into

prisons, but still there was not enough room. They were therefore forced to release some of the prisoners until they had sorted out the capacity problems.

Mukhamet's family were neither rich nor poor, but in 1931 his father was labelled a kulak, even though having one hundred sheep, twelve horses, eight cattle and two camels was relatively common-place. His animals and other family possessions were confiscated and redistributed to the needy. Some months later, his father was given a two-year prison sentence because he too had not been able to pay the taxes that the authorities claimed he owed.

He was now the son of a convicted kulak, so the nine-year-old Mukhamet was expelled from school. The children of kulaks did not deserve to be there. And even when the family had had all they possessed taken from them, the head of the family was in prison and the son had been thrown out of school, the authorities were still not satisfied. They visited the family a further three times to make sure they had not missed anything. On their final visit, they lifted his old, sick grandmother onto the floor and took away the bed, as well as her threadbare bridal shawl, two buckets and some old carpets, the family's very last possessions. His grandmother died two months later, a sad and bitter woman. A year later, Mukhamet's father died in prison. Almost six months were to pass before Mukhamet and his mother were told the sad news.

In the years that followed, Mukhamet, his mother and younger siblings moved from *aul* to *aul*, and from village to village. They scraped together a living by working at odd jobs, and slept in sheds and overfull dormitories. They stayed wherever they could for days, weeks or months, until the owners had had enough and threw them out. As the wife and children of a kulak, they had no rights, and could not get work in any of the growing number of collective farms.

At the beginning of the 1930s, the Soviet Union underwent a

long and catastrophic famine. It was triggered by a poor harvest followed by a drought, but there can be no doubt that the forced collectivisation of agriculture and the Soviet authorities' inflexible food distribution policies were contributing factors. In Ukraine, which was hardest hit, the famine was called *Holodomor*, which means "to kill by starvation". More than three million Ukrainians starved to death. The Soviet authorities showed no mercy: they continued to appropriate all harvests and sent the corn to other republics in the Soviet Union, even though the local population was dying in large numbers. Thousands of Ukrainian collective farmers were sentenced to prison or death for stealing corn.

The people of Kazakhstan suffered almost as much as the Ukrainians. Many of the nomads had slaughtered their animals rather than hand them over to the authorities. Over the course of three years, the number of cattle shrank from seven million to fewer than one million, and the number of sheep fell from nineteen million to fewer than two million. The Soviet authorities paid no heed to the fact that most of the terrain in Kazakhstan was not suitable for intensive farming, and the nomads, who had never cultivated the land before, did not have the skills required. All this, combined with slapdash planning and excessive haste, made the collectivisation process the greatest upheaval in the history of Kazakhstan. Many of the new collective farms existed only on paper. They were without houses, outbuildings, animals, water systems and, in some cases, without even arable land.

The unavoidable consequence was failing harvests and famine.

Initially, there were trifling attempts to feed the hungry. People from the worst-affected areas were evacuated to farming regions in the north. At the time, Mukhamet was living in one of the small towns that was not yet touched by the famine. He had no idea what the Kazakh word for "starving" meant, and none of the adults would explain. So, together with a couple of other children, he ran down to the train station to catch a glimpse of the evacuees and to find out what "a starving" was. He was never to forget what he saw.

> Out of the train's freight wagons came not people but walking skeletons. The skin on their faces looked as though it had been stretched and then stuck tightly to their bare skulls. It was impossible to tell whether their faces were black from the sun or smeared with dirt. Their arms looked unnaturally long and their eyes, sunken and terrifyingly lifeless, like sheep's. They could hardly stand, let alone walk, and kept stumbling and falling over . . . There were no elderly people or small children among the living corpses emerging from the wagons: they had not made it this far. They had either starved long before the resolution on famine relief or they had died during the journey. The corpses of those who had died during the last few kilometres were left in the empty wagons after the survivors had got out: their relatives were simply too weak to carry them out and bury them.

Mukhamet would soon experience for himself what hunger meant. The famine reached the eastern and northern parts of Kazakhstan in 1933. Finding enough food to survive another day, another week, until the next harvest became the sole purpose of their existence. There were beggars everywhere, bodies everywhere. Instead of introducing relief measures, the government's lackeys persisted with the complex five-year plans. So, as hundreds of thousands starved to death, the "modernisation" and industrialisation of Kazakhstan continued apace. "When you look at the archival documents relating to those tragic years, you can see how much public money was spent not only on industry, but also on endless conferences attended by thousands upon thousands of people from all over the Soviet Union. The funds squandered on those alone would have been sufficient to save many lives," was the author's incisive verdict.

When the famine finally came to an end in the autumn of 1934, more than one million Kazakhs, around a quarter of Kazakhstan's ethnic population, had died. Many of the nomadic traditions had died out along with the victims. The Soviet authorities' obsession with collective farming and heavy industry forced the Kazakh nomads into houses, factories and mines. The endless steppes, which only a few years before had been home to so many yurts, extended Kazakh families and animals, have remained empty to this day.

Later in the evening, the train stopped again. When I came back to the compartment, the young mother was alone. For the first time, she looked me in the eye.

"Why don't you drink tea?" she said.

"It's too warm."

"Does that matter?" she shook her head, disbelieving. "How old are you? Are you married?"

"I'm twenty-nine, and yes, I'm married," I said. My partner and I had even bought a proper wedding ring to support this practical little lie. They gave us a very strange look at the jewellers when they realised we only wanted one ring.

She nodded approvingly. "How long have you been married?"

"Three years," I said. It sounded like a suitable length of time for it to be solid.

"Do you have children?"

I shook my head.

"Why not?" She looked at me, astonished. "Is there a problem? Something wrong?"

Before I could think of an answer, her husband stomped back into the compartment with their son and within seconds my child-lessness and I were forgotten. I climbed up into my berth and lay staring at the ceiling. When the train started to move again, the young father made sure to shut the window and lock the door.

I vowed that I would never travel on the Trans-Siberian railway. Some dreams should remain just that.

The only high point of that day was when we could put our watches forward an hour at a specific point in the unending, flat steppe.

After exactly thirty-six hours, the train rolled into Aral station. The handful of passengers that got off disappeared swiftly into waiting cars. Wearing only sandals and thin cotton clothes, I stood there on the platform, shivering in the dark. The agreement had been that someone from the Aral Sea Foundation, who would arrange my accommodation, would also meet me at the station. But the platform was empty. I rang the number I had been given, but there was no answer.

"You can't stand out here, it's dangerous," the guard called from the door of his compartment as the train pulled slowly away.

"What should I do then?"

He shrugged. We were already several metres apart.

"You should have thought of that before."

The train picked up speed. The carriages thundered by. Then they were gone.

THE SEA THAT VANISHED

The guard was right, I could not stay standing on the platform all night. I wandered over to the station building and tried the door. It was open. The building was white and grand, with a small half-dome and large, arched windows. Cold and tired, I sank down onto a bench in the deserted waiting room. There was a big clock on the wall in front of me. A quarter to three. It was still hours until sunrise.

"Excuse me, *devushka*, can I see your papers?"

Three uniformed guards, two men and a woman, appeared out of nowhere. The oldest took his time looking through my passport.

"What are you doing here?" the woman said.

I explained the situation, that I had just arrived by train, that the representative from the environmental organisation was not there to meet me, and that I was going to see the Aral Sea in the morning.

"It's a long time until morning," the oldest guard grunted. "You can't sit here."

The guards spoke quietly among themselves, then turned back to me. "Can you follow us, please?"

I stood up obediently and followed them through a side door into what was clearly the actual waiting room. One of the walls was almost entirely covered by a colourful mosaic of solid, broad-shouldered men standing up to their waists in water, pulling up a net full of fish. There is an explanation above the mosaic to say that in 1921 Lenin had written a letter to his comrades in Aral asking them to send fourteen carriage-loads of fish to help their brothers in need. The young Soviet state had been drained by years of war and civil strife, and people everywhere were starving. But not in Aral.

A young couple was sitting in one corner of the waiting room. He was as strapping as a Viking with a long, wild beard, and she was small and slight, with Asian features.

"They don't speak Russian," one of the guards said. "Can you ask them why they are sitting here?"

The young man explained in English that they were waiting for daylight. They were going to stay with a local family, but did not want to wake them in the middle of the night.

"Tell them they can't sit here all night. They'll have to come with us to the hotel."

"Hotel?" The colour drained from the young girl's cheeks. "Are they open this late?"

"We have checked and it's open," the guard said. "We've already arranged for a car. It's waiting for you outside."

"Can't we just sit here for another couple of hours?" the girl said.

The guards were firm and shook their heads. The couple stood up, rather reluctantly.

"It's not far," the female guard assured us.

"We know, we went there earlier," was the young man's gloomy reply.

During the short journey there, I found out that he was Canadian and she was Japanese, and that they were here to do the final interviews for a documentary about the fishermen in Aral. They did not have time to say more before we arrived at Hotel Aral, the only hotel in the town. Two grey-haired women in red dressing gowns, one thin as a beanpole, the other big as a bus, were waiting at the door. They squinted at us, their eyes heavy with sleep, and let us in without a word. The big woman sank down onto a chair in reception with a heavy sigh, while the thin one continued to stand in the doorway, arms akimbo, staring at us with hostility.

"Three rooms?" the fat woman barked.

"A double room for them and a single room for me, please," I said.

"All the same price," she grunted. "We only have double rooms. Four thousand for each room."

We paid for both rooms with a five-thousand note each, equivalent to about seventeen pounds.

"I don't have any change." The receptionist glared at us, as though it was our fault.

"Not to worry." We were too tired to argue the point.

The thin woman snatched two keys from the hooks on the wall, marched past us and disappeared up the stairs. We assumed we were supposed to follow her. A couple of the treads on the stairs creaked alarmingly. We passed a sofa and some armchairs in the corridor that had no doubt been fashionable around the time that Stalin died. The carpet looked as though it had not been cleaned for at least forty years. The ceiling was covered in an even layer of mould, and every now and then a small shower of plaster fell.

The thin woman was standing at the end of the corridor waiting for us, clearly impatient. With a sniff, she gave the Canadian and me a key each, then turned on her heel and strode away. The room was big, if nothing else, but that is the only positive thing there is to say about Room 304 in Hotel Aral. There were two brown beds pushed up against the mint green walls. It was impossible to close the window, so there was a constant draught. A large, black insect that I could not identify was floating in the toilet bowl. It looked like it might have been there for some time. I tried to flush the toilet, but the only result was a violent gurgling in the badly insulated pipes. The insect bobbed around on the ripples. The bath worked

as a combined shower and sink, but not as a tub. It was too small.
And what was more, it was held together with brown tape and had
probably not been scrubbed since the dissolution of the Soviet
Union. When I turned on the tap, it produced a thin stream of
lukewarm water that smelled like sewage. I abandoned any plan
of taking a shower, and went straight to bed. The mattress was hard
and the bedlinen smelled like damp dogs. I fell asleep instantly.

When I woke up some hours later, the bathroom was flooded.
I quickly packed my things and left the room.

"Breakfast is included," the thin woman informed me, as I
checked out.

I said that I had to meet someone, and hurried out into the sun.
I looked back at the hotel's grey, sunken front. The top floors were
boarded up. I am sure that in Khrushchev's day, the hotel was quite
fashionable – an Aral pearl, built in concrete, the newest material
at the time, with modern lounge suites on every floor.

Time had not been kind to the model socialist town. The street
was dirty and unkempt. The road was full of broken glass and beer
cans, and there were syringes in the gutter. The handful of high-rise
blocks looked as though they might collapse at any moment. The
detached houses were hidden by overgrown gardens. I would never
have believed that this was Makataev Street, the main street in
Aral, had it not said so in the guidebook.

I rang the Aral Sea Foundation again. Still no answer. It was
one thing that they had not been there to meet me the night before
as agreed, but I was dependent on them to get me to the Aral Sea.
It turned out that the office was right next door to the hotel, but the
door was locked and the lights were off. Just as I turned to leave,
a young man came running towards me. He stopped in front of me
and held out his hand.

"Erika? I am Jedige from the Aral Sea Foundation. I thought

I would find you here. I am so sorry that there was no-one there to meet you last night! We had a lot of visitors yesterday and the driver was tired. He didn't get the message until today, and I had completely forgotten. But I promise you, there will be a trip. You can trust me." He spoke very fast, and was persistently apologetic and incoherent.

"What's done is done," I said, to appease him, just glad that I had met him in the end. "Where can I get breakfast?"

"Breakfast? I know *exactly* where we should go," Jedige said. "Follow me."

We set off through the dusty streets, negotiating the tumble-down houses, dodging donkeys, hens and scabby dogs, but we soon started to flag. Nearly all the restaurants and cafes were shut, most of them for good.

Eventually we found a bar that was willing to give me a fried egg. A handful of men were sitting in the corner drinking. They had already emptied a couple of bottles of vodka, even though it was not yet ten in the morning. While I ate, Jedige made some frantic calls. He dialled the same number again and again without getting an answer.

"Don't worry," he said, clearly upset. "I've got everything under control. I'll just try another driver."

The second driver answered his phone at the fourth attempt. They agreed he would pick us up in an hour. While we waited, Jedige took me down to the old harbour. A gate led into an over-grown cut in the landscape. To the right of the gate were four boats, painted in bright colours. They were kept there as a monument to the bustling harbour that had once been the heart and soul of the town. A skinny stray dog growled at us. The crane that was used to unload all the boxes of fish still stood outside the old fish factory. The factory itself lay abandoned.

"The factory here was huge," Jedige said. "Everyone in Aral worked with fish."

"What do they do now?"

He gave a nervous laugh.

"There aren't many jobs anymore."

The death knell sounded for Aral when the sea started to shrink in the 1960s – about the time that Hotel Aral was built. Until then, the town had grown and thrived as a fishing port, and the future looked rosy; the population was growing and the people of Aral lived and ate better than most other Soviet citizens. But when the sea and the fish began to disappear the town's very foundations were pulled out from under it. The population has more than halved to around thirty thousand since the sea vanished, and things look very bleak. Every year, hundreds of young people leave the former port town.

Even after Jedige had shown me everything worth seeing in Aral, and a few things more, there was still no sign of the driver. Jedige called him again.

"Erkut will be here in half an hour," he said, with an apologetic smile.

Two hours later we were on our way to the Aral Sea in Erkut's jeep. Erkut was a good-natured man with a very deep voice. His stomach was so large that it almost obstructed the steering wheel.

"In its time, the Aral Sea was the fourth largest inland sea in the world. It was 428 kilometres long and 234 kilometres wide, and covered a total of 68,000 square kilometres," Jedige told me from the back seat. He had all the figures in his head. "Now it is ten per cent of its original size."

"What happened?" I said.

"Two rivers fed into the Aral Sea, the Amu Darya and the Syr

Darya. In the Fifties and Sixties, the Soviet authorities had a dream that the union would produce enough cotton to be self-sufficient, so they diverted the water from the rivers into large irrigation canals for the cotton plantations. For a while they succeeded. But the irrigation canals were badly built and half the water either evaporated or leaked out along the way. The canals are still in use. We don't have enough water in the region as it is, and then we waste half of it because of these canals."

We drove through a small village where there seemed to be more horses than people.

"They used to live on the shores of the lake," the driver said, in broken Russian.

"When did people start to realise something was wrong?"

"It was slow to begin with," Jedige said. "From around 1960, the water level fell by around twenty centimetres every year. As more and more of the desert was made into cotton fields, which needed vast quantities of water, the process accelerated. By the 1980s, the water level was falling by almost a metre a year."

"How could the authorities just sit back and watch the world's fourth largest lake all but disappear?" It was an absurd question. The Soviet authorities had certainly not spared any resources when it came to achieving their goal of becoming an industrial superpower. The good old adage that the ends justify the means must have been repeated daily, like a mantra, in the Kremlin. But to wipe an entire lake from the map, with all the unknown environmental consequences that might entail, was that justified?

"They thought, in fact, that it would happen much faster," Jedige said. "It was a prudent calculation on their part. For them, cotton was more profitable than fish."

In some places, the sand we drove on was white with salt. Like the Caspian Sea, the Aral Sea had some salinity, but only a quarter of what would be found in normal seawater. As the lake shrank, the salt was spread by the wind, making the already thin soil in the region even more unfertile. There were broken shells everywhere, which crunched as the tyres rolled over them. Here and there camels nibbled at the tufts of grass that had sprung up from what was once the bottom of the lake.

Jedige, for some reason, was no longer talking about ecology, but about polygamy.

"Islam allows four wives," he was saying, "but I think two or three is enough, personally." He had told me earlier that he was studying Arabic in his spare time. His aim was to read the Qur'an in the original language so that he could live closer to God's laws.

"What about Kazakh law?" I said. Kazakhstan is the most northerly country in the world with a Muslim majority. Around seventy per cent of the population is Muslim. President Nazarbayev, who was brought up in the atheist Soviet Union, has worked hard to spread a secular form of Sunni Islam that accords with "traditional, Kazakh values". The Central Asian leaders all fear that more fundamentalist Islamic teachings, inspired by groups in neighbouring Iran and Afghanistan, will gain traction in their countries, and have taken different measures to prevent this from happening. In Kazakhstan, religious political parties are banned, and all religious groups are strictly monitored.

"It only allows one wife, but no-one cares about that," Jedige said. "The laws of Islam are more important than the president's laws."

"What does your wife think about your plans?"

"She was quite negative to begin with, because she wanted me to herself." He grinned. "But now she's more in favour. Lots of women are just pleased to get some help around the house."

"Can't *you* help her?"

Erkut and Jedige rolled their eyes at each other.

"It's the man's job to bring in the money and to look after things outside the house, and it's the woman's job to look after the house and the children. My wife isn't allowed to leave the house without my permission. The home is her domain," Erkut explained.

Jedige nodded. "My wife isn't allowed to go out without my permission either. I'm shocked that your husband allows you to travel alone. Has he ever considered getting another wife? It would be more practical for you too. Then you'd have someone to help with making the food and cleaning the house."

"He has never expressed the desire to have a second wife," I tell them.

"No doubt he's being polite. A man gets tired of his wife after a while, it's in our nature. And anyway, the first wife makes more of an effort to be attractive and beautiful if she gets some competition."

Erkut gave a knowing smile, but said nothing.

"He has already found a second wife," Jedige said. "A '93 model. They're getting married in the autumn."

Erkut's smile broadened. Then he stopped the car. We had arrived. Behind some dense, tall reeds, the lake opened out. The water was as blue as the sky. The birds twittered merrily and in the distance you could hear the screech of seagulls. A swan glided by. The air smelled of salt and sea. I had not imagined that an environmental catastrophe could be so attractive.

"Everyone is surprised to see how clean and beautiful it is here," Jedige said. "There are even fish in the water now."

"I'd heard that it was too salty for the fish to survive."

"The southern part is too salty. In 1987, the lake had shrunk so much that it split into two lakes: the North Aral Sea, or Little Aral, which is here in Kazakhstan, and the South Aral Sea, or Big Aral, which is on the other side of the border in Uzbekistan. In an attempt to save the North Aral Sea, the Kazakh authorities built a dam to stop the water running out into the South Aral Sea. They've also repaired a lot of the irrigation canals, so that more water is fed into the lake. The results have exceeded all expectations! The water level has risen by several metres, and the salinity has decreased. The lake used to be sixty kilometres from Aral, and now it's less than twenty. The aim is to bring the waterline back to Aral one day."

Perhaps Aral is not fighting a losing battle after all, I thought. I had expected to find the lake full of lifeless water, surrounded by fields of salt and depleted soil, but instead I was met with swans and the cry of seagulls. The North Aral Sea is living proof that man-made environmental disasters can be reversed, up to a point, if the authorities have the will and the resources to invest. The Kazakh government has taken steps, and succeeded.

In the world's largest country without a coastline, fish are once again more important than cotton.

Perhaps, after all, there is hope for the thirty thousand inhabitants of Aral, I thought. Perhaps the rusty cranes by the harbour will be repaired and put to use again. Perhaps the boats that are now lying on dry sand will once again go out to bring fish to the factories. And if that happens, it is even possible that they may renovate Hotel Aral.

THE EMPIRE

"The break-up of the Soviet Union was a tragedy," the ornithologist said. He had a full, white beard. He had just turned sixty, but looked closer to eighty. "The Americans won, they got what they wanted! People don't understand that we lost the fourth generation war, the information war. They don't understand that wars can be fought at that level." He was silenced by a coughing fit. When at last it stopped, he wiped his mouth on his sleeve, and continued undeterred. "Since the dissolution of the Soviet Union, everything has become clearer. We are not like the Europeans. We are different."

From his office window, there was a view to the snow-clad mountains in Aksu-Zhabagly National Park, and wild apple trees and green fields where cows and horses grazed side by side. The panorama could have been taken from an advert for the Swiss Alps. The green meadows were full of wild tulips. The ornithologist knew the national park like the back of his hand – he had been the director there until he retired.

The train journey here from Aral, which took seventeen hours, had been just as train journeys should be. A Russian security guard, Vladimir, had provided half the carriage with caviar and vodka, and everyone sat up until late in the night playing cards. I had won game after game, even though I did not know the rules.

"The *common good* is what is important for us," the ornithologist said. "*I* comes second, never first. Those of us who grew up in the Soviet Union have more in common than divides us."

He was by birth Ukrainian, but saw himself as Russian.

"Being Russian is not a nationality, it's a mentality, a state of mind!" he shouted. "Take Pushkin. His father was an Arab, but he himself was one hundred per cent Russian! These people here, the Kazakhs, had nothing before the Russians came. No schools, no literature, no civilisation or culture. And now you have to be fluent in Kazakh to get a job in the public sector! They barely had an alphabet before the Russians came. They owe *everything* to the Russians!"

Another violent coughing fit. He mopped the sweat from his brow and had a sip of tea to clear his throat. I took the opportunity to ask a question.

"Not *everything* can have been pink and rosy in the Soviet Union?"

"There were a lot of things that were not so good about the Soviet Union," the ornithologist conceded. "But there was a lot that was good as well. There is repression everywhere. All countries have prisons. There are more people in American prisons today than there were in the gulags."

"But what about developments after the Soviet Union? Kazakhstan has managed O.K., hasn't it?"

"What development?" The ornithologist gave a hoarse laugh. "Nothing has happened. We still work in Soviet factories. The Chinese are building the roads. The oil we sell will soon run out. And the saddest thing of all is that we're no longer experts or scholars." He pulled a well-thumbed reference book from the pile on the table and started to leaf through it. The covers were worn and the pages were yellow with age and use.

"This book contains everything I need to know about birds. They used to write books like this. But now students can't read Latin!" He was disgusted. "We sell oil and buy Chinese goods. We produce nothing ourselves. Everything I'm wearing is made in China. Look!" He bent down and pulled up his trouser legs to reveal white tennis socks. "My socks, shoes. Trousers. Everything. The idea that we have sovereignty is just a nonsense. We can only have real independence as part of the Eurasian Union."

The Eurasian Economic Union, also known as the Customs Union, officially came into force on January 1, 2015. To date, Russia, Belarus, Kazakhstan, Armenia and Kyrgyzstan are members, and Tajikistan is also expected to join. The protests in Kiev before Christmas 2013, which led to the dramatic fall of President Yanukovych, were the result of disagreement as to whether Ukraine should approach the E.U. or forge stronger bonds with Russia through the E.E.U.

According to President Putin, the union is of "epoch-making significance", but the form and extent of this primarily economic cooperation are not yet clear. There has been talk of a common currency between member states, but it is expected to involve free-trade agreements and the free movement of labour across borders. With its current five members, the union covers more than fifteen per cent of the earth's surface and supplies more than a fifth of the world's natural gas resources.

"Kazakhstan's president, Nazarbayev, first came up with the idea of a union in 1994," the ornithologist told me. "It's not like the Soviet Union, because each member state is still independent." He started coughing again. His face turned red. Tears ran down into his white beard. When he stopped, he lit up his pipe. "The most important thing, though, is *the moral stance*," he said, puffing on his pipe. The sweet smell of tobacco blended with the dustiness of old reference works. "*Morals*," he repeated. "*That* is what matters."

When I got up to leave, he asked me to sit for a little longer.

"I want to show you some pictures," he said. "Then perhaps you'll understand more." He started to look through the albums on his computer. Beautiful shots of laughing doves, griffin vultures, smews and alpine swifts flicked across the screen, all taken with a long lens from a considerable distance. The images were so sharp and well composed that they could have been used to illustrate a reference book, but it was not the birds in the national park that the ornithologist wanted to show me. It took some time before he found the picture he was looking for and leaned back in his chair, satisfied. It was a formal black and white photograph of a school class; the girls were wearing skirts or pinafores, and the boys were in shorts.

"All the boys had short hair back then," he said. The children on the next picture were even younger, but also well dressed and trimmed. "For as long as we were in kindergarten, we got to spend three months in the country every summer and didn't have to pay a penny, while our parents stayed in town to work. Imagine! Three months, completely free, every year!" A little cloud of pipe smoke filled the room. The young son he had with his second wife toddled into the room and started to drive his toy car around the carpet. His father barely noticed him, he just stared at the screen, transported.

"I had the best childhood in the world," he said. "The best in the world."

When travelling in the former Soviet Union, one seldom has to go far to find hardcore nostalgia and people who miss the good old days when the world was red, when school pupils were young pioneers, the shops were full of tinned food and unemployment was not to be found in the statistics. Nostalgia is not, of course, exclusive to the Soviet Union. My grandmother was also convinced that she had had the best childhood in the world. Everything has gone downhill since then. You only need to turn on the news, and the wretchedness of the world is streamed into your sitting room. The key difference between my grandmother and the Ukrainian ornithologist is that the social system in which he grew up no longer exists; the Soviet Union has dissolved and its fundamental ideology has been tossed onto the scrapheap of history.

Russians, in particular, seem to be prone to *nostalgia sovietica*. Many of them, quite rightly, associate the dissolution of the Soviet Union with loss and defeat. Overnight, the empire was reduced by more than one fifth, and Mother Russia was thrown into economic chaos and anarchy. In his annual speech to the federal assembly in 2005, Putin called the break-up of the Soviet Union the greatest geopolitical disaster of the twentieth century. He emphasised, in particular, the negative consequences that the collapse had had for the 25 million Russians living outside Russia. More than a third of them, that is around 9.5 million, lived in Central Asia. Between 1991 and 2003, eight million former Soviet citizens, primarily ethnic Russians, moved back to Russia. Of these, roughly four million people came from Central Asia.

Some of the Russians who have remained in the region have experienced a significant deterioration in status and rights. None of the post-Soviet states in Central Asia have taken de-Russification as far as Turkmenistan, where all traces of communism and the Russian language have been removed from the public sphere. The Turkmen government recently introduced a ban on dual nationality, which primarily affects the forty-three thousand Russian citizens who still live there. Since independence in 1991, that wealthy and eccentric country has gone its own way and prioritised cooperation and trade agreements with China and Iran, rather than with other post-Soviet states. The authorities have invested huge sums to increase gas exports to China, and China is now Turkmenistan's most important trading partner.

China has also penetrated the markets in the other Stans with the exception of Uzbekistan, which has chosen to go it alone to an even greater extent than Turkmenistan. Exports from China to Central Asia have increased more than a hundredfold since the dissolution of the Soviet Union, and China is, without a doubt, also the main trading partner for Kazakhstan, Kyrgyzstan and Tajikistan. While China's interests in the region are entirely financial, Russia's motives are more complex and it is not always easy to differentiate between financial and political interests. Soviet nostalgia may also play its part. The empire misses itself.

It is no surprise that both Tajikistan and Kyrgyzstan are considering membership of the E.E.U. These two mountainous, agricultural economies are among the poorest ex-Soviet states. Both are dependent on the money that migrant workers send home from Russia, which accounts for half and a third of their gross national product, respectively. Given these figures, it goes without saying that Tajik and Kyrgyz politicians are not much of a match for big brother Russia. Putin could at any point introduce visas for migrant workers and the politicians in Tajikistan and Kyrgyzstan are only too aware of this.

Kazakhstan's relationship with Russia is more complex. Kazakhstan is richer even than Turkmenistan and has secure financial foundations, but the bulk of its exported oil is transported through Russian pipelines. No other country shares a longer border with Russia – a total of 6,846 kilometres – and there are more Russians here than in any of the other Central Asian countries.

The Russian colonisation of Kazakhstan started in the eighteenth century, when the main Kazakh tribes asked the tsar for protection against invading hordes. In the course of the nineteenth century, more and more Russians settled on the Kazakh steppes, but it was not until the 1950s that people flocked there, when Nikita Khrushchev started a major campaign to cultivate the so-called "virgin lands" in northern Kazakhstan. His intention was that Kazakhstan, with its huge territory, would become the Soviet Union's corn basket. Hundreds of thousands of Russians and Ukrainians heeded the call and moved to what had previously been Kazakh grazing grounds. By the end of the 1950s, the Russians were in the majority in Kazakhstan, accounting for nearly forty-three per cent of the population. The Kazakhs accounted for only thirty per cent. The Virgin Lands Campaign was successful in the short term, but it soon became clear that the dry, salty earth of the steppes was not suitable for intensive cereal farming. The harvests were good for the first few years, but then they began to dwindle and continued to do so, year after year.

Despite the failure of the agriculture campaign, most of the Russians and Ukrainians stayed in the Soviet Socialist Republic of Kazakhstan until the dissolution of the Soviet Union. In 1989, there were more than six million Russians living in Kazakhstan. Today, that figure is closer to four million. In other words, Russians now account for less than a quarter of Kazakhstan's population. The Kazakhs, who have had a higher birth rate than the Russians, now make up nearly two-thirds of the population. President Nazarbayev has emphasised the importance of maintaining a good and close relationship with Russia, not least through the E.E.U., and Russian is still recognised as an official language, whereas Kazakh has been designated the "state language".

Even though Kazakhstan has chosen a different and softer line than, say, Turkmenistan, the balance of power lies without a doubt in the Kazakhs' favour. The Russians are no longer the lords. In the new constitution of 1995, Kazakhstan – land of the Kazakhs – is defined as "a state on the indigenous Kazakh land".

KAZAKH POLO

Victory Day on May 9 is one of the Soviet public holidays that is still widely celebrated throughout the former empire. In Turkobas, in southern Kazakhstan, not far from the Aksu-Zhabagly National Park, it was celebrated in true Kazakh style.

The grass plain was thronging with people. Women in long skirts and high heels struggled to keep their balance on the uneven ground. The bluish smoke from barbecues hung thick over the crowds. A cluster of older men stood pressed against the fence and followed the races with fierce concentration. The jockeys were young boys, some of them looking no more than eight or nine years old. They rode bareback, in jeans and trainers; none of them wore a helmet. The horses thundered past, circuit after circuit, with no sign of slowing down. The boys seemed to be glued to their horses' backs, apparently calm and relaxed, but with fixed, determined eyes.

Only two weeks earlier I had witnessed the president's fall in the marble-clad hippodrome outside Ashgabat, surrounded by men in dark suits and women in freshly pressed, long dresses. The contrast could not have been greater. Here in Turkobas, the track was a simple strip of sand out on a plain, with a basic, badly nailed picket fence. There were people, cars, horses and barbecues everywhere, and no one seemed to be in charge of the event. And yet there was something happening all the time. Between races, there was wrestling on horseback, and *kyz kuu*, literally, girl chasing. *Kyz kuu* is a popular sport among all the big, Central Asian horse tribes. The boy, most often dressed in traditional clothes – waistcoat, hat and all – sits waiting on his horse at the start line. The girl, generally in a long dress, starts some way behind him. As she gallops past, he gives chase. If he manages to catch her before she crosses the finish line, he can, according to tradition, steal a kiss from her. If, on the other hand, he does not catch up with her, the girl quite literally whips him back to the start line. Three boys tried their luck, and all of them were chased back to the start line by the girls, who galloped after them, dresses flapping, as they whipped their backs. The onlookers whooped and cheered. As a prize, each of the girls was given a vacuum cleaner.

The races were over by midday. The older men who were gathered by the fence were filled with a sudden reverence. Fathers called their sons. On the tracks, the kokpar teams got ready. Kokpar or buzkashi, as it is also called, is a national sport in Central Asia and Afghanistan. Some commentators have called it football on horseback, but it is in fact more akin to polo. The teams each have ten players and, instead of a ball, they play with a decapitated goat. At each end of the field, a circle is drawn that is about a metre and a half deep and three metres across. This is called a kazan, which is also the name of the iron pot used to make rice pilaf and other Central Asian dishes. Every time a player manages to get the goat into their opponent's kazan, his team scores a point. The carcass is then placed on the ground in the middle of the field again, and the game continues. These games can go on for days on end, but out of consideration to the spectators there is a now a limited match time.

The men by the fence stopped talking. A whistle blew and the game began. The goat, light brown and hairy, lay on the ground between the two kazans. Four riders were fighting to get hold of the carcass. They swung themselves down towards the ground like acrobats, without ever losing their balance. The muscular horses jostled each other, unaffected by the onlookers' cheers and shouts. The horses were specially trained for the game and could go from a standstill to a gallop within seconds, and the best of them could take the tightest corners without losing speed. The riders swung down on one side, then the other, as they tried to grab the more and more battered goat from their opponents. It was as though they were attached to their saddles by an invisible thread. Suddenly one of the riders broke loose from the scrum and galloped towards one of the white rings. The goat carcass dangled over his horse's mane. All the other riders swung about and took chase. The dust clouds trailed behind them like a tail. When a cheer rose up from the crowds, I realised one of the teams had scored a goal.

Archaeologists believe that it was here, on the steppes of Kazakhstan, that people first tamed a horse – around six thousand years ago. And the horse has been an indispensible and natural part of the nomadic steppe life ever since. Even though most Kazakhs have given up the nomadic life and have long since settled down, their culture is still closely linked to the horse. Horse competitions draw thousands of spectators, and every village with any self-respect has at least one good *kokpar* team. When the horses reach retirement age, they end up on the barbecue. Unlike the Turkmens, who would never eat horsemeat, the Kazakhs enjoy a good horse steak and horse sausages. *Kumys*, which is soured mare's milk, is considered a delicacy and is drunk every day and at celebrations.

Later on in the afternoon, the wind picked up. The tents were in danger of being blown away, and the women had to hold down their skirts. Plastic bottles and paper napkins swirled around on the gusts, and people and horses alike were covered in a film of reddish brown dust. The teams were not even halfway through the game when the public started to retreat from the fence, the tents and barbecues into their cars. In the end, only a few hardcore enthusiasts were left by the fence, and the area was otherwise deserted; tents had been packed away and the car park was abandoned. The riders on the field played on, unperturbed, raising clouds of dust as they galloped in clusters from one *kazan* to the other.

The sun would not set for hours.

—◊◊◊—

Earlier in the day, I had been to Shymkent, the regional capital of south Kazakhstan, and the country's third largest city. The Victory Day celebrations there were more traditional, with parades and speeches and tributes to war heroes. Those veterans who were still in good health had put on their finest garb to celebrate.

In the city park, in front of the grand monument to the Second World War, I met war veteran Sesembai Makhmytov and his equally celebrated wife, Kundus. Sesembai was so old that he almost disappeared in his freshly pressed, dark suit. His white shirt was immaculate and his black boots shone in the sun. His chest was laden with medals. The old couple spoke only Kazakh, but with some help from a passer-by, I found out that Sesembai had fought on the Eastern Front in the Second World War. He had been wounded in the shoulder during the battles in Eastern Europe, but had not given up and had carried on fighting until the end of the war. In April 1945 he marched into Berlin.

"The bullet's still in there," Sesembai said, pointing proudly at his shoulder.

Kundus had also been awarded a medal. It was polished, and twinkled in the sun. While their husbands, fathers and sons were away fighting the Nazis, the women worked on the collective farms and kept them going, throughout the empire.

"Was the work hard?"

Kundus looks at me, astonished. "Of course it was hard! And all the food was sent to the front. We were starving here at home."

The Second World War is called the Great Patriotic War in Russia, and no other country suffered such losses as the Soviet Union. Between twenty and thirty million people lost their lives, through either war, or starvation, or disease. The Central Asian republics paid their price too: it is estimated that more than three hundred thousand Kazakh soldiers were killed in the Second World War, and around three hundred and fifty thousand civilians died from hunger and illness at home. Ten per cent of Kazakhstan's population died as a result of the war, a loss on a par with Germany. Like Sesembai, many Kazakh soldiers could not speak Russian. Most of them had never left their village. Then, suddenly, they were called up, and, before they knew it, found themselves in an unknown part of the world in uniform, with a weapon in their hands, fighting for the world's largest country in the world's biggest war.

Despite these great losses, there was in fact pronounced growth in the population of Kazakhstan during the war years. Though there was fighting everywhere and soldiers were killed in droves, Stalin still took the time to move millions of people around within the empire during the war. As late as winter 1944, trainloads of people arrived in Central Asia. The deported people were simply dumped on the Kazakh steppes – women, babies and old people – thousands of miles from home, with no possessions other than the clothes on their back.

STALIN'S PAWNS

The cathedral, which is the largest in Central Asia, was almost full. Several hundred believers were at the service, dressed in dark suits and respectable skirts. Most of them had fair, European features, and all, down to the smallest child, were sitting in silence listening to the priest.

"For seventy years, good Christians were denied the right to practise their faith, and Catholics from far and wide were deported here to Karaganda in Kazakhstan, because of their nationality and faith." The priest spoke slowly, in correct Russian, but with a noticeable German accent. "For that reason, it is a particular pleasure to stand here in this newly consecrated church, Our Lady of Fátima. And could there be a more suitable name for a church here, of all places?"

The name of the cathedral refers to events that are alleged to have taken place in the Portuguese village of Fátima in 1917. In a series of apparitions, the Virgin Mary entrusted three secrets to three poor young shepherds. The first secret was about Russia: if Russia did not convert, mankind would suffer an even greater war and anti-Christian propaganda would spread falsehoods throughout the world.

"The Virgin's prophecies ended with the following illuminating words: *In the end, my immaculate heart will triumph.*" The priest allowed himself a smile. "Today we can confirm that her immaculate heart *has* indeed triumphed. The Soviet Union no longer exists, and Russia and Kazakhstan are now both independent countries where Christianity can be freely practised."

Three children in white tunics led the procession. They walked backwards as they scattered rose petals on the church floor.

The celebration of Fátima's prophecies continued in the basement of the cathedral, with soup and fizzy drinks. Kazakh pop music thundered out of the loudspeakers. The three children who had so solemnly scattered rose petals on the floor were bopping up and down on the dance floor, giggling and singing along. The grown-ups lined the walls and shouted to one another.

I must have looked as lonely and forlorn as I felt, because an older gentleman with a bald pate and broad shoulders came over and asked where I was from. He was very elegant, dressed in a dark suit and a black wool coat. He told me his name was Antonin, and he was a Pole, as were the majority of the congregation.

Tens of thousands of Poles ended up on the Soviet side of the border that was negotiated after the First World War. For the first few years, they enjoyed a degree of self-rule: they were allowed to speak Polish and their children went to Polish schools. Over time, however, concerted efforts were made to sovietise them, but the Poles opposed collectivisation and the religious ban, in particular. Then, in the mid-1930s, Stalin took off his kid gloves for good. Those Poles who were not imprisoned or executed were deported to Kazakhstan. Antonin's parents were exiled in 1936.

The Poles were among the first to be deported, but by no means the last. Not a few nationalities were declared to be "enemies of the people" and deported to Siberia or Central Asia, chiefly to Kazakhstan, home of endless steppes and not many people. Entire ethnic groups were transported here, then left to their own devices, with nothing more than their wits and the clothes they stood up in. With the outbreak of the Second World War, deportations increased in line with Stalin's paranoia. Anyone who might sympathise with the Germans or in some way be a threat to the Soviet Union was chased from house and home and sent east. Tartars from Crimea, Chechens and Ingushetians from North Caucasus, and Germans from the colonies on the Black Sea and Volga river – they were all sent to Central Asia during the war. It is estimated that six million people were deported in the 1930s and '40s. Around a quarter of them died in transit or within the first few years. To this day, there are more than a hundred different nationalities in Kazakhstan, a legacy of Stalin's brutal regime.

Antonin's parents survived the journey, but were not allowed to live together, not even after their son was born in 1939. His parents were both set to hard labour, his father on a collective farm in the country, and his mother as a lamp carrier in a mine on the outskirts of town. If the flame went out or altered in any way, it signalled danger and the mine had to be evacuated.

"It must have been tough work," I said with some sympathy.

"No, not at all," was Antonin's blithe reply. "It was very easy work. So in that sense, she was lucky."

The deportees in Karaganda lived under strict surveillance until Stalin's death in 1953. Antonin's parents were not allowed to leave their respective villages without permission, and minor offences were harshly punished. For example, being late for work could lead to a prison sentence. But worst of all was the knowledge that even the slightest misdemeanour could result in your children being taken from you and sent to a children's home.

"Did you have enough food?" I said.

"No, there was never enough," Antonin said. "We had ration cards for bread, but that didn't really help."

Hundreds of thousands of people lived like this. They were not imprisoned, but nor were they free. They were forced to work from morning to evening, and still were unable to feed their families properly. It was not always easy to differentiate between those who were in principle free and those who were prisoners. And there were plenty of them. The labour camp in Karaganda went under the name Karlag, and was one of the biggest in the Gulag system. It covered an area of land the size of Kuwait. Many of the prisoners were artists, intellectuals and scientists who had not necessarily done anything wrong, but were perceived to be a threat to the state because they were freethinkers. Others were in prison because, according to the state, they had been too wealthy, or stood out in some other way. And to be on the safe side, the wives and children of male prisoners were often sent to the camps too.

The camp inmates were very useful for the Soviet economy: Karlag provided the Soviet Union with light bulbs and rail tracks, among other things, but primarily with food. At its peak, there were more than two hundred thousand sheep and thirty thousand cows in the camp, which was known for far exceeding its production targets. The prisoners saw little benefit from the food they produced, and as a rule went hungry to bed.

More than eight hundred thousand people were detained in the camp over the course of its nineteen-year existence, from 1934 until Stalin's death. A total of twenty-five thousand people were executed there. When looking at the Gulag system as a whole, it is estimated that as many as eighteen million people were detained at some point in one of the Soviet Union's thousands of labour camps during the twenty-four years that they were fully operational, from 1929 to 1953.

Back in the crypt of the cathedral, some of the parents had ventured onto the dance floor. They danced with stiff legs, with stiffer smiles. Every one of them presumably had an equally dramatic family history. Antonin followed my gaze. He pointed to one of the fathers who had just joined the dancing.

"Polish," he said, then pointed at someone else. "Polish as well. Ukrainian. Polish. Russian. Polish. Korean. Kazakh. Russian. Polish."

Millions of people were first uprooted then forced to put down roots hundreds of thousands of mile away in barren lands. If nothing else, the experiment shows just how resilient people are. After Stalin's death, when people were gradually allowed to return to where they came from, many of them chose to stay. The country of their exile had become home.

Leaving was never an option for Antonin, even after the Iron Curtain fell.

"This is where I was born," he said, matter-of-factly. "This is my country."

As the son of Poles, Antonin too was labelled an enemy of the people, from the day he was registered in the population census. He was rehabilitated in 2002.

"Gosh, as late as that," I said.

Antonin shrugged.

"I got a thousand tenge in compensation."

"That's not much. It's . . ." I did a quick calculation, "four euros."

"It was worth a lot more eleven years ago," Antonin said, with a fleeting smile.

Even though the tenge has performed badly as a result of inflation, it could not have been so much more then, either, but it is not always the market value of compensation that matters most.

THE CAPITAL CITY

Sasha, my eighteen-year-old driver, was nervous and insisted that we go to a car wash before we left. He firmly believed that a shiny, clean car would increase our chances of getting in. The road north was flat and straight and there were fewer and fewer houses. Then, after a couple of hours, we spotted a faint glare in the distance. Astana. The capital.

"It's so beautiful, I'm sure you will love the city," Sasha said. "If we're allowed in, that is." He gave the dented bonnet a worried look.

The checks at the city gates were stricter than at most European border posts. Undesirables were not welcome in the Kazakh capital. An army of neatly dressed policemen watched the traffic with mean eyes. Buses were stopped and all the passengers had to show their papers and have their luggage searched. We, on the other hand, were let through without a problem. Sasha heaved a sigh of relief.

"It's a good thing we stopped to wash the car," he said.

The pale blue and yellow Kazakh flag fluttered in the evening breeze as we drove along Astana's wide, floodlit avenues.

"Isn't it beautiful?" Sasha said, entranced.

"Very nice," I said, to please him.

I disliked Astana from the outset. Perhaps it was the endless traffic jams that made me think of Moscow. By the afternoon, the cars were trapped in long, claustrophobic queues. I secretly suspected that the town planners had intentionally designed a road network that would result in queues to create the illusion of a bustling, pulsating metropolis. Astana is surrounded by miles and miles of nothing; the bare steppe to the horizon and beyond. Outside the city gates there is not a car or person to be seen, and scarcely a sheep or a camel. Yet the seven hundred and fifty thousand inhabitants who live crammed together within the city limits spend the greater part of the working day stuck in queues.

The side streets were often a kilometre apart, and the queues were as long as the blocks. Walking between attractions was not really an option, so you just had to sit out the queues. There was no underground system and no-one cycled. However, it was the atmosphere that unsettled me more than the queues. Men in dark suits rushed along the pavements. No-one looked up. No-one looked me in the eye. For the first time on my trip I felt invisible. The atmosphere in Astana was not so different from the business-like efficiency and briskness of any other capital, yet this city seemed to amplify the feeling of loneliness. Perhaps this was due to its rather peculiar inception. Kazakhstan's capital has not grown organically, like Moscow or London, honed and refined over the centuries. It came into existence as the result of a decree. In 1994, President Nazarbayev decided that the capital should be transferred from the city of Almaty in the south, with its population of more than one million, to the small and insignificant provincial town of Akmola, 970 kilometres to the north. The transfer was made in 1997, and the following year Akmola was renamed Astana, which simply means "capital".

No-one knows for sure why Nazarbayev chose to move the capital. Not only is Astana far from the populous regions in the south and surrounded by steppe, it has one of the most unforgiving climates in the world: it is the second coldest capital in the world after Ulan Bator in Mongolia. In winter, the temperature can fall to -40°C. Nazarbayev himself said that Almaty was too small, the city had expanded beyond capacity and there was no room for growth. He had also thought for some time that the capital should move to a more central location, and not be on the periphery like Almaty, which was close to the borders with Kyrgyzstan and China. Rumour has it, however, that Nazarbayev had so many enemies in Almaty that he had no choice but to move north. A more plausible explanation is that Nazarbayev wanted to create a power base in the Russian-dominated regions of the north, where almost sixty per cent of the population is ethnic Russian. And there really *was* more room for growth and expansion in Astana than in the densely built-up Almaty.

In recent years, Astana has become the very symbol of modern Kazakhstan. Vast sums have already been invested in developing the city, but the project is nowhere near finished: eight per cent of the national budget is earmarked for the development and expansion of Astana until 2030. There is construction going on everywhere. The buildings that are being raised are daring and futuristic and the centre is almost exclusively signature buildings. Astana's most famous building, the Bayterek Tower, designed by the award-winning British architect Norman Foster, dominates. The tower itself is exactly ninety-seven metres high, in honour of the year that Astana became the capital. The gold-mirrored sphere atop the tower is held up by a web of white, metal girders. There is a lift to an observation deck on top where the view over Astana's modern centre is astonishing. Straight ahead lies the Khan Shatyr shopping mall, also designed by Lord Foster. The structure is formed like a giant transparent tent, the largest of its kind in the world, and is full of European designer shops, cinemas, swimming pools and restaurants. The temperature inside the tent is a constant and pleasant 24°C, no matter how boiling hot or freezing cold it is outside. Then there is Astana's new concert hall that can hold 3,500 people, and the new mosque, richly decorated with gold and white marble, which is one of the largest in Central Asia. To the left of the mosque is the new presidential palace, a magnificent building with white pillars and polished glass surfaces, crowned by an enormous azure blue dome. The National Museum, where the development of Astana is to be given a prominent place, and the futuristic National Library, designed by the Danish architect firm BIG,[5] have yet to be completed.

Inside the golden egg on top of the Bayterek Tower is a round, malachite table. In the middle of the table is a circular, solid silver disc that weighs five kilos. And on top of the silver disc is a two-kilo triangle of pure gold, where the imprint of Nazarbayev's hand has been immortalised. No visit to Astana is complete unless you have laid your own hand in the gold impression of the president's right hand, closed your eyes and made a wish. But first you have to wish him well, the guides explain, or your own wish will not be fulfilled.

With the exception of Norman Foster, no-one has left a greater mark on Astana than Nursultan Nazarbayev, the city's midwife and chief architect. It is hardly a coincidence that Astana Day, which is celebrated with pomp and circumstance every year, is on July 6, Nazarbayev's birthday. "Some people approached me saying they would like to raise a monument to me as they do in Turkmenistan for Turkmenbashi," Nazarbayev said modestly to Hugh Pope, a visiting *Wall Street Journal* correspondent. "I asked, 'What for? Astana is my memorial.'"[iii]

Astana's modern buildings, designed only by renowned foreign architects are triumphant proof of a successful transition from Soviet rule and five-year plans to a market economy. Kazakhstan

5 No more than the foundations were laid for the National Library, as BIG with-drew from the original project. Foster + Partners completed the building in its current design. It is now the Nazarbayev Centre, and opened in 2012.

possesses enormous gas and oil reserves, as well as gold, coal and uranium, making it the richest country in Central Asia. Prices reflect this relative wealth: a hotel room in Astana costs as much as a hotel room in Oslo.

Nazarbayev attributes the successful transition from Soviet state to modern national state to his own wise leadership. Like Turkmen-bashi, Turkmenistan's first president, Nazarbayev comes from a humble background. He was born into a poor shepherd's family, but proved to be bright and did well at school. Anyone who would like to read Nazarbayev's school reports can visit the Nazarbayev Centre in Astana, where they are on display. Compared with his fellow pupils' grades, which are also on display, Nazarbayev did very well indeed at school. Like Turkmenbashi, he trained to be an engineer, a highly respected profession in the industry-oriented Soviet society. He spent several years working in smelting works, first in Ukraine and later in Kazakhstan. The work was well paid, but physically demanding. The temperature in the furnace was more than 2,000°C, and in the course of a shift workers had to drink half a bucket of water each to replace what they had sweated out. In his spare time, Nazarbayev took a correspondence course in economics – a sign that he had greater ambitions in life than to make steel. When he was twenty-two, he joined the Communist Party, and rose quickly through the ranks. In 1989, Gorbachev made him first secretary of the Communist Party of Kazakhstan.

Compared with Turkmenbashi – a comparison which is favour-able for most – Nazarbayev has adopted a moderate leadership style. In the 1990s, when all the former Soviet republics were struggling with unstable economies and rocketing inflation, he kept his country on a steady path. Kazakhstan has recorded consistent annual growth in G.D.P. of around five to ten per cent, and most people are better off. Nazarbayev has also made great efforts to keep the various ethnic groups united and to avoid any tension flaring between the Russians and Kazakhs.

But, like most of his Central Asian colleagues, Nazarbayev also suffers from dictator syndrome. He has held the post of president since 1991. No more than a handful of candidates have made any serious attempts at opposition over the years. They have all been outmanoeuvred in one way or another, and a couple of them have been killed. In 2007, the parliament approved a constitutional amendment that exempted Nazarbayev from the rule that the country's president can sit for only two consecutive terms. In practice, he can now be president for life. In 2010, the parliament awarded Nazarbayev the honorary title of "Leader of the Nation", despite modest protests from the person in question. At the same time, a law was passed that made it illegal to insult the president or deface his image. Nazarbayev was also granted lifetime immunity from prosecution and the right to decide over the country's policies after his retirement.

If the election results are to be believed, Nazarbayev is still extremely popular, even after all these years. In fact, his popularity has increased with each election, and in 2011, he was re-elected with more than 95 per cent of the votes, a feat that is even more impressive given that the turnout was 89.9 per cent. One of his opponents boasted that he had voted for Nazarbayev, out of "respect for the winner".

Nazarbayev's leadership style could at best be described as enlightened autocrat. It is Nazarbayev who makes all the important decisions – the parliament is more of an accessory. Nazarbayev has always insisted that Kazakhstan must be allowed to do things in its own way and to set its own pace – the transition from seventy years of totalitarian rule to democracy should be taken slowly. For the time being, the president is prioritising economic growth and the gradual development of national institutions. Freedom of the press, civil rights and democracy are way down the list of priorities, but fortunately there is still plenty of time: according to the president's long-term plan, Kazakhstan will not be a fully developed democracy until 2050. In every town, there are big posters of Nazarbayev, emblazoned with 2050, the magical year when all will be well. The obvious problem is, however, that Nazarbayev, who was born in 1940, is likely to be long dead by then. But instead of ensuring a smooth transfer of power after his death by naming his successor, Nazarbayev has donated substantial sums to Nazarbayev University in Astana for research on life-prolonging medicines.

Even though 2050 is still a long way off, Kazakhstan is in fact the most successful of the Central Asian countries, from an economic perspective at least. The country is so successful that Nazarbayev is considering changing its name from Kazakhstan to Kazakh Eli, which also means land of the Kazakhs but does not have the "stan" ending with all its negative connotations. The president is tired of Kazakhstan always being lumped together with its poor and badly run neighbours, and fears that investors may be put off by the similar name.

Even though the independent Kazakhstan, or Kazakh Eli, was lucky in terms of its geology and is now revelling in natural resources, the Soviet era still casts a shadow over the country. Many people still associate Kazakhstan with the atrocities of the gulags, Stalin's deportations and the terrible famine of the 1930s. In addition to the human cost, the environmental consequences were disastrous. The thin crust of earth on the northern steppes could not cope with Khrushchev's utopian Virgin Lands campaign; in the south what was once the mighty Aral Sea has now shrunk to a small lake; and in the east, great swathes of land are uninhabitable as a result of the nuclear arms race during the Cold War, and many of the people who do live there suffer from radiation-related health problems.

One of Nazarbayev's first independent decisions, which consolidated his popularity as president, was to close the Soviet authorities' controversial nuclear testing site in Semipalatinsk.

THE GREAT EXPERIMENT

The small airplane that would take me south-east to Semipalatinsk climbed slowly towards the clouds. Worn curtains fluttered in the windows, and a dusty carpet with faded squares ran down the aisle. Suitcases and overfull plastic bags bulged out over the edge of the open overhead luggage racks. The body of the plane shook like an old tumble dryer. And the flat landscape below fell further and further away.

Kazakhstan has a lot of airlines, but, with the exception of Air Astana, they are all on the E.U.'s blacklist of companies banned from flying in European airspace. Air Astana, however, no longer flies to Semipalatinsk. After the upgrade of their fleet in 2012, the scheduled flight to Semipalatinsk was stopped because the airport there did not "live up to international safety standards". So an airline with the rather less reassuring name of S.C.A.T. Airlines took over the route. It was clearly a while since S.C.A.T. had upgraded its fleet, as the propellers thundered and rattled. The ashtrays below the windows stank of stale cigarettes. The flight attendant had not bothered to do a safety demonstration before take-off, but if the plane fell out of the sky, we were without hope anyway.

When the landing wheels finally hit the runway with a thud, the passengers cheered and clapped. I joined in the applause whole-heartedly.

*

One of the Cold War's darkest chapters was played out on the empty plains outside Semipalatinsk: it was here that the Soviet Union carried out most of its nuclear testing. They detonated, on average, one nuclear bomb a month, 456 in total. And every explosion had an echo on the other side of the world, in the Nevada Desert and the Pacific Ocean, where the Americans did their testing; the two superpowers carried on like this for nearly forty years. A slow dance of sorts, a war of shadows in the shape of white mushroom clouds.

The driver who was going to take me from Semipalatinsk to the testing ground set off at breakneck speed. He just laughed when I asked him to slow down, and drove even faster. But then, when we were about halfway there, we spotted an old man walking along the side of the deserted road. For the first time in the journey, the driver slowed down, and the old man gratefully climbed into the back seat. He had narrow eyes and deep furrows in his brow. His gold teeth caught the sun when he smiled. He told us he was called Sadyk and he was fifty years old.

"If I'm lucky, I'll maybe live another five years," he said. "No-one lives to be old in these parts. My cousin died earlier this year. He was forty-two. Cancer, naturally. That's what people die of round here."

Sadyk only needed to go a couple of kilometres. He asked to be let off at the turnoff to a ghost town. Empty concrete shells yawned at us. The road leading to the abandoned apartment blocks was in part overgrown with weeds and scrub.

"That's Chagan, my hometown," Sadyk said, and nodded towards the derelict buildings. "In Soviet days, Chagan was a closed town, and only Russians and military people lived here. My father was in the army, that's why I grew up there. When the Soviet Union broke up, all the Russians left. Now there's nothing left. I pass the empty houses every day on my way to work, but try to look the other way.

Once upon a time, the town was full of life; there was a school, an outpatients unit, everything."

"Did you know about the nuclear tests that were being carried out nearby?"

"No, but we knew something was going on. When I was born, they had stopped atmospheric detonations, and instead did the testing underground. Sometimes the ground shook, especially on Saturdays. If we were at school when it happened, we were sent out into the street."

Sadyk got out of the car and started to walk towards the small village on the other side of the road, where he lived now. His gait was slow and stiff.

The driver put his foot on the accelerator, and after a surprisingly short time we arrived at Kurchatov. At the old checkpoint, only a few posts remained of the barbed wire fences that had once prevented unauthorised persons from entering the town. Today, they are no longer needed. People do not move to Kurchatov anymore, they move away.

Kurchatov, the administrative centre for the nuclear test ground, was built at top speed in 1947. Thousands of prisoners were used to build the houses and roads. The authorities had no time to lose. Two years had already passed since the Americans had bombed Hiroshima and Nagasaki, and the need to build a similar Soviet bomb was urgent. The physicist Igor Kurchatov – the town was later named after him – was put in charge of the programme. Stalin had set 1948 as the deadline for developing a Soviet atom bomb, and appointed the head of the secret police, the much feared and ruthless Lavrentiy Beria, to supervise the project. It was no coincidence that the experiments took place in Semipalatinsk. The Soviet leaders saw Kazakhstan as a barren wasteland, perfect for experiments of this kind. The few people who lived here simply made the testing more realistic.

At its largest, Kurchatov had forty thousand inhabitants. Officially, the town did not exist and it was not marked on any map. The area was sealed off to unauthorised persons and the road there was guarded by heavily armed soldiers. For a long time, the town did not even have a name, only a number. The area around the town, where the tests were carried out, was called Polygon 2. There was no Polygon 1: the number was chosen to confuse the Americans.

On August 29, 1949, the day had arrived. The operation had been given the code name "First Lightning" and Beria himself was present for the occasion. Seconds after a violent explosion, a fireball appeared in the sky. For a brief moment, the light from the fireball was stronger than the sun. The shock waves from the explosion were felt as far away as Karaganda and what is today Astana. Miners working hundreds of kilometres away from the testing site felt the ground shake. In the silence that followed, the fireball changed into a white mushroom cloud. After a few minutes, it disappeared. Everything had gone according to plan.

Over time, these test detonations became routine.

It was obvious that Kurchatov had been quite a smart town in its day. The houses on the main street were neoclassical in style and painted in muted colours. Through the broken windows it was possible to catch a glimpse of what must once have been elegant flats and offices. There were two hotels in the town, one of which was closed indefinitely for renovation, and the other only accepted guests who were associated with the nuclear institute.

"Are there any other hotels here?" I asked.

"Hotels, well," the driver muttered. "There's a kind of bed and breakfast for social occasions, pensioners and casual workers. I'm sure they'll have a room."

The bed and breakfast was surrounded by grim, grey concrete

apartment buildings. Every second block was derelict, with broken windows and gaping holes in the walls. Dogs had taken over in the corridors. The open green spaces between the blocks were witness to the town planners' best intentions: there would be plenty of green spaces and recreational areas; children would have playgrounds, and adults parks and benches. Kurchatov would be a good place to live.

No-one looked after the trees and parks now, and piles of rubbish lay hidden in the long grass between the buildings. A gaggle of more permanent guests were standing around talking, drinking and smoking outside the hostel; they seemed to have all the time in the world. A group of pensioners were sitting at a table playing cards. They stank of vodka, but the mood was jolly. As soon as they saw me and my companion, they started straight away to tell us about the good old days.

"Everything was better in the Soviet Union!" crowed a ruddy-cheeked man in his sixties. "Those were the days. Everyone had work, there were no differences. Everyone was a comrade!"

"It's another story now," sighed a woman with bleached, back-combed hair and pink lipstick. "Now a few people are very rich and the rest of us are poor."

"But what about the nuclear testing?" I said.

A toothless, old man coughed and spoke up. "My name is Vladimir Maksimovich and I worked as a driver in Polygon for forty years. I saw all the explosions!"

"What does a nuclear explosion look like?"

Vladimir stared at me for a long time, but said nothing. It was possible he had not understood my question.

"Most of us have never seen a nuclear explosion," I said.

"No. Well, first of all there is an explosion and then a mushroom cloud and then, after five minutes, it disappears," he said, very matter-of-factly.

"Weren't you frightened?"

"No, not at all! I didn't know it was dangerous. They didn't tell us."

The sun was about to go down when I wandered back to the bed and breakfast. An enormous, faded poster brightened the otherwise drab street. Under the photograph of a matronly nurse it said in big letters: "The people's health is most important". Stray dogs slunk out of back lanes and alleys with a growl and took over the night streets.

The next morning I was going to visit the testing site where Vladimir Maksimovich had worked as a driver all his life. A small part of me wanted to cancel the trip, even though that was the only reason I had come here. Who would voluntarily visit a nuclear testing site?

A small delegation was waiting for me outside Kazakhstan's Institute of Atomic Energy, the only building in Kurchatov that was reasonably well looked after. A young man with long hair and bad teeth introduced himself as Valentin, my guide. The institute's driver was sitting in the grey people carrier with a fierce-looking, bald man, whose arms were as stout as his thighs. Valetin explained that he was our orderly. He was there to make sure that everything was done according to the rules.

"He has experience from Chernobyl," Valentin whispered, so quietly that I could barely hear him. "He was actually there when it happened . . ."

It did not take long before we were out of Kurchatov and inside the testing ground itself. It was unguarded and unprotected; only a sign low down in the tall grass warned that the area was dangerous and that entry was strictly forbidden.

"The landscape is perfect for nuclear testing," Valentin said, full of enthusiasm. "It isn't flat, you see, but more like a huge bowl, with a gentle incline. Ideal conditions for explosions and shock waves, in other words."

We had the vast green area to ourselves. The test site covers an area that is a little smaller than Wales. We could have driven for several days without crossing the whole site. After two kilometres or so, we drove past a cluster of houses. Cows were grazing by the buildings. There was smoke coming out of the chimneys.

Valentin followed my gaze.

"This area has been declared safe," he said. "They've been given permission to farm here."

"But is it really safe to live and farm here?"

Valentin laughed.

"I *knew* you would ask that! People think it's so dangerous here, but there is only high radioactivity in a handful of zones. Most of the areas are perfectly safe." He got out a Geiger counter, which hovered around zero. "There you go, no radiation."

We drove further into the testing ground. The landscape was green and yellow. The grass had grown tall and was surprisingly lush, almost beautiful. After some time, I spotted a row of concrete constructions to the right. They were several hundred metres apart, and most of them appeared to be intact.

"Observation towers," Valentin said. "Before each test explosion, cine cameras and pressure-measuring instruments were installed in them. All the explosions were measured and documented. Sometimes, they built whole imitation towns around the detonation area before the explosion, complete with bridges and roads – and also helicopters, tanks and fire engines – to measure the effect of the explosion on various types of infrastructure and military equipment. They didn't experiment on people, naturally, but they did use cattle and pigs. Did you know that pig skin is very similar to human skin?"

The Geiger counter started to beep. Valentin looked at the small screen, very happy. The digits shot up: 2 . . . 3 . . . 4 . . . 5 . . .

"Almost there!" he said.

Our blue shoe covers rustled as we got out of the car. The Geiger counter beeped loudly with every step we took. The landscape around us was bare, empty. There is only one other place I can remember hearing such intense birdsong: on a guided tour of Chernobyl.

"We're lucky today," Valentin grinned. "Because it's just rained, the dust has settled on the ground and we don't need to wear gas masks."

The Geiger counter beeped furiously as we waded through the tall, yellow grass. Even though I know it is impossible to feel radiation, my entire body seemed to be fizzing and buzzing. I glanced over at the two-digit number on the Geiger counter and sent a worried apology to any potential offspring.

After a while Valentin stopped. He pointed solemnly at a modest reservoir.

"That is the crater created by the Soviet Union's first atom bomb. This is where the Cold War started."

The Soviet Union's successful nuclear test detonation was a cause of great concern in the U.S.A. American nuclear physicists began frantically to explore the possibility of making an even bigger and more powerful bomb. In 1951, Edward Teller and Stanislaw Ulam succeeded in developing a thermonuclear bomb, now known as the hydrogen bomb. The new bomb would involve a two-stage detonation: the primary detonation was a standard nuclear bomb, followed by the secondary, which was far more powerful and contained hydrogen isotopes. These would be heated to tens of millions of degrees by the power of the first explosion, which would make them race towards each other at such speed that they would fuse and create a third, heavier chemical element. This fusion would produce more energy than fission, or the splitting of the atom, which is the basis of the uranium bomb.

In 1952, the U.S.A. carried out the first successful controlled explosion of the new bomb. Unlike the uranium bomb, which explodes spontaneously if the size exceeds a critical limit, there is no limit to how big a hydrogen bomb can be. "Ivy Mike", as the bomb was called, had an explosion yield of 10.4 megatons, and was four hundred and fifty times more powerful than the atom bomb that had been dropped on Nagasaki in 1945.

In the Soviet Union, the physicist Andrei Sakharov worked extremely hard to develop a similar bomb. In summer 1953, the first Soviet hydrogen bomb was ready for testing at Semipalatinsk. There was only one problem: Sakharov's team had been so focused on getting the bomb itself ready that they had forgotten to calculate the damage area. When one of the scientists pointed this out, everyone panicked. A couple of intense days followed, and the team concluded that tens of thousands of people in the area had to be evacuated. Seven hundred military lorries were immediately procured and the evacuation began. Sakharov had some concerns about the way in which the evacuation was carried out; there were sick people, old people and children – would they all cope with being driven across the open steppe on the back of a lorry? These concerns were dismissed by those higher up: "Army manoeuvres always result in casualties – twenty or thirty deaths can be considered normal. And *your* tests are far more vital for the country and its defence," the then minister of defence, Alexander Vasilevsky, said. Comments like this only made Sakharov more anxious, and in his memoirs, he wrote: "Catching a glimpse of myself in a mirror, I was struck by the change – I looked old and grey." [iv]

And so, on August 12, 1953, Sakharov and the other scientists were assigned to an area thirty-five kilometres from the detonation. They were equipped with safety glasses and lay on their stomachs on the ground, facing the test site. Sakharov wrote:

> The minutes passed slowly. Sixty seconds. Fifty, forty, thirty, twenty, ten, nine, eight, seven, six, five, four, three, two, one. We saw a flash, and a swiftly expanding white ball lit up the whole horizon. I tore off my goggles, and though I was partially blinded by the glare, I could see a stupendous cloud trailing streamers of purple. The cloud turned grey, quickly separated from the ground and swirled upwards, shimmering with gleams of orange. The customary mushroom cloud gradually formed, but the stem connecting it to the ground was much thicker than those shown in photographs of fission explosions.

When the dust had settled, the scientists were driven closer to the epicentre, to have a look at the destruction. Sakharov recalled:

> We drove in open cars ... braking to a stop by an eagle whose wings had been badly singed. It was trying to fly, but couldn't get off the ground. One of the officers killed the eagle with a well-aimed kick, putting it out of its misery. I have been told that thousands of birds are destroyed during every test; they take wing at the flash, but then fall to earth, burned and blind.

The test was, to all intents and purposes, a success, but Sakharov had not yet fully understood the connection between radiation and the build up of heat in the first stage and the implosion of the second. The energy yield of the bomb was "only" 400 kilotons, and was primarily generated by fission, not fusion. It was not until November 1955 that Sakharov developed a true hydrogen bomb, this time with an energy yield of 1.6 megatons.

> I saw a blinding, yellow-white sphere swiftly expand, turn orange in a fraction of a second, then turn bright red and touch the horizon . . . Between the cloud and the swirling dust grew a mushroom stem, even thicker than the one that had formed during the first thermonuclear test. Shock waves criss-crossed the sky, emitting sporadic milky-white cones and adding to the mushroom image. I felt heat like that from an open furnace on my face – and this was in freezing weather, tens of miles from ground zero. The whole magical spectacle unfolded in complete silence.

Even though the bomb was dropped from an airplane this time to minimise the spread of radioactivity, several lives were lost. A young soldier died when his trench collapsed as a result of the blast wave. In a village beyond the testing site, a two-year-old girl died when the bomb shelter where she was sitting was hit by the blast wave and fell apart. In another village, the roof above the women's ward of the local hospital was destroyed. And in Semipalatinsk itself, which was 150 kilometres from the explosion, the blast wave blew out the windows in a meat-packing factory and the mince was contaminated with glass splinters. Even further away, in Ust-Kamenogorsk, the local population reported that, for some reason unknown to them, all the ash from the ovens had blown into the rooms.

The test was a success, and the military top brass were invited to a banquet the same evening. Sakharov, the hero of the day, proposed a toast: "May all our devices explode as successfully as today's, but always over test sites and never over cities."

Silence fell around the table. Everyone froze. Nedelin, the commander-in-chief of the test programme, raised his glass and replied with a joke: "An old man wearing only a shirt was praying before an icon. 'Guide me, harden me. Guide me, harden me.' His wife, who was lying on the stove, said: 'Just pray to be hard, old man, I can guide it in myself!' Let's drink to getting hard."

In his memoirs, Sakharov wrote that Nedelin's words were like a punch in the stomach. He suddenly realised what he had been part of: "We, the inventors, scientists, engineers and craftsmen, had created a terrible weapon, the most terrible weapon in human history; but its use would lie entirely outside our control."

As a result, Sakharov studied the long-term consequences of the tests. Even though no statistics were recorded, it soon became clear that the number of cancer cases in the Semipalatinsk area had rocketed since the testing began. An alarming number of children were born with deformities, and in some villages there was a very high incidence of mental health issues. Having looked at the human cost in detail, both Sakharov and Kurchatov became active opponents of nuclear weapons and nuclear testing. Their protests had some impact, and, in 1963, the U.S.A., Great Britain and the Soviet Union signed a multilateral agreement banning the testing of nuclear weapons in the atmosphere, outer space and under water.

Sakharov went on to become a passionate peace activist and advocate of universal human rights. He was awarded the Nobel Peace Prize in 1975 for his commitment and tireless anti-nuclear campaigning. The Soviet authorities refused him permission to leave the Soviet Union, and his wife, Elena Bonner, had to travel to Oslo to accept the prize on his behalf.

Sakharov became a very bothersome individual for the Soviet regime. He was strongly opposed to the Soviet Union's invasion of Afghanistan in 1979 and took every opportunity to explain why he was against the war. The following year, in 1980, he and his wife were arrested and deported to Gorky, a town four hundred kilometres east of Moscow that was closed to foreigners. He was kept under strict surveillance by the K.G.B., and was not allowed to have any contact with foreigners or with academic circles in Moscow. Drafts of Sakharov's memoir were confiscated on several occasions, and he had to start all over again. The renowned physicist wrote letters protesting about the way in which he was being treated, he even went on hunger strike, but to no avail.

At ten o'clock in the evening of December 15, 1986, there was a ring at the Sakharovs' door. Two electricians and a K.G.B. agent entered the flat and installed a telephone.

"You'll get a call around ten tomorrow morning," the K.G.B. agent said as they left.

On December 16, Andrei Sakharov and his wife sat waiting at home for the telephone call until three o'clock in the afternoon. Just when Sakharov was about to put on his coat to go out and buy some bread, the telephone rang.

"Hello, this is Gorbachev speaking," said the voice at the other end.

The new General Secretary was calling to inform Sakharov that he and his wife could move back to Moscow.

Even though test detonations in the atmosphere were stopped in 1963, the Soviet authorities continued to experiment in Kazakhstan. In the period to 1989, a further 340 underground detonations were carried out at the testing ground close to Semipalatinsk. When the Soviet Union collapsed, the site was closed. The Russians packed up and went home. In a very short space of time, the population of Kurchatov fell dramatically from forty thousand to fewer than ten thousand. Every second apartment block stood empty.

Looters had a field day. The Russians had left behind a dangerous legacy in Kazakhstan. In 1991, there were more than 1,400 nuclear warheads on Kazakh soil, which made Kazakhstan one of the world's leading nuclear powers. The following year, the new Kazakh government entered into an agreement with Russia for the transfer of all nuclear weapons back to Russia. Nazarbayev's goal was to make Kazakhstan a nuclear-free state.

The transfer of the weapons was relatively swift and painless, but it did not solve the problem. There were still several hundred kilos of plutonium and enriched uranium lying in the tunnels under the test site. As a young economy, Kazakhstan did not have the capacity to deal with the problem, and for several years the hazardous waste lay unguarded – waste that could be developed into powerful nuclear bombs if it fell into the wrong hands.

The Americans were worried. In 1998, Professor Siegfried S. Hecker visited Kurchatov. Hecker was the former director of Los Alamos National Laboratory, where America had developed its nuclear bomb. In many ways, Los Alamos is Kurchatov's twin city – it was built in the desert in New Mexico during the Second World War, with one purpose: to develop the world's first nuclear bomb. The town's existence and location were top secret. Like Kurchatov, it was not marked on any map and did not have a name, only a number. Leading scientists from the U.S.A. were sent there with orders to use their spare time to develop the atom bomb, under the code name the Manhattan Project. To make living in the middle of a hot desert more attractive, the town was equipped with every possible modern comfort and facility: swimming pools, air-conditioned buildings, well-stocked supermarkets and excellent primary schools. This intense work produced results: on June 16, 1945, America carried out the first nuclear test detonation. Three weeks later, the first atom bomb was dropped over Japan.

Only a few years earlier, it would have been unthinkable for a former director of Los Alamos National Laboratory to visit Kurchatov. The Cold War was not only over, it was already becoming history. But political relations change faster than the breakdown of radioactive waste: the physical legacy of the Soviet's nuclear testing still lay just below the surface and needed to be dealt with as soon as possible.

Hecker had heard that equipment and metal were being stolen from Polygon, but was shocked all the same by what he saw when he got there. He had expected to see men on camels dragging copper cables behind them, but instead he discovered that diggers had been used to excavate trenches kilometres long. The copper cables from these trenches had been sold to Chinese dealers. In other words, the looting was focused and organised. The local people told Hecker that of course they knew they were running an enormous risk by stealing materials from Polygon, but they saw no alternative, as they had lost their jobs and been abandoned.

In a report published in 2013, there is an account of how, for the first time in history, the U.S.A., Russia and Kazakhstan worked together to remove and decommission the hazardous nuclear waste. Following his visit to Kurchatov, Hecker was able to persuade the Russians to share secret documents that contained information about what kind of waste was where. The Russians were reluctant at first, but gave in when Hecker showed them photographs of the trenches. Kazakhstan was responsible for the actual work and the U.S.A. financed the project.

In autumn 2012, a group of Russian, Kazakh and American scientists gathered at the foot of Degelen Mountain in Polygon to celebrate. Fourteen years and 150 million dollars later, the supersecret project was finally completed and the tunnels had all been filled with a special cement. The scientists raised their vodka glasses and unveiled a three-sided stone monument. Engraved in English, Russian and Kazakh, it read: "The world has become safer."

No-one has a complete picture of the human cost of the Soviet Union's 456 test detonations in Kazakhstan. Radioactive waste was spread by wind and rain over an area of more than three hundred thousand square kilometres. More than two million people have been affected by radiation and radioactive fallout from the explosions in some way or another.

After three hours on a bumpy Soviet road, we arrive in Sarzal, one of the villages that has been hardest hit. The wind blows almost incessantly here and carries with it radioactive particles, making the villagers, who were totally unaware of this, very sick. But for this perpetual wind that whips up the sand and dust, making it hard to breathe, Sarzal would seem an idyllic little village. The houses were whitewashed, with blue window frames, enclosed by low blue fences. Sturdy horses were tied to the trees and posts. An old man stood by one of the fences, gazing up at the sky. I approached him, but he waved me off before I had a chance to introduce myself. The same thing happened when I tried to speak to a young mother pushing a pram.

A large white building dominated the other small houses around it. It had to be the town hall. I decided to try my luck – surely the council employees would be able to tell me how Sarzal had been affected by the nuclear testing. Perhaps they even had statistics, figures. There was no-one in reception, but one of the side doors was open, so I went in. All the offices were empty, but upstairs, at the end of the corridor, I found three men sitting on plastic chairs, drinking tea.

"Hello," I said. "I'm from Norway and—"

"Every year, journalists and academics from all over the world come here," the man in an expensive-looking leather jacket said, curtly. "They come from Japan, the U.S.A. and say they want to help, but they never come back! It's all talk. Nothing ever happens. You may as well just leave."

I made my way back out of the town hall. It seemed even windier outside. Sand was in my hair, my nose, my ears, under my nails, everywhere. The building next to the town hall was long and run down. A sign above the main door said that it was Sarzal Health Centre. I went in and was greeted by a young nurse who could not speak either Russian or English. Wordlessly, she showed me to a booth where a woman in a white coat was sitting. Her name was Laura, she had short hair and was a doctor, and had moved here after she got married twelve years ago.

"We have lots of problems here," she said, in a quiet voice. "About half of the two thousand inhabitants are ill. Children are born with anaemia or with six fingers. Lots of the young people have mental health issues. I am ill too, and that's since I moved here. My blood pressure is not what it should be. Almost everyone here suffers from high blood pressure."

"Why don't you move?" I said.

Laura shrugged. "My family is here. What can you do? You just have to live with it."

On the edge of the village, a group of men were loitering outside a corner shop that sold cigarettes and spirits. They agreed to talk about Polygon as long as they remained anonymous.

"Everyone knew what was going on, but what could we do?" said the most talkative one, a bearded man in his fifties. "It was us against the empire. They flew over the village in helicopters with banners warning that there would be an explosion at eleven o'clock. So, we had to make sure we were outside at eleven o'clock, for our own safety, in case the tremors flattened our houses."

"And the radiation made people ill?"

"Of course," the man said and pointed to a small hill full of grave-stones and crosses. "The ones that fell ill are over there."

"Aren't you worried about the health risks?"

"Why should we be worried?" His laughter was hoarse, and he lit up another cigarette. "We were born here, and we're going to die here. We got used to the radiation a long time ago."

As we were about to leave the windy and unfriendly village of Sarzal, an older woman in a brown coat and leather boots came strid-ing over to the car. She was carrying two heavy bags of shopping.

"I'm originally from Semipalatinsk, but moved to Sarzal in the '80s because money goes further here. As the village is so badly affected by radiation, you get a better pension," she said happily.

She did not, however, want to talk about the test detonations.

"Why should we talk about it? Talking doesn't help. No-one wants to remember. It doesn't do any good."

A WEAK HEART

The Russian tradition of sending troublemakers to the Kazakh steppes is not new. Arguably the most famous prisoner to live in Semipalatinsk arrived in 1854: Fyodor Dostoyevsky. He had spent four years in prison in Omsk in Siberia, for his participation in the liberal Petrashevsky Circle, and was now going to serve out the rest of his sentence as a soldier in Semipalatinsk. The years in the prison camp had taken their toll on his health. Like the other prisoners, his legs had been shackled all the time. The barracks were overcrowded and the prisoners were not alone for even a second. At night, thirty men had to squeeze together on the hard, bare bunks that were infested with fleas and lice. The floorboards were rotten and there were leaks in the roof. It was bitterly cold in winter, both inside and out, and in summer the weather was humid and sultry. Dostoyevsky later wrote that he had never felt happier than he did when he was being transported along the Irtysh river to a new military life in Semipalatinsk, "with the clean air around me and freedom in my heart".

Today, Semipalatinsk, or Semey, as it is called in Kazakh, is a polluted, rather drab provincial town, with wide streets and tall, grey, concrete buildings. The town is older than it looks, however. Peter the Great built a fortress here in 1718 as part of his expansion eastwards. Over the years, a town grew up around the garrison. In the quiet streets behind the university and the massive town hall, built in concrete for a socialist eternity, it is still possible to get an

impression of what the town must have been like when Dostoyevsky lived there. The roads are unsurfaced, and are lined by low,
solid timber houses from the 1800s. Back then, there were five to
six thousand inhabitants in Semipalatinsk. Dostoyevsky rented a
tiny room from a soldier's widow. The room was full of fleas and
cockroaches, but for the first time in four years the writer was by
himself. At last he could read and write again.

In the town's Dostoyevsky Museum, the curators have tried, as
far as possible, to recreate the author's hovel. There is a simple desk
in the small room, a narrow bed, a samovar and tea cups, and two
French clocks. The furniture is all from the 1850s or thereabouts,
but none of it belonged to the writer. Dostoyevsky had not yet had
his literary breakthrough when he lived there, and no-one thought
of saving any of his rickety furniture. And nobody knows for
certain what his room looked like. In other words, the museum is
an educated guess.

The art of recreating writers' homes is a Russian speciality. There
are hundreds of such ghost homes throughout the empire, with furniture appropriate to the time, sometimes the writer's own. These
hallowed shrines are generally guarded by stern women who rush
to turn off the lights as soon as the literary pilgrims have left the
room. The guide who showed me around the museum in Semipalatinsk was a large lady. She was so unfit that she had to stop and catch
her breath between the displays, but she knew the writer's life and
work inside out, minute by minute, sentence by sentence. She followed me, with contempt in her eyes, feeding me with details about
Dostoyevsky's time in the town.

"Shortly after he came here, he made friends with Baron Alexander Wrangel, who was a great admirer of his books," she told
me. "Wrangel did whatever he could to improve the poor author's
living conditions in Semipalatinsk, and soon became his confidant.

Around this time, Dostoyevsky also got to know the drunkard Alexander Isayev." The guide stopped for breath, then went on eagerly: "Isayev's consumptive wife, Maria, was desperately unhappy in her marriage. Her husband beat her when he was drunk. Because he was an alcoholic, he had lost his job and they had *no* money. Dostoyevsky had enormous sympathy for her, and soon was head over heels in love. But this love was *not* a blessing for the great man, in any way..."

Thanks to the book that Wrangel wrote about the years with Dostoyevsky, we know a good deal about the turbulent relationship between the author and the weak, consumptive Maria, who could also be passionate and capricious. "She was kind to him," Wrangel wrote, "not because she was fond of him, but, rather, because she felt sorry for him, an unhappy man who had been dealt a rotten hand by Fate. It is possible that she also became quite attached to him, but she was certainly never in love with him. She knew that he suffered from nerves and that he had no money. He was a man 'with no future', she said. But Fyodor Mikhailovich understood her sympathy to be love and fell for her with all the passion of a young man."

A year later, disaster struck: Isayev got a job at an inn in Kuznetsk, a town six hundred kilometres from Semipalatinsk. Dostoyevsky spent all his free time pining and writing letters. According to Wrangel, he filled entire notebooks writing to Maria. Unfortunately, only one of the letters has been saved. It is full of praise: "You are an admirable woman. Your heart holds a singular, almost childlike goodness. The very fact that a woman held out her hand to me is a great occurrence in my life." Maria replied with vivid descriptions of the torments of her illness and poverty. Dostoyevsky suffered terribly. "He became even thinner than before,' Wrangel wrote. 'He became melancholy, irritable and wandered around like a shadow. He even stopped his work on *Notes from the House of the Dead*."

In August 1855, Isayev died. Maria despaired. Who would look after her and their seven-year-old son? Dostoyevsky did what he could to help; he took out a loan and sent her money. While Isayev's death filled him with hope, it also gave rise to new anxieties. What if she fell for someone else? Surely her admirers were queuing at the door? "I live and breathe only for her," he wrote in a letter to his brother. "I am so unhappy! So unhappy! I am tortured, killed! My soul aches."

Maria knew how to play on his jealousy. What should she say if "an older gentleman with fine qualities, a wealthy official," came and asked for her hand, she asked in a letter.

"Great is the joy of love, but the sufferings are so terrible that it would be better never to love," Dostoyevsky said in a letter to Wrangel. We do not know what he wrote to Maria, but his reply must have touched her. In her next letter, she assured him that the wealthy official did not exist. She had wanted only to test his devotion!

However, it did not take long before Maria was once again tempted to sound the depths of the author's devotion. In her next letter, she told him about "a sympathetic young teacher, with a noble soul". Dostoyevsky could bear it no longer, and, during a tour of duty, secretly made his way to Kuznetsk to meet her. "What a noble, what an angelic soul!" he wrote to Wrangel, full of admiration after their meeting. He was beside himself with joy at having seen her again, but at the same time Maria had confirmed his worst fears: the teacher really existed. He was called Nikolai Vergunov, and, in tears, Maria admitted that she had fallen in love with him. And yet, she did not want to let go of Dostoyevsky. "Don't cry, don't be sad," she comforted him. "Nothing is decided yet, it is you and me and no one else!" Holding these words in his heart, Dostoyevsky went back to the garrison, his hope renewed. But only too soon he was overwhelmed with despair, as Maria wrote in her next letter that it was the teacher she loved, after all. To make himself more attractive in Maria's eyes, Dostoyevsky started a campaign to rise through the ranks. He wrote a touching and remorseful letter to his superiors, and was eventually promoted to the rank of officer. Maria continued to vacillate between him and the teacher, driving them both to distraction. "Have become an unhappy madman!" Dostoyevsky wrote. "A love such as this is a disease. I know it only too well."

Dostoyevsky visited Maria in Kuznetsk again at the end of November, this time in his officer's uniform. There is no way of knowing whether it was the uniform that did it, but by the end of the visit Maria had agreed to marry him. "She loves me, that I know for certain now," he wrote in triumph to Wrangel. But he had a bad conscience about his defeated rival, and asked Wrangel to ensure that he got a proper teaching qualification. His ecstasy about the forthcoming marriage was short-lived, however: in the letter that followed, there were no more eulogies or romantic outpourings, only dry, practical wedding preparations and money.

"They got married on February 6, 1857," the guide said, with feeling. "Fyodor Mikhailovich was thirty-four years old, and Maria Dmitrievna was twenty-nine. Vergunov, the teacher who was so in love with Maria, was a witness. Dostoyevsky was a nervous wreck! What if Maria regretted her decision at the last minute and chose the teacher instead? What if the teacher, beside himself with jealousy, attacked and killed him? The wedding was a success, but the marriage was short and unhappy. On the journey back to Semipalatinsk, Dostoyevsky had a bad epileptic fit. Marie started to regret that she had chosen the poor prisoner rather than the young teacher, and she did *not* keep her regrets to herself. One certainly could *not* say that." The corpulent guide seemed to be angered by Maria's behaviour, and stamped over to the next display case.

Dovstoyevsky suffered epileptic fits more and more frequently and eventually had to leave the army. "My life is hard and bitter," he wrote in 1858. The following year he was given permission to leave Semipalatinsk and the couple moved to St Petersburg. They lived there only for a short while, and argued most of the time. The climate in the Russian capital was not good for Maria's health, and she moved back to the provinces, to a town called Vladimir. Things did not go well for her. She became very ill and bitter. Dostoyevsky, for his part, fell passionately in love with another woman, Apollinaria Suslova. Together they went on a long trip to Western Europe, and there Dostoyevsky developed another passion: gambling.

In autumn 1863, Dostoyevsky was called away from the card tables in Homburg: Maria was dying. According to Wrangel, the couple were reunited on her deathbed. "Oh, dear friend," Dostoyevsky wrote to him. "Her love for me is boundless, and I love her eternally, and yet we could not live together happily . . . We could not stop loving one another; the more unhappy we were, the more bound we became to each other. It sounds absurd, but that is the way it was. She is the most honest, most noble and most generous woman I have ever known."

FATHER OF APPLES

An old propeller plane, once again courtesy of S.C.A.T. Airlines, took me from Semipalatinsk to Almaty, my final destination for this trip. The former capital is situated in dramatic surroundings, with snow-covered peaks all around. The city was totally destroyed by a powerful earthquake in 1887, and most of the buildings are Soviet style, with the same facades and design. The streets are straight and steep, a little like San Francisco. Almaty may have lost its status as capital, but it is still the financial centre of Kazakhstan, and possibly the most cosmopolitan city in Central Asia: you can hear many different languages in the pavement cafés, from Russian and Mandarin to French and English. Up in the mountains close to the city is Medeu, the famous skating rink where hundreds of world records were set.

The skating rink was completed in 1951 and Alma-Ata, as Almaty was then called, soon became a phenomenon in international skating circles. Only a year later, alarming reports began to circulate that Russian skaters had beaten the world records at 500, 1,500 and 5,000 metres. In Norway, there was speculation that perhaps the Russian clocks were slow, or that the measurements of the rink were wrong. But when non-Soviet skaters took to the ice and started to set world records as well, criticisms were silenced. In 1976, the Norwegian Sten Stensen became the first person in the world to complete 10,000 metres in under 14 min. 40 sec., when he finished in 14 min. 38.08 sec. In a race between Norway and the Soviet Union in 1977, Sergey Marchuk broke the record when he completed

5,000 metres in under seven minutes. However, his record of 6 min. 58.88 sec. did not stand for long: in a later race, the Norwegian Kay Arne Stenshjemmet achieved a time of 6 min. 56.9 sec.

Several factors helped to make Medeu the world's best skating rink: the rink's high altitude, at 1,691 metres above sea level, is one. Another was the wind; sometimes the wind came down off the mountain and gave the skaters a tailwind all the way round the rink. In 1972, the Soviet authorities invested a vast sum of money in modernising the complex, and installed an advanced watering and freezing system for artificial ice.

World records continued to be set in Medeu until 1986, the same year that the first indoor skating rinks were opened. After 1991, the ice rink was left to fall into disrepair as there was not enough money to maintain it. The young Kazakh nation had more urgent priorities. More recently, though, the Kazakh authorities have regenerated Medeu and the other winter sport complexes around Almaty, in the hope that they will one day host the Winter Olympics. Kazakhstan was beaten by Russia to hold the 2014 Winter Olympics, but did not give up the dream. They put in another bid in 2015, but once again a powerful neighbour stole the dream: the 2022 Games will be held in Beijing, not in Almaty.

Any future Olympic participants will not be able to benefit from the favourable winds in Medeu, however, as modern skating regulations now require that international competitions at that level take place under a roof.

—⚍—

Alma-Ata means Father of Apples.

The Soviet botanist Nikolai Vavilov, who with great patience and passion went to all corners of the earth looking for new plants,

wrote in his notes about the apples in Alma-Ata: "All around the
city, one could see a vast expanse of wild apples covering the foot-
hills which formed forests. In contrast to the very small, wild apples
in the Caucasian mountains to the west, the Kazakh wild apples
have very big fruit, and they don't vary from cultivated varieties.
On the first of September, the time that the apples were almost ripe,
one could see with one's own eyes that this beautiful place was the
centre of origin of the cultivated apple.'ᵛ

Vavilov's plant expeditions took him all over the Soviet Union,
to Japan, China and Korea, to the USA and Canada, to distant mountain passes in Afghanistan, to the Sahara and to Ethiopia, where
bandits attempted to rob him. He was always impeccably dressed in
a tailored, dark suit with a white shirt and tie, and his good humour
and boundless energy won him friends wherever he went. Vavilov's
plan was ambitious: he wanted to eradicate hunger by crossing
plant types to produce more genetically robust variants of foods
such as potatoes, wheat and rye. He believed that many of the
wild variants of these plants had valuable genetic qualities that had
been lost in the cultivated plants. Some of them could, for example,
survive extreme temperature changes. By crossing the wild and
domestic plants, it would be possible to cultivate varieties that
inherited the best qualities from both worlds. At the time, in the
infancy of genetics, this was groundbreaking.

Vavilov built up an impressive collection of seeds from his many
expeditions. This seed bank, the first of its kind in the world, was
kept at the Institute of Plant Industry that Vavilov had established in
Leningrad. Because of this work, Vavilov was one of the best-known
biologists in the world in the 1920s. Lenin understood the economic
value of Vavilov's research and gave him free rein. He was invited to
join the Soviet Academy of Sciences and was awarded the Lenin
Prize, the Soviet Union's most prestigious science prize, for his work.

When Lenin died in 1924, Vavilov's good fortune waned. Stalin favoured another botanist, Trofim Lysenko. Whereas Vavilov built on the nineteenth-century Austrian botanist Gregor Mendel's research on cross-cultivation and inherited qualities, Lysenko was inspired by the eighteenth-century French biologist Jean-Baptiste de Lamarck, who believed that acquired qualities could be passed on to progeny. If a plant had survived a long, cold winter and then flowered again in spring, Lysenko believed that its progeny would also flower in spring, irrespective of whether it had been exposed to a long, cold winter or not. In other words, he believed that it was possible to train plants to acquire different qualities, and that these would then be passed on to the next generation.[6]

Lysenko's misguided theories, which had long since been rejected in Europe, dominated Soviet agricultural policy until the 1960s, with catastrophic consequences for both Soviet agriculture and for Lysenko's staunchest critic, Vavilov. He was arrested during a research trip to Ukraine in 1940, and sentenced to death. Two years later, the death sentence was commuted to twenty years imprisonment, but on January 26, 1943, Nikolai Vavilov, a man who had dedicated his life to eradicating hunger, died of starvation in prison.

Thanks to Vavilov's dedicated colleagues, the seed bank miraculously survived the 28-month siege of Leningrad. The authorities had not given any instructions to protect the two hundred and fifty thousand seeds, but the employees at the institute took it upon themselves to do this: they put a selection of the seeds into a large chest and hid it in the cellar, taking turns to guard it. Not one of those guarding the collection was tempted to eat any of the seeds,

6 The belief that acquired qualities could be inherited by the next generation was also a central axiom of the Communists' treatment of "enemies of the people" and their children: they believed that the father's sins would literally be inherited.

even though nine of them died of starvation before the siege ended in spring 1944.

After Stalin's death, Vavilov's sentence was posthumously reversed, and he regained his position as one of the Soviet Union's leading scientists.

As I was in the city of apples, I went to the market to try the local produce. The big fruit and vegetable market was filled with mothers doing their shopping; the scent was earthy and sweet. Most of the vendors could tempt customers with large, juicy apples. I picked out a large, green apple, paid for it and took a bite. It tasted like a summer morning. Perfectly sour, perfectly sweet, with a perfect consistency.

"I think that this is the best apple I've ever tasted in my life!" I said.

The seller behind the neat piles of fruit lit up.

"All our apples are specially imported from China," he told me proudly.

THE TIRED ACTIVIST

Like most human rights activists, he did not have much time. Even before we had found a bench to sit on, he had managed to tell me about Kazakhstan's most pressing democratic challenges, about the president's three daughters, their various posts and duties and fat bank accounts, about the financial situation of many other people, and the increasing censorship.

"The situation is worse here than in Russia," he said. "Kazakhstan is more closed, we have no intellectuals. Nazarbayev rules the country like a thug. He keeps a flock of people close to him, who all get money and benefits, and are completely dependent on him. No-one knows how much money he and his family have, but we're talking about billions of dollars. Nazarbayev runs Kazakhstan like a limited company where he is the main shareholder and general manager."

Galym Ageleuov was thin, sinewy and forty-five years old. His narrow face and fine features were framed by a mop of unruly hair, which did something odd to the symmetry and somehow made his head too heavy for his slim body. His voice was quiet and gentle, and when he laughed it was with the same exasperation and irony that many human rights activists seem to have, the world over.

"There's no real opposition," he said. "The authorities systematically arrest any opposition candidates. You can talk freely as long as you don't make it official or start to organise anything. They'll stop you as soon as you do."

He himself was arrested following a demonstration in 2012 and sentenced to fifteen days in prison. He was held in a cell of eighteen square metres with fourteen other prisoners, and was not allowed to telephone anyone, and certainly not a lawyer. As it was summer, it was unbearably hot in the cell, and the inmates were allowed to wash only once a week. They were allowed out into the yard for one hour a day, but spent the rest of the time locked in the crowded cell. Galym was one of the lucky ones: a number of Kyrgyz and Uzbeks did not have even a cell and had to sleep on cold concrete floors, outside.

"Are you afraid you'll be arrested again?"

"No," he said, without hesitation. "I'm a human rights activist. I'm not afraid. But I don't speak in public as much as I used to – they would just arrest me again. I post my speeches and appeals on YouTube instead."

Some people leave and we sit down on a bench in the shade of a tree. We had agreed to meet in a square that was simply called Old Square, one of Almaty's green spaces. In December 1986, thousands of students and protestors gathered here to protest against the appointment of Gennady Kolbin, a Russian, as First Secretary of the Kazakh Communist Party. They felt that the first secretary should be a Kazakh. The demonstration got out of hand and on the afternoon of December 17 skirmishes broke out between the protesters and the police. A few weeks before my meeting with Galym, I had talked to a policewoman called Anna, who had been at the demonstrations.

"Special forces came to help us in the evening," she said. "As normal police officers we didn't have guns, we just had to stand there. The special forces were brutal. They went in with batons and water cannons and had cleared the streets within a few hours. I can still remember, word for word, what one of them said: 'The protesters are the enemy. Don't bother about the dead and injured. Just leave them there.'"

The day after, on December 18, several thousand more protesters came to the square, so the army fired shots to frighten them. As the detailed account of the demonstration is locked in an archive in Moscow, no-one knows how many people were injured or killed on those two cold December days. Figures vary from two to a thousand. Anna did not know the exact figure, but was convinced that it must be high. "It still hurts to think about all the dead and injured who were left lying all over the square," she said.

More than a thousand protesters were jailed, and dozens of them were given long sentences. Two were sentenced to death. Anna and her colleagues were given medals and declared heroes.

After the dissolution of the Soviet Union, the December demonstrations, in which the Kazakhs rose up against Moscow, have become an important element of national identity. The demonstrators did not want independence from the Soviet Union – in fact, when given the vote five years later, more than ninety per cent were against it – they just wanted a Kazakh first secretary. And in 1989, they got what they wanted: Nursultan Nazarbayev took over the top post. Two years later, when Kazakhstan became the last Central Asian country to declare independence from the Soviet Union – on December 16, 1991 – Nazarbayev became the country's first prime minister. No-one talks too loudly about the fact that he sided with the Soviet authorities during the demonstrations, least of all himself.

Ten years after she was declared a hero by the people, Anna had to give the medal back. She was told that the Kazakh authorities now saw her as an "enemy of the people" and that she no longer had a job.

History is always written by the victors.

*

Exactly twenty years later, in December 2011, there was another bloody protest in Kazakhstan. Several hundred oil workers in Zhanaozen, a poor town in the west of the country, not far from the border with Turkmenistan, had been on strike since the summer, because, among other things, they had not been paid. Human rights activist Galym Ageleuov watched developments carefully, and documented the arbitrary arrests and the physical abuse of some of the strikers.

Galym had a feeling that it would not end well, but he had not anticipated just how bad things would get. On December 16, armed police arrived to move the protesters away from the large central square, which they had occupied for months. The official explanation was that the square had to be cleared in preparation for the Independence Day celebrations. What happened next is unclear, but the end result was that fourteen demonstrators were shot and killed. Some claim that the number of people killed was much higher.

"I believe it could be as many as two hundred," Galym said.

"But how is it possible to hide that many deaths?" I said.

"They might have bribed the families of those killed to say nothing. They might have made unofficial graves. There are lots of ways they could do it."

It is hard to see how the Kazakh authorities could have concealed such a large number of deaths, even in a remote industrial town. Conspiracy theories tend to flourish under regimes that lie so much to the people that they get used to it. Conspiracy theories were rife in the Soviet Union. The authorities never told the truth, everything was embellished and glossed over. Many of the leaders of former Soviet republics attained their positions of power in the Soviet Union, and have continued to rule their countries in the same authoritarian and opaque tradition. In other words, conspiracy theories still have perfect growing conditions in Central Asia.

Instead of conducting an open and independent investigation of events in Zhanaozen, which might have helped to curb the speculation and cynicism, the authorities instead ordered a ban on any speculation regarding the number of deaths. Officially, fourteen people were killed. Full stop.

Anna, the former policewoman, told me that her youngest son did his military service in Zhanaozen. He was shot during the massacre on December 16, and lost consciousness, but he was not seriously injured because he was wearing a bulletproof vest. The military wanted to give him a medal afterwards.

"I told him there was no point in accepting it, as they would only take it back later," Anna said. "He listened to me, and declined to accept it."

"The government's plan is that we will be an ideal society by 2050," Ageleuov told me. "They keep moving the date. First it was 2020, then 2030. And now, in 2050, everything will be fine, at last." He laughed briefly. "The problem is, things are going the wrong way. Earlier this year, thirty-two media outlets were closed down, including the critical weekly newspaper *Respublika*. Everything in the newspapers is controlled and dictated. On the radio and television as well. The only place where you might find any criticism of the president is on social media. But the Internet is restricted too, of course, and hundreds of websites are blocked."

"Do you think you're being watched?" I said.

"I *know* I'm being watched."

"Do you think they're listening to us now?"

He felt for his mobile in his trouser pocket.

"Yes, that is the case, unless I take out the battery or put the mobile in another room. But it's fine to talk like this. I say what I want, as long as I don't do it from a lectern, with a microphone and an audience."

The sun was about to dip down behind the trees. All of a sudden, Galym looked pale and tired. He was so thin that there was practically nothing of him in the big, black T-shirt and baggy jeans. He laughed quietly, almost to himself.

"The ironic thing is that we only meet our ombudsmen at conferences abroad," he said. "They come and find us, tell us what to say and think. And of course they always take the government's side, not ours."

Presumably a healthy dose of black humour is needed to survive as a human rights activist in Central Asia. Many of the activists operate under extremely difficult conditions. In Uzbekistan and Turkmenistan, the countries with the most oppressive regimes, human rights campaigners work almost exclusively underground, risking their lives. Even in Kyrgyzstan, which is now deemed to be the most democratic country in Central Asia, their work is not without personal risk. In 2010, Azimzhan Askarov, one of Kyrgyzstan's best-known human rights campaigners, was sentenced to life imprisonment following a highly controversial court case. Kazakhstan is not a stronghold of liberty, but, in this part of the world, simply being able to meet and talk to a human rights activist openly provides a glimmer of hope.

A HARD BLOW

BIFATIMA was written in big blue letters on the corrugated iron wall facing the road. We had arrived.

I got out of the car and crossed the small yard. There were hens and geese wandering between the basic houses, but no people to be seen other than an old, hunchbacked woman, wearing a headscarf and a plain, green dress.

"Is it possible to meet Bifatima?" I asked the old woman.

"Yes," was her short reply. Her face was weather-beaten and fierce. "I am Bifatima."

"Ah, wonderful! My name..."

Bifatima was not interested in my name. She ambled over to the house closest by and pointed in through the dark doorway.

"Go in and drink tea first. That's how we do it." She turned her back on me, then rounded the corner of the house and disappeared.

The traffic queues out of Almaty had been massive. It was the last day of school before the summer holidays, a day that was celebrated throughout the former Soviet Union. It was also the final day of this part of my journey. The following day, I would board an airplane bound for Oslo.

Somewhere on this trip, I no longer remembered where, someone, and I no longer remembered who, had told me that if I went to Almaty, I should visit Bifatima. "You won't regret it," they said. And even though I had forgotten how I had heard about Bifatima, her name had lodged firmly in my mind.

The journey out here had taken longer than expected. We had driven through endless green fields dotted with wild red tulips. But it was not difficult to find. Everyone the driver asked along the way knew where Bifatima lived.

Hesitantly, I entered the dark room. There was a little kitchen in the corner, where the flies buzzed around some leftovers. Three women were sitting at a table at the other end of the room, drinking tea. I sat on a chair and was served some steaming hot tea, as if it were the most natural thing in the world. None of the women asked me any questions, but they were more than happy to answer mine.

The women were sisters, they told me. They had come here because they had various problems. The youngest, Rimgul, a lively woman in her late forties, had with increasing frequency woken up in the morning with no feeling in her arms. So, for the past few nights, and always at night, Bifatima had massaged her arms. Two nights ago, Bifatima had said thoughtfully that she believed another woman was robbing Rimgul of the feeling in her arms. A neighbour, perhaps. Someone with ill intentions. Rimgul had immediately thought of a neighbour who was difficult and she found hard to get on with. It had to be her.

The evening before, the women had all performed a ritual together. Bifatima had mixed blood from a hen and a goose, then they had sat in a circle and said *Allah, Allah* repeatedly as Bifatima smeared them with blood. It had been so powerful that Rimgul started to cry. She had cried and cried. And now she felt much better, she said. Cleansed. Full of zest and energy.

A young, fair woman appeared in the doorway.

"She's ready for you now," she said.

Rimgul put a hand on my shoulder. "It'll be fine," she whispered.

Bifatima was waiting for me outside in the yard.

"Find a coin," the fair woman said.

I rummaged in my pockets. The three sisters discussed whether I should use a coin from my own country, but I had no Norwegian coins left, so it would have to be a Kazakh tenge. After further discussion, the sisters decided that would be just as good.

"Put the coin in one of your hands and hold them both out," the young woman said.

Bifatima mustered her strength and hit my hands hard.

"Bend forward."

I bent my head. Bifatima hit me again, making my head sing. I cried out. Next it was my neck. I cried out again.

"Lean even further forward."

I was utterly bewildered, but I did as I was told, even though I had no idea what would happen next. Seconds before Bifatima's fist hit my spine, I screamed again. She sent me a disapproving look.

"Take off your shoes."

Bifatima gave the soles of my feet a well-aimed blow. Then she filled her hands with water from a grubby, blue bucket and held them out.

"Drink."

I bowed my head and drank.

"Drink more."

I drank more. It tasted like bog water and old ladies. Then Bifatima emptied the rest of the bucket over my head. It was ice cold. I screamed. Bifatima nodded to herself and went over to the house to get another bucket. This time she threw it in my face. Then she clapped her hands and wandered off towards the henhouse.

"Look after the coin well," the blonde woman said. "It will make you rich. Now we're going to visit the Sacred Hill."

She took me up to the ridge of the hill on the other side of the road. She told me that she had come all the way from Moscow, but nothing else. She was reluctant to say where we were going.

"Wait and see, wait and see," she said in her gentle, ethereal voice, each time I asked. She was a few paces ahead of me. Her long batik skirt flapped in the wind.

On the top of the hill, there was a circle on the ground. The crust of the earth in the middle of the circle had collapsed to create a kind of channel. According to the young woman, it was the grave of someone from the village. She kneeled down by the hollow and said a prayer, and asked me to do the same. To make it more atmospheric, she got out her mobile and played an imam chanting. Then we stood up and walked on to a small rocky outcrop. Two stones had been placed on top of it. One was a woman stone and the other a man stone, she explained. We kneeled down, and she said another prayer. Then I was told to sit down between the stones and make a wish. I did as I was told, but could not think of a wish. The only thing I could think was how bizarre it was to be sitting like this, between two stones, far out in the Kazakh countryside, accompanied by an imam chanting from a tinny mobile.

Central Asia is full of mysterious traditions and sacred places like this. The belief in evil spirits and witchcraft, which has presumably survived from pre-Islamic times when the nomads prayed to nature deities and had shamans, lives side by side with Islam, and very few people see it as problematic. Sufism, the strain of Islam that focuses on individual, spiritual experiences, has traditionally had a strong following in Central Asia. There are hundreds of pilgrimage places across the region, everything from holy men's graves to hot springs and other special places that for some reason have been credited through the centuries with supernatural healing powers. During my trip to Turkmenistan, we stopped at many such places, included Kyrk Molla (Forty Mullahs Hill), one of the country's most sacred pilgrim destinations. In the past, men who wanted to become mullahs had to fast and pray on top of the hill for forty days. Today, childless women from all over Turkmenistan make a pilgrimage there. They have with them a doll in a small cradle, as a symbol of the child they long for. They leave the cradle on the top of the hill, alongside the hundreds of cradles left there by other women before them. Then they lie down on their side and roll down the hill. Three times they roll down, faster and faster, getting dizzier and dizzier each time. It is quite a sight. If they then give birth to a child, they have to go back and collect the cradle.

"That's us done then," the fair-haired woman said and silenced the imam. She stood up and started to walk back down with quick steps. I hurried after her. I wanted to know more about her. Who was she? How had she ended up here?

"Where are you from?"

"Moscow," she said curtly, without slowing down.

"Why did you come here?"

"People come here for many different reasons," she said, not answering my question. "Some come because they're sick, others come to open their soul and gain insight."

"Did you come here to gain insight?"

She smiled, but did not answer.

"How long have you been here?" I said.

"A long time."

"Are you a Muslim?"

She laughed and looked down.

"God is one and the same, it doesn't matter who you pray to. The people here are Muslims, so it's most natural to do things the Muslim way."

When we got down to the house, Bifatima was nowhere to be seen. The sisters had brewed more tea. Dusk was falling. I had to get back to Almaty, to my hotel room and to my suitcase that still needed to be packed.

The first part of my journey was over. Summer was just around the corner, and in Central Asia it can be intense. In many places daytime temperatures rise to 40°C and more. I would be back, but not before the summer heat had faded and autumn had come. The oil-rich desert countries were behind me. It was now the turn of the poor mountain states.

I was sorry to say goodbye to the three sisters.

The traffic jams had dispersed and we had the road to ourselves. The lush fields were grey in the twilight. The tulips had closed.

When I got back to the hotel, I discovered that the coin for which I had endured so many hard blows had fallen out of my pocket. My key to wealth. Gone for ever.

I had an upset stomach for weeks after I got home. I cannot be certain, but I suspect that Bifatima's holy water was the culprit.

TAJIKISTAN

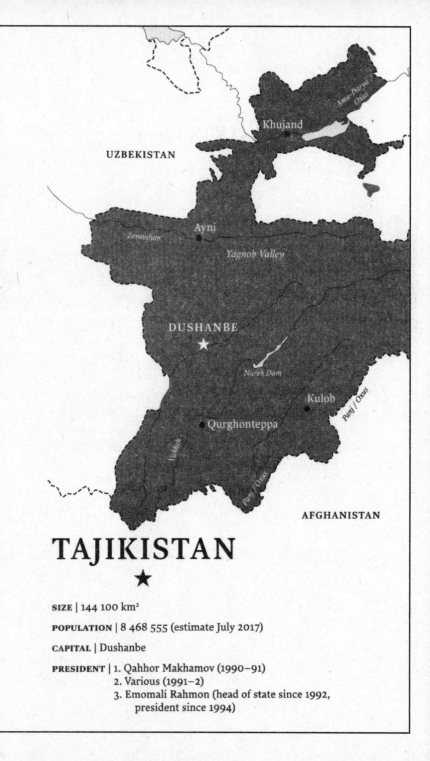

TAJIKISTAN

★

SIZE | 144 100 km²

POPULATION | 8 468 555 (estimate July 2017)

CAPITAL | Dushanbe

PRESIDENT | 1. Qahhor Makhamov (1990–91)
2. Various (1991–2)
3. Emomali Rahmon (head of state since 1992, president since 1994)

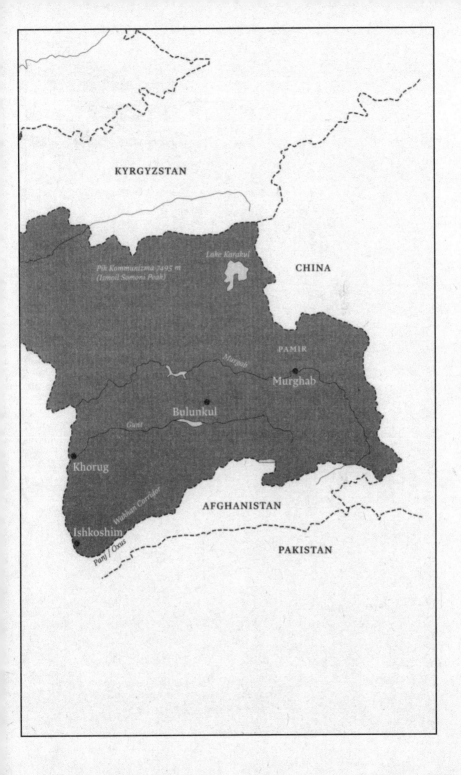

MERCEDES BENZ CAPITAL

The first light of dawn was visible above the trees. In the distance, the red, white and green flag of Tajikistan fluttered on the morning breeze. The flag, which weighs three hundred kilos and is sixty metres long and thirty metres wide, is impressive enough in itself, but even more so is the flagpole from which it hangs: at 165 metres, it is the tallest free-standing flagpole in the world – for now. Tall flagpoles have become a bit of a thing recently.

It started in 2001, when a company ordered a 123-metre flagpole to celebrate national day in Abu Dhabi. People from the United Arab Emirates could already boast the world's tallest hotel, the world's biggest chandelier and the world's largest prayer mat. And now Abu Dhabi's red and white flag was flying from the world's tallest flagpole. But the glory did not last long. In 2003 King Abdullah of Jordan raised a 127-metre flagpole in the capital, Amman. The following year he ordered another flagpole, which was three metres taller than the first. So, for a short while, the two tallest flagpoles in the world were in Jordan. Then in 2008, Turkmenistan was the first former Soviet state to enter the competition, and snapped up the record with its 133-metre tall flagpole in Ashgabat. Two years later, the Azerbaijanis broke all previous records with a 162-metre flagpole, which stands in Baku. But once again the joy was short-lived, as, less than a year later, the Tajik flag was flying from the 165-metre flagpole in Dushanbe.[7]

7 The 160-metre flagpole in North Korea, which is strategically placed on the border with South Korea, is not included here, as it is in fact a very tall radio tower with a flag on top. It is not free-standing, as a traditional flagpole should be.

But the real winner of this international flagpole competition is without a doubt Trident Support, the company that has built every single one of these record-breaking flagpoles. Following the success of the Abu Dhabi flagpole, the company discovered there was an almost insatiable market and that few others, if any, had the skills needed to make record-breaking flagpoles. Trident Support has produced only flags and flagpoles since 2001. On their website, it says that they build monumental flagpoles from 90 metres to a record-breaking 165 metres – or taller. So we will just have to wait and see if Tajikistan can hold on to the record. Rumours abound already that both Saudi Arabia and Dubai plan to invest in new flagpoles.[8]

The fact that oil-rich nations such as Azerbaijan, Dubai, Turkmenistan and Saudi Arabia can afford to compete for the tallest flagpole should come as no surprise. But where do the Tajik authorities get the money?

Tajikistan is much the poorest of all the post-Soviet states. The country has neither oil nor gas, and ninety per cent of the territory is mountainous. Only seven per cent of the ground area can be cultivated. The country's industry, to the extent that it exists, has been mismanaged, and the state is dependent on foreign aid organisations to keep things going. Half the population are deemed to be living in poverty, with around twenty per cent of the eight million inhabitants surviving on less than a pound a day.

And yet, the world's highest flagpole today stands in Dushanbe.

—〰—

Dushanbe is said to be Central Asia's most beautiful capital. Avenues of big, leafy trees cast long shadows over the low, pastel-coloured neoclassical houses. The streets were dusty and wide, built for a

8 The Jeddah flagpole in Saudi Arabia is currently the tallest in the world at a staggering 171 metres. It was completed in 2014.

socialist future, and half the pavement was reserved for cyclists, who were clearly a thing of the future. In the four days I was in Dushanbe, I saw only one cyclist; an old man on a rickety, rusty old bike. The pavements seemed to be the domain of women, who wandered along in groups of two or three, dressed in colourful, patterned knee-length cotton tunics and matching loose trousers. Most of them let their long black hair hang loose or kept it in a single plait: only a few had covered their heads with a scarf. Their faces were light and oval, with brown, almond-shaped eyes and straight, narrow noses. In contrast to the Kazakhs and Turkmens, who are descended from Mongolian and Turkic tribes, the Tajiks are of Persian descent, and the Tajik language is so like Persian that many students of Farsi spend their year abroad in Dushanbe rather than the more politically charged Teheran. The major difference between the two languages is the alphabet: Farsi is written with the Arabic alphabet, while Tajik still uses Cyrillic letters.

The morning sun had warmed the air, which was now as pleasant as a summer's day in Norway. At the other end of the large square, behind an oval fountain, stood a building that was both modest and grand. It was rather small, as prestigious buildings go, and oddly squat and boxy, but the facade was lifted by proud, classical pillars. This was the home of the Tajik Academic Theatre of Opera and Ballet. Even though Dushanbe lay at the eastern limit of the empire, on the border with China and Afghanistan, the Soviet authorities provided the city with its own opera and ballet, as befitted a capital. I wandered past some old women feeding the birds by the fountain, and headed for the box office to find out what was on over the next few days. The box office was closed, and the repertoire on the poster, which included productions of Tchaikovsky's operas and ballets, was from the year before.

Before Tajikistan was given the status of a Soviet socialist republic in 1929, having first been part of the socialist republic of Uzbekistan, Dushanbe was little more than a village with three thousand inhabitants. The new republic needed a capital, and the choice fell on this village that was famous for its big Monday market: Dushanbe means Monday in Tajik. From 1929 to 1961, the town was called Stalinabad, and it was in these decades, the post-war period in particular, that the neoclassical buildings sprang up.

Today, the once modest village is the largest city in the country, with seven hundred thousand inhabitants. Since 1991 many of the low, pastel-coloured houses have been pulled down and replaced by modern apartment blocks, but something of the old village atmosphere persists: no-one seemed to be in a rush, people walked slowly along the pavements, and, with the exception of the rich people who cruised by in their large 4×4s, no-one honked their horn or raised their voice. And the enormous red, white and green flag flew above the rooftops.

By steering a steady course towards the flagpole, I came across a large, lush park. At the far end of the park, not far from the flagpole, was a magnificent palace with a gold dome and so many pillars that it seemed pointless to start counting. Dushanbe's new presidential palace is in no way inferior in size or style to those in Astana or Ashgabat. Such extravagant buildings are perhaps to be expected in oil-rich nations like Turkmenistan and Kazakhstan, but what was all this luxury doing here, in the poorest of the post-Soviet states? Where did the money come from?

The presidential palace and flagpole are not the only surprises of this kind in the capital. Beside the Hyatt Regency Hotel, the construction of the world's largest teahouse[9] was well under way, and just outside the city centre they were building what was going to

9 Completed in 2014.

be the largest mosque in Central Asia. It will, apparently, be able to hold 150,000 people, which is more than a fifth of Dushanbe's inhabitants. By way of comparison, Hazrat Sultan Mosque in Kazakhstan, which is currently the largest mosque in Central Asia, can hold ten thousand. The Emir of Qatar has offered to pay the lion's share of the cost of the giant mosque, but there is no such clarity as to how the teahouse, which it is estimated will cost sixty million dollars, is being financed.

Not far from the presidential palace is another massive building: Tajikistan's national library, the biggest library in Central Asia. It opened in 2012 and covers an area of forty-five thousand square metres over nine floors. It has room for ten million books and, in order to fill all the shelves, each household was asked to donate books for the opening. Journalists who have been inside have said there are only books in one of the halls; in the rest the shelves stand empty.

The door in the impressive main entrance with its tall, slender columns and dark glass surfaces was locked. Some boys explained that the door in the basement was for everyday use. An elderly security guard in a tight, blue uniform stood by the dimly lit basement door, and turned away anyone who wanted to go in.

"I'm sorry, the library is closed today. – Sorry, closed. – We've closed for today."

"But it's not even half past ten," I objected.

The security guard looked around surreptitiously. "We don't have electricity today," he said very quietly. "Try again another time. Perhaps we'll have electricity tomorrow."

Outside an official-looking building on the other side of the road, there was a gigantic poster of a besuited man in a cornfield. The man had thick, bushy eyebrows, a pronounced widow's peak and a head of thick, dark hair. From what I had seen in Turkmenistan and Kazakhstan, I realised that this man could be none other than the president of Tajikistan, Emomali Rahmon.

Like that of so many of his colleagues, Rahmon's career has followed a steep curve. His parents were farmers in Kulob, a province in southwest Tajikistan. He studied economics at university in his twenties, as did Turkmenbashi and Nazarbayev, before moving back to Danghara, where he slowly rose through the ranks of the collective farming system. From 1987 to 1992, he was chairman of the collective farm Lenin, and in 1990 he was elected as a people's deputy to the Supreme Soviet. During the civil war, which lasted from 1992 to 1997 and cost the lives of between fifty thousand and one hundred thousand people, Rahmon's career was stellar. In November 1992 he was appointed chairman to the Supreme Soviet, and in 1994 he was elected president by 59.9 per cent of the voters. If the Tajik authorities are to be believed, the election turnout was 95 per cent, even though there was a civil war raging.

When a person moves into the presidential palace of a Central Asian republic, it is very hard to get them to move out again of their own free will. True to tradition, Rahmon has stayed there, and, having led the country into the twenty-first century, has continued to tighten his grip on power. He and his wife Azizmo have seven daughters and two sons, all of whom have respectable jobs in the government apparatus: one of his daughters is the first deputy minister of foreign affairs, and his elder son is currently head of the customs service.[10] The personality cult around Rahmon is not comparable to that enjoyed by the president of Turkmenistan, but there can be little doubt he is heading the same way: on official occasions, Rahmon is addressed more and more frequently as *Janobi Oli*, meaning "His Highness". In 2007, he removed the Russian-style ending

10 That was in 2013. He is currently the mayor of Dushanbe.

from his surname and changed it from Rahmonov to Rahmon, which means "merciful" in Tajik. And on top of his daily workload as president, he has found time to write a dozen books, including his masterpiece, *The Tajiks in the Mirror of History*, in which he draws extravagant parallels between the present day and the Tajiks' glorious past during the Sasanian empire in the sixth century. The book is Rahmon's "spiritual gift to the Tajik nation".

In the 1999 presidential election, two years after the ceasefire, Rahmon won an incredible 97.6 per cent of the votes, with a record turnout of 98.9 per cent. In the 2006 election, which was boycotted by the opposition parties and described as peaceful, but lacking in "genuine choice and meaningful pluralism" by the O.S.C.E., Rahmon was re-elected, with 79.3 per cent of the vote. Once more turnout exceeded 90 per cent. In November 2013, only a few weeks after I had been there, there was another election. And even though Rahmon, in theory, was up against six other candidates, there was little excitement about the outcome. Rahmon himself was so confident that he would be re-elected that he did not even bother to campaign. But he made sure that the opposition were given only minimal coverage in the media, so that they, effectively, could not run a campaign either.

There is no lack of grand architecture in Rahmon's capital, but the same is not true of good places to eat. Having walked past countless shops specialising in second-hand mobiles and pirated D.V.D.s, I eventually found Tajikistan's only continental café, which was busy with international aid workers. I sat down at a table outside and watched the traffic. It was not heavy, but there were a striking number of B.M.W.s and Mercedes. The shiny white and black vehicles rolled by like pearls on a string. Again, I wondered where the money came from. Most Tajiks earn less than eighty dollars a month, and a third of the population is malnourished. The Tajik state cannot provide its citizens with sufficient electricity in winter, let alone vaccinate its babies against the most dangerous childhood illnesses. And yet there were more luxury cars to be seen here than on the streets in Ashgabat and Astana.

Only once I was back in Norway did I find the answer – not to where the money came from, but to the mystery of the cars. They came from Germany. A thorough investigation and the use of modern G.P.S. equipment enabled the German police to trace two hundred stolen luxury cars, including many B.M.W.s and Mercedes. The police had assumed that the cars had been sold on to criminal gangs in Eastern Europe or Russia, but, to their surprise, they discovered that the new owners of the cars were in fact senior officials in the Tajik presidential administration, as well as friends and family of President Rahmon.

OUT OF TIME

Popularly known as the Doomsday Tunnel or Tunnel of Death, the Anzob Tunnel is a catastrophe. The first few kilometres were relatively smooth: there was a surface on the road, lighting and emergency telephones on the wall. Everything seemed to be fine. But then, at roughly the halfway point, the tunnel deteriorates. Pipes and cables dangled from the roof, and there were no light bulbs. We drove on through the mountain in the pitch dark. The air in the tunnel was full of fumes that seeped into the car. Asphalt was a memory: the road was reduced to gravel and potholes full of black, oily water. It was impossible to guess how deep they were. The driver hung over the steering wheel and peered into the dark with narrowed eyes. He zigzagged as best he could to avoid the worst potholes and the oncoming cars that came towards us like jumping cones of light.

The tunnel was built with help from Iran, but for one reason or another it was never finished.[11] It is the only direct route between Dushanbe and Khujand in the north, the second largest city in Tajikistan. Before the tunnel was built, the road to Khujand passed through Uzbekistan, and the neighbours have a somewhat fraught relationship. The alternative was to fly, which very few Tajiks could afford. And now, even though the Anzob Tunnel is often closed in winter, locals generally prefer to bribe the tunnel guards and

11 Work on the tunnel was completed in 2015 and it was officially inaugurated in August 2017.

take the risk than to pay through the nose for a plane ticket.

"It's actually worse in summer," my guide Muqim said. "Then the tunnel is full of water. It's like fording a river."

It took almost half an hour to drive the last few kilometres. The driver, a chain-smoking, taciturn man in his fifties, let out an almost imperceptible sigh of relief when we saw light at the end of the tunnel.

The landscape was magnificent. On either side of the road, the glittering, snowy mountains rose up sharply into the deep blue sky.

"My mother doesn't understand why all these foreigners want to come here on holiday," Muqim said. He was a qualified English teacher, but had made his living as a guide in recent years. "I've explained to her that they come to see our majestic mountains, but she thinks that's ridiculous. For her, the mountains are a nuisance." He smiled. "I used to think the same, but now I see our country through the tourists' eyes. It's not always easy to understand that what you see every day is beautiful."

Muqim was twenty-six, and even though he had recently discovered the beauty of the mountains, he was obsessed with getting away from Tajikistan. He became quite emotional when he told me about the six months he had spent in the U.S.A. on a work-exchange programme.

"The sun had just risen as we started our descent into New York. We flew over all the advertisements and skyscrapers. It was just like a film." He stared out at the dark, pointed mountains. "All my siblings have gone to work in Russia, as people here do. But I don't want to go there, I want to go back to the West."

When we got to the Yaghnob Valley, our destination, the road was much worse again. It was no longer surfaced, but bumpy and full of potholes. The fact that here in this remote valley they had anything that resembled a road at all was thanks to the ambitious Soviet authorities. There was no road connection to the valley until the 1970s.

The first village, Margib, lay on a verdant slope by the end of the road. The gardens were full of apple and plum trees. Following a sumptuous meal of dried fruit, nuts, pilaf rice, yoghurt and vast quantities of green tea, I was shown to my room, which was simple but sparkling clean.

The inhabitants of Margib are all Tajiks, but there are still villages in the valley where only Yaghnobis live. The Yaghnobis have almost mythical status and are descendants of the Sogdians, an ancient people who lived in Tajikistan and Uzbekistan until the early Middle Ages. It was the Sogdians who founded Samarkand, and for centuries they dominated trade along the Silk Road. The Sogdians were largely Zoroastrians. Zoroastrianism was established by the Persian prophet, Zoroaster (or Zarathustra, as he is also sometimes known), in the second millenium BCE, and was one of the world's first monotheistic religions. As the Zoroastrians placed great importance on the various elements, in particular fire, they were sometimes mistakenly known as "fire worshippers". But Zoroastrianism also has a lot in common with Christianity: among other things, the Zoroastrians believe in redemption and resurrection, and that there is a heaven and a hell.

In 1722, when the Arabs conquered Penjinkent, one of the most important cities in Sogdiana, some Zoroastrians escaped to the almost inaccessible Yaghnob Valley to avoid being forced to convert to Islam. Here they continued to practise Zoroastrianism long after the rest of Sogdiana had been converted. The descendants of these rebels, the Yaghnobis, have been so isolated over the centuries that they still speak Sogdian, a language that scholars until recently thought had died out.

A yellow full moon illuminated the village as night came. I fell asleep to the sound of scurrying mice, clearly busy under the floorboards.

Early in the morning Muqim and I set off with an old pack donkey and its owner, a toothless, retired geography teacher. The pension for teachers is about thirty pounds a month, which is not enough to live on, so he had to earn extra money from freelancing as a donkey driver. The little donkey was laden with clothes, water bottles, bread, fruit and tinned food. The Yaghnobis are among the poorest people in Tajikistan, and even though Muqim assured me that they would share their last potato with us, it was better that we took our own supplies.

A path ran from the village up over the hill. From here, we followed a new dirt road into the valley. As we walked, Muqim told me more about his time in the U.S.A., where he had worked in an amusement park and as a waiter at weddings.

"I knew nothing about waiting, but learned fast! Everyone was so kind and friendly, and the tips were good, even in the amusement park!"

"The U.S.A. can hardly be compared with this," I said, looking up at the mountains that surrounded us. The snow-clad peaks on the horizon were five thousand metres high.

"Perhaps not, but in America you can build a future."

After a couple of hours, we came to the ruins of a village. Only the foundations of the houses remained. Nature had reclaimed the village. There were trees and bushes growing in all the kitchens and bedrooms.

"The villagers were deported in the 1970s," Muqim told me. "The people who lived here never moved back."

The deportations in the 1970s are one of the most dramatic

chapters in the history of the Yaghnobis. The Soviet authorities wanted to increase cotton production in Tajikistan and invested heavily. Unlike in Uzbekistan and Turkmenistan, the main issue was not the water supply but labour. The authorities' solution was to deport people from mountain villages to the collective farms in the lowlands. The Yaghnobi people, who lived so remotely, were the last to be deported. There was an attempt at first to get people to move voluntarily, but this failed; when the deadline passed, only a few families had left the valley. The rest of the families were removed by force in helicopters, in an operation that lasted just under two years. The villages were systematically emptied of people until there was no-one left in the valley. Any Yaghnobis who returned to the valley were picked up by helicopter and taken back to the collective farms, again and again, year after year, until finally, after a decade of this, the authorities gave in. By the 1980s, it was clear to everyone that Russia's iron grip was weakening and the families that moved back to the Yaghnob Valley were allowed to stay.

The majority of Yaghnobis chose to stay in the lowlands, where there were roads, electricity and running water, as well as nearby schools and hospitals. But some families decided to leave these comforts behind and returned to their homes. As the houses were built from stone, clay and cow dung, they did not withstand the test of time. One snowy winter without care and attention was all it took for the roof to cave in and the walls to collapse. The villages were in ruins after being unoccupied for a decade.

We carried on along the new dirt road. The Yaghnob River gurgled and clucked companionably alongside us. Until only a few years ago, the Yaghnobis had lived in splendid isolation, without roads, but now it was possible to drive to the villages in the lower part of the valley, in the summer months at least. In winter the valley is covered in a thick layer of snow and the roads and paths are impassable.

When we paused to catch our breath on a slope, Muqim asked for advice.

"I want to apply to do a Masters in economics in Germany next year. What are my chances of getting in, do you think?"

"Are you not a qualified English teacher?"

"Yes, but I started a part-time course in economics this autumn."

"If that's your only grounding in economics, I think it might be better to apply for a bachelor degree," I said, diplomatically. "Or something more connected to your English studies."

Muqim pursed his lips. His brown eyes flashed.

"A friend told me that you can become whatever you want in this world," he said. "You just have to believe in it."

We trudged on in silence. Summer was retreating and some of the trees already glowed orange and yellow. The air smelled of earth and sun. Muqim did not sulk for long and was soon telling me his plans for a future life in the West.

"I hope I'll find a wife in Europe," he said. "It doesn't matter if she's German or Russian, Christian or Jewish, she just has to live in Europe. I want to have European children. All doors will be open to them."

"What about your wife here, and the child you're expecting?" I said. He had shown me a photograph of her. She looked like him. Their faces were open and friendly, and she had big brown eyes and round, almost childlike cheeks. They had grown up together. She had just qualified as a nurse and was now heavily pregnant.

"That's not a problem," Muqim said, with a shrug. "She's fine with me finding myself a new wife, as long as I send money home. And I'll come and visit them at least once a year."

"And you think your European wife will be O.K. with you having a wife and child in Tajikistan as well?"

"Why wouldn't she be?" Muqim looked at me, puzzled. "I'll be with her most of the time."

The sun was going down when finally we saw the first village, Bidef. It stood on the top of a hill, some way from the river. A narrow path snaked up the hillside. It was steeper than it looked, and we were already at three thousand metres. I had not noticed how thin the air was until now. My legs felt like jelly when we cleared the first slope, and the sweat was running down my back. I was gasping, without managing to catch my breath. A little boy in plastic sandals ran past us with a light step. He waved as he passed and disappeared over the brow of the hill.

As we approached the earthen houses, I heard rhythmic drumming. It sounded a bit like shaman drums. Was it the rhythms of a secret Zoroastrian ritual? That was more than I could have hoped for. I looked at Muqim with excitement.

"Should we wait until they've finished?"

"Finished what?"

"Their ritual. Can't you hear the drums?"

Muqim burst out laughing.

"That's a disco. If we're going to wait for them to finish we may as well set up camp here."

We followed the noise, past a field of potatoes and through a narrow passageway between the houses. This led to a small square where two loudspeakers were blasting out Tajik pop music. The square was teeming with men and women; some were just standing there, others were running back and forth. The women were dressed in simple, bright cotton dresses and the men were in jeans and tracksuits. One man was standing by a wall stirring something in a huge iron pot. He was moving in time to the music and singing as he stirred.

"We're in luck," Muqim said. "It's a wedding."

The ceremony itself was the following day, we were told, but the preparations were in full swing, and most of the guests had arrived already. Only four families lived in this tiny village, but now it was bursting with people. A steady stream of guests went in and out of the houses carrying teapots and traditional round breads. Some of them had crossed the river from the neighbouring village, which lay like a reflection on the opposite side of the valley. Others had travelled from Zafarabad in the lowlands, where the Yaghnobis had been deported in the 1970s. Some had come all the way from Dushanbe.

Every square metre of floor space in the village was needed to accommodate the guests, but there was still room for us, and we were immediately invited to join the wedding celebrations the following day.

"Oh no, we don't want to gatecrash," I protested politely.

"It would be an honour if you came," the host assured us – a thin man in a blue Adidas tracksuit with a face covered in fine wrinkles. A young lad showed us to a room where we could sleep, at the far end of the village beside the communal privy. As we sorted out our things, another boy came in with fresh bread and green tea.

Muqim got out a Russian book and started to read the chapter about the Yaghnobis. "Until the deportations of the 1970s, the Yaghnobis were isolated from any other people, and though they have gradually converted to Islam, some pre-Islamic, Zoroastrian rituals have survived in the valley."

While we were drinking the warm, bitter tea, a tall, older gentleman appeared in the doorway, with his back to us. He had a grey beard and was dressed in a thick, blue kaftan, with a small, flat black hat on his head. He stood like this for a while, rocking back and forth, then he started to recite the words that are called from minarets all over the Muslim world, five times a day, all year round: *Allah-u-akbar! Allah-u-akbar!* God is great. A flock of older men with beards, kaftans and round, flat hats started to gather. They stopped at the threshold and took off their shoes, then they went into the spartan side room that served as the village mosque.

While the old men said their afternoon prayers, the young men and women carried on with whatever they were doing, running here and there with food and tea, or standing around in groups, chatting. When the prayers were over, the old men trooped out again, put on their shoes and went back into the village.

The man who had chanted the call to prayer sat down beside us and poured himself a cup of tea. He told us he was seventy years old.

"Are you from here?" I said.

"No, I live in Zafarabad," he said in perfect Russian, but with a thick accent. "I've lived there since we were forced to move in 1970."

"Where did you learn to speak Russian?"

"In Moscow. I did my military service there from 1962 to 1965."

"It must have been quite a shock to move from the Yaghnob Valley to Moscow."

"Moscow was just like the Yaghnob Valley," the man said, after some thought. "It was cold there too."

"Have you never wanted to move back here, to where you grew up?"

"Never." The answer was instant. "Life here in the valley is hard. I got a job driving tractors in Zafarabad, so I could feed my family."

"Have you managed to preserve the Yaghnobi culture in Zafarabad?"

He looked at me blankly.

"Have you managed to keep any traditions and customs that are unique to the Yaghnobi?" I tried again. "It must be difficult when you're surrounded by Tajiks, far away from home."

"But our culture is the same as the Tajiks," the man said. "We're Muslims, like them. There's no difference."

"So you don't have any customs that are special to the Yaghnobis?"

"No. We're good Muslims, and we have been ever since we were converted by the Arabs in the eighth century."

Muqim could not hold back. "That's not true. In the books that I've read, it says that the Yaghnobis fled from the Arabs to avoid being converted, and that they became Muslims much later."

"No, we've been Muslims since the eighth century, just like the Tajiks," the man said. He got up from the mud floor without any difficulty. "Let's go and join the others. They will all say the same as me, just wait and see."

We followed the old man along a path between the low, rundown houses. Mounds of grass had been left to dry on some of the roofs, in preparation for winter. The sweet smell of hay, manure and fresh bread hung over the village. The man stopped in front of one of the houses and gestured that we should follow him in. All the men who had been to pray in the mosque were sitting inside on a small platform. There were soft colourful mats everywhere. And the lower part of the walls was covered in orange hardboard, so that the guests did not have to lean back against the mud. In the middle of the room, on a large tablecloth, was a spread of small plates, pots of tea and bread. The old men were all dressed in kaftans and had short, well-groomed beards in various shades of grey. The younger men and boys sat at the end of the platform where there was no wall. They all stood up when we came in, and one of them immediately poured us some tea.

I asked if any of them could tell me what was unique about the Yaghnobi culture, but I was left none the wiser.

"Other than our language, there's no difference between the Yaghnobis and the Tajiks," said a toothless man beside me.

"We're Muslims, just like the Tajiks," another chimed in.

"In the towns, Yaghnobis live just like Tajiks – they've got nice houses and a good education. No-one can tell the difference," said a third.

When I asked if any of the Zoroastrian traditions had survived, they all shook their heads.

"We are *Muslims*, not heathens," the toothless man beside me said, categorically.

Muqim, who was a Tajik, knew more about Zoroastrian customs than the Yaghnobis. His village lay in the far north of the country. After the birth of a baby, a candle was left to burn in the baby's room for forty days, and when someone in the house died, they burned a candle day and night for three days. When he was little, they used to have a bonfire on a particular Wednesday every year. Everyone in the village jumped over the fire three times, then each of them threw something old and something new on the fire – a mug, for example. This was to protect them against future ill fortune.

Even though there are still some traditions and customs from pre-Islamic days, Tajikistan is now largely Muslim. Tajikistan is in fact the only post-Soviet country to have a state religion, and ninety-eight per cent of the population is Sunni Muslim. President Emomali Rahmon, who is himself a Sunni Muslim, has a rather ambiguous relationship to Islam. He knows perfectly well that Islam is an important identity marker for most Tajiks, but like the other Central Asian presidents he is worried that Islamic fundamentalists might gain a foothold in his country. In an attempt to counteract the growth of extremist groups, he has introduced a ban on hijabs in schools and universities. Long beards are also forbidden and teachers are not allowed facial hair at all. In 2007, the authorities closed four out of every five mosques in Dushanbe. These were then renovated for non-religious use, as had been the case in the Soviet era.

Rahmon has tried to construct a unifying, post-Soviet national identity by looking back to the time before Islam, when the people who lived in what is today Tajikistan were Zoroastrians. He proudly reels off these Zoroastrian traditions, that Tajiks are kind to animals, for example, as proof that the heritage is very much alive. After considerable pressure from the Tajik government, U.N.E.S.C.O. decided that the three thousandth anniversary of Zoroastrianism should be marked in 2003. There were celebrations throughout Central Asia, not least in Tajikistan. According to Rahmon, the Zoroastrian sacred book, *Avesta*, surpasses Homer's *Odyssey*, because it is older and has more words. *Avesta* is also the name of Tajikistan's official news agency.

Here in the Yaghnob Valley, however, where the Zoroastrians hid from the Arab conquerors, no-one wanted to talk about the old religion. The Yaghnobis are good Muslims, just like the Tajiks, that was the mantra.

But why was it so important for the Yaghnobis to be like the majority?

When I was twenty-four, I went on a field trip to North Ossetia to do some research for my Masters dissertation in social anthropology, which was on the consequences of the Beslan school siege. On my first day there I committed the cardinal sin of referring to my sources as Russians. I was immediately corrected: "We are *not* Russians, we are *Ossetians*." If I asked an Ossetian what was typical of Ossetian culture, I would get a long lecture. If the greatest enthusiasts were to be believed, the Ossetians had contributed to pretty much everything in history, from the founding of London to the fall of the Roman empire. As I went west to Ingushetia and Chechnya, these claims became even more outrageous. Some people I met did nothing but talk about their people, their origins and their uniqueness.

But not the Yaghnobis. These rare people, of whom there are only a few thousand left in the world, whose language is modern day scholars' only link to the extinct Sogdian language, insist that they are just like the Tajiks. Perhaps the lack of pride and confidence in their own people can be traced to the Soviet Union's policy on minorities: there were not enough Yaghnobis for them to be given the status of separate nationality. Following the deportations in 1970, the Soviet authorities went as far as to delete Yaghnobi as a separate ethnicity from all registers. They simply decided that the Yaghnobi people no longer existed. All Yaghnobis were instead registered as Tajiks. And that is still the case today, as Tajikistan has the same lower limit for a nationality to be recognised. The minimum number is fifty-two thousand people. The Yaghnobis are nowhere near as many as that.

"When my son was born, I asked the nurse to write *Yaghnobi* under nationality," said one of the men who had not spoken until now. "She didn't listen to me, and wrote *Tajik*, and I'm very glad of it now. If she had done what I said, my son would probably have faced countless unnecessary problems."

The man who was talking seemed to be poorer than the others in the room. He was wearing a threadbare, checked shirt and a pair of jeans that were so old they were about to fall apart. A trim white beard framed his sharp, fox-like face.

"My name is Mirzonazar, and I was born in Nometkon, not far from here, in 1941, the year the Great Patriotic War broke out," he said. "Of all the men in the room here, I am the only one who has come back to the valley. I had just finished building a new house for me and my family when the helicopters came to get us. If I'd known that they were going to force us to move, I would never have built the house. I ruined my back doing it."

Mirzonazar, his wife and four children were forced aboard the helicopter and taken to a collective farm in Zafarabad, in the low-lands. The eldest son, Sohibnazar, was eleven. Kholmahmad was eight. Gobinazar was seven. And Shohibi, the little girl, was only one.

In less than a week in Zafarabad, Sohibnazar, Gobinazar and Shohibi had all died. As the children had lived in the isolated valley all their lives, they did not have the immune system to deal with the illnesses in the lowlands.

In 1981, after eleven years on the collective farm, Mirzonazar, his wife and their one surviving child moved back to the Yaghnob Valley.

"When I left, my beard was black," Mirzonazar said. "When I came back, it was white."

Mirzonazar's house had been empty for eleven years and the elements had destroyed it. The walls and roof had collapsed, and local shepherds had helped themselves to what there was of wood and used it for fuel. The small family had to live in the barn, the only building in the village that was more or less intact, until Mirzonazar had rebuilt the house.

"Now I only go back to Zafarabad to visit the children's graves," he said. "Sohibnazar was very special. He was an intelligent boy and did well at school. When he came to ask for ten roubles to buy a notebook and pen, I always gave him twenty, I was so fond of him. Buy yourself some biscuits or pierogi with the extra ten roubles, I told him."

"It must have been hard for your wife to lose three children in such a short space of time," I said. The other men in the room listened in silence.

Mirzonazar sighed and laughed. It was a bitter laugh, and his eyes dulled.

"It was she who suggested we should move back," he said. "My father advised us not to. He didn't think there would be enough food. I told him that three mouthfuls of water from the Latabandsoi source by the village was enough to satisfy my hunger."

A month after they had moved back, ten policemen and a lawyer came to persuade them to go back to the lowlands.

"You *have* to leave, the helicopter will be here soon," the policemen insisted.

When the policemen were out of hearing, the lawyer told Mirzonazar that he could refuse to leave. According to the lawyer, the police did not have the authority to use force, but he would have to be firm and clear.

"My friends, you can take me back to Zafarabad, but not alive," Mirzonazar told the policemen. "I may not feel the first bullet, or the second, but I would feel the tenth. And yet I'm not afraid of you."

When the helicopter came, the policemen and the lawyer boarded without Mirzonazar and his family.

"What is it like, living in the valley?" I said.

"Everything about the life here is good, otherwise I wouldn't have come back. I can list the seventy-six types of plant that grow here. When they start to grow in spring, we can eat the shoots and buds. I could talk about the clean air. You don't get air like this in the lowlands! But if I was to choose one thing, it would be the cold water. You can only find water like this here. In this valley, there's only one illness, and that's death!" Mirzonazar grinned, revealing his pointed eyeteeth, which made him look even more like a fox.

Men kept arriving and we had to squeeze together to make room for everyone. Young men came in with warm, fresh bread and pots of newly made green tea. Every time an older man came into the room, the younger men got up and stood until he had sat down. Only the older men answered my questions, in fact, it was only the older men who spoke. The younger ones listened. Stood up and sat down again. Made sure there was always enough bread and tea on the cloth.

"Is it important in Yaghnobi culture to show your elders respect?" I said to the man next to me.

"In the Qur'an, it says that the young shall show respect for the old," he said. "Old people only pray for those they like, and the prayers of the old are more valuable to God than those of the young."

The older men chatted away amongst themselves. Many of them had not seen each other for more than a year, so there was plenty to talk about.

"Old people like to talk about their lives," Muqim remarked wisely.

"What are they talking about?"

"I don't understand a lot of what they're saying, just the odd word here and there," he said. "They speak Yaghnobi to each other."

I sipped my tea and tried to savour the foreign sounds and words in this world of hats, beards and kaftans. Perhaps it was the intonation, but did it not sound a bit harder and more staccato than Tajik? As I spoke neither language, it was not easy to hear the difference. And yet the knowledge that I was listening to Yaghnobi, the closest one can get to Sogdian, the main language in ancient Sogdiana, made my ears tingle. This was the language in which the Zoroastrian priests chanted and sang to their god two thousand years ago. This was the language in which the indigenous people must have begged, threatened and negotiated with Alexander the Great, as he conquered country after country from Greece to India, in his legendary campaigns in the fourth century BCE. This was the language in which the merchants haggled about slave prices along the Silk Road. Sogdian was the *lingua franca* of trading, and was spoken from Turkey to China.

"Can all Yaghnobis speak the language?" I asked the man beside me.

"No, there are fewer and fewer who really master the language. Most of the Yaghnobis who live in and around Dushanbe speak only Tajik. Those of us who live in Zafarabad have managed to keep the language alive, even though it's not used or taught in schools. Nowadays, a lot of Yaghnobis marry Tajiks or Uzbeks, and, as a rule, their children do not learn Yaghnobi. It's one of our greatest fears, that the language will die out."

There are fewer than fifteen thousand Yaghnobi speakers in the world today. The people who still live in the Yaghnob Valley – four to five hundred – all speak Yaghnobi, and many of the children do not learn Tajik until they start school, where only Tajik is spoken. But it is questionable how long people will continue to live in the valley, where poverty and isolation make for a hard life. How long is it possible to preserve a minority language when the minority is not even recognised as such, and the language is not a written language and no longer taught? The fact that their language has survived until now bears witness to the Yaghnobis' resolve and pride. Though many of them lived in isolation in the valley until the 1970s, most now live in the lowlands, surrounded by Tajiks and Uzbeks. How long can a language survive in those circumstances?

As soon as I left the men, a young woman with a lined face and mouth full of gold teeth grabbed hold of me. She said something to me in either Yaghnobi or Tajik.

"She's inviting you to the women's party," Muqim said.

"Oh, great!" I said. "Come on!"

Muqim hesitated. "It's not really my place, as a man. Would it be alright if you went on your own?"

The women's room was almost identical to the men's room. Women were sitting all along the walls, drinking tea, eating fresh bread and chatting. Every time an older woman came into the room, the younger women got up and remained standing until she sat down. They were all dressed in colourful, ankle-length skirts and dresses, and many of them had white scarves on their heads. Once again, as in the men's room, I was invited to sit in the best place, furthest in, and a young woman immediately poured me some tea. But here I was helpless without Muqim. Neither the younger nor the older women could speak a word of Russian. I sat there smiling and nodding and listening. As soon as I put down my tea bowl, it was filled by one of the young women. The woman beside me broke the bread and held it out to me. I smiled, broke off a piece and ate, drank more tea, then my bowl was filled again. All the young women stood up politely when I finally got up to go, having drunk eight or nine bowls of green tea. I thanked them all and left.

The meal was rice pilaf, the food of celebration in Central Asia. The cook, a smiling, bearded man, served up generous portions from an enormous iron pot. The fried rice was dripping with lamb fat and smelled of onions, carrots and roast meat. Muqim and I got a portion to share, and ate with our hands, as was the custom in the valley.

At half past nine, everyone went to bed. I, who was very much treated as the guest of honour, was allowed to sleep in the men's quarters with Muqim, the geography teacher and a tall, wiry fellow. Because the village was so high in the valley, the temperature dropped as soon as the sun went down. The houses were poorly insulated, so it was soon almost as cold inside as it was outside. The arthritic old men, who had been given the inner room where there was a wood burner, lay chatting in the dark for hours. As most of them were hard of hearing, they talked in loud voices. Where the rest of the guests slept was a mystery. There were perhaps eight small houses in total in the village, and there were nearly a hundred guests there already. Thanks to my hat, scarf and earplugs, I fell asleep straight away, and barely noticed the small insects that crawled out of the holes in the wall and over my face.

The sun had not yet risen when the older men went out into the blue light of dawn to wash and say their morning prayers. By six o'clock, they were chatting away again in the next room, and by seven the disco rhythms were pounding from the loudspeakers by the outdoor kitchen. It was the day of Mirzo and Nisor's wedding and the whole village was busy with last-minute preparations.

When I wandered out into the cool morning air, I saw the bridegroom for the first time. He had big, brown eyes, thick eyebrows and high, fine cheekbones; he looked remarkably like Franz Kafka as a young man. He was small and slight, shorter than me, and did not look a day over fourteen. The other guests had told me that he was eighteen, and old enough to get married, according to Tajik law. Maybe he really was eighteen years old – most children in the valley were so malnourished that they looked much younger than they actually were. The opposite seemed to be true of the adults: even the twenty-five year olds had lined faces and rounded backs.

Mirzo sat solemnly on a chair. Behind him, with a large pair of scissors, stood an old, white-haired man who was careful to catch Mirzo's black locks of hair in a white scarf. Many of the guests darted forwards and dropped rolled banknotes in the scarf as well.

"Money for the barber," Muqim told me.

Haircut over, the bridegroom disappeared into his parents' house. We stood outside and waited. After a short while he came back out in a black, shiny suit that was at least one size too big. The guests, now well over a hundred of them, followed him to the end of the village. Here they all stopped, and the oldest men said prayers for him and gave their blessings. Mirzo could not stop smiling, despite the ceremony and circumstance.

His bride, Nisor, came from a village called Qul, a few hours away. Mirzo had chosen her himself, I was told. He had noticed her once when he visited the village, and told his parents that that was the girl he was going to marry. The two youngsters had never been alone together; they had never touched, and had barely spoken to one other.

When the elders had blessed Mirzo, the bridegroom set off for the bride's village with a small group of companions. They started out on foot, down the steep hillside, but would then drive as far as they could on the dirt road. When the road stopped, they would continue on to the village of Qul on donkeys and horseback. They reckoned they would be back again by early afternoon.

We ate in the meantime. First we were given fresh bread and tea, then a young girl served us with newly prepared pilaf rice. We were then given lentil soup, followed by a steaming vegetable soup. One of the younger boys made sure that there was always warm, fresh tea in the pot.

Just after five o'clock, the bridal party appeared at the foot of the steep hillside. The first up were a long line of women with small children in their arms; they huffed and puffed and paused frequently. Then some boys rode up on donkeys, followed by the bridegroom, the only male in the party wearing a suit. He was on a horse, surrounded by his friends who were running alongside. He was grinning from ear to ear. His big eyes sparkled. Behind him came the bride. She was sitting on the back of a brown horse, her arms around a lean, tanned man dressed in jeans and a tracksuit top, who was her uncle. Her face was covered with a veil which was so thick that it was hard to get any impression of her face, but she was said to be beautiful. She had white, baggy trousers on under a plain, white bridal dress. The cheap fabric appeared to be hiding a child's body.

The loudspeakers had been moved from the outside kitchen to the roof of the couple's house for the wedding. In the room where they would sleep, seven mattresses had been laid out on the floor, as was the custom. The guests had been standing waiting outside the house for several hours now already. When the bride finally reached the village, the women started to wail in the traditional manner, with their right hands over their mouths. They flocked around the bride's horse and showered her with sweets. Some of the women started to dance spontaneously; with their arms above their heads they moved slowly in a ring to the disco beat.

The bride was helped down from her horse and led into one of the houses to eat the wedding meal. She would then be accompanied to her new home, where she and the bridegroom would spend the rest of the evening and night while the guests continued to celebrate in the village.

Yet more guests had arrived at the small village in the course of the day. To make room for the new arrivals, or at least some of them, Muqim, the geography teacher and I loaded our things onto a donkey and got ready to leave. The bridegroom's father protested a little. It was almost dark, he objected, could we not stay until the morning, but we thanked him politely and set off on our way to the next village, which was about an hour further down the valley.

"Well, I guess there will be dancing here until the early hours," I said, as we made our way down the steep slope.

The geography teacher looked at his watch.

"Only until nine," he said. "The president has decreed that a wedding cannot last more than three hours, and there must be a maximum of one hundred and fifty guests. And no more than a hundred guests at funerals, and sixty at circumcision ceremonies."

These rules are not plucked from thin air. Presumably there has been a problem with families using all their money on extravagant weddings for the extended family that have lasted several days. In a poor country like Tajikistan, laws like this can make it easier for families without means to have scaled-down celebrations without losing face. The question is whether these rules also apply to the president's family. A famous YouTube clip that was posted in May 2013 shows a very drunk Rahmon performing a karaoke number at his son's wedding. In the clip, the president sings out of key as he dances around unsteadily. The guests appear to have drunk quite a lot, so one can only assume that they have been partying for well over three hours.

The clip was so popular that the Tajik authorities felt compelled to block YouTube for a while.

We arrived at the next village, Nometkon, in the magical light of a full moon. The village was abandoned, empty. A dog barked somewhere close by. We could not see a single light, other than that of the moon, which shone on the simple mud houses. A man appeared and welcomed us. He explained that he was alone in the village, as everyone else was at the wedding. We were shown to a room where we could sleep, and were then served bread and green tea.

Night fell over the Yaghnob Valley. I slept like a log. When I woke up, it was broad daylight.

"Did you sleep well?" Mirzonazar, the old man with a fox-like face from the wedding celebration, gave me a knowing look. He had left Bidef after morning prayers and had already been home for a few hours.

"Very well," I nodded.

"I should hope so too," he said, with a wily wink. "You were sleeping on the couple's mattresses!"

It was late September and the harvest was nearly finished. In the coming weeks, until the first snow was due, there would be a wedding every week in the valley, sometimes one day after the other. People went from one to the next, without much time for anything else. It was the turn of one of the young men from Mirzonazar's village the following week, and everything was ready for the wedding. There was a pile of soft, colourful mattresses in the corner, and a large wooden chest full of cups, knives, bowls, plates, other kitchen utensils that the newly-wed couple would need, and fabric for clothes. A smell of fresh paint lingered in the room, and against the end wall was a small T.V. set, which the happy couple could enjoy in the evenings.

We sat and sipped our tea. Muqim talked about when he was in America, and Mirzonazar listened for a long time without saying anything. Then he looked out of the window, suddenly restless.

"It's getting late," he said. "There's work to be done. I don't have time to sit here chatting."

Muqim and I started to pack our things, but Mirzonazar made no sign of getting up.

"My wife died on February 14 this year," he told us. "So after fifty-eight years of being shackled by marriage, I'm a free man again." He jumped up from the floor without difficulty. "No, this won't do. I'd better get to work. I can't sit around wasting time."

But he stayed standing where he was. When we were ready to leave, he started to talk about Sohibnazar again, his firstborn, who had died in Zafarabad when he was eleven.

"I wish he was still alive! He was the smartest of the four hundred pupils in school, and the best behaved. Five hundred people came to his funeral."

He blinked furiously, then gave us another wry smile. "When you get back home to your country, you can write that in a place far,

far away, in a distant valley, in a remote part of the world, you met an old man with a tragic story."

After we had walked for about half an hour, the dirt road ended. A yellow digger had been abandoned on the verge, awaiting better days. Beyond, a narrow path snaked its way along the green hillside. And across the river stood the valley's new, half-finished school. A couple of times along the way we were overtaken by Yaghnobis riding donkeys laden with onions, which was one of the things they had to get outside the valley, along with other basic products such as rice, oil, soap and flour. They could only grow a few varieties of corn, potatoes and carrots in the poor soil. In order to augment these basic supplies, the men rode to the head of the valley once or twice a year and exchanged goats and sheep for the necessary wares. No-one in the valley had much money to spare, they were largely self-sufficient and relied on bartering.

We followed the narrow path for two to three hours until we came to Pskon. Today, only thirteen families live here, but it is still one of the biggest villages in the valley. We made our way between the buildings until we came to the house at the top of the village, where Saidmurod, the village mullah and healer, lived. People from all over the valley came here to be healed.

Saidmurod was sitting in the reception room. There was very little furniture, but it had large windows and a magnificent view of the mountains. He was talking to another guest, a shepherd who was on his way south with his flock. He welcomed us graciously and showed us straight away to the guest room, where we could stay the night. No matter how poor a Yaghnobi family might be, they always have a house or at least a room standing ready for unexpected guests. And here in the valley, where there is no mobile coverage, no landline or Internet, more or less all guests are unexpected.

Saidmurod was forty-seven and had a very calm and pleasant nature. His family was the first to return to Pskon in 1980. The only building that was still relatively intact when they came back was the barn, or *saraiet*. His parents had swept the floor and cleaned it as well as they could, so that they could live there while they rebuilt their house.

"They say that if Pskon is abandoned, everyone will leave the valley," Saidmurod told us. "My father, who was the head of the village, therefore felt it was incumbent upon him to move back. And he was very unhappy in Zafarabad. The heat and the different climate made both him and my mother sick. I was sick too, and my brothers and sisters. But when we came back here, we all got well again."

Now that his parents are dead, Saidmurod is head of the village, as well as being a mullah and healer. He has also fathered seven sons and two daughters, but only six of them are still alive. Two sons and one daughter died before they were five. There are a lot of stories about dead children. Nearly everyone has lost someone. In the Yaghnob Valley, people have no access to doctors or medical care. In winter, the paths and roads are blocked by snow, and no one can get anywhere. The only thing they can do when a child falls sick is to pray. Sometimes their prayers are heard, other times not. A simple illness like appendicitis can be fatal for both adults and children. When someone has stomach pains, they start to count the days. Sometimes it passes.

"We still live in the nineteenth century here in the valley. It's a hard life, but we're happy," Saidmurod said.

Before dark fell, Muqim and I walked around the village. We met two sisters-in-law outside the barn; Bibinasab was forty-six and Narzimoh was twenty-six. Bibinasab was married to Narzimoh's brother, and, as Narzimoh was divorced, she lived with them. They were standing by a pile of dung cakes that the women in the village made, stacked and dried for fuel. Both were wearing wide, colourful dresses and baggy trousers. Their long, dark hair hung loose under faded scarves.

"It's a hard life," Bibinasab said and giggled. She had big, brown eyes surrounded by a web of fine wrinkles. "But we were born here, we're used to it."

Bibinasab had no children. Soon after she was married, she had given birth to a son, but he died. A few years later, her husband found himself a second wife.

"How did you feel about that?" Muqim translated for me. They only spoke Yaghnobi in the village, but the women had learned some Tajik from the shepherds and others who visited the village.

"I agreed to it, of course," she said, and giggled again.

"Was she younger than you?"

"Oh yes, by about ten years, I think, but I'm not sure. I didn't go to school, so I don't know anything." She sniggered. "But my husband loved us both just as much, he didn't treat us any differently. And we got on well, the new wife and I, so there wasn't any problem. I made the food and we always ate together."

"What did the other wife do, if you made the food?"

"She cleaned the stable," Bibinasab said, and tried not to laugh. "After a few years, she got fed up of living here and left to find herself another husband. The life here was too hard, she wasn't used to it. And she didn't have any children – she took medicine to stop that, so it didn't really matter when she left."

Suddenly the two women excused themselves and hurried off, they had to milk the cows. But they left the door open so we could continue to talk while they worked.

Narzimoh did not have any children either. She had married when she was fifteen, and after three years of marriage her husband had sent her away when she was heavily pregnant. Her first son was stillborn. The second died when he was three.

Neither Muqim nor I could make sense of her story. Why would her husband send her away when she was pregnant?

"It wasn't actually my husband who sent me away," Narzimoh admitted. "His parents weren't nice to me and didn't treat me like a human being. So I left."

"Did they try to get you back?"

"No," she said at once. "They never came."

There was still something odd about her story, but we gave up trying to understand the family relations and marriage stories.

"Would you like to get married again?"

"Oh yes!" Narzimoh shouted from the barn. Her voice was almost drowned out by the cow's happy mooing.

The following morning, I met Saidmurod's wife, Umrimoh. She was sitting on a slope by the kitchen drinking tea with a friend, surrounded by their children, when Muqim and I stopped for chat.

"Oh, oh, oh, it's so hard, everything in Yaghnob is hard!" She said and laughed, when I asked her about life in the valley. She had a high-pitched, girlish voice, bright eyes and a smile that lit up her face. The youngest daughter, an infant, was feeding at her breast. A happy, snotty boy of around three or four was sitting beside them.

Umrimoh was born in Zafarabad in 1972, and was married to Saidmurod when she was sixteen.

"We don't have a proper stove and use cow pats for fuel. It stinks!" Umrimoh laughed. "And look at my clothes, how dirty they are!" She lifted the hem of her flowery cotton dress, which was worn and threadbare and discoloured by dirt and smoke.

"Would you have preferred to live in Zafarabad?" I said. Muqim translated.

. "Life in Zafarabad is better, of course it is," she replied. "But I don't have any money. There's no work for us either. I don't have any education, I can barely read and write. So it's better for us here." She put down her youngest daughter. The happy, snotty little boy immediately took the opportunity to clamber up onto her lap. He had clearly done this before, as he took hold of her vacant breast and started to suckle.

"I want my children to have an education," Umrimoh said, suddenly serious. "We sent our two eldest sons to a boarding school in Ayni, the regional capital, but they came home again after a year. We've tried everything to get them to go back, but they refuse. They said they would rather throw themselves in the river than go back to school." She sighed. "They say the food there is terrible. And the pupils often go hungry and are given bread that's not good ... Hopefully we'll have our own school here soon. The building is nearly finished – down by the road. Did you see it?"

We nodded.

"Sadly, it's not very well built. Most of the money disappeared, so the builders had to use cheap bricks and the flooring is so bad that it won't last through the hard, snowy winters. But the main problem is that we don't have teachers. Who would want to work as a teacher here, in this remote valley?"

When we mentioned the two women we had met by the barn the evening before, Umrimoh and her friend had plenty more to tell us.

"Narzimoh came from a rich family here in Pskon, but her husband was poor," the friend said. "She liked her husband, but didn't get on with his family and was very unhappy in his village. It was too much for her in the end. His family came to get her back, but she refused to go."

The relationship between Bibinasab and wife number two had not been as rosy as Bibinasab liked to claim it was.

"Bibinasab was so jealous, they even fought!" Umrimoh said. "The new wife was more beautiful and stronger than her. In the end, Bibinasab had had enough and went home to her father's house. When she came back, her husband had done what she wanted and got rid of the new wife."

"No, no, she didn't take any medicine. Where would she get that? If she did, I wouldn't mind some myself," the friend said, pointing to a little girl with short, curly hair. "She's my seventh child. I didn't want her. I took medicines and herbs, anything to avoid having more children, but she came all the same. Our men won't leave us alone."

"What about pregnancy and birth?" I said. "Do you really manage to do everything without help?"

"This time last year I was out cutting the corn," Umrimoh said. "Suddenly I felt the pains in my stomach. When I got home, I gave birth to my daughter. It all happened so fast that the village woman who was going to help me didn't manage to get here in time. My husband didn't believe me and shouted to me to come out again and help him."

"After giving birth, we have one day's rest," the friend said. "Then it's up and back to work. The other women make fun of anyone who's lazy and doesn't work."

"If a baby is stillborn, or dies, we cry," Umrimoh said. "We don't grieve for long, as life goes on. But we do cry and that helps."

A boy came over and sat down beside us.

"This is Rajabal, my second oldest," Umrimoh smiled. "He's fourteen."

He was so small and thin that he did not look a day over eight.

"And what do you want to do when you grow up?" I asked. "Do you want to be a doctor, or a teacher, or maybe a football player?"

"I want to get married in two years' time," he said, without a flicker of a smile.

"I want him to study, but all he cares about is getting a wife and some cows," his mother complained.

"Have you found a wife?"

"No, not yet," the boy said, just as seriously. "But I'm keeping an eye out. I want a clean wife, the best. Maybe from Zafarabad or Dushanbe."

"Whenever relatives come to visit from town, he studies the girls carefully," his mother teased. "She has to be so pure, so clean, not like the girls from the village, who have cow dung under their nails!"

Umrimoh and her friend laughed heartily, but the boy did not bat an eyelid.

We went back the same way we had come, past the digger at the end of the road, past the unfinished school, through the village where the old man with the foxy smile lived. This time we stayed the night in a village on the other side of the river, with a view over to Bidef, where the disco rhythms were now silent. On our last day, we passed the ruins of the abandoned village, and went over the ridge of the hill and down to the geography teacher's lush village. The taciturn driver was there, waiting for us, and once again we set off down the bumpy dirt track, through the Tunnel of Death and back to Dushanbe, where the enormous flag fluttered lazily in the evening breeze. Seeing all the Mercedes and B.M.W.s on the main street, the wide pavements, the empty library, the president's huge palace, made my head spin. It felt as though I had been away for months, for years, as though I had been out of time. Had it all been a dream?

When I crept into bed, that wonderful invention, and pulled the white, freshly ironed sheets over me, I noticed that my legs were covered in hundreds of small, red bites.

A greeting from the Yaghnob Valley.

So it had been real, after all.

THE SAD SERVING LADY

Even though Qurghonteppa is the fourth largest town in Tajikistan, it was not even mentioned in the guidebook. The only attractions were the Museum of History and Regional Studies, a version of which was to be found in all Soviet towns, and Tajikistan's first tractor, mounted on a plinth in the middle of a roundabout. There was nothing else to see or do.

Having trudged up and down the main street a couple of times, I chanced upon Karina's Café. I was the only customer in the gaudy premises. With its velvet sofas and enormous disco ball, it was clearly not geared towards lunch guests.

"It's not often we get foreigners here!" The waitress looked at me, elated. Her shoulder-length hair was dyed red, she was slim and well groomed, with varnished nails and high heels. When she came over with a pot of tea a few minutes later, she had with her a photograph of three children. The oldest looked around eighteen, and the youngest boy was probably four or five.

"Could you maybe sign this for me?" She looked at me hopefully. I took the pen she gave me and wrote my name on the back of photograph. She thanked me profusely.

My Greek salad was accompanied by the waitress's tragic life story. Her name was Sveta and she was thirty-seven. She had a daughter of eighteen and a son of twelve from her first marriage. The youngest son, who was five, was from her second marriage. When she was pregnant with him, her husband had done what so many Tajik men do: he had gone to Russia to earn money. Between one and two million of Tajikistan's eight million inhabitants are at any one time working in Russia. The money they send home accounts for half of Tajikistan's gross domestic product. No other country in the world is so dependent on the wages of migrant workers.

"For the first few months, he called regularly and sent money," Sveta, who had now sat down at my table, told me. "After about six months, he said that his employer had tricked him, so he wanted to find another job. And I haven't heard from him since then."

She smiled sadly, and I saw that she was missing two teeth.

"I was worried to begin with and did everything I could to find him. I contacted friends and acquaintances and tried to track him down. I didn't even know if he was alive! I've just accepted that I'll only find him if he wants to be found. He knows where I live. I haven't changed my SIM card since he disappeared, so I still have the same mobile number. My boy only knows his dad from photographs. Every time he meets a new man he's thinks it's him."

Sveta's Russian was perfect, without even a hint of an accent. There was a simple explanation, as it turned out: her mother was Russian. As a young woman, her mother had fallen in love with a Tajik man and converted to Islam. After living in Russia for a few years, the young couple had moved to Qurghonteppa, the man's hometown, and built a life together here.

"I spent my first five years in Russia," Sveta said, lighting up a thin cigarette. The smoke formed blue clouds in the thin strip of daylight that slipped through the curtains. "I was baptized, but I'm not sure if I'm Christian or Muslim. Probably a bit of both, half-half, maybe? Apart from those first five years, I've lived here all my life. Well, except during the war, of course. When it got too bad, I fled to Russia. I even lived in Moscow for a while. They've got everything there! Electricity, gas . . . There's nothing you can't get."

"Why did you come back?"

"My children were here! I wanted to be with them. But I wish I could go . . ." she sighed. "It's just that I don't have a Russian passport. I suppose I could get one, but then I would have to go to Dushanbe and that's two hours away, and it costs money. Everything costs money. I don't get a salary, just a share of the tips, and that's not enough. We don't even have guests here every day. A trip to the market, a bag of food, and whoosh – the money's gone." She sighed again. "Living here is not a life, Erika. I hope that my eldest son can go to Russia."

"What about your daughter? Does she want to go to Russia?"

"She's just finished school and is at home looking after the little one," Sveta said. "She's met a boy and they're going to get married soon."

Sveta leaned over the table and lowered her voice to a conspiratorial whisper.

"Our president only thinks about himself. He never does anything for the people. In winter, we only have electricity for a few hours a day. We sit shivering in candlelight. We don't have gas either and there's practically never any hot water. My flat is so high up that I don't even get water in the taps. I have to go down to the cellar and carry up buckets of cold water. Every winter, small children and old people freeze to death. It's no life, this. We're not living, we're surviving. I sometimes come here with my friends, when I have time off, to dance. To forget our troubles for a short while."

She apologised and lit up another thin cigarette.

"I only started smoking when my husband disappeared. I drink a bit as well, but not much. The other Russians who are still here are all alcoholics. The women too."

Most of the Russians fled the country during the civil war in the

1990s. Today, fewer than one per cent of the population are Russian, which makes Tajikistan the country with the lowest number of Russians in the whole of the former Soviet Union. And yet, no country is more dependent on Russia than Tajikistan. If the Russian authorities were to introduce a visa requirement for Tajik migrant workers – which they threaten to do every time President Emomali Rahmon does not dance to Russia's tune – the country's economy would immediately collapse.

Many of the Tajik migrant workers find themselves Russian wives. However, this does not stop them from coming back to their village once a year and making their Tajik wife pregnant, perhaps even giving her an S.T.D., before returning to Russia. But then the visits and money transfers become less and less frequent, until they take the final step and apply for Russian citizenship and stay there. As it is sufficient in Sunni Islam for a man to repeat *talaq*, the word for divorce, three times for a couple to be divorced, many Tajik women have received the following text message from their husbands in Russia: "Talaq, talaq, talaq".

In 2011, the Council of Ulema in Tajikistan banned divorce by mobile telephone.

In the evening, I went back to Karina's Café. It was transformed. There were now big and small groups of men at the tables upstairs. I was the only female guest there, and the only one sitting alone. The disco ball showered the room with small squares of light, and the loudspeakers pumped out music, while sexy pop videos flickered across the big screen. The lights were so low that I gave up trying to read the book I had with me.

Sveta was transformed as well. She was enveloped in a cloud of heavy perfume and had put on a metallic lipstick and thick, dark, glittering eye make-up. She sat at the tables with the men, and listened attentively, putting her hand on their thigh when they whispered something in her ear.

The night version of Sveta came over to me with a Greek salad and some bread, and told me excitedly that the young gentleman in the white shirt, the one sitting in the corner smoking, had expressed an interest in me. He wondered if he could come and sit at my table.

"But," she whispered in warning, "don't believe any of his stories. Don't let him fool you."

"I was just about to leave," I said. "I only came to say hello to you." She gave me a sad smile.

"You know, I still haven't lost hope that I might meet a new man," she said. "A woman has to hope, or what's the point?"

THE FACES OF WAR

Stories of war are stories of chaos. They are fragmented, episodic, hard to comprehend, in the way that war itself is fragmented, unpredictable and incomprehensible.

When the war is over, it is broken down into numbers, and thus we create order from chaos and make the incomprehensible more manageable. The civil war in Tajikistan lasted for five years. The first few months from early summer 1992 to late winter 1993 were the bloodiest. Between 50,000 and 100,000 people were killed, and more than one million were forced to flee their homes.

When war is raging, surviving from day to day is about all one can do. Batten down the hatches, try to control the fear and uncertainty, and find enough daily bread.

"I remember the queues," said Soraya, an old woman I met in a small, simple hut in the Yaghnob Valley, where she and her husband grew potatoes in summer to top up their meagre pension. "I got up at the crack of dawn to get a place in the queue. And that was the morning gone. If I was lucky, I got a loaf of bread before they ran out. And it was the same again the following day. By midday, the streets were deserted. Criminal gangs took advantage of the security vacuum and roamed the streets, looting and causing trouble. It was total anarchy."

Every day, while his wife was in the bread queue, Sanginmurat went into the centre of Dushanbe, to the Philharmonic, where he worked as a security guard. As there were no concerts during the war, he was the only person in the building. Sanginmurat sat alone in the dark in the security booth for ten to twelve hours at a time, seven days a week. He did not dare to turn on the lights for fear of being shot.

"Every time I went into the centre, I wondered if I would come home alive," he told me. "Things were relatively calm where we lived, but it was all out war in town."

One day, a group of young rebels broke into the Philharmonic. Sanginmurat did nothing to resist, and instead helped them as best he could to pick out objects of value and to get hold of the money in the safe. The next day, the director came by. He praised the security guard for staying so calm and instructed him not to resist if the rebels came back. He should just let them take what they wanted, and certainly should not contact him, the director.

The gang did come back. They were young men with no education and no manners. They tramped over the expensive carpets in their muddy boots. They boasted in loud voices. There and then, they were the victors. As Sanginmurat was always helpful, they did not harm him, but gradually they started to bring in other people with them from the street. They would strip them in his security booth and confiscate anything of value. And sometimes they punched and kicked them. When they had finished, they let them back out onto the street, often without giving them their clothes back. One time, Sanginmurat had had enough and shouted at them to stop. A man came over and wanted to cut off his ear. And he would have done, if one of the leaders had not defended Sanginmurat.

On his way to and from work, Sanginmurat was sometimes stopped by young men with knives and guns. "Who do you side with, the state or the opposition?" they shouted at him. As Sanginmurat never knew who they supported themselves, his reply was always as diplomatic as possible. "I side with peace," he said. Again and again, he repeated this. "I don't side with anyone. I just want peace."

In the end, he could not bear it any longer. In 1994, he fled to Russia and stayed there for three years, until the Philharmonic in Dushanbe opened its door to the public once again.

To begin with, everything had looked rosy. In autumn 1991, Tajikistan was the first post-Soviet state to hold a free election. In contrast to Turkmenistan and Kazakhstan, several different parties and presidential candidates were allowed to stand in the election. But as expected, the Communist Party candidate, Rahmon Nabiyev, was elected president. He had previously been chairman of the Communist Party of Tajikistan, but was removed from office by Gorbachev following a corruption scandal in 1985. However, he managed to climb back to the pinnacle of power in autumn 1991.

The opposition, which included the Democratic Party and the Islamic Renaissance Party, had taken thirty per cent of the vote, but Nabiyev still refused to give them any ministerial posts in his government or share power with them in any way. The fact that Nabiyev was from Khujand in the north, where many Communist party leaders had been recruited, was not in his favour. Tajikistan is a very clan-based society and people from the other regions felt overlooked. And it did not help that Nabiyev had a number of bad habits from the Soviet era: he drank and smoked huge amounts, turned up to the office late and too often went home after lunch. When thousands of dissatisfied citizens gathered to demonstrate in the capital in spring 1992, he did nothing until May, when finally he intervened and tried to stop the protests with force. But by then it was too late. He formed a coalition government in June in an attempt to placate all sides, but it did not survive long and the tensions escalated. The country was divided into more or less four factions: the pro-Nabiyev camp in Khujand in the north, the anti-Nabiyev alliance between the Islamic Renaissance Party and pro-democracy groups in and around Dushanbe, the pro-Nabiyev camp in Kulob in the south-east, and the Islamists in the south-west, based around Qurghonteppa. They also had a strong hold in the poor and sparsely populated Pamir region.

On September 7, 1992, Nabiyev was captured by opposition supporters and forced to step down. The same autumn, Emomali Rhamon was appointed chairman of the Supreme Soviet. Thanks to military support from Uzbekistan, which did not want the Islamists to gain power, Rahmon and the Communists managed to take control of Dushanbe and Qurghonteppa. Tens of thousands of people were killed or forced to flee the fighting.

Having regained power in parts of the country, the Rahmon government chose revenge rather than reconciliation, in keeping with old clan culture. The hardest hit were the people in the Gharm area in mid-Tajikistan and Pamir in the east. The opposition had been supported with a passion in both places. In spring 1993, more than a thousand Gharmis and Pamiris were quite simply liquidated in Dushanbe by militia that operated with the government's silent blessing. More than two hundred thousand Gharmis and Pamiris fled to the mountains in the east during this period, and many of them sought refuge on the Afghan side of the border, where the Taliban gave them moral support and practical help to continue their fight. And in the midst of all this turbulence, opium smuggling from Afghanistan increased by an estimated two thousand per cent.

Even though the worst fighting was over, peace had still not come to Tajikistan. As soon as the snow melted in Pamir, the Islamist rebels renewed their attacks on Russian posts and military buildings along the border. Every now and then bombs went off in Dushanbe.

The U.N., Russia and Tajikistan's Central Asian neighbours tried for several years to negotiate a peace treaty between the parties, but did not apply any real pressure until the Taliban seized power in Kabul in autumn 1996. For Russia, Tajikistan was an important buffer against Afghanistan, and the Russians wanted to prevent the Taliban from gaining any influence on the Tajik side of the border. The other Central Asian countries did not want the Taliban to expand into Tajikistan either, and they urged Rhamon to agree to a peace settlement with the Islamists in Pamir.

Rahmon came under a lot of pressure, and finally, in 1997, he reached an agreement with the leader of the Islamist movement, Said Abdullah Nuri. The peace treaty was signed on July 1, 1997. Rahmon agreed to give at least thirty per cent of seats in the parliament to the opposition, as well as several important ministerial posts. This promise has gradually been diluted; today, the opposition has no ministerial posts, and the Islamic Renaissance Party[12] has only two of sixty-three seats in the parliament. Members of parliament no longer have much influence, as the president has, with increasing frequency, made unilateral decisions in recent years.

Qurghonteppa was the town that suffered most damage during the civil war. Tens of thousands of people were killed there, and entire neighbourhoods lay in ruins. Today there are no visible signs of the war, not even a modest memorial, only newly painted, four-storey Soviet apartment blocks, as far as the eye can see.

But the memories are everywhere.

"Civil war is the worst thing there is," said the caricature artist. He was a small man, almost bald, but with a trim, grey beard. His eyes were bright with laughter all the time. He often giggled at his own

12 The party was banned by the government in 2015.

jokes or the drawings he showed me, and there were a lot of them. Hundreds. On the wall behind him, between all the diplomas and honours, there were foxes, knights and princesses, all from the play he was about to put on. In addition to being the only caricature artist in Tajikistan, he was also a poet, actor, set designer and puppet-maker.

"Caricatures were more powerful during the Soviet era," he said, in excellent Russian. "Now I draw more everyday situations."

He pulls out a pen-and-ink drawing of a bureaucrat sitting at a table clutching a large rubber stamp. There's a coin slot on the top of his head.

"Every time someone puts in a coin, he stamps a document," Khairullo said, and laughed. Then he showed me a drawing of Father Christmas being interrogated at the Tajik border.

"If he can't provide an acceptable address, the border guards won't let him into the country. Not even Santa Claus can avoid our nit-picking bureaucrats!" Khairullo explodes with laughter.

In the Soviet Union, Khairullo was recognised as a great artist and invited to conferences all over the vast empire. In August 1991, he was a guest at a conference for artists in Moscow. While he was there, a new world was born. The caricature artist from Tajikistan witnessed the mass demonstrations in Red Square. The tanks. Yeltsin's passionate speeches. All flights back to Dushanbe were cancelled, and he did not manage to get a seat on an airplane until August 27. By then, there were demonstrations in the streets of Dushanbe as well. Two weeks later, on September 9, Tajikistan declared its independence.

"It was like a tsunami. Suddenly the Soviet Union was history."

At that point, Khairullo was leader of the Democratic Party in Khatlon province, and was also on the city council in Qurghonteppa. But he did not fight. Not even when the battles reached

Qurghonteppa in February 1993. There was shooting in the streets, and children and adults panicked and ran to dodge the bullets. Thousands of people fled the city.

"Then everything fell silent, and we went back," Khairullo said. "There were bodies everywhere. We had to make a new graveyard for the victims outside the city, because there wasn't room for them all in the old one."

Later that year, Khairullo and his wife and five children had to flee. For three to four months they hid in a barn by the Afghan border. Some five hundred to a thousand people were squeezed together under the same roof, neighbours, friends and relatives. The men and women slept separately, but everyone lay close together in order not to freeze. Fortunately, the snow was late that year and did not come until February. Then they had to move on. Khairullo's wife and children found a safe place nearby, but he had to go further, as he was so well known. Before they left Qurghonteppa, they had sold the car, as the money would come in handy. At the first road block that Khairullo came to, everyone from Qurghonteppa was shot – unless they could pay. Khairullo also managed to pay for a pass which allowed him to move freely through the various war zones.

He spent one year in hiding on a collective farm in Turkmenistan. Then he moved on to Ukraine, where he stayed with a friend for a few months. From there, he went to a small town in Russia, where he had some relatives. And stayed there until 1995. To make ends meet, he sold bananas at the local market. One day, a customer noticed that he sat drawing when he had nothing else to do. The customer came over and asked if he could draw Christ for him. So Khairullo did, and when the man saw the drawing, he burst into tears: "To think that such a great man, an artist, is sitting here selling bananas! If you were from here, you would be driving a Land Cruiser!"

The man bought the drawing for the equivalent of two weeks' banana sales.

"Even though I have seven or eight different jobs now, and I no longer sell bananas, I still can't afford a Land Cruiser," Khairullo said. He got up from his chair and pulled a leather-bound notebook out from a drawer. The book was full of tightly written verse. Each stanza was two lines, and each poem was illustrated with intricate pen-and-ink drawings. One of the illustrations was of a man sitting on the ground with his head between his knees. The man had no eyes, no mouth. Another showed a lion that had lost its battle with a forest fire: "The giant that lived and died." All the poems were from his time in exile in Russia. I asked if he could read a poem from the collection, but he shook his head.

"It's a closed chapter now."

When the war was over, Khairullo returned to his family in Qurghonteppa. It took him two years to restore his flat, which had been destroyed by one of the many fires started during the civil war. He was eventually employed by the theatre and was able to rebuild his life. His poems are now being set to music, he makes sculptures on commission and has been given several film roles.

"When I die, the city won't lose just one man, it'll lose many!" Khairullo said, and smiled. Then he was serious again. "As long as I'm useful to them, they leave me be. But I still haven't been given any honorary titles or medals, even though I've been drawing for thirty years. I'm probably on some blacklist."

Of the many caricatures that Khairullo drew in the Soviet era, only two survived the war. One is called "Human Evolution" and shows a man being awarded more and more medals. The more that he is weighed down by the honours, the more visible his dissatisfaction and the more evil he looks.

When I asked him what he thought of the current situation in

Tajikistan, he gave a fleeting smile and for the first time said nothing.

"A man who has been bitten by a snake will fear a coiled rope and cables," he said eventually. "A child who has burned himself on the teapot takes care not to do it again. I'm done with politics now. I never draw the president or any other politicians, I'm happy with everyday situations. There's enough inspiration for me there."

"Who will you vote for in the election?" I asked.

"I'll probably be working both Saturday and Sunday, so there won't be time to vote," he said promptly. "The most important thing now is that we have peace. It must never happen again. Civil war is the most terrible thing that can happen in a country."

THE GREAT GAME

*"Now I shall go far and far into the North,
playing the Great Game."*
Rudyard Kipling, *Kim*, 1901

The body of the helicopter vibrated as the rotors lifted us from the ground. The exterior had been refurbished and now wore the Tajik national colours. The interior, on the other hand, looked as though nothing had changed in the past fifty years. Around twenty of us were squeezed together on two long benches, our backs to the oval windows. The pilot sat on a stool in the cockpit. As there was only space for one person there, the co-pilot had to sit on the narrow bench with the rest of us. The door into the cockpit was open, so the two pilots could communicate.

It was a beautiful morning. The sun shone and there was barely a cloud in the sky, as is always the case when an airplane – or, in this case, a helicopter – flies from Dushanbe to Khorog. As the pilots have to fly without radar, they are dependent on good visibility over the mountains. And for the pilots to be given the go-ahead for landing, there has to be almost no wind. The slightest gust can be fatal, as the small aircraft that are used on the route fly at a maximum height of 4,200 metres, and many of the mountains they pass are higher than 5,000 metres. In other words, we were going to fly between the peaks and not over them. In the Soviet era, this was the only route on which Aeroflot pilots were awarded danger money, and not without reason.

Once we reached cruising altitude, the flat, green plains around

Dushanbe were soon replaced by barren mountains. We passed over peaks with what felt like only a few metres to spare. The co-pilot smiled happily. The mountains got steeper and steeper, and more jagged, and there were no man-made structures in sight, just brown rock face and snow-capped peaks as far as the eye could see. Most of the passengers were surprisingly indifferent to the magnificent panorama and took the opportunity to have a snooze. As one mountainside loomed dangerously close, the man sitting beside me opened his eyes. He glanced out of the window, then leaned over and shouted in my ear loud enough to be heard above the noise of the rotors: "AFGHANISTAN!"

How many have not paid with their lives attempting to tame and subjugate this country? If the Afghans are half as unyielding as the mountains they live in, it is a mission that is doomed from the outset. And yet so many have tried. The British made their first attempt in 1839. Dost Mohammad Khan had been reigning in Kabul since 1818. He had always been well disposed to the British, but in 1837 there were worrying reports that he was about to form an alliance with Russian envoys in Kabul. This was a cause for concern for the British, whose greatest fear was that Russia would invade India through Afghanistan. After some to-ing and fro-ing, the British decided to restore to the throne their previous ally, Shah Shujah, who had been exiled from Kabul thirty years earlier.

In December 1838, more than twenty thousand British and Indian soldiers set off from India. By the time they reached Kabul in April 1839, they had crossed mountain passes at four thousand metres and conquered several smaller Afghan towns without any great losses. Dost Mohammad was forced to flee, and Shah Shujah reclaimed the throne. But Shujah was not a strong leader, and in order to ensure that he stayed on the throne, the British had no choice but to stay in Kabul. The Afghans disliked the British presence intensely, and, in

November 1841, riots broke out. The British realised that they were no longer in control and decided to withdraw. On January 6, 1842, a party of sixteen thousand people from the British-Indian cantonments in Kabul set course for the British garrison in Jalalabad, 145 kilometres away. It was bitterly cold, and already on the first night there were deaths from hypothermia, while others suffered from frostbite. After three days, they reached the Khurd Kabul pass, where the Afghans were lying in ambush. The British and Indian soldiers did not stand a chance. Of the sixteen thousand that had left Kabul, only William Brydon, a British army surgeon, made it to the garrison in Jalalabad. On January 13, 1842, one week after the withdrawal from Kabul, he rode in, bloody and exhausted, on a badly wounded pony. The entire British-Indian column, with the exception of fewer than one hundred British soldiers who had been taken prisoner by the Afghans and a few hundred Indians who managed to escape, had been killed in the ambush.

A few months later, Shah Shujah was killed and Dost Mohammad reclaimed the throne.

There are a number of striking similarities between the British attempt to conquer Kabul and the Soviet Union's invasion in 1979, more than a century later. The Russians also wanted to install a regime-friendly leader in Kabul. As a result, fourteen thousand Soviet soldiers were killed in the nine-year war. More than one million Afghan civilians lost their lives and at least as many were forced to flee. When the Soviet tanks withdrew in 1989, they had achieved nothing.

There is a saying that only a fool learns from his own mistakes; the wise man learns from the mistakes of others. It appears that the British have not learned from their mistakes or the mistakes of others, as they were keen supporters of the N.A.T.O. invasion in 2001. After twelve years of fighting, thousands of people have been killed on both sides and the Taliban are gaining ground again, even in areas of Afghanistan where they previously had no influence.[13]

Through the window, I saw the sun rise between the steep mountains. The snowy peaks glittered in the morning sun. The landscape opened out below us and not long after we landed smoothly in Khorog, the regional capital of Pamir. As soon as the helicopter was on the ground, my fellow passenger sprang to life. Within minutes, there was no one to be seen on the runway.

I took my first step on Pamiri soil in the cool morning air. Pamir is often called "the Roof of the World" and stretches over an area of 120,000 square kilometres covering five countries: China, Pakistan, Kyrgyzstan, Afghanistan and Tajikistan, which is home to the greater part of the mountain range. Three of the mountains in Pamir are higher than seven thousand metres – the highest is Kongur in Xinjiang in China, at 7,719 metres. The highest mountain on the Tajik side is Ismail Samani Peak at 7,495 metres. This was once the highest mountain in the Soviet Union. From 1932 to 1962 the mountain was called Pik Stalina (Stalin Peak), and from 1962 until 1998 Pik Kommunizma (Communism Peak).

Until relatively recently, Pamir was one of the most inaccessible regions in the world. This remote region is now more open to adventurous visitors, as a result of changes in visa policy in the past few years.

The border between Tajikistan and Afghanistan is 1,206 kilometres long and follows the river Panj. Ergash, my local driver, took me south along the river. There were no soldiers or barriers to be seen. The border between the two countries is as leaky as a sieve: literally tons of cigarettes and opium are smuggled over the river every year,

13 Peace talks between the Afghan government and the Taliban are ongoing. The U.K. officially withdrew from Afghanistan in 2014, but still has troops in the country.

then on to Kyrgyzstan and Kazakhstan, and from there to Russia and finally Europe. Entire villages on either side of the border are dependent on smuggling. The network probably extends up into Tajik government echelons, which would help to explain both the luxurious cars and extravagant buildings in Dushanbe.

About mid-afternoon, we get to Ishkashim, the most southerly point in Tajikistan and our destination. I wander along the riverbank and find somewhere to sit in the shelter of some big boulders. There is not a cloud in the sky and the sunbeams twinkle on foaming waves. Old plastic bags in the grass dance on the gusts of wind.

This is where Russia's expansion into Central Asia stopped, here on the eastern banks of the Oxus river. On the other side, some fifty metres away, is Afghanistan. Even though the currents are strong, the water is so shallow that it would presumably be possible to wade across. The people on the other side speak the same language as those on this side of the river: Wakhi. For centuries, it was not the river that was the border between the peoples of Pamir, but the brown mountains that tower into the sky on either side of the valley. The current border is a result of the geopolitical power play between the Russian and British empires in the 1800s, each vying for supremacy in Central Asia.[vi]

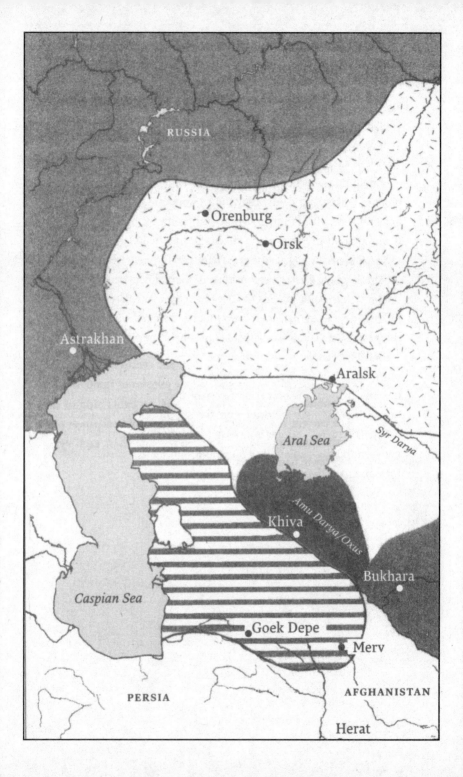

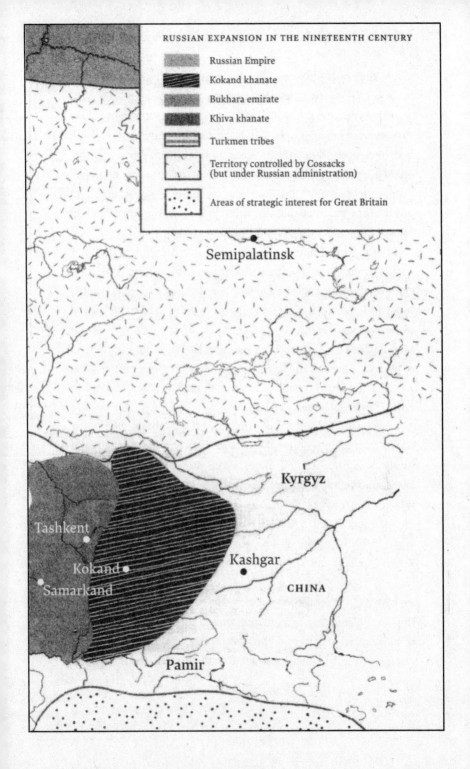

RUSSIAN EXPANSION IN THE NINETEENTH CENTURY

Russian Empire

Kokand khanate

Bukhara emirate

Khiva khanate

Turkmen tribes

Territory controlled by Cossacks
(but under Russian administration)

Areas of strategic interest for Great Britain

Semipalatinsk

Kyrgyz

Tashkent

Kokand
Samarkand

Kashgar

CHINA

Pamir

When the rivalry between Russia and Great Britain escalated in the latter half of the nineteenth century, there had long been rumours that Peter the Great had left a secret will. According to these rumours, the mighty tsar had urged his descendants, from his death bed, to do everything in their power to fulfil Russia's true mission: world domination. This could be achieved if the Russians conquered Constantinople and India. Even though no-one has been able to produce any evidence that this will ever existed, the story lived on for several generations after his death.

In 1807, when Napoleon suggested to Tsar Alexander I that they should combine forces and march south to India together, the suspicions of many an Englishman were confirmed: that Russia wanted to get its hands on India. Nothing ever came of the planned union of Russian and French troops, as Napoleon decided to march on Moscow instead – a campaign that was the beginning of the end of his rule. And even though the alliance with Napoleon never materialised, the British continued to fret about Russia's next move in Asia. The Great Game had started.

Lieutenant Arthur Conolly first coined the phrase "the Great Game" in 1839, to describe the struggle between Great Britain and Russia for domination and influence in Central Asia. The phrase was later immortalised in Rudyard Kipling's *Kim*. By that time, the game was in its final stages. The borders had been drawn and the balance of power had tipped in Russia's favour. But the game had just started when Lieutenant Conolly first got involved, and the khanates in Khiva, Bukhara and Kokand were still independent. Central Asia was seen as wild and dangerous territory; very few white men had ever been there, and they were clearly not welcome. Pioneers in the Great Game therefore often disguised themselves as holy men or horse merchants to avoid being recognised as Europeans, taking notes and drawing maps in secret. Conolly himself was most often disguised as a doctor or native. On the occasions he dressed up as a native, he made sure that he looked as poor as possible, so that bandits and robbers would pay him no attention. Many of the Turkmen tribes had specialised in attacking and robbing merchants, and foreign caravans were a popular target. In other words, the first British and Russian explorers exposed themselves to great personal risk in order to fill in the white spaces on the map. The greatest danger, however, was not hostile tribes or capricious khans, but nature itself. The cities and towns in Central Asia were protected by some of the highest mountain passes in the world and enormous deserts that were savagely hot in summer and could plummet in winter to -50°C.

In the winter of 1839–40, the Russians were unfortunate enough to experience just how bitterly cold it could get in the desert. They had made their first serious advance in Central Asia in more than a century. The initial attempt in 1717 had ended in disaster. At the start of the eighteenth century, the khan of Khiva had sent a letter to Peter the Great, asking for his protection against hostile tribes in the region. He promised that if the tsar was willing to do this, Khiva could become a Russian vassal state. Some years after he had received this request, Peter the Great decided to respond and sent an army of four thousand soldiers to Khiva. The army was led by Prince Alexander Bekovich-Cherkasky. It took the men all summer to cross the hot, unforgiving desert and they did not arrive in Khiva until August, by which time they had been on the move for four months. The khan welcomed the Russian soldiers, and explained to them that it was not possible to house and feed so many men in Khiva itself. He therefore asked if they could divide themselves up into five smaller units, and set up camp at specific locations outside the city. The prince, who wanted to be agreeable to the khan, did as he was asked. During the night, the unsuspecting Russians were

attacked and killed. Only a handful of soldiers survived the massacre. Fortunately for the khan, Peter the Great was busy trying
to conquer the Caucasus and therefore did not have the capacity to
send an army to wreak revenge. But the khan's deceitful attack was
not forgotten in St Petersburg.

In November 1839, 122 years later, the Russians attempted once
again to take Khiva. General Vasily Perovsky set off through the
Karakum Desert with an army of 5,200 soldiers and 10,000 camels.
The official reason was to free the hundreds of Russians who were
being held as slaves in Khiva. Perovsky hoped they would get there
before February, when the real winter cold set in.

Meanwhile, the British in India had got wind of the Russians'
plans. They immediately sent a delegation to Khiva to persuade the
khan to release the slaves, so the Russians had no reason to attack.
The last thing they wanted was the Russians to conquer more parts
of Central Asia, thus getting closer to India.

The first of the British emissaries was Captain James Abbott.[14]
He managed to get to Khiva unharmed, and was possibly the first
Englishman ever to do so. On his way through the desert, he had
seen several groups of captive men, women and children being
escorted to Khiva by Turkmen guards.

> The men are chained together by the throat at night, so that
> rest is scarcely possible, whilst the contact of the frozen iron
> with their skin must be torture. My heart is full of heaviness,
> when I think of all the heart-rending misery of which this
> system is the cause. Alas, he who enters Khiva abandons all
> hope, as surely as he who enters hell. His prison-house is

14 James Abbott founded the city Abbottabad in Pakistan. Abbottabad hit the
headlines in 2011 when Osama bin Laden, who had been hiding in the city for some
time, was killed there by U.S. special forces.

girdled with trackless deserts, whose sole inhabitants are the sellers in human flesh.[vii]

Abbott was made to feel welcome by the khan, who proved to be remarkably ill-informed about the world. The captain had great difficulties in getting him to understand that the British were not some insignificant tribe who were subjects of the Russian tsar. But he was also somewhat ignorant when it came to Russia: he thought that the Russian khanate was of a similar size to his own. And when the khan heard that the king of Great Britain was in fact a woman, there was no end to his questions: did they always crown a woman as king? Did the minsters also have to be women? How many cities did she rule over? How many cannons did she have? Would her husband become king if she got married?

In the meantime, General Perovsky had to admit to defeat by the weather gods. Winter came early that year, with the first major snowfalls in December. Soon the soldiers were wading through snow up to their waists, and the temperature kept falling. It turned out to be the worst winter in living memory. In January they lost on average a hundred camels a day. After three months, Perovsky admitted that they would never make it to Khiva and ordered a retreat. When they got back to the Russian garrison in Orenburg on the border of what is today Kazakhstan, a thousand soldiers had died. And of the ten thousand camels, only fifteen hundred survived. Not a shot had been fired.

When the khan heard that Perovksy and his army had turned back to Orenburg, he lost interest in the British and dismissed Abbott, who returned to India having achieved nothing, other than having given the khan of Khiva an elementary course in geography and politics.

The British general, Richmond Shakespear, went to Khiva the

same year and, unlike Abbott, managed to persuade the khan to release the Russian slaves, all 416 of them. He then escorted them to the Russian garrison in Orenburg, which was several weeks' march from Khiva. When Shakespear popped up in St Petersburg shortly afterwards, Tsar Nicholas I had no choice but to give a warm welcome to the saviour of the Russian slaves. In political circles, however, it was no secret that the tsar was furious that he no longer had an excuse to attack Khiva, which of course had been the intention of the British all along.

Shakespear's compatriot, Lieutenant Arthur Conolly, was to have less luck in the Great Game that he himself had named. In autumn 1841, he set out for Bukhara to rescue fellow countryman Charles Stoddart, who had been held prisoner by the emir for three years. Conolly was an experienced explorer and had many long expeditions under his belt. He not only hoped to persuade Nasrullah, the emir of Bukhara, to release Stoddart, but also to get him to agree to a peace treaty with the khanates of Khiva and Kokand. If the khanates in Central Asia stopped fighting each other and instead were united, they would have a greater chance of withstanding the Russians, who were on the move again in the north.

Stoddart had been taken prisoner when he went to meet the unpredictable emir on a similar mission three years earlier. His aim had been to persuade the emir to release the Russian slaves in Bukhara, so that there too the tsar would no longer have reason to attack. Emir Nasrullah, like the khan of Khiva, had no understanding of how big and powerful Russia was, and only a vague idea of the British empire. His response was to throw Stoddart into the city's infamous prison.

Conolly, who had been cordially welcomed by the khans in Khiva and Kokand, was not well received by the emir of Bukhara.

The emir accused him of being a spy, and it was not long before Conolly was put into the same prison as Stoddart. When the emir heard a year later that the Afghans had massacred the British colony in Afghanistan, he concluded that he need not fear the British. On June 17, 1842, Conolly and Stoddart were taken out of prison, forced to dig their own graves, and then beheaded in front of the emir's palace.

Following the catastrophic retreat from Afghanistan in January 1842, the British changed their strategy in Central Asia. "Masterly inactivity" was the new mantra. To do as little as possible, to wait and see what happened. By happy coincidence, the Russians adopted the same strategy, though for different reasons: they had more than enough on their hands with the rebels in the Caucasus, and, following their humiliating defeat in the Crimean War, there was no appetite for any further risks on foreign fronts. There was also an uprising in Poland, and social unrest in Russia had forced Tsar Alexander II to abolish serfdom, which in turn had angered the aristocracy.

In 1864, after half a century of fighting, the Russians finally managed to subjugate the Circassians, the last of their opponents in the Caucasus. Tsar Alexander II then once again turned his attention to the khanates of Central Asia. The import of cotton from the southern states of the U.S.A., on which Russia was so dependent, had stopped entirely as a result of the American Civil War. And he believed that the soil in the fertile Fergana Valley, which was part of the Kokand khanate, would be well suited to growing cotton.

The Russians advanced slowly. In winter 1864, they took a number of small rural border towns in Kokand. The khan protested and turned to the British for help, but they politely dismissed his request.

In anticipation of protest, the Russian imperial chancellor and minister of foreign affairs, Prince Gorchakov, wrote a shrewdly worded memorandum that was circulated to the European governments:

> The position of Russia in Central Asia is that of all civilised states which are brought into contact with half-savage nomad populations possessing no fixed social organisation. In such cases, it always happens that the more civilised state is forced, in the interests of the security of its frontiers and its commercial relations, to exercise a certain ascendancy over those whose turbulent and unsettled character make them undesirable neighbours. First, there are raids and acts of pillage to be put down. To put a stop to them, the tribes on the frontier have to be reduced to a state of more or less perfect submission. This result once attained, these tribes take to more peaceful habits, but are in their turn exposed to the attacks of the more distant tribes.
>
> The State is bound to defend them against these depredations, and to punish those who commit them. Hence the necessity of distant, costly and periodically recurring expeditions against an enemy whom his social organisation makes it impossible to seize. If, the robbers once punished, the expedition is withdrawn, the lesson is soon forgotten; its withdrawal is put down to weakness. It is a peculiarity of Asiatics to respect nothing but visible and palpable force; the moral force of reason and of the interests of civilisation has as yet no hold upon them. The work has then always to be done over again from the beginning.
>
> In order to put a stop to this state of permanent disorder, fortified posts are established in the midst of these hostile tribes, and an influence is brought to bear upon them

which reduces them by degrees to a state of more or less forced submission. But soon beyond this second line other still more distant tribes come in their turn to threaten the same dangers and necessitate the same measures of repression. The State thus finds itself forced to choose one of two alternatives, either to give up this endless labour and to abandon its frontier to perpetual disturbance, rendering all prosperity, all security, all civilisation an impossibility, or, on the other hand, to plunge deeper and deeper into barbarous countries, where the difficulties and expenses increase with every step in advance.

Such has been the fact of every country which has found itself in a similar situation. The United States of America, France in Algeria, Holland in its colonies, England in India – they have all been irresistibly forced, less by ambition than imperious necessity, into this onward march, when the greatest difficulty is knowing where to stop.[viii]

Gorchakov did not spell it out, but intimated that Russia would stop at the Kokand border: "We find ourselves in the presence of a more solid, less unsettled and better organised state, fixing for us with geographical precision that point at which we must halt."

When Gorchakov was on later occasions confronted with Russia's expansion into Central Asia, which soon went well beyond what was indicated in the memorandum, he often laid the blame on adventurous generals. He claimed that they sometimes acted on their own initiative and exceeded the tsar's orders. And, in fact, that is precisely what happened when the Russians annexed Tashkent a year later, in 1865.

At the time, Tashkent had one hundred thousand inhabitants and was the wealthiest city in Central Asia, thanks to a combination of fertile soil and extensive trading with Russia following Russia's conquest of Kazakhstan in the 1700s. In spring 1865, yet another conflict blew up between the Bukhara emirate and the Kokand khanate, which included Tashkent. General Mikhail Chernyayev, the commander of the frontier garrison by Kokand, decided to take the opportunity and attack before the emir's army had reached the city walls. There was, however, one major problem: Chernyayev's company was only 1,300 strong. And inside Tashkent's city walls, there were at least 30,000 soldiers, ready to defend their city. In St Petersburg, the general opinion was that it was too risky to attack with such a small army, so the tsar sent a telegram with instructions not to attack. Chernyayev must have known what the telegram said, and chose not to open the envelope. He presumed that the tsar would forgive him if he succeeded.

When Chernyayev's small army reached Tashkent, they discovered that soldiers from Bukhara had got there before them and taken over the defence of the city. Any hopes they may have had of resolving the conflict with the help of the city's many Russian-friendly merchants were now crushed. And they could not turn back, as that would be the same as admitting defeat, which would then send the wrong message to the Central Asian peoples. Chernyayev had no choice but to win the battle for Tashkent.

They attacked in the early morning of June 15. A couple of hundred men were sent to another part of the wall in a feigned attack to distract attention. Chernyayev had had the wheels of the gun carriages covered with felt so they could be moved as silently as possible to where they intended to launch the surprise attack. Just outside the city wall, they came across a couple of men who had clearly come out through a secret passage. Chernyayev's soldiers then forced the men to show them where it was, thus some of the soldiers were able to enter the city through the secret passage. The rest climbed over the wall with the help of ladders. The emir's soldiers were busy trying to fend off the feigned attack on the other side of the city, and did not notice until it was too late that the Russians had managed to get in.

Even though they were inferior in terms of numbers, the Russians were better trained and had more powerful weapons than the local soldiers. The following day, the inhabitants of Tashkent surrendered. Only twenty-five Russian soldiers were killed in the daring attack, which was successful, against all odds.

As expected, Chernyayev was celebrated as a hero in his home country. Not only did the tsar forgive him for defying orders, he awarded him the highest honours.

Not long after, the skilled and experienced General Konstantin von Kaufman was appointed as the first "General Governor of Turkestan", based in Tashkent. The days of the free khanates truly were numbered, even though the Russians declared that they had no plans to conquer any more regions.

Three years after the annexation of Tashkent, the Russians got the excuse they had been waiting for. The emir of Bukhara had been rash enough to gather his troops in Samarkand, which was within his emirate, with the aim of forcing the Russians out of Turkestan. General Kaufman immediately sent 3,500 men to meet them, as many as he could do without himself. The emir's army was plagued by internal conflict and, to the Russians' astonishment, surrendered within a day. And so Samarkand, the jewel of Central Asia, became Russian territory on May 2, 1868. Shortly after, Bukhara also fell. The emir remained on the throne, but in reality was nothing more than a Russian vassal.

The following year, in 1869, the Russians started, in secret, to build a fort on the Caspian Sea. They had learned from their mistakes in 1717 and 1840, and realised that they needed a more strategically located base than Orenburg, in order to conquer Khiva, which lay much further west than the other khanates. The fort was named Krasnovodsk. In 1873, five years after the taking of Tashkent, General Kaufman marched towards Khiva with an army of thirteen thousand men. The khan knew that he did not stand a chance against Russia's modern army. He fled, and, on May 28, 1873, the once so rebellious Khiva khanate finally became part of the Russian empire, almost without bloodshed.

Two years later, in summer 1875, the people of Kokand revolted against the Russians. This gave Kaufman the justification he needed to gain control over the last remaining towns and cities in the fertile Fergana Valley. In March 1876, the Kokand khanate was formally abolished and incorporated into Russian Turkestan.

In no more than a decade, Russia had conquered three major khanates in Central Asia, covering an area half the size of the U.S.A. However, there was still the problem of the wild Turkmen tribes, who, according to Prince Gorchakov's memorandum, were the very reason that the Russians had felt obliged to penetrate further and further into Central Asia.

In 1879, the Russians launched an attack on the Turkmen fort Geok Tepe, which was one of the Turkmen tribes' main bases. The Russians had only fought with the khans' poorly disciplined armies in recent years, and were not prepared for the Turkmens' combat skills. The furious Turkmens pursued the Russian soldiers as they fled, and they only just managed to escape. The battle at Geok Tepe ended in the most humiliating defeat for the Russians since 1717.

"It is a peculiarity of Asiatics to respect nothing but visible and palpable power," Prince Gorchakov wrote in his memorandum. A little under two years later, the Russians attacked again. And this time they were going to win. The 7,000-strong army was led by General Mikhail Skobelev, who was known as "the White General", as he always wore a white uniform in battle. Skobelev was also known for his brutality and lack of scruples. Inside the city walls, ten thousand Turkmen warriors and forty thousand civilians stood ready. The Turkmens had clearly expected another attack, as they had reinforced the walls in the meantime. The Russian bullets did not even graze the Turkmens' simple but solid fortress of dried clay. But Skobelev knew what to do: he ordered the soldiers to dig a tunnel. It is said that he himself stood at the start of the tunnel and timed the different digging teams. If the soldiers did good work, the officer in charge was given champagne and vodka. If, on the other hand, the work was too slow, the officer was physically punished in front of his men.

On January 24, 1881, the tunnel was finished, and two tons of dynamite were placed under the fortress walls. Hundreds of Turkmens were killed in the resulting explosion. The Russian soldiers stormed the fort while everyone was still in shock. The Turkmens quickly realised that all was lost and fled as fast as they could. But instead of letting them go, the Russians pursued them on horseback. For three days on end, Skobelev's soldiers plundered, raped and killed. The soldiers killed everyone they came across; not even children or old people were spared. As many as eight thousand of those who fled were killed, and inside the fort, a further 6,500 were massacred.

The Russians lost only 268 men.

Only Merv remained, the famous Turkmen capital. In order to impress the Turkmen tribal leaders, representatives were invited to the crowning of Tsar Alexander III in St Petersburg in 1883. There they could see with their own eyes how enormous, modern and rich the capital of the Russian empire was. When Russia then started to put military pressure on Merv a year later, and also seized one of the neighbouring cities, the tribal leaders decided, after much discussion, that it was best to submit voluntarily to the Russians. The massacre at Geok Tepe was still fresh in their minds and they realised that their oppressor was simply too big. And so the once powerful city fell into Russian hands without a drop of blood being spilled.

The British, who had watched with a certain stoicism the Russians conquer one khanate after another, were now worried. Merv was strategically placed on the road to Herat and Kandahar in Afghanistan, so not far from India. The tsar's diplomats appeased the British by telling them that the Turkmen themselves had wanted to become part of the Russian empire. They had wanted to end the anarchy, so they could enjoy the benefits of civilisation. And what could the British say to that? They had themselves given similar explanations to justify their presence in their own colonies.

"The greatest difficulty is to know when to stop," to quote Prince Gorchakov again. In order to smooth ruffled feathers, it was decided that representatives from Great Britain and Russia would meet in autumn 1884 to agree on the border between the Russian empire and Afghanistan, which was so important to Britain as a buffer state to India. The Russians kept finding new excuses to postpone the meeting, however, so it never took place. When winter started to loosen its hold early on in 1885, the Russian forces crossed the Oxus river and laid siege to the oasis town of Panjdeh, which was in Afghanistan. It was in clear contravention of all agreements, and the British were enraged. The Russian forces did not want to be accused of firing the first shot, so did nothing other than wait, patiently. On March 31, one of the Afghan soldiers shot and wounded a Russian horse, if we are to believe Lieutenant Alikhanov, who led the attack. This was what the Russians had been waiting for. More than eight hundred Afghans died in the fighting that ensued. And so Panjdeh also became part of the Russian empire.

Never before in the Great Game had Russia and Great Britain, the two greatest empires in the world, been so close to war. Fortunately, the emir of Afghanistan, Abdur Rahman, took the Russian annexation of Panjdeh lightly and chose to see the whole thing as an insignificant border tussle.

The planned border negotiations between Russia and Great Britain did not take place until 1887. The Russians kept Panjdeh, but only when they yielded a strategic mountain pass to the Afghans. It was also agreed that the Afghan border would follow the Oxus river, with the exception of Panjdeh, and the Russians promised to respect the border forthwith. Even though people on the British side were sceptical, the Russians kept their promise. Almost a century passed before Russian soldiers once again crossed the Oxus.

The only area in Central Asia where the borders were not yet fixed was the sparsely populated Pamir plateau, where Russia, China, British India and Afghanistan met, several thousand metres above sea level. The British were nervous about what the Russians might do. From Pamir, it would be very easy to cross India's poorly manned northern border. The Russians were busy building railways through the former khanates, which would facilitate the movement of military forces. A British delegation was sent from India to Kashgar in China in order to persuade the Chinese to annex part of Pamir, thus ensuring it would not fall into Russian hands. And the Chinese were easily persuaded, but local Russian spies understood what was going on, and made sure that Russia got there first.

In summer 1891, a unit of around four hundred Russian Cossacks invaded Pamir from the north. According to the Russian authorities, it was not an invasion, the Cossacks were simply investigating what the Chinese and Afghans were up to there, so they could report back to Moscow. Not long after, two British officers were accused by the Russian soldiers of being on Russian territory, and expelled from Pamir. This provoked a diplomatic crisis, and the Russians quietly withdrew. The Russian empire was, meanwhile, struggling with crop failure, famine and a financial downturn, and Tsar Alexander III could ill afford to fall out with Great Britain.

In the following year, 1892, the Russians returned, just as quietly as they had withdrawn. And over the course of that year, they built a garrison in the Pamir mountains.

In 1895, delegations from the two empires met once again to discuss the borders in Central Asia. The British had realised there was little they could do to prevent the Russians from annexing Pamir, as, in effect, they already had. Their main concern now was to plug the hole between Pamir and British India, so that the two empires would not have a direct border. They therefore asked Abdur Rahman, the Afghan emir, to add the southern end of the Wakhan Corridor to Afghanistan's territory. The corridor runs like a long finger between today's Tajikistan and Pakistan. Abdur Rahman did not need to be asked twice. Even though the Afghan side of the Wakhan Corridor was only a few kilometres wide in some places, Afghanistan was now a buffer, however narrow, between Pamir and India. The people who lived on the banks of the river, and who suddenly found themselves on either side of a national border, were not, of course, consulted.

So at the end of a power play that had lasted almost a century, the Russian empire had finally reached its outer limit in Central Asia. Their expansion south had ended. The Russians had, to a great extent, achieved what they wanted to, and were the winning party. At the start of the century, Russia had been two thousand kilometres away from British India, and now the distance in some places was less than twenty kilometres.

Russia turned her sights further east. The Trans-Siberian railway was being built, so claims were made on territories in Mongolia and a big port was built on Korean territory. The Japanese kept an anxious eye on developments, and in 1904 they launched an attack. The war with Japan was catastrophic for Russia, and indirectly led to the revolution and downfall of the tsar thirteen years later.

Following the bitter defeat by Japan, Russia entered a secret pact with Great Britain whereby the two empires divided their areas of interest in Central Asia. It was decided that Tibet was within China's sphere of influence, whereas Afghanistan was within Great Britain's. In return, the British promised not to interfere in Central Asia, and to advise Afghanistan to do the same. Persia was divided into three zones according to Russian and British Indian interests. On August 31, 1907, the parties signed the Anglo-Russian Convention.

The friendship between the two great powers was short-lived, however. The Bolsheviks, who took power in Russia in 1917, regarded the Anglo-Russian Convention as worthless. Lenin shared Peter the Great's dreams of world domination and of conquering India. But despite these ambitions, the borders in Central Asia did not change in Lenin's lifetime. Neither the Soviet Union's nine-year occupation of Afghanistan, nor N.A.T.O.'s twelve-year fight against the Taliban, have resulted in Afghanistan's northern border moving by so much as a millimetre. The border today is as it was in 1895 and follows the Oxus river, except through the area around Panjdeh. Panjdeh, which very nearly triggered a major war in its time, now lies in Turkmenistan. Panjdeh, or Serhetabat, as the little town is called today, was the southernmost point of the Soviet Union.

The grey river water is cold. I dip my toes in and quickly pull them out. On the other side, the mountains rise up sharply into the blue sky. There are a few simple houses, which are well camouflaged in the brown, sandy earth. A couple of men dressed in light tunics trundle along patiently behind an ox, and a woman in a red tunic stands bent over in a small field. A narrow road, apparently brand

new, cuts into the terrain. As we drove in from Khorog, I saw only
one car on the Afghan side – a white jeep with the logo of an international aid organisation on the side.

The village on the other side is called the same as the one on the
Tajik side, Ishkashim. The two are divided by a river and a century.
There is a bridge over to the other side, and, once a week, there is a
joint market. Otherwise, there is no contact between these people
who once were the same.

I stand and make my way over the remains of picnics and broken
vodka bottles, and wander back up to the straighter, more ordered
streets of Ishkashim. There are an astonishing number of official
buildings on the main street, given that only two thousand people
live here. There is a town hall, a community centre, a health centre,
and various council administration buildings. It was presumably
of particular importance for the Soviet authorities to build their
socialist paradise here, on the peripheries of the empire, where the
contrasts would be visible. A bust of Lenin still stands outside
the small town hall. An old man with a hunched back notices me
standing there looking at the bust, and comes over.

"Here stands Vladimir Ilyich Lenin," he declares. "Our *beloved*
Lenin," he adds, with respect, and runs his hand over the communist
leader's head.

A giant poster of Tajikistan's president, Emomali Rahmon, has
been hung up opposite Lenin, to keep the balance.

On my way back to the guesthouse, I pass the school. The
pupils are doing gymnastics in the playground. An energetic teacher
ensures that the boys do enough press-ups. The boys wear white
shirts and black trousers, and the girls wear white blouses and black
skirts, as is still the rule throughout the former U.S.S.R.

On the other side of the river, there is a shortage of schools and
teachers, and many children become goat herders instead of going

to school. The Wakhan Corridor has generally been a peaceful part of Afghanistan, untouched by the wars and unrest, but recently the Taliban started to move in here too. There are fears and concerns in Tajikistan about what will happen when the U.S. and other N.A.T.O. forces withdraw. Will the Taliban try to cross the river? And if they do, who can stop them?

THE LAND AT THE FOOT OF THE SUN

High up on the Pamir plateau, surrounded by an other-worldly landscape of bare rocky outcrops and rounded peaks, and lakes with the bluest water you can imagine, lies the village of Bulunkul. All kinds of metallic overtones are visible in the earth. Some of the outcrops are green, other peaks more blue, in some places the earth is rusty red and in others golden yellow. Forty-six families, that is to say 407 people, scrape together a living in this lunar landscape, at the end of the road, with no mobile or Internet coverage, miles from the nearest village.

I was given lodgings by the school director, who ran a guest-house. Despite the biting wind and barren surrounds, everyone in Bulunkul was always smiling. At one end of the small village, wedding preparations were under way. Tipsy men were busy chopping meat and mounds of onions in the middle of the improvised outdoor kitchen.

"Bulunkul is the coldest place in Tajikistan," the school director's husband boasted. "The record is -53°C."

"How do people manage to live here in winter?"

"We're used it. We just put on a coat."

Pamir accounts for more than a third of the territory of Tajikistan, and yet only a couple of hundred thousand people live here. And it is not hard to understand why. The climate in Pamir is one of the harshest in the world, with long, cold, snowy winters. The soil is poor and the landscape barren. Most of the plateau lies at between three to five thousand metres above sea level, and is surrounded by some of the highest mountains in the world. A lot of people who come here suffer from altitude sickness, owing to the thin mountain air, especially if they do not take time to acclimatise – Pamir is not called the roof of the world for no reason. Marco Polo, who crossed the plateau on his way to China in the thirteenth century, described the journey as a strenuous enterprise: "The plain is called Pamir, and you ride across it for twelve days together, finding nothing but a desert with no habitation or any green things, so that travellers are obliged to carry with them whatever they have need of. The region is so lofty and cold that you do not even see any birds flying. And I must notice also that because of this great cold, fire does not burn so brightly, nor give out so much heat as usual, nor does it cook food so effectually."[ix]

Cows, goats and ordinary sheep cannot cope with the tough climate, so most farmers keep yaks. The Marco Polo sheep, a hardy, wild breed, has adapted to the barren terrain; other than that, not many animals live up here. The sheep breed was first described by Marco Polo, and therefore named after him: "[Their] horns are a good six palms in length. From these horns the shepherds make great bowls to eat from, and they use the horns also to enclose folds for their animals at night." Today, the Marco Polo sheep is on the brink of becoming an endangered species. Tourists who still want to hunt the sheep have to pay at least 25,000 dollars per expedition.

No-one knows what the word "Pamir" actually means. The name first appears in Chinese travelogues around the seventh century and then again in Marco Polo's travel notes some six hundred years later. One theory is that it derives from the old Persian word *bom-ir*, land of the Aryans. Several nineteenth-century explorers came across this theory and believed that Pamir must have been the cradle of the Aryan race, as so many of the inhabitants here do not resemble other Asians, but instead are tall, fair and blue-eyed. Another theory is that the name comes from *pa-i mir*, "land at the foot of the mountain peaks". And a third is that it comes from the Turkish word for desert or plateau. But the most poetic theory is that it has its roots in the old Persian expression *pa-i mehr*: "land at the foot of the sun". Looking around Bulunkul took no time at all. The school director's tall, unmarried brother-in-law showed me the school. It was built in the 1950s, like most of the other houses in the village. Despite being one of the most isolated villages in Pamir, which in turn was one of the most isolated regions in the Soviet Union, the Communists also made their presence known here. As well as the school, they built the weather station where Tajikistan's lowest ever temperature was recorded. The locals were organised into collective farms, as they were everywhere else, and modern equipment was sent out from the Soviet tractor factories to make agriculture more effective. When the Soviet Union collapsed, all the Russians left, taking much of the technical know-how with them, as well as the supply of equipment and spare parts. The local people who were left behind had forgotten how to farm in the traditional way. Everything had to be learned again.

The classrooms were small, with only four or five desks in each. The walls in the corridors were decorated with posters from various aid organisations.

"The children get school lunches from the U.N.'s World Food Programme," the brother-in-law told me. "They also give us flour, oil and potatoes. As we're so high above sea level, it is difficult to get anything to grow. Our yaks give us meat, yoghurt, butter, milk and clothes, but everything else has to come from outside."

He took me to a small greenhouse where tomato plants peeped out from rows of pots.

"Another organisation built this greenhouse for us, so now we have cucumbers and tomatoes as well." He frowned, thought hard. "It might have been the Aga Khan Foundation, I can't remember."

"Aga Khan?" I looked at him, surprised.

"Yes, he is our religious leader. We're not Sunni Muslims like the Tajiks, here in Pamir, we're Ismailites, which is a branch of Shia Islam. The Aga Khan, our leader, lives in Switzerland and has lots of money. His foundation has helped the people in the Wakha Valley, and us here in Pamir, with all kinds of things: money, schools, health services, roads . . . Without their help it would impossible to live here. The government doesn't care about us."

"Do the Ismailites practise a stricter form of Islam?"

"Not at all!" The brother-in-law laughed so loudly he had to put his hand in front of his mouth. "Other Muslims pray five times a day, whereas we only pray once or twice. It's enough. We don't fast during Ramadan, as the climate here is too harsh. It's not good to walk around in the mountains all day when the sun's beating down and you haven't had anything to eat or drink. And the Aga Khan believes in education. That's the key, he says. Girls, in particular, should be educated, so they can get a job and not just sit at home with the children. The Ismailites are modern Muslims!"

Later on in the evening, once the yaks had been milked and were safely in the byre, when the yoghurt had been set to ferment and the butter had been churned, the school director finally had time to sit down and chat with me. She smiled all the time, and her smile lit up the room. Unlike most of the others I had met in the village, she looked younger than her years. Her voice was soft and gentle, almost a whisper, though she was not talking quietly. Her brother-in-law had told me that the children used to beg her to keep teaching them, even after they had moved on to a new class and a new teacher. She seldom had the heart to say no.

"I don't like towns," she said. "And nor do my children. After a week in town, they ask if we can go home. They miss the fresh air, nature, home-made food. We make everything ourselves here, we don't buy things. People live from what their yaks can give them and the fish in the lakes. There aren't many jobs here, so a lot of our young men go to Russia for a few years to save up some money. Then they come back." She smiled warmly.

"Isn't it hard on their wives and children who are left here alone?" I asked. The school director was the most positive person I had met on my travels, and for some reason I found it hard to believe her. Everywhere I had gone, I had heard complaints and grumbles about the challenges of daily life, or, as was the case in Turkmenistan, parroted praise of their wonderful president. Surely living here was not *that* idyllic – three thousand metres above sea level, miles from the neighbouring village, surrounded by soil where nothing would grow and frozen, snowy winters when the temperature dropped to minus fifty?

"It's not difficult at all," the school director said, with a smile. "Everyone helps each other. For example, my husband was away for five months last winter. And all the neighbours helped me with my practical tasks and looking after the guests and things like that."

"In other words, you live like true communists?"

She nodded and laughed.

"I work all the time," she said. "If I have quarter of an hour to spare, I knit or sew. I only rest when I'm sleeping. On Sundays I do the laundry. And I never have time to watch T.V., but that doesn't matter, I like being busy."

She is from Pamir, but from a village further to the west. She moved to Bulunkul seventeen years ago, when she got married.

"My parents found a husband for me," she says. "That's how it's done here."

"And are you happy with him?"

"Oh, yes!" She beamed, brightening the room. "And even if I wasn't happy with him, I would have stayed. For us Ismailites, the first marriage is the only true marriage. If the first doesn't work, the second and third won't work either."

We went together to the wedding celebrations at the other end of the village. The small room was packed with people and the music was playing at full volume. The children were crying with their hands over their ears. A young man in a leather jacket sat down beside me. He told me that he was recently divorced and looking for a new wife.

No-one in Bulunkul paid any attention to the president's wedding rules, and the party carried on into the small hours, but we did not stay that long. The music echoed in our ears as we wandered through the village on the short way back to the school director's house. There was no moon; it was so dark that we could scarcely see the wall in front of us. Suddenly she stopped.

"Look," she said, tilting her head back. "Isn't it beautiful?"

I looked up at the sky. I have never seen so many stars as I did there, on the roof of the world. They were strewn across the black night sky like luminous grains of sand.

—⁓—

After a long winter at the Pamirsky Post, the Russians' first military garrison in Pamir, Captain Serebrennikov was fed up. In summer 1894, he wrote about his melancholy in his diary: ". . . we were all so tired of the vast, monotonous Pamir, which would be the ideal landscape for a pessimist, should he ever need it. In fact, I cannot think of a more fitting image of the most extreme melancholy than a pessimist reading Schopenhauer in Pamir. It is a place without hope."[x]

Russian soldiers were posted here until 2005, long after Tajikistan had become an independent country, to help guard the border with China. When they withdrew, having been there for more than a century, they took with them all hope of a future and fixed monthly wages for the inhabitants of Murgab, as Pamirsky Post is now called. Murgab is still a godforsaken place. The contrast to Bulunkul, which is only a few hours' drive away, could not be greater. Murgab lies in the middle of the Pamir plateau, at 3,650 metres above sea level. Around seven to eight thousand people live here. They are all poor and many of them are sick and alcoholics, but they stay here because there is nowhere else to go. If they could, they would have left a long time ago. Gone to Dushanbe, to Kyrgyzstan, to Russia. Anywhere is better than here.

The buildings are low and miserable. Only a very few people have bothered to paint or whitewash the grey concrete walls. A long row of sparsely furnished containers constitutes the town's bazaar, the shopping street and local drinking holes. There are very few cafés in the town, and they too are in containers, done out with narrow benches, churlish waitresses and gleaming bottles. As evening falls, the streets are filled with blue exhaust from the generators. The smoke blends with the dust that swirls up from the roads as cars pass, which then takes a long time to settle. Women cover their faces with the edges of their headscarves to protect themselves from the poisonous air. They look like Ninja soldiers as they walk along wrapped in colourful cotton fabrics, with only a small opening for their eyes. Even though it is still some hours to the border, one is in many ways already in Kyrgyzstan. The indigenous faces here are very different from the soft Persian features of the Tajiks, and the people are much shorter than the tall Pamirs. They have high, defined cheekbones and Mongolian eyes. They are Kyrgyz.

It is not possible to see the stars through the thick layer of smoke and dust. Night falls quickly and there is no street lighting. There is no electricity supply to Murgab in the evenings, hence all the generators and the stench of diesel and petrol that settles over the town. It is every man for himself. The electricity supplied by the generators is not strong enough to recharge mobiles or run other electrical appliances, it is just enough to make the bare light bulbs glow faintly inside the houses.

"I'm going to move to Kyrgyzstan as soon as I can," muttered Ibrahim, the proprietor of the guesthouse where I stayed. "There's no future here."

Ibrahim's niece is to be married the same evening, and, before I know it, I am a guest at yet another wedding. I am shown into the rectangular room. People are sitting squeezed together along the walls. The women, who are all wearing scarves, sit along one side, and the men, who are all wearing high, white felt hats, sit on the other side. Unbelievable amounts of food are arranged on a cloth in the middle. Hundreds of round loaves of bread, small dishes with different salads, jam, fruit and juice. A short while after, the hosts appear carrying large dishes of pilaf rice. Then a soup is served. When the soup has been eaten, big bowls of mutton fat are sent round. People help themselves in silence and eat in silence. When the fat is finished, an oval plate full of mutton is passed round. People pile up their plates with meat. This is followed by a dish of home-made butter. The guests help themselves, putting a generous portion of butter next to the meat. The young woman beside me does not let me pass on the butter until I have taken a large helping myself.

"I don't think I can eat that much butter," I whisper.

The young woman just laughs. She is the only Tajik in the room and the only woman without a headscarf. She tells me in a whisper that she is the bride's best friend. She is not yet married herself, even though she is thirty, but it is her turn next. The wedding will be in November. I congratulate her, but she shakes her head sadly in response. "I'm a qualified nurse, but he has no qualifications. After the wedding, I have to move to Ishkashim, to my brother-in-law's."

"Are you not going to stay with your husband?"

"He'll go back to Russia as soon as I'm pregnant."

"But he'll come back and visit you regularly, won't he?"

She shakes her head.

"At least you'll have your freedom," I say, trying to comfort her.

A quick, firm shake of the head again.

"His brother will keep an eye on me. It's not going to be easy, and it'll be lonely. My parents don't even like him. They say he drinks too much. But he's got a good personality. He's a good man. And it's not that easy to find good men around here."

"But why do you want to marry a man who spends all his time in Russia?"

"There's no-one else here."

"Can't you go to Russia with him?"

"No, we can't all leave. Someone has to stay."

A boy comes into the room carrying a pile of plastic bags. In the blink of an eye, the mounds of meat and butter disappear into the bags. The generous offerings of food on the cloth also disappear into the bags. Then the guests stand up and march out, each with a plastic bag in their hand.

The next day, the same ritual is repeated with just as much food and as many dishes, but in another house. This time it is the neighbour who is hosting. When I leave in the afternoon, there are still a number of feasts in prospect. The groom's family, friends and colleagues must be welcomed properly. In some Kyrgyz families, these feasts go on for weeks, with a constant stream of new guests:

friends, acquaintances, new and old neighbours, close and distant relatives. Everyone is welcome.

Full of bread, jam, pilaf and green tea, I haul myself up into the passenger seat. As Ergash pulls out onto the M41, the jeep leaves behind a trail of dust. We turn onto the Pamir highway and head for the Kyrgyzstan border. On top of my rucksack are four plastic bags full of fresh mutton and newly churned butter.

LET'S FIGHT CORRUPTION TOGETHER!

A fence cuts across the flat, dusty landscape. The posts are two metres high and exactly two metres apart. Between the posts, the barbed wire has been put up in a carefully designed pattern so that not even a fox could sneak through. This meticulous barbed wire fence stretches for kilometres. It must have been an enormous job to put it up! Post by post, metre by metre, at four thousand metres above sea level, with the bitter winds of Pamir at your back and whirling desert sand in your eyes. The most ironic thing about the fence is that it was not erected until the 1980s, when it had been agreed that a buffer zone of fifty metres should be established between the Soviet Union and the Chinese border. Only a few years before it collapsed, the Soviet Union was still building for eternity, and was passionate about securing every single metre of the border, not so much to keep other people out as to keep its own people in.

The sight of this painstaking buffer zone brings to mind one of the most fascinating sections in the Polish foreign correspondent Ryszard Kapuściński's great work, *Imperium*:

> The surface of the Imperium measures more than twenty-two million square kilometres, and its continual borders are longer than the equator and stretch for forty-two thousand kilometres. Keeping in mind that wherever it is technically possible, these borders were and are marked with thick coils

of barbed wire . . . and that this wire, because of the dreadful
climate, quickly deteriorates and therefore must often be
replaced across hundreds, no, thousands, of kilometres, one
can assume that a significant portion of the Soviet metallur-
gical industry is devoted to producing barbed wire. . . . If one
were to multiply all this by the number of years that the
Soviet government has been in existence, it would be easy
to see why, in the shops of Smolensk or Omsk, one can buy
neither a hoe nor a hammer, never mind a knife or spoon:
such things could simply not be produced, since the necessary raw materials were used up in the manufacture of barbed
wire. And that is still not the end of it! After all, tons of this
wire had to be transported by ships, railway, helicopters,
camels, dog teams to the furthest, most inaccessible corners
of the Imperium, and then it had to be unloaded, uncoiled,
cut and fastened. . . . It is also easy to imagine telephone
calls from officials in Moscow to their subordinates in the
field, telephone calls characterised by a constant and vigilant
concern expressed in the question: "Are you all properly wired
in?" And so instead of building themselves houses and hospitals, instead of repairing the continually failing sewerage and
electrical systems, people were for years occupied (although
fortunately not everyone!) with the internal and external,
local and national, wiring of their Imperium.[xi]

There are no longer any telephone calls from Moscow. The fences
are falling into disrepair. In some places, the barbed wire has been
cut, and in other places gates have been forced and left wide open.
The Tajik authorities have clearly given up trying to keep strangers
out and their own people in. In many ways, life was perhaps easier
before, when orders, fence posts and barbed wire were sent from

Moscow. Now it is the migrant workers' illegal wages, also sent from Moscow, that keep the country afloat.

The Tajik border post with Kyrgyzstan was so modest that I thought it was just another checkpoint. A sleepy narcotics dog sniffed our wheels without much enthusiasm. The border guards were accommodated in a small hut where there was just enough room for four bunks and a table. Three of the soldiers were playing cards. When they noticed me, they woke the fourth guard, who crept down from one of the upper bunks and pulled on some clothes, then searched around for two notebooks. I was invited to sit down on one of the bunks – there were no chairs in the room – and was offered some lukewarm tea, while the young soldier wrote my passport information down in very neat writing.

"How long do you have to stay here?" I said.

"Two years," he replied grimly.

As soon as we were on the other side, the landscape changed. The ground became greener and the mountainside redder. The peaks were covered in glittering snow.

The Kyrgyz border station was much grander. On the other side of the barrier stood five or six brand new brick buildings. Ergash, my driver, sounded the horn impatiently, but no-one came out to open the barrier. There was no-one to be seen. It was only when I got out of the car and passed the barrier on foot that anything happened. A fat customs officer waddled out and demanded to see our passports and vehicle registration papers. Ergash popped a Kyrgyz 200-som banknote in his passport (equivalent to a couple of pounds or so) and handed it over to the fat customs officer. He took the banknote and handed back the passport.

"I drive through here every week, so I have a good relationship with them," Ergash told me in English, so the customs officer would not understand.

We were shown over to the passport controller's house. On a sticker by the door, it said: "Let's fight corruption together and work towards a better Kyrgyzstan!" The passport man was sitting by a big, old-fashioned computer. We gave him our passports and he started to look through them, very slowly. When he noticed the banknote in Ergash's passport, he quickly sat up. He put the passport on his lap, so that it was hidden by the desk and out of sight. In a slightly agitated voice, he said that it was perhaps best if I went out and waited in the car. It would take no more than five minutes to record the information he needed from my passport.

"He was upset, because tourists aren't supposed to know about the bribes," Ergash told me when he came back. "I assured him that you hadn't seen anything."

"Did he take the money?"

"Of course."

Once three banknotes had disappeared into three different pockets, we were allowed through the open barrier and into Kyrgyzstan, the only relatively free and democratic country in Central Asia. The people here have rebelled and twice deposed the president. It is also the only country where western tourists do not need a visa.

Something was definitely different on this side of the border. It was noticeable from the start, but it took several days before I was able to put my finger on what exactly it was that was missing.

KYRGYZSTAN

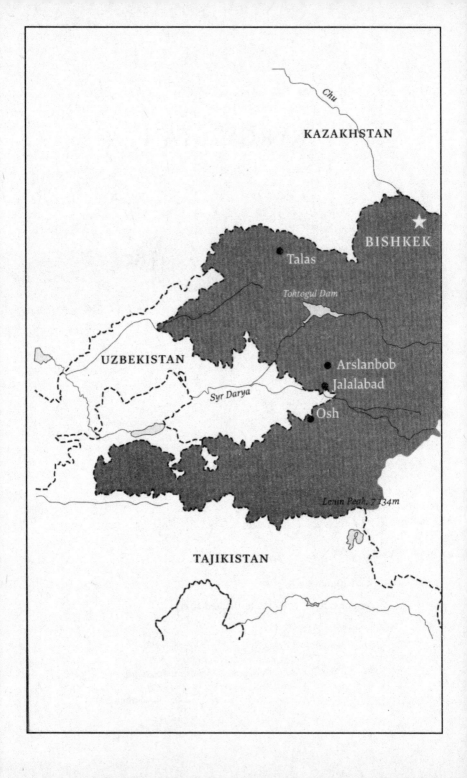

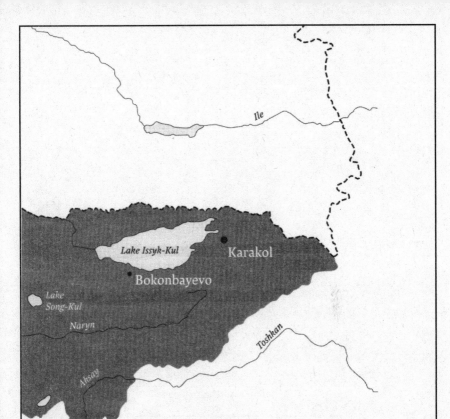

Ile

Lake Issyk-Kul

Karakol

Bokonbayevo

Lake
Song-Kul

Naryn

Toshkan

Aksay

CHINA

KYRGYZSTAN

★

SIZE | 199 951 km²

POPULATION | 5 789 122 (estimated 2017)

CAPITAL | Bishkek

PRESIDENT | 1. Askar Akayev (1990–2005)
2. Kurmanbek Bakiyev (2005–10)
3. Roza Otunbayeva (interim, 2010–11)
4. Almazbek Atambayev (2011–17)
5. Sooronbay Jeenbekov (since November 2017)

TURKMENISTAN

Top: Rush hour in Ashgabat. "Long Live Neutral Turkmenistan!" is the message to all motorists.

Bottom: Ruhnama, "The Book of the Soul", still has pride of place in central Ashgabat, but no longer opens up in the evening.

Above: The Turkmen Horse Beauty Contest. The audience holds its breath.

Right: The president prepares for the special horse owners' race. So far, so good.

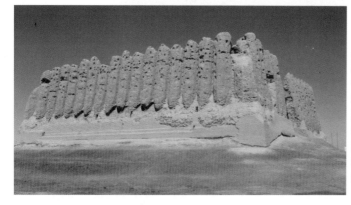

Left: It is no longer known why this fort outside Merv's city walls is called Kyz Kala, the Maiden's Castle.

KAZAKHSTAN

Below: The Bayterek Tower in the futuristic centre of Astana.

Traditional Kazakh wrestling. On horseback, of course.

Point Zero. The Soviet Union carried out 456 nuclear tests at Polygon.

TAJIKISTAN

Above: Dushanbe: the world's tallest flagpole (the presidential palace to the left is included to give a sense of scale).

Left: Nisor on her way up the last slope to her new home in the Yagnob Valley. She has never been alone with Mirzo, her groom, before.

By the Kyrgyz border. The journey's highest point.

KYRGYZSTAN

Right: Rot-Front: When the Soviet Union dissolved, the majority of Germans moved, but the sign still stands.

Below: Talgarbek, "The Eagle Man", and Tumara, his prize-winning golden eagle.

UZBEKISTAN

Above: The old town in Khiva is one enormous outdoor museum.

Left: The fishing boats at Monjnak are moored up for good.

Samarkand: final destination.

MOMENT OF FREEDOM

Kyrgyzstan is the only post-Soviet country in Central Asia where a sitting president has stepped down of his own volition. The country also holds the Central Asian record for the number of presidents, even if it is not very many. By way of contrast, the leaders in Kazakhstan and Uzbekistan were both appointed by Gorbachev in his time, and even though they are now greyer and have more wrinkles, the overwhelming majority of people still support them, if their election results are to be believed.

All maps illustrating freedom and democracy rankings show Kazakhstan's smallest neighbour in a different colour from its surrounding countries. Kyrgyzstan is the most democratic country in Central Asia. Not only does it allow its press the greatest freedom in the region, but the tiny, impoverished, mountainous country also makes the top one hundred with regard to economic freedom, way ahead of its autocratic neighbours. And it is the only Central Asian country to have introduced parliamentarianism, thereby limiting the power of the president. All the other Stans are autocracies, albeit, in the best cases, enlightened.

Is this freedom tangible? Is the air different? No, the freedom is just there, without any great fuss. It is not so much the freedom that is noticeable, rather the absence of fear. People do not lower their voices when they criticise the authorities. They do not look around in fear if they make a throwaway comment about the government. People laugh at politicians here, even the president. They openly make fun of them. Nothing seems to be taboo. The first Kyrgyz I meet, Ubraim, boasts about how corrupt he is. He guffaws as he tells me that he is receiving unemployment benefit, even though he owns two grocery shops. It was not his idea, he claims, it was the benefits officer who suggested it. They made a deal whereby Ubraim receives unemployment benefits for ten months of the year and the officer keeps the remaining two payments. A win-win situation for them both. The dole does not amount to much, just under forty pounds a month, but luckily Ubraim is not dependent on the money to survive. Corruption is the only category in which Kyrgyzstan scores lower than some of its neighbours: it is ranked 150th of 177 countries, below Kazakhstan and Russia, but still higher than Turkmenistan and Uzbekistan, which are unbeatable when it comes to many of these rankings.

The capital, Bishkek, still feels very Russian. There are not many headscarves or white felt hats to be seen. Most people wear modern clothes: jeans, trainers and timeless leather jackets. And you can hear almost as much Russian as Kyrgyz spoken in the street. The situation in Kyrgyzstan in the 1950s was very similar to that in Kazakhstan, in that the Kyrgyz accounted for only forty per cent of the population, so were a minority in their own country. The first Russian and Ukrainian settlers had appeared on the Kyrgyz steppes towards the end of the nineteenth century, and there were almost as many Russians and Ukrainians as Kyrgyz in the country under Soviet rule. Following the collapse of the Soviet Union, many of the Russians and Ukrainians moved back west, and the Kyrgyz now make up more than seventy per cent of the population. Today, there are fewer than 370,000 Russians in Kyrgyzstan, and most of them live in Bishkek.

Bishkek is the greenest capital in Central Asia. The meltwater from the surrounding mountains supplies its many parks and trees with fresh water, giving the city a friendly, almost rural feel. Exploring Bishkek's wide, shaded streets is like going back several decades in time. Little has changed, other than the name: until 1991, the city was known as Frunze, after the Bolshevik leader who was born there. Following independence, it was given a variant of the old name Pishpek, which is apparently derived from the Kyrgyz word for the milk pail that is used to make *kumys*, or fermented horse milk. But if one goes as far back as Sogdian, Pishpek may also mean something like "town at the foot of the mountains". True or not, it is a fitting description of the city's location. Behind the socialist tower blocks, the majestic Tian Shan mountains reach into the sky.

Many of the streets have been given new names, much to the confusion of the taxi drivers, even after twenty years: Lenin Prospect became Prospect Chui, Pravda was changed to Ibraimov, Karl Marx was replaced by Junusaliyev, and so on. Bishkek has none of Ashgabat's marble glory or Astana's cool modernism, it does not even compare with poor Dushanbe, which can, after all, boast a very tall flagpole, a brand new presidential palace and a library so big that not even all the books in the country can fill it. Bishkek is instead an unpretentious capital, everywhere wide streets, solid Soviet architecture and spacious, open, concrete squares. A number of Turkish shopping malls have appeared among the Soviet concrete in recent years, and old reliable Russian restaurants have been reinvented as cool sushi bars. The red propaganda banners with quotations from the latest party congress have long since been replaced by advertisements for cosmetics and electrical goods, but the big Lenin statue is still standing, only now in a less prominent place, behind the history museum.

It would seem that the number of extravagant buildings and marble facades has an inverse ratio to a country's democratic development. Kyrgyzstan is the only Stan that has not afforded itself a new presidential palace. The "White House", a Soviet mastodon that mixes neo-classical and brutalist architecture, is still where the president and government sit.

Things looked promising to begin with, as was the case in Tajikistan. The first elections that were held in the early 1990s were relatively open and free. Only one man qualified as a candidate for the presidency, but various parties were allowed to stand in the parliamentary election. Kyrgyzstan's first president, Askar Akayev, differed from his opposite numbers in neighbouring countries in a number of ways: he was not an engineer but rather a qualified physicist; and he did not have a long political career behind him when he was elected to the Kirghiz Soviet Socialist Republic's Supreme Soviet for the first time in 1987. He started out as a champion of democracy and transparency, but, as the years passed, the gap between theory and practice widened, along with more and more fantastical election results.

The economy also deteriorated. When it was a part of the Soviet Union, subsidies from Moscow accounted for three-quarters of Kyrgyzstan's total budget. With the exception of agricultural produce and gold from a mine that is now Canadian-owned, Kyrgyzstan still has no exports of any significance. After only a few years of independence, foreign debt outstripped gross national product, prices rocketed in tandem with periods of galloping inflation, and wages did not keep pace. When Akayev tried to amend the constitution in 2005, so that he could be re-elected for a fourth term, enough was deemed to be enough. Furious demonstrators stormed the presidential palace and government buildings on March 24, and, in the south of the country, they took control of important administrative buildings. Akayev and his family fled to Moscow, where they were granted political asylum.

As wild tulips flower all over Kyrgyzstan in spring, the uprising was called the Tulip Revolution, following on from the Rose Revolution in Georgia in 2003 and the Orange Revolution in Ukraine in 2004. Secret diaries and documents have since been found that reveal just how corrupt the Akayev government was: detailed price lists show that a seat in parliament could be had for thirty thousand U.S. dollars and an ambassador's post in a nice, western capital cost close to two hundred thousand dollars.

Akayev's successor, Kurmanbek Bakiyev, proved to be no less corrupt, quite the opposite, in fact. He immediately made sure to appoint several family members to key positions, and during his presidency a number of members of parliament, opposition politicians and journalists died in mysterious ways. The corruption persisted and the people were no better off. In 2010, the price of fuel and electricity more than doubled. When the authorities then arrested some opposition politicians in April of that year, in advance of planned public meetings in Talas, Naryn and Bishkek, the people's patience ran out. On April 7, angry demonstrators once more stormed the White House. This time eighty-seven people were killed. The ousted president and his brother, Janysh Bakiyev, were later sentenced *in absentia* to life imprisonment for ordering the guards to open fire on the demonstrators. The Bakiyev family live in Belarus, where they have been granted political asylum.

In order to ensure that the next president would not be as bad as the previous two, Kyrgyzstan introduced parliamentarianism – a first in Central Asia. The president is accountable to the parliament and prime minister, and has limited powers. Roza Otunbayeva took over from Bakiyev as interim president until the next election in 2011. She was not only the first female president in the region, she was also the first to step down voluntarily, as agreed.

Little Kyrgyzstan is the only one of the five Stans to rise up against the state and oust an incumbent president. Not once, but twice. So why Kyrgyzstan? Or, more to the point, why has it not happened in any of the other countries? One possible explanation is poverty. Revolutions tend to flourish in poor countries, or countries where a large proportion of the population is poor. The Russian Revolution, in its time, was driven by anger at the enormous gulf between rich and poor, and the triggers for both the Orange Revolution and the Arab Spring were poverty and increased living costs.

Kyrgyzstan is among the poorest post-Soviet republics. More than a third of the population live below the breadline and, like Tajikistan, the country is dependent on the income of migrant workers, sent back from Russia, to make ends meet. While the situation may not be acute, there are signs of poverty everywhere, such as the improvised flea markets on the pavements where pensioners try to sell any valuables they have: a candlestick, an old vase, four unread books. Some sit with nothing more than a jar of sunflower seeds in front of them, or some old bathroom scales that passers-by can use for the equivalent of five pence.

Both Turkmenistan and Kazakhstan have substantial oil and gas reserves. The upper classes are rolling in money and the middle classes also have opportunities to succeed. The Tajiks, on the other hand, are understandably so scared that the country will once more disintegrate into fighting and chaos that the majority of people are willing to vote for the same president over and over again. They can live with the corruption, the nepotism and the failing economy as long as the country is stable. As long as there is peace. Uzbekistan, to the west of Kyrgyzstan, is also poor, though richer than its neighbour, and the president will stop at nothing to keep hold of power. The Uzbek regime is one of the most repressive in the world, almost on a par with Turkmenistan and North Korea. And this is another important factor: the regime's ability and willingness to resort to violence. Kyrgyzstan's first president, Akayev, gave orders not to shoot the demonstrators in Bishkek. His successor was less principled, but then dropped everything and ran when he realised the battle was lost. The Uzbek president, on the other hand, has already used tanks and automatic weapons to deter demonstrators and is unlikely to hesitate to do so again.

Whereas the other post-Soviet countries in Central Asia are far safer than most European countries, thanks to the large number of police, people are advised not to go out alone in Bishkek after dark. Crime is on the rise, and there are more and more incidents of assault and theft.

One evening when I got a taxi back to the hotel, I was astonished to see a young woman behind the wheel. She must have noticed my surprise, because she immediately started to explain: "I've got four kids, and no husband and my parents are dead. I'm actually a qualified teacher, but the salary is only 150 dollars a month, and you can't live on that, certainly not when there are four mouths to feed. So driving a taxi and taking the risk is my only choice, even if you do get all sorts in the car, especially at night . . ."

As I walked the few metres from the taxi to the hotel entrance it dawned on me what was missing. I had been in Kyrgyzstan for more than a week and still did not know what Almazbek Atambayev, the president, looked like. The walls in Bishkek were plastered with cinema posters and cosmetics advertisements. The few men who were given any space were all bronzed and handsome, with shining white toothpaste smiles and broad, muscular shoulders showing off designer clothing.

DON'T CRY, YOU ARE MY WIFE NOW

Nineteen-year-old Mariam felt very pleased for her friend as she got dressed and ready for the engagement party. The date for the wedding had been set and Mariam was going to be a witness. She did not know the bridegroom well, but her friend seemed to be happier than she had been for a long time, and that was what mattered. It was exactly a year since Mariam had left her small village and moved to Bishkek to study German. In the course of that year, she had fallen in love with a fellow student and they were now a couple, but they felt it was too early to think about marriage. Mariam still had four more years left at university and intended to move to Germany when she graduated.

Shortly after Mariam arrived at the party, her friend's husband-to-be asked if she would like to go for a little walk. Once they were out on the pavement, he asked her to get into a car. A young man she recognised from her village was sitting behind the wheel.

"I'm going to take you to my parents," her friend's fiancé said. Mariam thought he was joking and tried to laugh it off. He laughed too, but a moment later five of his friends appeared in the doorway. They bundled Mariam into the car, then jumped in themselves. The car moved off.

Mariam soon realised what was happening. She knew that she had to act quickly, while they were still in the city. When the car stopped at a red light, she managed to get out. She ran over to a mini-bus that was standing at a bus stop, and scrambled in. But the man's friends followed her and pulled her back out onto the street. Mariam fought as hard as she could, but did not scream or shout. She did not want to make a scene. After all, she knew who the men were; they had grown up in the same village.

During the long car journey, her friend's fiancé did all that he could to convince Mariam. He told her that he had never been in love with her friend, and that he had only got engaged to her so he could be near Mariam. He said that he loved her. That he could not live without her. If she did not stay with him, he would take his life. He also threatened her: if she did not marry him, he would continue to pursue her. He would never leave her in peace. Mariam was scared, not that he would do anything to her, but that he would harm himself.

As there had been so many witnesses to the abduction, Mariam knew that her family and friends would be told. When they got to her abductor's house, they were all there: her parents, her friends, her boyfriend. Her mother wept. Mariam wept. Her boyfriend wept and begged her to go back with him.

"I was young and really believed that he would take his own life if I left," Mariam says. It is seven years since she was kidnapped, and she is now twenty-six. Her face, which is still without wrinkles, is big and angular. She is wearing a red velour tracksuit and while she tells me her story she breastfeeds her younger daughter, who is five months old. As she is visiting a friend, and well out of earshot of her mother-in-law and husband, she can speak freely, but she does not want to tell me her real name. To be on the safe side. This is not something that is generally discussed.

The wedding would be held a month later, but Mariam stayed with her future husband and his parents in the meantime, as is the tradition. In the course of one day, her whole life had turned upside down: her studies and life in the city were over. She was to marry her friend's fiancé, a farmer who lived at home with his parents. In those early days, Mariam cried a lot.

"He comforted me and said that I mustn't cry," she says. "He was kind and patient. With time, things got better. Luckily."

Instead of finishing her degree and moving to Germany, Mariam is now a hard-working farmer's wife. Her husband and his parents have fifteen cows, one hundred sheep, fifty hens and fifteen geese. There is more than enough to do. She is also the mother of two little girls, and dreams of having two more children, boys.

"I think I'm happy. He's a good man. I used to think about my old life a lot before the children were born, but I don't think about it anymore." She lifts her youngest daughter from her breast and looks at her lovingly. The little girl whimpers unhappily, but Mariam just glows at the sight of her. "I want my daughters to have the life they choose, for them to get proper jobs and have good careers," she says. "I don't want them to get married as young as I did. And I want them to choose their own husbands. Bride kidnapping is one of our traditions, but it's wrong."

Mariam's mother too was abducted. A colleague from the factory who was three years older than her kidnapped her on the street one day, after work. She wept bitter tears, but she had to stay with her future husband, who would become Mariam's father.

"Taking your daughters back when they've been kidnapped is seen as shameful," Mariam explains. "Especially if they're not virgins anymore. It would have been a scandal if I had not agreed to the wedding. It's not easy for the men, either. I have never seen my old boyfriend again. Last year, my brother's girlfriend was kidnapped. She chose to marry the man who abducted her, even though she was in love with my brother."

—m—

Roza had been living in Bishkek for three years when she was kidnapped on her way home from the cosmetics shop where she worked. Nothing had been left to chance: the man who abducted her knew when she finished for the day and the route she normally took. He struck when Roza was alone on a dark, empty street. He had borrowed a minibus and had ten friends from the village with him. The friends pulled Roza into the minibus and tied her to one of the seats.

"I've kidnapped you. You're going to be my wife," the man behind the wheel declared. Roza vaguely remembered him from her village and had no wish to move back. She and her sister lived in the city now. Both their parents were dead. The village belonged to another life.

The men in the minibus were tipsy and continued to party on the long journey back to the man's family. It took hours. The vodka bottles clinked and were passed around, and they were all very merry. None of them were bothered by Roza's tears. When they got to the village, his grandmother was standing ready with a big, white shawl. Roza knew that if she let her put it on her head it was a sign that she agreed to the marriage. His family had prepared the wedding feast, or *toj*. Many of the guests were already eating.

Roza did not want to get married. She liked her life with her sister in Bishkek and was happy. What is more, she did not like the man who had kidnapped her. He was not at all her type, coarse and boorish and anything but handsome. He was five years older than she was and worked in the construction industry. But she let the grandmother put the white shawl over her head all the same.

"I was tired of crying," Roza said. She was small and slender, dressed in a long, black sweater and jeans. Her round face was framed by short hair.

She had insisted that we meet in my hotel room, so that no-one could hear what we were talking about, and I had promised not to reveal her real name. We were in a small provincial town that nestles below the mighty Tian Shan mountains, in the far west of the country. Everyone knows everyone here and there are ears everywhere.

She did not have sex with him the first night, but they slept next to each other in the same room. The following day, the imam came to see them. He read from the Qur'an and performed *nikah*, the Islamic wedding ceremony. She slept with him on the second night, when they were husband and wife.

The first year was hard. Roza did not want to live with her husband or his parents, but she did not feel she could divorce him.

"The Kyrgyz do not approve of divorce," she said. The tears ran down her cheeks. She sniffed.

"Do you love him?"

"No, but I've got used to him."

"Has he explained why he kidnapped you?"

"He said he liked me."

"Is that all he said?"

"Yes."

Just before their first child was born, Roza and her husband moved out of his parents' house. They could not forgive their daughter-in-law for saying that she did not want to live with them, and they treated her badly. Their elder child was now six, and their second child, also a boy, was born a year ago.

"When I had my youngest, I stopped thinking about leaving him," Roza told me. "I knew then that I had to stay with him, for the children's sake. I no longer had a choice. And where would I go, anyway? I don't have a job, I have no education, no money of my own. And he's not a bad man, really. He doesn't drink. He doesn't hit me. He respects me."

She dried her tears and got ready to leave. I gave her the money for a taxi home, as she had none of her own. The fare was about sixty pence.

—⁓—

"You're welcome to use my name," Elena says. She has been sitting quietly listening to Roza's story. Occasionally, when either Roza or I got stuck and could not find the right Russian word, she helped out. She is twenty-three, and dressed in jeans and a leather jacket. Her chestnut hair sticks out from under the scarf she is wearing because of the rain. Her face is tanned, which makes her blue eyes even bluer.

"I didn't think they kidnapped Russian girls," I say.

"Neither did I!" Elena says. Then she starts to tell me: five years ago, when she was eighteen, she moved to Bishkek to study economics. In the winter break, she went back to her village to visit her mother. As her mother was in the village hospital, she was at home alone. Her father had died some years earlier, and her sister was in Bishkek. A couple of days after Elena got there, the neighbours called to say that their youngest child was ill, and asked if she could go with their daughter to get some medicine. Elena had known the neighbours all her life, and their daughter, Bubusara, was one of her best friends. Bubusara's parents organised a car for them, and the two girls got into the back seat. Elena had not seen the young men sitting in the front, but Bubusara knew who they were. The men drove them to the hospital. The pharmacy was closed. On the way back, the car stopped and Bubusara's uncle got into the back seat with them. As he slammed the door shut, the driver accelerated away. They drove out of the village and through the next two villages at top speed. Elena and Bubusara started to cry and tried desperately to get them to stop, but to no avail. The men had been expecting a fight. The uncle held Bubusara in a tight grip and one of the young men got into the back to hold Elena. Elena could not believe this was happening to her. She was Russian, after all!

Elena eventually managed to persuade the men to stop so they could go to the toilet. As soon as they were out of sight, she took her friend by the hand: "Come on, let's run!" The two friends ran as fast as they could. As it was winter, it was already dark and the snow lay thick on the ground. They had no idea where they were going, they just needed to get away. But they were not wearing warm clothes. What if they had to stay out all night? What would they do if they met some wolves? Elena need not have worried, because the three men soon caught up with them and forced them back to the car.

"Let me out!" Elena screamed. "I want to go home!" She screamed and kicked and punched.

"Calm down, it will only get worse," the driver muttered from the front.

They reached the driver's house at nine in the evening. His relatives were all there, and in one of the rooms the table was set for a feast. Elena and her friend were taken into another room, and soon after an old, hunchbacked woman came in with a white shawl.

"I'm not going to put that on!" Elena screamed. She was never going to marry that man. She did not know him, or anything about him! To her, he was just a man. More of his relatives came in to negotiate, but Elena just screamed at them. When one of the aunts tried to get her to put on a warm sweater, she pushed her away so hard that she fell down.

At some point, Elena and Bubusara were left on their own. Elena did not waste a moment. She got a stool and tried to push open a window high up in the wall. She had just succeeded when her kidnapper appeared in the doorway.

"Where do you think you are going?" he said.

"I've got a boyfriend," Elena screamed. "I'm pregnant!" She would say anything to get away.

"Is that true?" The colour drained from the young man's face. "I'm not going to look after another man's child, just so you know."

"Then let me go!"

But he was not prepared to do that. When the two friends were left alone again, Elena got out her mobile and rang her sister, who was a lawyer. At first, her sister was angry. How could she be so stupid as to get into the car? What was she thinking? Then she demanded to speak to the kidnapper's family.

"You have kidnapped a Russian girl. If you do not drive her home immediately, I will go to the police," she told them.

After an hour, and presumably a lot of discussion, the family drove Elena home. It was now eleven o'clock. All Elena could think about was how relieved she was to have escaped and to be back home. Bubusara, on the other hand, had to stay. She had asked Elena to tell her parents so they could come and get her. But what they did not know, at that point, was that Bubusara's parents had been party to the whole thing.

Her kidnapper continued to try to persuade her in the car on the way back, albeit less forcefully.

"Why do you want to go home? Tell your sister you want to live with us."

The same evening, the driver married Bubusara instead. She did not have the will to resist, and agreed to the wedding.

After what had happened, Elena could not get back to Bishkek fast enough. She stayed away from the village for the next two years and did not even go home for holidays. Bubusara's marriage was not a happy one. It turned out that her husband was violent, and she ran away to Elena's mother on several occasions. On one occasion,

Elena was at home. When he came to collect his wife, repentant as always, Elena asked him why he hit her friend.

"It would have been different if I had married you," he said.

Bubusara has two small children. She lost her third child, as her husband beat her when she was pregnant.

"He's got a second wife now," Elena says, shaking her head. "Kyrgyz men are worse even than Russians!"

Three years after the kidnapping, Elena met a Kazakh man on the Internet. They are going to get married in two months' time, when Elena has qualified as a bookkeeper, and then move to St Petersburg to start a new life. She worries about her friend, who has chosen to stay with her violent husband, but is so thankful that she managed to get away.

"Staying was never an option. I felt no shame in leaving. I'm not Kyrgyz. I just wanted to go home."

—〜〰〜—

Ala kachuu, "snatch and run", is what the tradition of bride kidnapping is called in Kyrgyz. There are no reliable statistics for how many young women are abducted and forced into marriage in Kyrgyzstan each year. Russell Kleinbach, professor emeritus of sociology and one of the founders of the Kyz Korgon Institute, an organisation that aims to end this practice in Central Asia, has researched the phenomenon for many years, and estimates that around one third of all marriages in Kyrgyzstan occur in this way. The figure rises to fifty per cent in rural communities, in other words, 11,800 young women every year, or thirty per day. More than ninety per cent of these wives stay with their kidnapper.

"Lots of people say that ala kachuu is an ancient, nomadic tradition, but that's just nonsense," says Banur Abdiyeva, a lawyer and head of the women's rights organisation, Leader. "People think that it's mentioned in 'Manas', a national epic poem, but that is a misinterpretation that has spread because so few people have actually read the whole thing. *Ala kachuu* is not mentioned once in 'Manas'! In the olden days, women were sometimes kidnapped during wars, or a young couple might elope together if their parents did not agree to the marriage, or if the bridegroom wanted to avoid paying *kalym*, the bride price. That still happens today, but it's not *ala kachuu*. It is only *ala kachuu* when the woman is taken against her will. The so-called tradition started in the Soviet era, during collectivisation, and has become even more prevalent after the break-up of the Soviet Union."

Kidnappers previously risked a fine of up to 100,000 som, which is just over a thousand pounds, and three years of restricted movement. The penalty for stealing sheep was harsher. After much hard lobbying by Leader, among others, the legal punishment has increased to seven years' imprisonment, or ten if the girl is a minor. According to the Kyz Korgon Institute's figures, only one in 1,500 men are sentenced for bride kidnapping, and to date only two men have been imprisoned in line with the new law: in one case, the young woman committed suicide, and, in the other, a divorced man kidnapped a sixteen-year-old girl three times. He raped her on the first night. Her parents did not want her to marry a man like that, and came to get her. Then he kidnapped her again. In the end, her parents reported it to the police. During the trial, the girl had to answer questions from the prosecutor as to why she had said no to a secure life with the man and his family. Was he not good enough for her?

Banur believes that attitudes to *ala kachuu* run deep: "The whole way we think about women and children in this country has to change. There's no tradition of romance here. Men in rural communities don't know how to get a wife, other than to kidnap and rape her.

That's how their grandparents got married, how their parents got married, how everyone else in the village got married. The whole family is part of it. The grandmother is standing ready with the white shawl when the man comes home with his weeping, kidnapped bride. His older female relatives are there to add to the psychological pressure: "We were kidnapped too, we cried too, but then we had children and forgot about it. Look at us now! We've got children and grandchildren and live in a nice house!" The men remain indifferent to the women's pain. They think the crying is part of the tradition, and don't understand that she's actually suffering. If a woman loses her virginity, it is the same as a life sentence. Then she has no choice but to marry. But even when the man doesn't touch her, she worries that no-one else will marry her if she goes home to her parents. The social and psychological pressure is intense, which is why such a high percentage of the women stay. In the seven per cent of cases where the girl does not agree to marry the man, the man is blamed: what sort of a man is he, if he cannot keep hold of the bride?"

Many of the girls who are victims of ala kachuu are raped or forced to have sex with a man they knew nothing about until a few hours earlier. When the imam has blessed the couple, it is expected that the marriage will be consummated the same night. There are many tragic stories about wedding nights. One young woman told me that she had never met the man she married until the imam came to bless them. On the night she was kidnapped and married, she and her husband were locked into the bedroom. His female relatives stood outside the door listening and waiting. As the young couple did not know each other, they sat there and talked. She did not want to have sex with a total stranger, and presumably he was nervous as well. After a few hours, one of the women knocked impatiently on the door. "Are you a man, or what? What are you waiting for?" The man started to chase the girl round the room. She screamed and cried when he raped her, but no-one cared. All the women were interested in was the bloody stain on the sheet to prove that the bride was a virgin.

"Our society is extremely aggressive," Banur says. "For all its generosity and warmth, Kyrgyz society is hard. It doesn't take much for people to flare up and shout and scream at each other, or to start a fight. There's a lot of domestic violence, inter-generational as well. We have to develop a more tolerant and peaceful culture. But how do you do that?"

THE EAGLE MEN

"I am the Eagle Man." He was dressed from head to toe in leather, and held his hand out in a very business-like manner. He was wearing a traditional, tall Kyrgyz felt hat. His face was both gentle and weathered. His handshake was firm. He opened the car door and indicated that I should take my place in the worn passenger seat. The engine coughed and spluttered before starting.

"It's old, but it's done me proud for three years now," he said, patting the dashboard.

Something tickled my feet. I leaned over and spotted a rabbit trying to make itself as small as possible under the glove compartment.

"I thought we were going to go on a proper hunt up in the mountains?"

The Eagle Man shook his head.

"The horses are grazing up in the mountains at the moment. It's too far to go. You'll just have to be happy with the usual rabbit show."

A loud screech whipped through the air. Startled, I turned around and saw the feathered head sticking up from the boot. The bird was hooded. The long, hooked beak opened as she let out another screech, longer and more indignant this time.

"She's hungry," the Eagle Man said.

The rabbit trembled with fear.

We drove through the dusty village streets of Bokonbayevo and out onto the steppe and there we stopped. The Eagle Man pulled on a long, thick glove, opened the boot and lifted the golden eagle onto his arm. He carefully removed the leather hood. A pair of black, beady eyes appeared.

"Say hello to Tumara, my best eagle." The Eagle Man took a few steps back and gave me some well-practised poses from different angles. Tumara shifted her weight from foot to foot, but was obedient and stayed where she was. As soon as she was given the order, she flew around in a small circle then settled on his arm again.

"Well, we'd better get started!" The Eagle Man put the leather hood back on Tumara, opened the door to the passenger seat and let the terrified rabbit out. It did not know what to do with its new-found freedom and darted here and there in confusion. Eventually it stopped in the middle of the plain, as though it hoped someone would come and rescue it. The Eagle Man ambled up onto the nearest ridge.

"Are you ready?" he shouted from the top.

I zoomed in on the rabbit, ready to immortalise its death. With a predator's cry, the Eagle Man let Tumara loose. She flew low over the ground, straight towards her prey. The rabbit must have realised that something terrible was about to happen, but had clearly not given up hope that someone would come to its rescue, as it stood stock still. Within seconds, Tumara had it. Her talons sank into its fur, so that it was unable to move. And there she sat until the Eagle Man came down from the ridge and with a single syllable gave her permission to start. She did not need encouragement. Without even bothering to kill her victim, her beak tore through the grey fur and she started to eat. The rabbit lay there, helpless, with frozen eyes and a hammering heart. Everything was devoured. The fur, bones, liver, blood, heart.

"What do you think?" The Eagle Man looked at me expectantly. "She's good, isn't she?"

"Yes," I mumbled. "Very good."

Golden eagles are fantastic hunters. They can apparently spot their prey from several kilometres away. For that very reason, it was not so impressive that Tumara had managed to catch a petrified rabbit that was only a few hundred metres away. It was the least she could do.

On the way back, we did not hear a sound from the bird. She was sated.

"I took her from the nest when she was a fledgling," the Eagle Man said. "I waited until she had started to flap her wings. Then she was ready. After only a few months, we could go hunting together. I'm her mother and father now, and she's like a daughter to me. She obeys only me, no-one else. I've trained three golden eagles, and Tumara is the best. She's twice been the national champion and even caught a wolf once in a competition."

He found two chairs that we could sit on in the overgrown garden. We had to stay out of the house because his eleven-year-old daughter was doing a major clean. Behind the house, Tumara was tied to an improvised perch made from an old pot. Her yellowed beak was still spattered with blood. Beside her was a larger, less sleek eagle that had only recently been caught. The Eagle Man threw it some meat, which it wolfed down. When he turned his back, it screeched furiously for more.

The Eagle Man was called Talgarbek. He had started working with birds when he was seven or eight years old. No-one had encouraged him, still less taught him. His grandfather had kept many birds, but he died when Talgarbek was six. His father was a teacher and had more than enough to do.

"We were not encouraged to keep up Kyrgyz traditions under Soviet rule," Talgarbek said. "I think my father would have been mortified if he had turned up at school with scratches from birds of prey." He pulled up a sleeve. Old scars and new wounds formed an intricate pattern on his tanned skin. Talgarbek was often told off at home for spending all his time in the mountains, from morning to night. He wore out more pairs of boots every year than his siblings did.

"I talked to the old men who were hunters, and they taught me everything they knew. I suppose it was in my blood, because I was quick to learn. I now know all there is to know about birds, and I have my own apprentices."

Talgarbek stopped working for Kyrgyz Telecom nine years ago and now makes a living solely from his rabbit shows. Tourists come here every day in summer. And thanks to their money and many martyred rabbits, he has managed to build his own house.

"My wife has always supported me, even when I haven't been earning much. A friend of mine had to give up birds because his wife didn't support him. They live in Bishkek now."

"How did you meet your wife?"

Talgarbek burst out laughing. "I stole her. We sat chatting in a café in Bishkek and then I forced her into my car. Two friends were there to help me. I was twenty-six and she was twenty-three. She cried and screamed, of course, that's the tradition. We brought her back here and told her parents that we'd kidnapped their daughter. Then my grandmother put the white shawl on her head and we got married."

"Why did you choose her in particular?"

"It was time to find a wife, so I went to Bishkek. Some friends introduced us, and it was love at first sight. She was working as a product designer and modeller in Bishkek. Now she's a housewife and pregnant with our fourth child. We're happy."

"Would you think it was O.K. for someone to kidnap your daughters?"

"As long as they had a good house, why not?" Talgarbek shrugged.

"Daughters have to be married anyway. But since *ala kachuu* was banned and you can end up in prison, it's become less common. Some men are frightened of talking to women. So now that the law has been introduced, they may never get married."

While we talk, a boy of about eight or nine comes out into the garden. He has a small falcon on his arm.

"Azim will be a fourth generation eagle man," Talgarbek said, and patted the boy on the head.

I caught a glimpse of his eleven-year-old daughter through the doorway. She was too busy sweeping the hall with a large brush to look up.

—⁓—

"Talgarbek is not a proper eagle man!" Ishenbek said with indignation. "I taught him everything he knows about birds, but for him it's just business. He sits and waits for the tourists to ring. He doesn't bother to go out hunting, he only takes part in competitions and festivals. That rabbit show he does is a disgrace. A disgrace!"

Ishenbek and his wife Zina lived about twenty kilometres west of Bokonbayevo in a village by Lake Issyk-Kul, the second largest alpine lake in the world. The blue, slightly saline lake makes for a milder climate than elsewhere in Kyrgyzstan – the winters are never extremely cold and the summers are seldom unbearably hot. During the summer months, Kyrgyz tourists flock to the beaches, whereas foreign tourists head for Ishenbek and Zina's simple guesthouse.

"You're lucky," Zina told me. She was a robust, down-to-earth woman. Before she retired, she had worked as a doctor in the village. "A Russian T.V. crew is coming tomorrow. They're going to film a fox hunt in the mountains. And, for a small fee, you can go with them."

"Is it a real hunt? Authentic, with horses and the whole shebang?"
I did not want to see another version of the rabbit show.

"Yes, yes, of course, it's a real hunt, with horses, everything,"
Zina assured me.

"And the fox is wild, isn't it? It's a real hunt?"

"Yes, the fox is wild, of course."

Ishenbek was a large, short-winded man. His voice was deep
and hoarse, owing to years of smoking. He had thick, grey hair, and
broad cheekbones. He started working with eagles in 1980, when he
was twenty-five, after his father and grandfather, who both hunted
with birds, had died. He had envisaged a more normal life for himself. He got himself a degree in economics, a sensible and practical
training, and had expected to divide his time between his family
and the office. And yet something in him made him carry on the
old family tradition. A yearning to be out of doors, an endless
fascination for birds of prey. According to Ishenbek, there was
only one eagle man left in the whole of Kyrgyzstan at the time, an
old man called Kutuldo. Kutuldo had feared that the art would die
with him, and was therefore delighted to take Ishenbek under his
wing. He even gave him one of his eagles, and taught him everything
he knew.

It is hard to grasp just how radically the lives of the traditional,
nomadic people of Central Asia changed under the Soviet regime.
They had no desire to settle. They lived in their yurts and moved
around with their animals according to the seasons, as they had
done since time immemorial. The Soviets thought this traditional
lifestyle was primitive and inefficient, and did everything they could
to stop it, to stamp it out – with catastrophic effect.

"Our ancestors did not have weapons and used only birds for
hunting," Ishenbek told me. "The prey gave them meat, and wolves
and foxes gave them fur to keep them warm. The birds also protected

them from predators. So the eagles gave them three things: food, clothes and protection. For them, the birds were indispensible."

Under Stalin, the nomadic people were forced to move out of their round yurts into square houses, and were required to stay in one place throughout the year. The new life was a psychological shock for them. They had to learn to understand time and space in another way. They had to learn new ways of farming. Everything was new, absolutely everything. The Soviet authorities gave them an infrastructure, with schools and a health system; they got kitchen equipment and tractors, but they lost their culture and their trad-itional way of life. Today, only around ten per cent of Kyrgyz live as nomads, and then only in the summer months. Much of the knowledge about the cycles of nature has been lost. Inevitably over-grazing is a problem in many areas.

"Today there's only a handful of genuine eagle men in Kyrgyz-stan, but sadly there are many pretend *bükütchüs*," Ishenbek said. "The pretend ones pose with an eagle on their arm for the tourists to take photographs. Some of them even wear shorts." He snorted in disgust.

Ishenbek left his accountancy job some years ago, in favour of tourism, and since then has worked full-time with eagles.

"An eagle is only with me for ten to fifteen years," he said. "Then I have to release it. That is the tradition. They also have to have the opportunity to find a mate, build a nest and have young. Contrary to what you might read in books, they soon become wild again and forget me. Even when they have lived with humans all their lives, they know how to build a nest. There are tears, of course, because it's always sad to say goodbye. But they have to get married. That's the tradition."

Ishenbek recently got himself a new eagle, so now three golden eagles live in his big, bounteous garden: Turman, who is ten, Dzjanar, which means spark, who is also ten, and the new bird, which has no name yet. Ishenbek took it from a nest in the middle of July, when it had just begun to flap its wings. A boy climbed up a rope to get to the nest, while Ishenbek and the rest of his group stood at the bottom and waited. They had guns with them to frighten off the parents, should that be necessary. For the next few months, Ishenbek fed the bird every day so that it got used to him and learned to trust him.

Zina has not always been as keen on her husband's interest in eagles, but is considerably more positive now that it brings in an income, as well as fame and honour: Ishenbek has become something of a local celebrity and has taken part in many documentaries.

"Nearly ready!" Ishenbek, who had put on the traditional suede clothes, appeared carrying a big, black box. Dzjanar, the golden eagle, was ready and waiting in the jeep, with a leather hood over her head and a strap round her feet. The morning dew still hung like a cobweb blanket over the garden. Ishenbek went over to a small concrete silo in the middle of the garden and climbed into it. A high-pitched, frightened bark echoed at the bottom of the silo. I went over and looked down. The stench of urine and excrement hit me. A thin, mangy-looking fox was cowering by the wall. Its eyes were big and scared, its fur was matted and covered in muck. Ishenbek drove the fox into the black box with a stick and closed the front. Then he put the box on his shoulder, climbed out of the silo and put it in the boot of the jeep beside the eagle. You could hear the fox tearing at the wood inside the box. The eagle became agitated and called from under her leather hood.

"There, now we're ready to go," Ishenbek said, and clapped his hands. "Nice fox, isn't it? We caught it a few weeks ago, when it was just a young cub."

Half an hour later we came to a parched brown plain, surrounded by hillsides with woods blazing in autumn colours. There were five people in the Russian film crew, of which only three seemed to do anything. The other two wandered around without purpose and were shouted at by the director every time they got in the frame.

On a signal from the director, the presenter jumped out of the driver's seat and stood in front of the camera. She had long, blonde hair, and was wearing a woolly hat and impractical shoes. She exclaimed dramatically that she was in Kyrgyzstan, home of the nomads, country of the yurt, land of mountains and traditions, and that she was about to meet Ishenbek, the Eagle Man. Ishenbek was standing ready with Dzjanar on his arm, and gave a succinct lecture on the hunting bird's capabilities.

"They hunt rabbits," he said, "and foxes, and sometimes wolves..."

"Wolves," the presenter squawked, leaning in to the camera. "*Volki!* They can catch wolves? *Woooolves!*"

The director was careful to keep the box with the fox in it away from the camera's view.

"Can't we let it try to hunt for real?" he suggested hopefully. "Maybe it will find something?"

Ishenbek shook his head.

"She won't find anything. It's too early in the year."

The director insisted that we should try all the same. Ishenbek and the energetic presenter made a couple of attempts to get the eagle to hunt. Each time, she flew no more than ten metres or so before settling on a stone, where she then waited for Ishenbek to fetch her. There was no choice: if the viewers were going to see the eagle in action, the fox had to be sacrificed.

The film crew lay down behind a pile of stones and were ready when the small, frightened fox was let out of the box. First it ran in one direction, then another. Then it stopped and had to be hounded on. Ishenbek took the leather hood off Dzjanar and gave her the signal to hunt. She rose with a screech. A few seconds later she had her talons in the bewildered fox, her beak deep in its fur, and she started to eat. The fox stared helplessly up at the sky. Its eyes dulled and at last its life was over.

The cameraman zoomed in on the bloody feast. The bird spread her wings over her prey and continued to eat, deliberately and systematically. Her sharp beak hacked at the fox fur again and again. The presenter had to turn and stagger away, bent double, her hand over her mouth. When she came back, she still had tears in her eyes.

"This is not suited to female sensitivities," she said to the camera. "I understand that it's nature, and nature can be brutal, but we women don't have the stomach for it. We're sensitive souls and such a sight is not for us, even though it is natural and all that. It's simply not something for sensitive women."

And yet she could not keep her eyes off the eagle and its prey. Ishenbek surveyed the scene with stoic calm.

"As soon as women see blood, they start to cry," he said to the camera. "I knew she would start to cry. They always do."

He walked slowly over to Dzjanar, picked up the remains of the fox and threw them into the wooden box. Then he clapped his hands, all part of the show.

"There now, you've got all you need, haven't you?"

THE LAST GERMANS IN ROT-FRONT

"No-one will want to talk to you," Herr Wilhelm said on the telephone. "*Niemand!* They're sceptical of strangers and have had some very bad experiences with journalists. It took me over a year to win their trust. I would therefore strongly advise you not to go to Rot-Front, *verstehen Sie?*"

Herr Wilhelm's warning took me by surprise. I had called him to get some background information about the German community in Rot-Front, since he was the person who had worked most closely with the village in the past few years. Our conversation unsettled me, but at the same time made me even more determined to go there. Why did they not want visitors?

The young driver who took me to Rot-Front had a name that was difficult to pronounce and impossible to remember. As he was blond, I assumed he was a Russian, but it turned out he was a Tatar. Central Asia is a jumble of different nationalities, cultures, faces, languages and traditions. Many of them, like the Crimean Tatars, ended up here during the Second World War. In 1944, Stalin decided that all Crimean Tatars, more than 230,000 of them, should be deported to Central Asia. Around 30,000 Tatars still live in Kyrgyzstan, along with a number of other nationalities, including 17,000 Koreans who originally lived in Vladivostok, 19,000 Azerbaijanis who hailed from the Caucasus, and 8,500 Germans from the Volga district and the Black Sea. Before the Soviet authorities allowed free movement in 1989, more than a million Germans lived in Central Asia, chiefly in Kazakhstan. But Kyrgyzstan was also home to 100,000 ethnic Germans. What is special about the Germans in Kyrgyzstan is that they came there in the nineteenth century when Russia was still ruled by tsars. Those who came in the first wave of migration were Mennonites, a Protestant Christian denomination born from the Anabaptists of the sixteenth century, established by the Dutch priest, Menno Simons. The German Mennonites had migrated all the way to the Black Sea in order to avoid military service in the tsar's army. There are still a few Mennonites left in the small village of Rot-Front, to the north of Bishkek.

The driver slammed on the brakes. He swore under his breath. Just in front of us, a rickety old lorry pulled out into the road. The tyres screeched and there was a faint smell of rubber.

"No-one can drive in this country," he grumbled, as professional drivers do all over the world.

"Is it expensive to get a driving licence?" I asked.

"It costs a hundred dollars, but the price is the same regardless of whether you choose to have driving lessons and an exam, or just get the piece of paper."

"What did you do?"

"Well, because I could already drive a car, there was no point in taking lessons. It would have been a waste of time."

Had we not on the way picked up a hitchhiker who knew the area well, we would never have found the village. A bewildering number of roads led us to different villages. The signage was, at best, haphazard.

A rusty Soviet sign welcomed us to Rot-Front. It proved to be a peaceful, idyllic place: two long, straight streets, and that was it. The houses were white, with blue or green window frames. Prolific gardens sheltered behind high fences. One or two farm labourers hurried along the side of the road, but otherwise the village appeared to be empty. My driver seemed to have a talent for spotting where the Germans lived.

"Germans, definitely Germans." He pointed to a neat, well-kept garden. We drove past a house where the paint was peeling from the walls. "But I can guarantee you that a Kyrgyz lives there." The garden was a mess of tools, old cars and children's toys. "Kyrgyz. Kyrgyz there too. Kyrgyz. German!" Again we passed an attractive, tidy garden. The house was old and sunken, but it was freshly white-washed, without so much as a crack, and the window frames were glossy in the autumn sun. The driver laughed. "Germans must have a special orderly gene that the Kyrgyz didn't get."

A man in working clothes walked towards us. He was tall, his fair hair was bleached, he had a thin, fair moustache and his face was weathered. With Herr Wilhelm's warning words fresh in my mind, I got out of the car and walked towards him.

"*Guten Tag.*" It felt strange to greet him in German in the middle of a Kyrgyz village.

"*Guten Tag.*" The fair man gave me a friendly smile. "Are you perhaps a journalist?"

"Yes. Well actually, I'm writing a book."

"You're in luck then. No-one knows the history of Rot-Front better than I do. How much time do you have?"

"All day."

"*Sehr gut!*" He held out his hand and introduced himself as Ernst Koop, one of the oldest Germans in the village. Then he began, without moving from where he was standing by the side of the road. He was a living encyclopaedia and knew the history off by heart.

"The Mennonites were persecuted during the War of Religions between the Catholics and Protestants in the 1500s. We have a lot in common with the Protestants, but unlike them we are pacifists and practise adult baptism. To avoid conscription, many of the

Mennonites moved from Friesland and Flanders, where the movement originated, to places in what today is Poland. In 1772, these
were taken over by Prussia. The Mennonites who lived there were
forced to pay a high price for military exemption. Eventually even
this option was closed. Catherine the Great invited the Mennonites
from Prussia to come and settle in the farming regions of south
Russia, today's Ukraine. As they were promised religious freedom,
exemption from military service and the right to run their own
schools, many of them accepted the empress' invitation. The
Germans established their own villages, built schools, hospitals and
churches, and generally got by without any help from the state.
But in the 1870s, the Russian authorities started to interfere in the
Mennonites' way of life and, among other things, demanded that
they do their military service like everyone else. Many Germans
emigrated west in protest, to the U.S.A. and Canada. But a large
group also headed east, towards Central Asia. In 1880, they arrived
in Tashkent in Uzbekistan, and for two years they looked for land.
The Russian governor general eventually gave them land in the
fertile Talas valley, which today lies in west Kyrgyzstan."

Ernst spoke perfect German, with meticulous pronunciation and
model clarity. He rolled his "r"s and pronounced every letter in each
word. He could perhaps have been mistaken for an old-fashioned
southern German or Austrian.

"As families had on average ten to twelve children, the German
villages grew fast," he said. We were still standing by the side of the
road. There was a breeze, but the sun was shining in a cloudless sky.
"It became harder and harder to find enough land for everyone.
Eventually, in 1927, a group of Mennonites – my grandfather was one
of them – left Talas and headed east. They walked for three to four
hundred kilometres until they found a place to the north of Bishkek
where they could settle. Here they established the village of Bergtal."

Three young Kyrgyz horsemen galloped by. The hooves rang out on the asphalt. Ernst followed them with his eyes.

"This used to be a purely German village," he said. "In the 1980s, there was only one Kyrgyz family here. But that's jumping the gun a bit. I'd only got to the 1930s, when the Soviet authorities started to show who was in charge down here, and the name of the village was changed from Bergtal to the more revolutionary Rot-Front. The Mennonites were no longer allowed to practise their faith and all private property was confiscated. Aron Wall, my maternal grand-father, refused to give up his horses and cows. He was not particularly rich, but he had around ten horses, which in those days was enough to be categorised as a kulak. Because he did not cooperate, he was arrested and sent to prison in Leninpol, three hundred kilometres away. My mother, who was thirteen at the time, told us that the police came and put everything they owned out onto the street. Plates. Beds. Knives and forks. Everything. And then the famine hit. The Germans in particular suffered. My mother buried food and things in the garden so no-one would find it. Throughout her youth, she secreted things away for later. Meanwhile, my grandfather escaped from prison and found himself a job in a sugar factory in Kazakhstan. My grandmother, mother and the rest of the children moved there to be with him. They stayed in Kazakhstan until 1937."

"And did they come back again then?" I said. I could feel that I had been too long in the sun. My scalp was burning, and my fore-head felt red and warm. We had been standing by the edge of the road for an hour. It did not seem to affect Ernst, though he was fairer than me. He carried on tirelessly.

"No, my grandfather never came home again. They came to get him in the middle of the night. They wouldn't tell my grandmother where they were taking him or what they were going to do with him. She found out later that he had been killed after only one month.

Lots of men from Talas and Bergtal suffered the same fate that year, the worst of Stalin's rule of terror. The men were killed, without a trial, simply because they were German. When the war started, all Germans over fifteen were sent to *trudarmiya*, the labour battalions. In practice, it was a labour camp. Their work was to build canals. Many of them could not speak a word of Russian, they spoke only German and Kyrgyz. It was hard work and they didn't get much food. In winter, they were cold all the time. Illness and disease were rife. A third of those conscripted never returned."

Ernst, the youngest of eight, was born in 1957 after the persecutions were over. The Kyrgyz Germans had been rehabilitated and once again had plenty of food.

"I was lucky to be born then," Ernst said. "After Stalin died in 1952 the Soviet authorities left us in peace. We could live as Germans. I didn't know a word of Russian until I started school, because everyone spoke German at home, or rather *Plattdeutsch*, which is our language. Every now and then inspectors turned up at school to instruct us in atheism, but we were all believers. Other than that, there was nothing to complain about. We didn't have many cars, but we were not freezing. We had food. Then, in 1989, when the Russian borders were opened and people could emigrate to Germany, nearly everyone left. I did too. I remember the stopover in Moscow was pretty awful. There were German emigrants everywhere."

All the houses in Rot-Front were put up for sale. People who had applied time and again for travel visas, and been rejected, were suddenly able to leave. All the doors were open wide. Ernst had never really wanted to go to Germany, but felt that he had to take the opportunity while he could. But he never really settled in his new country.

"It was a constant battle between the migrants and the natives," he said. "The Germans felt they were better than us *Zuwanderer*. Before

I went to Germany, I thought I could speak German, but when I got there I couldn't even understand what was being said on television. The Mennonites had not had any contact with Germany for several hundred years, so the language we spoke was ridiculously old-fashioned. Unlike the Germans, we pronounce words as they are written. And with all the abbreviations they use now, I could not work it out."

Ernst stayed in Germany for twelve years, in the course of which he got married, divorced and then married again. In 2001, he moved back to Kyrgyzstan, to Rot-Front, with his new Russian bride.

"I was shocked by how much had changed. The houses were so dilapidated. The village looked old. There are really only Kyrgyz living here now. Five years ago there were thirty German families in the village, now only ten. And presumably in fifteen years or so, there will be no Germans left at all in Rot-Front.

"Now, is there anything more I can tell you? That, basically, is the history of Rot-Front. You were indeed very fortunate to bump into me, *gnädige Frau!*"

Ernst gave me a friendly smile and held out his hand again in parting. Dizzy and sunburned, with a face that lived up to the village name, I tottered back to the car.

The following day was a Sunday. The church was easy to find, a simple grey building at the top of the village that had been built when Gorbachev was in power, with financial support from Germany. There were already twenty to thirty people in the pews. I sat down on the left-hand side, where the women were. I noticed people looking at me; I was the only woman wearing trousers, and the only foreigner. Most of the women wore headscarves, none of them had any jewellery and their faces were free of make-up. There were fewer men, and they sat on the right-hand side. The older men all wore dark suits. Ernst Koop, my friend from the day before, was not there. The church was as plain as the congregation. The walls were muted brown, beige and bare, with no colourful stained glass or paintings. There were Bible quotes in Russian on the wall behind the choir.

By a quarter to ten, more than a hundred people had gathered: there were a fair number of Germans, but most were Russian or Kyrgyz. At ten o'clock they started to sing: slow, melancholy songs from the Russian psalm book. Everyone sang. The high women's voices floated up to the ceiling. It went on and on. I thought it would never end. As soon as they had finished one psalm, they turned the page and started another.

When the last note did finally die away, a woman in early middle age stood up. She was eloquent and spoke for some time in a quiet voice that carried well. As human beings, we have to dare to be open and tolerant, she said in Russian. We have to dare to look those who do not belong to our community in the eye, to embrace their stories and their pain, to talk to them, to be open and friendly. When she sat down, another woman stood up. In a trembling voice, she told us how Jesus had helped her through difficult times. Then a young man. And a young woman from the choir. The rest of the congregation listened to what they had to say. Three fair-haired children sitting behind me were reading a German book. Noiselessly they turned the pages, looked at the letters, devoured the words. They were patient, invisible, silent.

Finally, the man who seemed to be the leader of the congregation got up to speak. He was lean and upright, with an air of authority that none of the others had. He positioned himself by the simple lectern and started to talk about God. His voice was firm and sincere, and he did not need to raise it. He spoke Russian, as the others had done, though it was clear that he was of German descent. My thoughts drifted on the gentle Russian sounds and were somewhere else all together when suddenly a word caught my attention: *journal-ist*. The elder was no longer talking about God, he was admonishing journalists.

"Journalists have come here and written erroneous things about us," he said. "It is therefore best not to talk to journalists." He looked in my direction as he spoke, but would not meet my eye.

Another prayer. A weeping woman stood up to speak. More singing. Then everyone who was not a member of the church was asked to leave. All the children and many of the adults stood up, as I went out into the sun. I felt the piercing looks of those who remained seated.

Shortly after, the rest of the congregation came out. The elder stood in the doorway. He beckoned to me.

"No doubt you already know my name," he said, as I approached him.

"No," I said, and it was the truth. "But I assume that you are the church elder?"

He nodded.

"Heinrich Hann. I understand that you have already spoken to Herr Wilhelm?"

"Briefly, yes," I said.

He nodded again. Then he launched into a longer speech, which he had obviously prepared: "I apologise, our experience with jour-nalists is not the best. Not just one, but several. They come here and write things that are untrue. And a number of books have already been written about us. Why should any more be written? What is the point? I think it would be best for everyone if you left now. No-one wants to talk to you."

I tried to get him to tell me what these journalists had written that was so wrong, but Herr Hann pursed his lips and refused to say more. He turned on his heel and disappeared into the church.

Before heading back to Bishkek, I asked my driver to stop at the graveyard. It lay undisturbed on the other side of the river, surrounded by a mixture of pine and deciduous trees. The ground was covered in dry, yellow leaves. The graves were simple and well tended. Former members of the congregation looked out at us from portraits on the headstones, timeless in their suits and respectable dresses, with combed hair and no jewellery or make-up. The headstones, however, were decorated with edifying, religious quotes: *Die Liebe weint. Der Glaube tröstet.* Love weeps. Faith heals. *Durchs Kreuz zur Krone.* Through the Cross to the Crown. *Ich bin Dahin! Kommst Du auch?* I am there! Are you coming too? From the years, we could see that it was not long since they were with us: 1988. 1987. 1989. 2009.

Herr Hann was locking the doors as we went past the church on the way out of the village. He turned and scowled as we passed.

GREEK NUTS

Legend has it that Arslanbob, the village's great benefactor and namesake, first came there in the eleventh century. The Prophet Mohammed had sent him on a mission to find heaven on earth. Arslanbob visited various places and countries, but he did not find heaven – until he came to a fertile valley surrounded by green slopes, with rivers and streams full of fresh, sparkling water. Arslanbob knew then that his mission was accomplished. The only problem was that the heavenly place had no trees. Arslanbob spoke to Mohammed, and told him that he had found heaven on earth, but there were no trees there. So Mohammed sent him a bag of nuts and Arslanbob climbed to the highest point in the valley and scattered the nuts.

And that, according to the tourist office, was the origin of the walnut forest of Arslanbob. Asilbek, the holy man of the village and guardian of the town mausoleum, told me a variation of the same story.

"Arslanbob was a close friend of Mohammed," he said. He had a long grey beard and full lips, and was dressed in worn suit trousers and an oversized brown jacket. He had a small, white hat on his head.

"The Prophet told Arslanbob that he had three tasks for him. The first was to look after the seeds of the orange kaki fruit. One day he would meet the man who was to have the seeds, and he should give them to him. Arslanbob kept the seeds under his tongue until he met the man, and he gave them to him, as he had promised the Prophet he would. The second task was to go to a green hill and plant a big garden. And Arslanbob did this. Then, finally, he would meet the angel Gabriel, who would give him some nuts. This time, he was not to give them away, but to plant them himself, which he did, here, in our village, in Arslanbob." Asilbek smiled. "And now forty generations have passed since Arslanbob came here, and I am a direct descendant."

The other walnut story that the local tourist office liked to tell involved Alexander the Great and contradicted the first two. When Alexander was travelling east with his army, they passed Arslanbob. To show the soldiers that they were not enemies, the locals welcomed them with baskets of walnuts. The soldiers were so taken with the tasty nuts that they took some back to Greece. There they planted the walnuts that grew into forests; thus the walnut trees of Arslanbob are the source of the European walnut. In Russian, walnuts are called *gretsky orekh*, Greek nuts, but if the legend is to be believed, a more apt name would be *kirgisky orekh*, Kyrgyz nuts.

In a fourth story about the origins of the walnut forest of Arslanbob, Alexander the Great brought the nuts with him from India, in great sacks, which he used as payment whenever he was taken across a river. When he got to Arslanbob, he and his soldiers planted what was left of the nuts. The two guides at the tourist office told me that the story was nothing more than lies and fabrication, and not to believed.

While there may be some disagreement as to how the walnut came to Arslanbob, no-one can deny that the walnut forest that surrounds the village covers an area of roughly six hundred square kilometres and is thus the largest wild walnut grove in the world. Arslanbob was the greenest and most fertile place I visited on my entire journey. The forest stretched eastwards in great green waves, kilometre after kilometre, until it met the blue mountains on the horizon. The houses were almost engulfed by the trees and it was only when I looked down on the village from a hill in the woods that I realised how big it was. Hundreds of houses and gardens were more or less hidden by the green canopy. And the houses were bigger and better built than any I had seen in other villages. They were made from bricks, freshly painted, with large, shining windows. The gardens were a joy.

A network of paths and gravel tracks led into the woods. There were allotments divided by low fences that families from the village could rent. Ten per cent of all income from the walnut sales goes to the local walnut association, which is responsible for looking after the forest and planting new trees. Some colourful tents had been pitched between the solid trunks, and there were children playing and running around everywhere. It was October and walnut season. Every autumn, the villagers have four or five weeks to pick the ripe nuts. If the snow comes, it is too late. Many families move out into the forest for the duration, so they do not lose valuable time walking to and from the village.

Abidshan and his family had been living in the forest for several weeks already. The whole family helped to gather, shell and clean the walnuts, even the youngest daughter, who was two. How the parents and four children coped in the small plastic tent that was barely bigger than a Volkswagen Beetle was a mystery. Colourful mattresses, rugs, cooking utensils and food were all stored under the tent flap. Hens pottered around between the tent lines. The family's donkey was tied to a tree. Their cat and dog had come with them too.

Abidshan's face was so weathered that he looked far older than his forty-five years. His gold teeth and protruding jaw did not help much. But his body was as slender and supple as a twenty year old's.

His arms and legs were strong and sinewy. He climbed into one of the trees like a monkey, using only a bit of rope and no safety equipment. He soon was no more than a dark silhouette up in the crown, thirty metres above the ground. He gingerly stepped out onto one of the branches. It curved down, but did not break. When he was almost at the end of the branch, which arched down under his weight, he squatted and started to bounce. The air was full of falling leaves and walnuts. The children darted about, gathering up the green, wrinkly nuts that were everywhere. Before the nuts can be sold, they have to be shelled and cleaned. The children's hands were already coloured black.

"Isn't it dangerous?" I asked when Abidshan had come down again.

"No, not if you respect the tree," he said. "Sometimes young men fall and injure themselves, but that is nearly always because they've been reckless. Personally I have never had an accident, thanks be to God."

The family have one hundred and twenty trees. In a good year, they harvest five hundred kilos of nuts. In early autumn, the price for a kilo of walnuts is sixty som, around seventy pence. In a country where the gross domestic product per inhabitant is less than seven hundred pounds a year, the nuts provide a considerable amount of extra income. The family rarely eat nuts themselves, everything is sold. If they waited until the high season in December to sell their nuts, they could earn twice as much, but very few people can afford to wait.

"Is it nice living in the forest?" I asked the eldest son, who was twelve.

"Oh, yes!" he said. His young face lit up. "The nuts mean money, lots and lots of money!"

Like most of the inhabitants of Arslanbob, Abidshan and his

family were Uzbeks, not Kyrgyz. According to the tourist office, Arslanbob's demographic composition can also be explained by a legend: many hundreds of years ago, an Uzbek princess was given in marriage to a Kyrgyz king. To show his thanks, the king gave Arslanbob to the princess's father. So Arslanbob became Uzbek, even though most of the neighbouring villages are Kyrgyz.

Regardless of how true the legend may be, Arslanbob is a good example of how misleading the borders in Central Asia can be. It would be natural to assume that the Kyrgyz live in Kyrgyzstan, which, after all, means Land of the Kyrgyz, and the Uzbeks live in Uzbekistan, Land of the Uzbeks, and so on. But that is not the case. Nearly half the Turkmens in Central Asia live outside Turkmenistan, many of them in Afghanistan and Iran. There are more Tajiks in Afghanistan than in Tajikistan. In Samarkand and Bukhara, both in Uzbekistan, the main language is Tajik. The Uzbeks, for their part, account for a sixth of the population of Kyrgyzstan and at least a fifth of the population of Tajikistan.

The Soviet cartographers did not have an easy task creating order out of the Central Asian patchwork of different peoples, languages and clans. Until 1924, the Russians treated Central Asia as one big region which they called Turkestan – Land of the Turks – as most people who lived there spoke Turkic languages. The Russians knew perfectly well that the people of Central Asia belonged to different clans and cultures, but saw no reason to complicate things further. It was difficult enough as it was. People often did not know which nationality they were. In the 1926 consensus, people could name their tribe and family, but could not always answer if they were Uzbek, Kyrgyz or Tajik.

In the same way that Turkestan had never existed as a unified, organised entity until the Russians invented it towards the end of the nineteenth century, the five post-Soviet republics that exist today had never been defined as such prior to 1991. The new countries follow borders that were drawn up in the Twenties and Thirties under Stalin, and which have no historical basis whatsoever. If the Russians had followed the more fluid borders of the khanates, Uzbekistan would have been divided into three states. Instead, the Soviet authorities chose to work along ethnic and linguistic divisions, without really caring much whether the map fitted reality or not.

The interesting question is why the Soviet authorities bothered to divide up Turkestan into five republics in the first place. It was partly due to the Communists' understanding of nationhood. They believed it was an important stage in the movement towards worldwide revolution, and used nationality as an organising principle across the union. It was also in part motivated by a fear that the Muslims in Turkestan would unite under a pan-Turkic nationalism. By emphasising how different the Central Asian languages were, when in some cases the similarities were in fact greater than the differences, as with Kyrgyz and Kazakh, and by highlighting the different cultures and histories, the Soviet authorities contributed to the construction of new linguistic and cultural divisions between the Central Asian tribes.

The strategy succeeded. Throughout the Soviet period, there was more contact and trade between the five Central Asian republics and Russia than there was contact and fraternisation between the five republics themselves. To this day, the Stans have closer economic and political ties with Russia than they do with each other. And indeed, it is to strengthen this relationship with Moscow, rather than any cooperation between the Stans that Kazakhstan has become a member of the Eurasian Economic Union, as has Kyrgyzstan. And Tajikistan will soon follow suit.

The borders between the different tribes and people were, as mentioned, approximate. As the different nationalities lived side by side in many places, one would have had to move hundreds of thousands, if not millions, of people if the borders were to delineate ethnic lines with greater precision. Stalin was not normally shy of taking on such tasks, but he did not pursue it in Central Asia. "Divide and Rule" was the policy from Moscow.

In the fertile Fergana Valley, where Tajikistan, Kyrgyzstan and Uzbekistan meet, the borders make for a confusing zigzag pattern on the map. The Kyrgyz, Tajiks and Uzbeks have lived side by side here for centuries. Large areas that were mainly settled by Uzbeks ended up on the Kyrgyz side of the border under the Soviet Union. When the Soviet Republic of Tajikistan was divided from the Soviet Republic of Uzbekistan in 1929, several hundreds of thousands of Tajiks ended up on the Uzbek side and vice versa. To make matters even more complicated, small Tajik and Uzbek enclaves were established in Kyrgyzstan, as well as Kyrgyz enclaves in Uzbekistan. These enclaves still exist today, and are an annoyance for other citizens who often have to make time-consuming detours around them. In the Soviet era, when controls were generally a formality, the borders and enclaves posed no real problem. The various republics leased land from each other as needed, and people could visit relatives in neighbouring republics without any restrictions.

Today, however, the borders that were previously no more than lines on the map are now physical barriers. People who lived together peacefully in Moscow's iron grip are now bitter enemies. The relationship between the Kyrgyz and the Uzbeks, who account for a third of the population in south Kyrgyzstan, is particularly complex. Historically, Kyrgyz have been wary of the settled Uzbeks, while the Uzbeks, for their part, have looked down on the Kyrgyz nomadic culture. As Uzbeks have traditionally worked with crafts and trade, they are generally better off than the Kyrgyz, who started

moving into the towns comparatively recently, and often struggle
to find work.

The underlying conflict was kept in check until the final years
of the Soviet Union. In June 1990, when the union started to come
apart at the seams, the first sparks flew. The conflict began when
an Uzbek nationalist group and a Kyrgyz nationalist group got
embroiled in a dispute about the ownership of a former collective
farm. The sparks quickly developed into a wildfire. In a matter of
days, three hundred people had been killed and twelve hundred
more had been injured. The battles were primarily fought in south
Kyrgyzstan, in Uzgen and Osh, which is the second largest city
in Kyrgyzstan. Three days after the riots began, Gorbachev sent in
troops. The highly trained soldiers quickly gained control of the
situation. Peacekeeping forces remained in the region for a further
six months to prevent the conflict from flaring up again.

When the Soviet Union collapsed, many Kyrgyz were worried
that the Uzbeks would have too much power and influence in
Kyrgyzstan. They had just been freed from the yoke of the Russians
and wanted to rule themselves. The Uzbeks, for their part, were sick
and tired of being known as the "Uzbek diaspora", as though they
were only temporary guests driven from their own country when
in fact they had lived on Kyrgyz territory for several centuries. The
Kyrgyz history books do not even mention the Uzbeks, and, following the introduction of the new language act in 2004, the use of
Uzbek in formal documents is no longer permitted. Uzbeks are also
excluded from holding political posts or positions of power.

Twenty years were to pass before the Uzbeks and Kyrgyz clashed
again in Osh. This time the number of people killed was higher than
in 1990.

FIVE DAYS IN JUNE

On June 12, 2010, two days after violent clashes had broken out in Osh, the unrest had spread to Jalal-Abad, a provincial town with around one hundred thousand inhabitants close to the border with Uzbekistan. Nigora, a 26-year-old Uzbek woman, was in her aunt's back garden in Lenin Street, together with her sister, aunt and cousin, and her cousin's two small children, when they heard the first gunshots. The women and children hurried into her aunt's house, locked all the doors and hid in a room without windows. They heard men's voices outside on the street and the tinkling sound of breaking glass. Nigora was worried about her three-year-old son, who was with her sister-in-law nearby, but she did not dare go out, however much she wanted to be with her son.

Dozens of shops were looted that evening. The jewellers further down the street had more than three thousand pounds' worth of jewellery stolen, which amounts to a fortune in Kyrgyzstan. Kyrgyz gangs drove around areas where only Uzbeks lived. They went from house to house, and loaded carpets, fridges, washing machines, T.V.s and jewellery into their vans before setting fire to the homes. Throughout the day and night, Kyrgyz came down from the villages to fight. An entire village outside Jalal-Abad went up in flames, and hundreds of people were killed or seriously injured in the clashes between Uzbeks and Kyrgyz.

The next morning, Nigora's sister-in-law rang. They did not know yet that Timur, her twenty-year-old son, was one of those who had been killed. She told Nigora that her little boy was frightened and was asking for his mother. Could she try to come by? Things had quietened down outside. They could no longer hear voices or gunfire from the street. Nigora and her sister, who offered to go with her, opened their gate with caution and went out into the deserted street. There were no cars and all the shops were closed. The smell of smoke lingered. When they got to the traffic lights, they saw two big Kyrgyz men coming towards them on the other side of the road. The men stopped when they spotted Nigora and her sister. They were no more than thirty or forty metres from them. They pulled out two long knives from a plastic bag. Further behind them, a group of nine or ten Kyrgyz appeared. "Stop those Uzbeks!" one of them shouted. Nigora and her sister turned and ran as fast as they could back to their aunt's house. They heard the men chasing them. The gate to their aunt's house was locked. "Auntie, open the gate!" Nigora shouted, and hammered on the gate. The aunt opened the gate and the two sisters managed to slip in just before the men were upon them. Their pursuers stood outside on the pavement and thumped and kicked the big metal gate.

Two hours later, the Kyrgyz came back. They kicked and thumped on the gate again, but it was big and solid, so they did not manage to get in. Instead they broke into the neighbour's house and stole his car. The women were frightened that the men would come back a third time and manage to force open the gate, so they fled to the house on the other side, where their blind neighbour lived with his son. The son showed them into a small storeroom, where he said they would be safe. "Don't go anywhere, stay here until we come to get you," he said, and locked the door, as a precaution.

Two other families had already sought refuge there, and nine women and ten children were now crammed into the small, dark room where the blind man and his son stored their potatoes and

onions in winter. It was summer outside and extremely hot. The air
in the small space was thick with the smell of sweat, fear and onions.
The minutes ticked slowly by, and when they had been there for
about an hour, they heard the old man begging and crying: "No, no,
don't do it, please, don't do it!" Then they heard the unmistakable
crackle of flames. They felt the fire getting closer, smoke filled the
small storeroom, and it got hotter and hotter inside. But the door
was locked, and they could not get out. Soon the roof caught fire.
The heat was unbearable and the air was full of smoke, and they
coughed and cried. They all prayed to God. Nigora did too. She
prayed that they would escape. This single prayer was the only clear
thought in her head. She waited, waited to be rescued, waited for
something to happen, waited for it to end. The flames licked the feet
of a fourteen-year-old girl. Both her legs caught fire, but she was so
terrified she did not notice. Nigora had started to accept that they
were going to die when the blind man's son came and opened the
door. The fire was about to engulf the house. Flames leaped out of
the windows. Nigora ran out with the other women and children.

When they reached the cul-de-sac behind the neighbour's
house, they stopped, uncertain what to do. Was it safe to leave? Four
kind Kyrgyz men standing further up the street saw the hysterical
women and came over. "Don't be frightened," they said, "we're your
neighbours, we'll help you." They took them to a nearby flat. They
were safe there. Other Kyrgyz neighbours came with food and did
what they could to help.

The following day it was over. The Kyrgyz gangs had gone and
it was safe to go out. But the women did not dare leave the flat until
later in the day. Nigora's son was so happy to see his mother again
that he forgot in an instant how frightened he had been. Nigora,
on the other hand, was terrified by sudden, loud noises for months
to come.

"It takes time to forget," she tells me. She is a slight young woman, dressed in a hijab and tight jeans. Her face is open, almost childlike. "Slowly, slowly, I stopped being frightened. Life returned to normal. But some things will never be the same. Something was broken for ever. Timur will never come back. My neighbour, who was pregnant, was so frightened when the shooting started that she lost her baby. And the relationship between the Uzbeks and the Kyrgyz will never be the same. I feel a shiver down my spine whenever I hear the word Kyrgyz."

As is often the case in chaotic situations, there are different explanations as to why and how the riots erupted that summer. Eyewitness accounts are disjointed and contradictory. One incident that prevails in many of the testimonies is an argument between an Uzbek and a Kyrgyz in the 24 Hours gambling hall in Osh on the evening of June 9. The Uzbek guest had apparently lost a large sum of money and started to quarrel with a young Kyrgyz man. The confrontation escalated and several Uzbeks on the premises rang other Uzbeks for help. Soon the whole town knew that there had been a clash between Uzbeks and Kyrgyz, and gangs of young men started to gather in the city centre.

No-one could explain later how the rumour had started. But in the space of a few hours, the whole town suddenly "knew" that something had happened at a university accommodation building. As the minutes and hours passed, the stories become wilder and wilder. Even though the dormitory building was still standing, the whole of Osh was soon convinced that a group of Uzbeks had razed it to the ground after raping, maiming and killing the young female students. Some days after the state of emergency had been lifted, a lawyer described what had happened as follows, fully convinced that this was the truth: "The crowd breaks into the dormitory and rapes female students. Others beat up male Kyrgyz students and break the windows inside the building. Eight bodies of female students who had been raped and cut up and who have signs of being burnt have been found. On some of them, they had ripped open their stomachs and thrown garbage in there, and poked out their eyes."[xii]

The reality is that no-one broke into the dormitory that night, neither Uzbeks nor Kyrgyz, and no-one was raped or killed. But the rumour had a life of its own, as rumours are wont to do, and incited the city's young Kyrgyz men. In the course of the night, the situation got out of control and Osh became a war zone. The streets were full of armed gangs and tanks. Big, black letters were painted on houses and shops. Those that were marked KYRGYZ remained untouched.

On June 12, the violence reached Jalal-Abad, a hundred kilometres north of Osh. The authorities in Bishkek were powerless. They asked Russia for help, but President Medvedev did not want to get involved in Kyrgyzstan's internal affairs.

It was not until June 15, five bloody days later, that the authorities were able to put a stop to the violence with the help of the army. More than 420 people had been killed and more than two thousand injured. Several thousand had fled to the border area and into Uzbekistan. Two thousand buildings had been destroyed by fire.

There are many similarities between the events of 1990 and 2010. In both cases, the violence erupted in a power vacuum, when the government was weak. In 1990, the Soviet Union was on its last legs; in summer 2010, Kyrgyzstan had just started to recover from the revolution earlier in the year when President Bakiyev had been forced into exile. In 1990, there was a downturn in the economy, as there was in 2010, in the wake of the international financial crisis. In both 1990 and 2010, the majority of the casualties were Uzbeks.

There is, however, one significant difference. In the court cases that followed the 1990 disturbances, which, incidentally, were the first trials resulting from an ethnic conflict in the Soviet Union, forty-eight people were found guilty of murder, attempted murder and rape, and given long sentences. Eighty per cent of them were Kyrgyz. Following the events in 2010, four out of five of the seventy-one people found guilty of murder were Uzbeks. And of these, seventeen – all Uzbeks – were sentenced to life imprisonment following trials that have been severely criticised by human rights organisations. In all the cases, the judges and the lawyers, including the defence lawyers, were Kyrgyz.

Three years after these dramatic events occurred, many of the burned-out sites in Jalal-Abad remain. The skeleton buildings serve as a reminder of the hate that spilled over on those sunny days in June. The highly esteemed Kyrgyz-Uzbek University of People's Friendship has not opened its doors since. Burnt curtains flutter behind broken windowpanes and the walls are covered in soot.

The relationship between the Kyrgyz and the Uzbeks is still tense, and very few of them have a good word to say about the other. Many Uzbeks have moved, either to Uzbekistan or to Russia. Nigora, however, has chosen to stay in Jalal-Abad.

"Most of my friends have left in protest, and gone to Russia," she says. "They don't want to be Kyrgyz citizens anymore. Obviously, we're all frightened that it could happen again, but Kyrgyzstan is my home. Jalal-Abad is my home. I don't want to move away."

SILENCE IN THE WAITING ROOM

They sit side by side in a long row against the wall. For some reason, very probably coincidence, they are all dressed in black. Black leather jackets, black scarves, black skirts, worn black shoes. They are all ages, from hunchbacked old women to lanky young men. The youngest cannot be more than two or three years old. He is sitting on his mother's lap, whimpering. Otherwise, there is silence in the corridor.

"They have to come here every morning for their medicine," the doctor says, as he closes the door behind him. He is a compact man in his fifties, with thick, grey hair and tailored but not ostentatious clothes. "A number of our patients don't believe the pills really work, which is why they have to come here, so our nurses can make sure they actually swallow them."

I express my surprise that even little Jalal-Abad has its own T.B. clinic. The doctor does not raise an eyebrow.

"Of course we do. We have T.B. clinics all over the country now. Here alone, we are seeing around eighty new cases a year. There are more than ten thousand people in the country with T.B. At least ten per cent of them have the aggressive multidrug-resistant strain."

The Central Asian republics have all had to fight a resurgence of tuberculosis since the Soviet Union collapsed. Kyrgyzstan is one of the countries that has been hardest hit – not just in terms of the region, but on a global basis. Multidrug-resistant T.B., in particular, which is difficult and expensive to treat, is on the rise.

"Things have got worse since the dissolution of the Soviet Union," the doctor says. "All the vaccination programmes fell apart at the same time. There's more unemployment now and more poverty. And there's no social security and no support network. Many of those affected are young adults in their prime. Unfortunately it's often people between twenty and forty-five who are worst affected. Officially, there are 700,000 Kyrgyz migrant workers in Russia, and most of them are young men. They live in poor conditions, with up to twenty-five people sharing a small flat. It's not strange then, really, that they all get ill. Prisons are incubators as well. The prisoners have a poor diet and live in close proximity to each other in cold, badly insulated cells. There's only one cure for this epidemic, and that's work for everyone and better pay. I earn a little more than one hundred dollars a month, and that's seen as a good wage in this country. Is it strange then that all the specialists go to Russia? They can easily earn 1,500 dollars a month there."

"Well, it's a good thing that you, at least, stayed," I say. "If all the doctors had gone to Russia, there would be no-one to treat the ill."

The doctor shrugs.

"If I got a good offer, I'd go."

DO YOU HAVE ANY PORN
WITH YOU, MISS?

If you are travelling from Kyrgyzstan to Uzbekistan, it is recommended that you cross the border during the cotton season. Usually the queues stretch for miles, and if you are unlucky you can look forward to hours of waiting, endless formalities and yet more waiting. In the cotton season, however, you will have the border more or less to yourself.

In order to discourage people from missing the annual communal work fest, the border to Uzbekistan is closed to everyone except foreigners. Every autumn, hundreds of thousands of doctors, teachers, nurses, bureaucrats and other public sector employees, as well as students, are called on to pick cotton – an old tradition from Soviet times that has been maintained; the only difference being that in the Soviet Union, the majority of the harvesting was done by machine, whereas now it is done by hand, as no-one has troubled to maintain and repair the machines. As the flowering season is so short, the 1.4 million hectares of cotton have to be picked in the space of a few frantic weeks and many people have to sleep under the open sky or on cold, crammed floors. An impressive number of public sector employees and people from other affected groups used to take long family holidays to neighbouring countries during the cotton harvest, but a stop has been put to that now.

"From Norway? Oslo?" The passport control officer smiled at me. "Samarkand, Bukhara, Khiva?"

I nodded. Another broad smile, stamp and hey presto, I entered one of the world's worst dictatorships. Well, not quite yet. The customs check is the real challenge, not passport control. Having gone through my luggage, the customs officer then wanted to know what I did. I had to lie again.

"Student! At your age?" He gave me a stern look. "I am twenty-five and I graduated from the military academy when I was twenty-two. And I have worked ever since. I take it you're not married?" It was more of a statement than a question.

"No, I'm not married."

He shook his head and waved me on to his colleague, who was responsible for moral checks.

"Do you have any porn with you, Miss?" The customs officer looked at me with interest.

I shook my head.

"What about bibles? Religious propaganda?"

I shook my head.

To be on the safe side, he asked if he could check all the books and photographs I had with me. He studied each picture on my telephone. Sometimes he asked a question: is this from Oslo? Does it get cold there in winter? Is that your mother? When he found the German Gender app with the symbols for male and female on the German flag, he lit up like a teenager. He pressed the symbol and the alternatives popped up: *Der. Die. Das.* Not to lose face, he tried with a couple of words. Got both wrong.

"Are you travelling alone?"

I nodded.

"Aren't you scared?"

"Uzbekistan isn't a dangerous country, is it?" I said.

"No, you're safe *here*, but . . ." He nodded pointedly towards Kyrgyzstan. "It's dangerous over *there*. Very dangerous."

He waved me through and I walked past the barrier into Uzbekistan.

"Be careful!" he called after me.

UZBEKISTAN

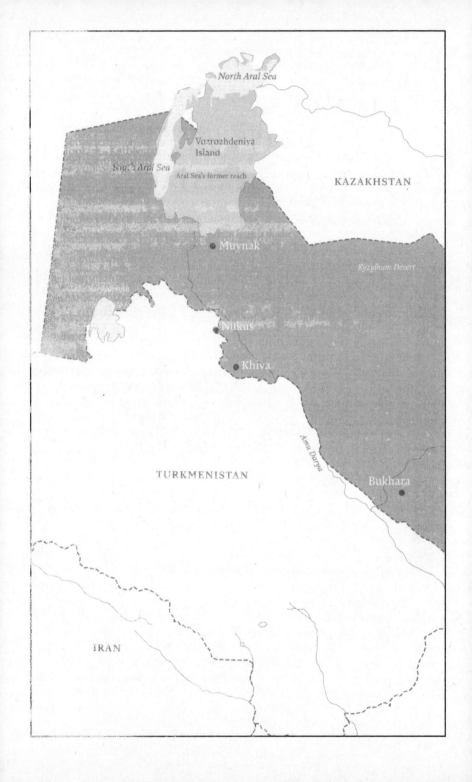

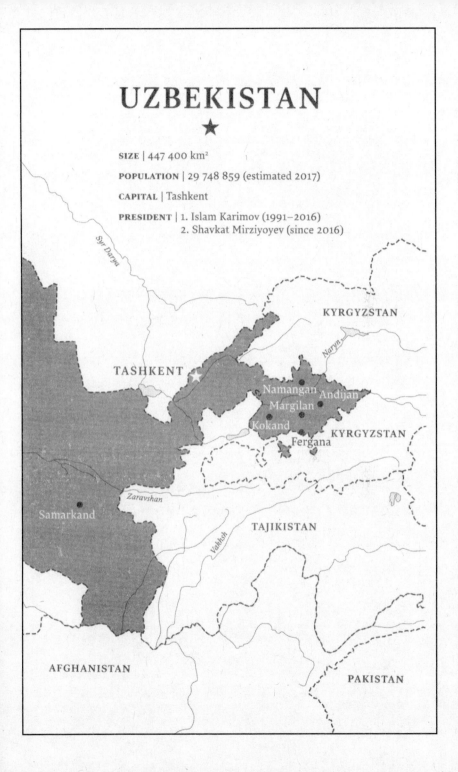

UZBEKISTAN

★

SIZE | 447 400 km²

POPULATION | 29 748 859 (estimated 2017)

CAPITAL | Tashkent

PRESIDENT | 1. Islam Karimov (1991–2016)
2. Shavkat Mirziyoyev (since 2016)

Syr Darya

KYRGYZSTAN

Naryn

TASHKENT

Namangan
Andijan
Margilan
Kokand
KYRGYZSTAN
Fergana

Zaravshan

TAJIKISTAN

Vakhsh

Samarkand

AFGHANISTAN

PAKISTAN

THE ART OF KEEPING UP APPEARANCES

The hotel's enormous restaurant looked as though it had been decorated for a wedding, but I was the only guest. While I was eating, a blonde girl approached the table with a smile. She held out her hand and introduced herself as Maria. "They said I might find you here," she said in perfectly accented English.

"Who are 'they'?" I asked warily. I had been warned that the secret police were omnipresent in Uzbekistan and that all foreigners, particularly those travelling alone, were kept under surveillance. As it is nigh on impossible to get a press visa to Uzbekistan, the handful of foreign journalists that are at any one time in the country generally operate undercover. If caught, they risk deportation. Which is nothing compared to what local journalists and contacts might suffer: being sectioned, torture, plain old murder (which no-one bothers to investigate) or long prison sentences in inhumane conditions. All that is standard treatment for champions of the free press in Uzbekistan.

"The receptionist, who else?" the friendly, blue-eyed girl said. "He said that a tourist had just checked in and I would probably find you in the restaurant. I'm a journalist for the state television channel, *Uzbekistan 1*, and I'm doing a report on private entrepreneurs in Andijan."

She did not need to tell me it was a state-run channel, as all T.V. channels in Uzbekistan are.

"There are many private entrepreneurs in Andijan, and that

makes the region pretty unusual," the girl told me. "Do you have time for an interview? It would be interesting for our viewers to know what you, a foreigner, think of our country."

"I've only just arrived," I said. "So I'm afraid I don't really have much to say." In a moment of paranoia, I got it into my head that Maria had been sent by the S.N.B., Uzbekistan's answer to the K.G.B., to find out what I was doing in their country and the interview was just an excuse to interrogate me.

"That doesn't matter," Maria assured me with another big smile. "Just give us your first impression of the city."

"I haven't got much of an impression . . ." I started. The smile disappeared from Maria's eyes and she seemed to crumble.

"Just let me finish my salad first," I said. "Then we can start."

As I ate, Maria told me about her dream to move away from Uzbekistan. To Germany, preferably. As an ethnic Russian, she felt foreign in her own country. Following the collapse of the Soviet Union, as many as half the ethnic Russians had left Uzbekistan and moved to Russia or to Kazakhstan. There are now fewer than one million left. Russian is no longer an official language, and many young Uzbeks would rather learn English. Maria spoke Uzbek, but with an accent.

"I can't leave until I've done my obligatory three years for the state," she said with a sigh. "Everyone who graduates from a state institution in Uzbekistan has to work for the country for at least that long."

Any aspiring Norwegian journalist would jump for joy if they were guaranteed work experience with the national broadcasting service, but Maria longed to get away. She wanted to start a new life in Germany. She was under no illusion that her training and experience as a journalist with Uzbek state television would be of an advantage in the West and was prepared to retrain.

When I had finished, we went out onto the veranda, which had a panoramic view of what Maria called the old town. None of the shiny brown facades looked older than a year at most.

"Here we are with Erika Fatland, a Norwegian tourist," Maria said earnestly to the camera. "What are your first impressions of Uzbekistan, Miss Fatland?"

"Everything is surprisingly modern here," I said, and immediately regretted using the word "modern". Could that be seen as offensive? Maria just smiled with enthusiasm, and I realised that she wanted me to elaborate.

"There are so many great new buildings here," I said.

"In Andijan, there are more than fifty thousand entrepreneurs and small businesses, a fantastic example of the kind of commercial activity that is encouraged and supported by our government. Do you have any comments?"

What I really wanted to say was that it sounded like pure dictator propaganda to me, but instead I heard myself saying: "That's wonderful. Burgeoning entrepreneurship is positive for a country's economy and growth, and helps to keep unemployment down. I've just been to Kyrgyzstan, where unemployment is very high and young people have to go to Russia to get work. That is so sad."

Several million Uzbeks earned their living as migrant workers in Russia, but I guessed that only the president would be allowed to comment on that, on state television. A few months earlier, he had in fact expressed his views in rather crass terms: "There are very few lazy people in Uzbekistan now," he said. "I describe as lazy those who go to Moscow and sweep its streets and squares. One feels disgusted with Uzbeks going there for a slice of bread."[xiii] Perhaps he feels equally disgusted by the idea that the money Uzbek migrant workers send home from Russia accounts for a fifth of the gross national product.

"What do you think about the fact that ninety per cent of the cars here in Andijan are manufactured in Uzbekistan?"

"That is impressive and so positive for the Uzbek economy," I said, with a smile. "It's great that the Uzbeks are so supportive of the local car industry."

Maria thanked me profusely for the interview and said again that she was so pleased that she had found me. "The viewers really do appreciate an outsider's perspective," she said.

Andijan. The name speaks of blood and death. If you look up the name on Google, "Andijan massacre" is one of the first choices. Tourists who come here from Kyrgyzstan generally move swiftly on. There is nothing worth seeing here. The only mosque that survived the earthquake in 1902 was destroyed by fire in the 1980s and all that remains is part of the facade around the entrance.

Before I left Andijan, I wanted to see Bobur Square, where the massacre took place. According to official figures, 187 people were killed in the clashes. Independent sources say that it was at least three times that number. Before I could go sightseeing, however, I had to solve a practical but precarious problem: I needed cash.

Uzbek money is a chapter unto itself. As part of the strategy to make it as difficult as possible for inhabitants to get hold of foreign currency, paying in anything other than Uzbek som is forbidden. The value of the som is extremely volatile and inflation is out of control. When the som replaced the rouble in 1993, the exchange rate with the dollar was set at seven Uzbek som. Now you have to pay 2,800 som for one US dollar on the black market. The official exchange rate is of course lower, at around 2,200 som, but it is all but impossible for normal people and honest business folk legally to get hold of dollars. Even state businesses have to wait weeks to get foreign currency, and there are strict quotas. The authorities have done nothing to adjust the difference between the black market and official exchange rate, and have instead exploited the discrepancy to the full in terms of export and import. In other words, they sell goods at the official exchange rate, and then they exchange the money on the black market.

As is the case with Turkmenistan, foreigners have to take sufficient dollars with them when visiting Uzbekistan. Plastic is not much use here. There are, in theory, A.T.M.s in Tashkent that accept VISA and Mastercard, but these are, most of the time, out of order. A couple of banks in the capital offer "cash advance", but only for a sizeable fee. So it really is down to dollar notes and the black market. All hotels give their prices in dollars, which they convert to the local currency at the day's exchange rate. With the exception of state hotels, which are obliged to use the official exchange rate, all of them use the black market. In other words, you too have to use the black market – not for gain, but to guard against loss. Technically, it is illegal to exchange money on the black market, but everyone does it, even the police. The dealers stand in fixed places, usually close to the markets, with plastic bags full of banknotes.

On black-market corners in central Andijan, currencies are whispered like monetary poetry.

"Kyrgyz som!"

"Dollar!"

"Russian rouble!"

"Euro!"

I approached a man with gold teeth and a two-day stubble.

"I'd like to change three hundred dollars, please,' I said, quietly.

"Only three hundred dollars?" he shouted back. "Not more? No euros? No Kyrgyz money?"

I shook my head.

"O.K., at today's rate, that's eight hundred and forty thousand."

I nodded. He made no attempt whatsoever to hide this illegal transaction, just fished up eight bundles of notes from a dirty plastic bag, which came to 800,000 som. Then with furious speed counted out forty 1,000-som notes, which he gave me along with the eight bundles.

"If you need to change any more, you know where to find me," he said and winked.

Because of the crazy inflation, Uzbeks are masters at counting money. They can count big bundles of notes like lightning, without losing track of the conversation or looking at their fingers as they leaf through the worn 1,000-som notes. A 5,000-som note had just been introduced, but it was clearly not in general circulation yet, because everything, even if it amounted to several million, was paid in 1,000- and 500-som notes.

If I ignored the fact that my bag was stuffed with banknotes, it felt a bit as if I had arrived in the Midwest. Compared to Tajikistan and Kyrgyzstan, Uzbekistan was incredibly modern. The brand-new, brown facades were built in a modern style and there were neon signs everywhere advertising FAST FOOD. In fact, there were no other restaurants on the main street, there was no slow food to be had. Nearly all the signs were written in the Latin alphabet. I still did not understand the Uzbek words, but as they were in Latin letters, they felt less foreign. The pavements were full of people. Most were dressed in western clothes, though some of the women had their hair covered. None of the men had long beards, as was the norm for Uzbeks in Kyrgyzstan. In Jalal-Abad I had even seen women in black niqabs, which would be unthinkable on this side of the border. Letting your beard grow or wearing Islamic clothes in Uzbekistan was asking to be arrested.

Despite their many conflicts and differences, the former com-

munist leaders of Central Asia are united on one front: they want
to prevent Islamist fundamentalism from gaining a foothold. They
have therefore all championed a moderate state Islam, based on
what they believe are traditional, Central Asian values. And they
have, to varying degrees, succeeded. Parallel restrictions have been
introduced in Tajikistan and Uzbekistan: Islamic clothing is banned
and only state-authorised mosques are permitted. In Turkmenistan,
suppression is so fierce that it is hard to find divergent religious
or political groups, and people are only allowed to pray in state
mosques or at home. The Kazakh authorities also keep a close eye
on the country's religious groups, but Islamic fundamentalists have
not as yet been a major problem – the Kazakh nomads have never
practised a strict form of Islam. Nor have the Kyrgyz. The heartland
of Central Asian Islam has traditionally been the fertile Fergana
Valley, which is now divided between Uzbekistan, Kyrgyzstan and
Tajikistan. Before the revolution in 1917, there were mosques on
every corner here, and women in *paranjas* were a common sight. The
paranja is a traditional woman's robe that was widely worn by Uzbeks
and Tajiks. It covers the body from head to foot, with a horsehair
veil to cover the face. These garments come in many colours, but,
as a rule, the veil is black. When the Communists came to power,
Central Asian women were liberated from the *paranja* and veil,
whether they wanted to be or not.

Following the dissolution of the Soviet Union, religion has once
again flourished in the Fergana Valley, and radical Islamist groups
such as Hizb ut-Tahrir, the Islamist Liberation Party, have taken
root. Many of the most active members served on the Soviet side
during the war in Afghanistan. There, the young men met Islam
for the first time, a profound experience for many of them.

Dzhumaboy Khodzhiev was one such. He served as a para-
trooper during the Soviet–Afghan war. In 1991, by now twenty-two,

he took the *nom de guerre* Juma Namangani and established the Sal-afist group Adolat (Justice) in his hometown of Namangan in the Fergana Valley. Adolat called for the imposition of Sharia law in Uzbekistan and for a short period managed to gain power in parts of the Fergana Valley. Close to a third of Uzbekistan's population lives there, and the bulk of the country's agricultural produce is grown in the valley. It was therefore imperative for Islam Karimov, the presi-dent, to regain control of the valley. He made his move in 1992: Adolat was banned and several of its members were arrested. Namangani and his followers escaped over the border to Tajikistan, where they fought alongside the Islamists in the civil war. When their support dwindled, they fled to Afghanistan and Pakistan, where they made contact with Osama bin Laden, among others. In 1998, Adolat was reborn as Uzbekistan's Islamist movement. The following year, when several bombs exploded in Tashkent in what was presumed to be an assassination attempt aimed at President Karimov, the authorities were quick to blame the Islamists in general, and the Uzbekistan Islamist movement in particular. Sixteen people were killed in the explosions. Karimov escaped without a scratch.

Like many of his Central Asian colleagues, Uzbekistan's presi-dent has had a remarkable career. He was born to a very poor Uzbek-Tajik family in Samarkand in 1938. He was able to complete his schooling thanks to scholarships, and graduated from the Central Asian Polytechnic Institute with a degree in mechanical engineering. The path from engineering to lifelong dictator is obviously very short in Central Asia. Karimov initially earned his living as a mechanic at the aircraft factory in Tashkent, while also studying economics. In 1966, he was appointed to a position in the Ministry of Finance and made steady progress up the ladder. After several changes at the top following corruption scandals and ethnic unrest in the Fergana Valley, Gorbachev appointed the relatively unknown Karimov as First Secretary of the Communist Party of Uzbekistan in 1989. Karimov made a name for himself as an authoritarian leader who toed the party line, but he was sceptical of Gorbachev's reforms. He gave wholehearted support to the conservative Communists' attempted coup in Moscow in August 1991. The coup was unsuccessful, and on August 31 Uzbekistan declared its independence. The primary motivation was not a strong desire for national independence, but rather the wish to sidestep Gorbachev's liberal reforms and keep the system as it was.

Uzbekistan has become one of the world's most ferocious dictatorships. With great cunning, Karimov has used the fear of ethnic violence, Islamist fundamentalism and unstable neighbours as an excuse to rule with an iron fist. Stability is the number one priority. Democracy, human rights and economic growth come second. The Uzbek regime is notorious for its violations of human rights. In order to stem population growth, for example, obstetricians in some regions have been ordered to sterilise a certain number of women every month. The women go into hospital for a caesarean section and leave without knowing that they can no longer have children. Prisoners are routinely tortured and raped as a means of forcing confessions. One of the preferred torture methods is to put a gas mask on the suspect and close all the valves. More than ninety-nine per cent of cases that go to court result in a prison sentence. In 2002, there was outrage when two young men who had been arrested on suspicion of religious fundamentalism were boiled alive. This is just one example. The former British ambassador to Uzbekistan, Craig Murray, describes in his book, *Murder in Samarkand*, how dead prisoners are frequently delivered back to their families in closed coffins, accompanied by a guard who is there to make sure that the relatives do not open the coffin before the funeral.

For a long time, the West turned a blind eye to Uzbekistan's human rights violations. When the U.S.A. went to war in Afghanistan after the terror attacks on September 11, 2001, the Karimov regime made a lucrative deal with the Americans for the lease of military bases on Uzbek soil. The U.S.A. and Uzbekistan were suddenly allies in the war on terrorism, and President Bush expressed great sympathy for his colleague's fight against Islamist fundamentalism. But just how dangerous was the fundamentalist threat in Uzbekistan? And was it really Uzbekistan's Islamist movement that was responsible for the bombs in Tashkent in 1999?

Today most terrorism experts, such as the Joint Terrorism Analysis Centre (J.T.A.C.), believe that it is unlikely. The bomb attacks were simply too professional, and the Uzbekistan Islamist movement has not been associated with similar actions before or since. There are several factors to indicate that it was either the government itself that carried out the terrorist attack, or factions within the government that wanted to get rid of Karimov. A wave of arrests followed the attacks and hundreds of people were locked up on suspicion of illegal religious activities and conspiracy against the state.

Even if many experts believe that Uzbekistan's Islamist movement was not behind the bombs in 1999, they were most definitely behind the kidnapping of the mayor of Osh in Kyrgyzstan in the same year. They were also behind the kidnapping of a group of Japanese geologists in south Kyrgyzstan. The mayor and the geologists were later released. In 2000, the following year, members of the movement then kidnapped four American climbers in south Kyrgyzstan. The Americans managed to escape after only a few days, but these incidents severely damaged the reputation of the Uzbek Islamists both in the West and in the rest of Central Asia.

On the morning of March 29, 2004, the Uzbek capital was again shaken by a series of attacks: a female suicide bomber killed six policemen at the Chorsu Bazaar in Tashkent. One hour later, another female suicide bomber was shot by police at a bus stop elsewhere in the city. And shortly after that, a man was killed by a presidential security guard as he drove through a checkpoint outside the president's palace. The car was apparently rigged like a car bomb, but it left no crater when it went up in flames. Nor did the bomb at the Chorsu Bazaar, if we are to believe former ambassador Craig Murray, who arrived at the scene soon after. The day before, eleven people had been killed in a police raid in Bukhara. The police said that they had raided a bomb factory and that one of the home-made bombs exploded during the raid. According to witnesses, however, the police threw hand grenades into the building. Over the next few days, a further thirteen people were killed in the course of police operations.

The authorities were quick to blame Uzbekistan's Islamist movement, Al-Qaeda and Hizb ut-Tahrir, the Islamist liberation party. Terrorism analysts are less certain that these organisations were behind it. There are too many things that do not fit: neither of the bombs left a crater; the parents of one of the so-called suicide bombers were taken into custody by police several hours before the supposed suicide bombing took place.

More arrests followed in the wake of the Tashkent bombs, including twenty-three businessmen from Andijan, who were suspected of being members of Akramija, an organisation on the government's list of terrorist bodies. Presumably the arrests were motivated by other things related to money and power. Following a long trial, the judgement was to be heard on May 11, 2005. That morning, several thousand supporters gathered outside the courthouse to await the verdict, and, as a result, the judge decided to delay the judgement. The following day, several of those who had initiated the demonstration were arrested. That night, a group of armed men broke into the prison where the businessmen were being held and several hundred prisoners managed to escape. The armed men then took more than twenty people hostage from various administrative buildings and demanded that Islam Karimov step down as the country's prime minister.

At the same time, several thousand people gathered at Bobur Square in the centre of Andijan. This quickly developed into a protest, not so much against the arrest of the businessmen, but rather the economic situation in Uzbekistan. Several protestors were outspoken. "Why is Uzbekistan ranked 137th out of 159 countries in the corruption index?" one of the demonstrators wanted to know. There were anti-Karimov chants. More and more people came to the square throughout the afternoon of May 13, and several thousand armed soldiers took up positions nearby. The demonstrators stayed where they were. There were rumours that President Karimov was on his way to speak to them.

Late in the afternoon, the soldiers closed off all the streets leading to Bobur Square, and then started to fire. The demonstrators were trapped. No-one knows how many people were shot and killed that day. Foreign journalists put the figure at somewhere between four and six hundred; some claim it was higher. Many of the witnesses have said that they saw soldiers shooting people who were already lying wounded on the ground. Some of the bodies were flown out of the capital on a specially chartered plane, others were buried in mass graves on the outskirts of Andijan.

I am not entirely sure what I had expected. More police, perhaps. A great security presence, barriers, secret agents with sunglasses and black leather jackets. But the square was empty save for a young couple who were sitting on a bench gazing into each other's eyes. There was not a trace of the massacre. The facades of the buildings

that looked onto the square were new and shiny. And in the middle
of the square there was a large statue of Zahir-ud-din Muhammad
Babur, the founder of the Mughal dynasty in India in the sixteenth
century. He was born in Andijan in 1483. The first Mughal emperor
gazed out over the vast square in lonely majesty.

The massacre in 2005 led to serious criticism from western
governments. Not even the U.S.A. could pretend to be blind to
such blatant abuse of power. The warm relationship cooled, and
Americans were told to leave Uzbek territory by the end of the year.
All western journalists and organisations were thrown out.

The Uzbek authorities have always asserted that the events in
Bobur Square were triggered by Uzbekistan's Islamist movement,
which was later seriously weakened by the death of one of its
founders in Afghanistan. Today it is most active in countries struggling with civil unrest, and in Pakistan and Iraq, and no longer has
a foothold in the Fergana Valley.

According to the government, the threat from extremists is still
critical. The authorities have therefore come down hard on various
religious groups, and several thousand Uzbeks are still behind bars,
accused of religious extremism or conspiracy against the state.

The greatest threat to stability in Uzbekistan, however, is not
Islamist fanatics, but Islam Karimov's deteriorating health. The
president is now seventy-six years old. Rumours about his health
have been circulating for some time now, and when he does not
make a public appearance for a few days, commentators start to
wonder if he might have had a stroke and be in a coma. Karimov has
long since passed retirement age, which is sixty in Uzbekistan, and
is eleven years older than the average life expectancy of Uzbek men.

What will happen when his iron fist no longer holds the country
together?

SUCH STUFF AS DREAMS
ARE MADE OF

An elderly woman sat in the middle of the dimly lit room, stirring a metal tub full of boiling water. Several thousand cocoons floated on the surface. They looked like small, smooth pebbles. When the woman lifted them with a wooden stick, the thin, cobweb threads loosened. With a practised hand, the woman gathered forty or fifty of these feather-light, almost invisible filaments and spun them together onto a bobbin on an old-fashioned spinning wheel. When the bobbin was covered by a thin layer of silk thread, she dropped it into a bowl of cold water. Here it was left to soak for an hour or so, before the threads were wound together into loose skeins. At the end of this treatment, the thread was still hard and dry, and a light corn colour.

"Each cocoon can contain up to four thousand metres of silk fibre, but only about a quarter of that gives strong, unbroken thread," my guide Emilbek explained. He was a serious young man, who had taught himself English. His language was functional. "The rest is sorted and hung on hooks to dry." He pointed at the thick skeins of coarse yellow thread that hung on the wall behind us. "We use it for the carpets."

The raw silk was then soaked in a tub of water with soap, sodium bicarbonate and an ingredient that Emilbek could not reveal, as it was the factory's secret. When the woman fished the thread up from the steaming, soapy water an hour later, the coarse, stiff fibres had been transformed into the softest, smoothest, whitest silk.

There were grey sacks hanging on the walls that were full of fluffy, pale-white cocoons. Each cocoon was about three to four centimetres long and a couple of centimetres wide, and so light and porous that it weighed little more than a sparrow's feather. The dry cocoons were supplied by professional silkworm farmers from Andijan.

Silk farming is an art and a highly demanding profession. The precious cocoons come from the Bombyx mori moth. In her final days the female lays around five hundred tiny eggs, and then she dies. The silk farmer has to care for these tiny eggs – a thousand of which weigh one gram. In the course of a few hectic weeks in spring, the larvae hatch. Farming families often move into an outhouse or barn during this vital phase, in order not to disturb the silkworms when they are growing. The newly hatched larvae start to eat straight away. Even though they cannot see and can barely move, the tiny larvae are picky to the point of obsession: they eat only fresh white mulberry leaves. The leaves have to be gathered when the dew has dried and are ideally served at half-hourly intervals.

For the next month, the little silkworms do nothing but eat and excrete. In these few weeks, the farmers have time for little else but feeding the larvae, cleaning, and ensuring that the hungry little creatures have perfect light and temperature conditions at all times. Silkworms are so sensitive that sudden loud noises, strong smells, changes in temperature or even bad hygiene can kill them. The farmers and their families sleep in shifts, so that someone is constantly on duty. Two thousand kilos of white mulberry leaves are required for the production of one kilo of silk.

When the larvae have moulted four times and have grown to just over five centimetres long and several thousand times their original weight, they suddenly stop eating and start spinning. For three days, the larvae produce from their salivary glands a material called fibroin. The fibroin comes out as two long threads that are immediately bound together by a secretion, sericin, which is produced by another gland. Sericin hardens as soon as it comes into contact with air, so binds the threads together into one. The silkworm spins this thread around its body in a figure of eight. The sericin dissolves in warm water which is why the cocoons are soaked in boiling water before the fibres are extracted. The butterfly itself emerges between twelve to sixteen days after chrysalisation, but very few larvae live to experience what it is like to have wings. As soon as the silkworms have stopped spinning, the cocoons are lowered into boiling water or left in hot steam, so that the larvae die. The cocoons are then left in the sun to dry before being sent to the silk factories where the fibroin is transformed into colourful silk shawls.

According to legend, it was Xi Ling Shi, the wife of the Yellow Emperor Huang Di, who discovered silk in 2640 BCE. As she sat drinking tea in the shade of a mulberry tree one day, a cocoon fell into her cup. When she tried to remove the cocoon, she discovered that it unravelled into a long, thin thread. And thus, if we are to believe the old story, the idea of silk production was born. More recent archaeological finds have shown, however, that the secret of the silkworms had been known in China for 1,500 years by the time that cocoon is supposed to have fallen into Xi Ling's teacup.

Emilbek showed me into the pattern room. It was a huge, dimly lit hall, and eight young men were sitting on the floor in deep concentration, bent over layers of white silk threads. Without a measuring tape or ruler, they drew intricate patterns on the white threads. Every now and then they might glance at the prototype shawl they had lying in front of them, which was already dyed blue, yellow and black. The men who were responsible for tying up the marked areas – with either string or tape – stood by the walls. Tying the threads ensured that only one of the marked areas was exposed when the dyers dipped the silk in the dye. When the colours were fixed, the threads were taken back to the tape men, who tied and covered the newly dyed areas and removed old string and tape to expose new parts of the thread. And so they continued until the threads were coloured in the pattern that the men on the floor had drawn on them, which the weavers would then complete.

The dying process was the most magical. The factory uses only natural colours, and there were great piles of onion skins, crushed walnuts, dried pomegranates, herbs and spices in the middle of the room. These natural dyes gave the silk clear, vibrant colours. In the next room, two sturdy men held a pole between them with silk threads hanging over it. Their white clothes were flecked with different earthy tones, and their hands had long since lost their natural colour. The threads were tied so that only about a quarter of the silk would be exposed to the dye. With controlled movements, the men lowered the threads into the huge iron vats where the dye bath bubbled and steamed, then quickly lifted them out. The exposed areas were now reddish-brown. They repeated the movement a couple of times before they hung the yarn up to dry.

"We also have a modern silk factory here," Emilbek said. "They produce several million metres of silk a year, and the whole process has been modernised and automated. But here we do it in the old way that's been used for thousands of years. Even our buildings are old." He pointed at the old, intricate carvings still visible on the ceiling. "More than a hundred people work here, and we do everything by hand, from treating the cocoons to weaving the fabric. It's a long process, but the quality makes it worthwhile. The silk from Margilan is famous throughout Uzbekistan."

Margilan is today a busy provincial town at the southern end of the Fergana Valley, not far from the border with Tajikistan, and is home to about two hundred thousand people. Most of them are

Tajiks, like Emilbek. The town is famous for its many canny traders, as well as for its silk. In the Soviet era, Margilan was the centre of the black market in Uzbekistan, but the town's proud trading history goes back much further than that: in the ninth century, Margilan was an important stop on the Silk Road between Samarkand in the west and Kashgar, which lies just inside modern day China.

It was called the Silk Road for good reason. Even though many other goods, such as horses, porcelain and paper, were also transported from east to west for many hundreds of years, silk was the most important and precious item. And in the first century BCE, silk was in great demand among the Roman aristocracy.

The Romans valued the exclusive fabric, but had little knowledge of its origins and production, which only served to increase the mystique. The distance from Xian, the most eastern town on the Silk Road, to Rome is eight thousand kilometres as the crow flies. In those days, the journey took more than a year. The goods often changed hands several times en route, so by the time they were sold to the rich and respected in Rome, the merchants might know nothing about their origins in the east.

There was no shortage of theories, however. Virgil believed that silk threads came from special leaves, whereas the Greek geographer Strabo thought they were extracted from the dried bark of trees that grew only in India. Pliny the Elder assumed it was a kind of wool from the forests of the Far East.

The Chinese understood the value of the silk monopoly. Anyone who told foreigners the secret origins of silk risked being sentenced to death. But as the years and centuries passed, the secret of the silk spinners and mulberry leaves spread. Farmers in India started to produce silk and then, the story goes, around 550, two Nestorian monks managed to smuggle a silkworm egg from China to Constantinople, in a bamboo stick. No-one knows exactly when the Central

Asians started to produce silk, but by the tenth century Merv, in what is today Turkmenistan, had surpassed China to become the biggest exporter of silk to the European market. It was not until the thirteenth century that silk production started in Western Europe. Silk from the Asian countries is still deemed to be the finest, however, and over the centuries the Uzbeks have perfected the art.

From the dyeing room, we went to the embroidery studio. As it was nearly lunchtime, there was only one embroiderer still there sewing; a beautiful, shy young girl who concentrated on the pattern she was creating. Emilbek could not take his eyes off her and hurried over. With flushed cheeks, he whispered something in her ear. She was quick to answer, then looked back down at her work.

"She's my girlfriend," he said. We wandered around looking at the various machines and settings in the studio.

"I could tell," I said. "Are you going to get married?"

He stiffened. "No, we're too young. I'm only twenty, and she's nineteen."

I asked no more questions, and he started to elaborate on the demanding work of the embroiderers. Then suddenly, in the middle of this, he could not help himself, and blurted out: "She's going to marry someone else! It was arranged two days ago, on Wednesday. I've only just found out." He stared straight ahead, blinking furiously.

"Had you been together long?" I said.

"Yes. A long time. I wrote so many letters to her, but she never answered."

There was an uncomfortable silence in the studio. The girl pushed her needle into the silk material, pulled it through, pushed it in, pulled it through, without looking up. Eventually Emilbek pulled himself together and carried on with our tour, but he was mechanical, detached.

When we were outside in the yard again, he told me with great bitterness that his mother had gone to see the girl's mother a couple of weeks before.

"She was going to ask if her daughter would marry me. But there was no one at home. My mother decided to try again another day. There was no rush..."

"Does she want to marry the other man then?" I said.

Emilbek's face clouded over. "Yes."

Before the lunch break, Emilbek showed me the rug weaving studio, where six young women with nimble, dancing fingers sat in a row and knotted the intricate patterns. It took two weavers a full year to make the biggest rugs. Emilbek rattled off a few phrases about the making of rugs, then led me into a room where they were weaving shawls. Here, a dozen women sat at big looms and transformed the silk yarn, prepared by the men in the pattern and dyeing rooms, into colourful, striped shawls. Every time the women pressed the threads into place, there was a firm thump from the beater. There were pearls of sweat on the women's faces as they sat there, rhythmically moving their hands and feet, the same movements over and over again. They wove at the same speed, but not in time, and the regular thumps sounded like syncopated music.

Later, Emilbek showed me the factory floor where grey power looms from the Fifties recalled bygone visions of the future. When the weavers were all at lunch, I wandered around, having a look at the machines by myself. Emilbek said he would wait outside, but came back in a couple of minutes, his face wet.

"It hurts so much right now," he said.

"There are a lot of beautiful young girls here," I said to console him. "I'm sure you will find someone else."

He shook his head in despair.

"This is not a good day for me."

When we had visited the whole factory, we passed the embroidery studio again. The girls were having lunch together. The one
Emilbek was in love with held up an iPad. The three other girls
giggled and leaned forwards to look at the screen, oblivious of the
scorned suitor.

"I don't like that sort of modern technology," Emilbek muttered.
"I think reading a book is a better use of time. When I have any to
spare, I read books. Preferably in English. At the moment, mostly
Shakespeare."

When we got to the shop, where all guided tours ended, he pulled
himself together and became a guide again.

"Do you know why Margilan is called Margilan?"

"No."

"The name comes from Alexander the Great," he said. "He
stopped here to eat lunch on his way east. The lunch consisted of
bread and milk. Milk is called *marg* in Persian, and bread is *nan* in
Persian and Uzbek."

"Everyone here always mentions Alexander," I said with a laugh.
"It's incredible how many places he stopped on his way east. Half
of Central Asia says they're his descendants!"

"Alexander the Great was an Uzbek," a voice behind me said, in
perfect English. It was the only other customer in the shop, a tall,
dark man in expensive jeans and a leather jacket.

"I'm not sure the Greeks would agree," I said.

"Yes, he was Uzbek," the man repeated confidently. "He was
actually called Ishkander, and his grandfather was also Uzbek."

"Well, that's certainly news to me," I said. "And I'm sure it would
be to most Greek historians as well."

The man was undaunted.

"The Greeks were also Uzbeks," he said. "There were originally
three types of Greeks, and the black Greeks were actually Uzbeks."

"Were the Uzbeks not originally nomads who came here in the sixteenth century from somewhere north of the Aral Sea?" I looked around for Emilbek for some moral support, but he had vanished.

"No," the man said, sure of himself. "They came from the south. They were Greeks."

"But you just said that the Greeks were Uzbeks."

"Yes, that's what I'm saying. The Uzbeks were Greeks."

There is little point in arguing with such ideas, but they demonstrate how linked Central Asian history and understanding are with developments in the rest of the world. The peoples of Central Asia have never lived in isolation, and over the centuries have had to deal with invading armies from the east and west, and north and south. People have come here from all directions; some have settled for longer or shorter periods, some have made the steppes their home. Central Asia has been shaped by its position in the heart of Asia, midway on the trading route between east and west. And indeed it is this location, and the constant flow of people and ideas, that enabled cities like Samarkand, Buhkara and Merv to become centres of learning.

The decades of Soviet rule, when Central Asia was at the periphery of the empire and closed in behind barbed wire barriers, is an anomaly in its history. But it is precisely because of this unusual period of isolation that a totally unique collection of Soviet art has survived to this day.

Thanks to the incredible efforts of a passionate Russian.

THE MUSEUM IN THE DESERT

From the moment I stepped inside, I was overwhelmed by colours and impressions. Intricate jewellery, bracelets and earrings, Karakalpak wedding dresses in thick, blue denim, created hundreds of years before Levi Strauss made a similar fabric from the Mediterranean available to all, 2,000-year-old pots and sculptures from the old Khwarazm, all from perhaps one of the most important and overlooked archaeological digs of the twentieth century. But it was the paintings, signed by some of the best Russian and Uzbek artists, which made the greatest impression on me. A treasure trove of light and contrast, inspired by European masters such as Picasso and Gauguin, yet with their own unique style, enriched by the exotic Central Asian landscape, the desert's changing skies, and the indigenous people's ancient traditions. Some of the motifs were extremely bold in their criticism of the Soviet regime, in a period of history when such frankness could be punished with exile or death, if discovered. Many of the artists had paid a high price for their brushstrokes.

There were only two other tourists there, and they were as overwhelmed as me. Every now and then I heard a hushed gasp, an expression of wonder, a drawn-out *ooooh* and *aaaaah*, or a quiet, happy sigh. Otherwise, I had the museum to myself. The attendants discreetly turned the lights on and off as I moved from room to room, from masterpiece to masterpiece.

Apart from the art collection, which is said to be the second most important collection of Russian avant-garde art in the world, the most striking thing about the museum is its location. Nukus lies two thousand kilometres south of Moscow in Karakalpakstan, a very isolated region in the far west of Uzbekistan, surrounded by nothing but sand. The flight from Tashkent to Nukus took an hour and a half – ninety uneventful minutes crossing an empty, dusty desert.

Even though Karakalpakstan covers a third of the territory of Uzbekistan, only 1.7 million people live here, which is less than six per cent of the country's population. Of these, around a quarter are Karakalpaks, whereas the rest are Kazakhs, Uzbeks and Turkmens. Karakalpak means "black hat", but no-one remembers any longer why the Karakalpaks were called this in the first place. If they once wore black hats, it is certainly no longer the case. Nearly all the old Karakalpak traditions and cultural traits were wiped out during the Soviet era, but not the language, which is closer to Kazakh than Uzbek. The tradition of bride kidnapping is also more widespread here than in the rest of Uzbekistan, which seems to be a hard habit to break once it becomes entrenched in a culture.

Nukus, the capital of Karkalpakstan, is a grey provincial town full of Soviet tower blocks and wide, soulless streets. Approximately two hundred thousand people still live here, but the figure falls with every year that passes. Those who can escape the poverty, pervasive desert sand and unforgiving climate do so at the first opportunity. In summer, the temperature can rise to 50°C, while the winters are cold and windy. And the winds carry with them salt and poisonous substances from the Uzbek side of the dried-out Aral Sea. Traces of pesticides, fertilisers and even biological weapons find their way over the sand dunes into the heart of the city.

After the Second World War, the Soviet Union intensified its work on biological weapons, and in the 1960s, when these activities were at their peak, as many as fifty thousand people were involved in the secret programme at fifty-two different test sites. Two of the sites where work on deadly microbes was carried out were the islands of Vozrozhdeniya and Komsomolsky in the Aral Sea. The research here focused on anthrax, smallpox and bubonic plague. In 1971 there was an accident. A boat sailed too close to Vozrozhdeniya and the crew came into contact with the smallpox virus, which they carried with them to the port of Aral in Kazakhstan. Of the ten people who developed the disease, only seven survived. Today, neither Vozrozhdeniya nor Komsomolsky exists – when the Aral Sea disappeared, they became part of the mainland. There are still spores and bacilli present in the topsoil of the former islands, so every time the wind blows, they swirl up and are carried in all directions.

Because of these military installations, the whole of Karakalpakstan was sealed off during the Soviet era, and no foreigner or outsider was allowed to visit the region. The official reason given was that there was no infrastructure for tourism, which, to be fair, is the truth.

The Russian artist Igor Savitsky came to this godforsaken place in 1950.

He was born in Kiev, Ukraine, in the summer of 1915 and had a privileged childhood with French governesses, surrounded by well-travelled and educated relatives. His father, Vitaly Savitsky, was a well-to-do and respected lawyer. His great-grandfather had been a professor at the theological faculty in St Petersburg and a priest at the Peter and Paul Cathedral. His maternal grandfather, Timofey Florinsky, was an assistant professor at Kiev University, and head of Slavic Studies. He was widely known for his private collection of more than twelve thousand books, to which his students had access. His grandson, Igor, would take the family collecting mania to new heights. Despite the fact that a war was raging in Europe, life in

Kiev carried on pretty much as normal, and the first years of Igor's life were very happy.

Then came the revolution and civil war. His privileged background turned into a curse. Timofey Florinsky was arrested and executed by the Bolsheviks. His book collection was scattered to the winds. Most of Igor's maternal relatives emigrated in the 1920s to France, where they could live freely. But Igor's parents refused to leave Russia, and instead moved to Moscow, where they lived with his mother's brother, Dmitry. He was head of the protocol office for the People's Commissariat for Foreign Affairs – a good, safe position, one would think, but, in the 1930s, nothing was safe in the Soviet Union. In 1934, during the first purge and wave of terror, Dmitry was arrested. We do not know what became of him, or of Igor's parents, for that matter, as Savitsky never spoke about his family or background, not even to close friends.

In order to fit in with the proletariat, Igor started an apprenticeship as an electrician. He took private evening classes in drawing and painting, which was where his true dreams and ambitions lay. He was an enthusiastic student and used all his free time to draw, paint and perfect his technique. In 1941, he was accepted to study at the Surikov Art Institute in Moscow. He was not called up for military service – due to poor health – so could continue with his education. In 1943, the whole Surikov Institute was evacuated to Samarkand. This encounter with Central Asia made a huge impression on the young Savitsky and changed the course of his life for ever.

In 1950, he was invited to be the expedition artist for a group of archaeologists who were going to excavate the ruins of the old Khwarazm civilisation in Karakalpakstan. The discovery of Khwarazm in the 1930s is now compared by some archaeologists to the discovery of Tutankhamun's tomb. Around 500 BCE, there was a large and progressive civilisation to the south of the Aral Sea, in what is today Karakalpakstan. The inhabitants were Zoroastrians and lived in a hierarchical, highly developed society that placed particular importance on science and mathematics. Savitsky, who was already infatuated with the people and landscape of Central Asia, accepted the invitation straight away. He was the expedition artist for eight years. While the archaeologists rested in the shadows to avoid the afternoon heat, Savitsky stood at his easel and eternalised the desert. He never tired of the colours and changing light in the limitless landscape.

Today Savitsky is recognised as the founder of the Karakalpak school of landscape painting. He had found his Tahiti. Like Gauguin, Savitsky was captivated by the indigenous culture, but his fascination was expressed differently: in his spare time, he travelled to remote villages to collect handicrafts, jewellery, carpets, embroidery and other Karakalpak artefacts. The Karakalpaks did not have a written language, but they did have an extraordinarily rich tradition in craftsmanship. Savitsky collected more than eight thousand objects that he stored in his home. People could not understand what he wanted with all that old junk. These were modern times and not even the Karakalpaks themselves saw any value in the old handiwork.

When, after eight years, the archaeologists finished the dig, Savitsky installed himself permanently in Nukus. He continued to collect Karakalpak artefacts, but also started to teach local artists. He believed an art museum was needed in order to do this properly. After several years, he managed to convince the local authorities to loosen their purse strings. On May 1, 1966, the Art Museum in Nukus opened its doors. From that day on, Savitsky ceased to be an artist. He did not think it possible to be a serious artist and a museum director at the same time.

The museum became his life. As a rule, he slept for only a few hours a night, did not eat much and owned very few things. He certainly did not have time for a family – all his energy was poured into the museum and collecting art. During his time in Central Asia, he had made an important discovery: there were great treasures to be found in the studios and the flats of the widows of half-forgotten or banned artists that nobody seemed to care about. When Stalin tightened his grip in the Thirties, only edifying art that promoted an idealistic, Soviet reality – so-called socialist realism – escaped censorship. Russian artists were not as blinkered as the Soviet authorities, however, and there was a wealth of gifted individuals whose paintings were inspired by European avant-gardism, cubism, Dadaism, surrealism and other modern movements. This work was not exhibited anywhere, but was hidden away in chests and attics.

Savitsky exploited to the full the fact that censorship was more relaxed in the Sixties than it had been in Stalin's day. He started to visit the studios and relatives of dead artists in search of forgotten works from the Twenties and Thirties. To begin with, he focused on Uzbekistan, as many Russian artists had fled there at the time, but then later widened his search as far as Moscow. Savitsky found gem after gem, by both known and recognised artists such as Ural Tansykbayev and unknown artists such as Konstantin Suryayev. Savitsky bought hundreds – if not thousands – of paintings that had been too colourful, too expressionistic, too critical or too experimental for the regime. Some of the paintings were in terrible condition and needed extensive restoration, a job that Savitsky often did himself. One artist's widow had used a painting he bought to plug a hole in the roof. During the war, the family of the painter Alexander Volkov had been forced to use his picture frames as firewood so they would not freeze to death. When Savitsky went to see them, the paintings were in a critical state. The family were delighted that someone still cared about Volkov's art, and donated the entire collection to Savitsky, who took them back to his museum in the desert and over time restored them.

The museum in Nukus soon became famous throughout the Soviet Union, and Savitsky was celebrated for his refined taste. He had extraordinary powers of persuasion and managed to convince even the most sceptical widows that they should bequeath their husbands' work to his museum. Friends and colleagues started to call him "the widows' friend". Savitsky paid the artists and their families as much as he could afford, and was always concerned that the impoverished widows should be treated fairly. If he did not have the money to hand, as was often the case, he gave them a handwritten I.O.U., which he, the director of the Nukus Art Museum, promised to pay in full. Remarkably, they often agreed to this. As soon as Savitsky had any money to spare, he conscientiously paid off those debts.

Not surprisingly, given the amount of art that Savitsky collected, the money he got from the local authorities in Karakalpakstan was never enough and he exceeded the budget time and again. He was repeatedly ordered not to buy more, but he could not stop himself. What is even more remarkable is that he bought with government money thousands of artworks that in no way complied with the regime's demands for edifying art – and by artists who had not been rehabilitated. The museum would certainly never have survived in Moscow or Leningrad, but things were more lax in Nukus. Whenever an inspector from Moscow paid an occasional visit, Savitsky removed the most controversial paintings. He put on his only suit and gallantly showed his guests around. Some works of art were captioned "Artist Unknown", for tactical reasons. And when the museum exhibited Nadezhda Borovaya's drawings from the gulag where she spent seven years in the 1930s, the text in the brochure said that the drawings were of imaginary scenes of daily life in the Nazi concentration camps.

Savitsky became very ill in 1983. He continued to work as before, even though he struggled to breathe. His doctor, Sergey Efuni, eventually managed to get him admitted, against his will, to hospital in Moscow. Following several thorough examinations and tests, the doctors discovered that the patient had neither cancer nor tuberculosis, as was originally suspected, but was suffering from chronic lung disease caused by the careless use of dangerous chemicals over a long period of time. Savitsky swore by the traditional method of cleaning bronze artefacts and had not used any form of protection when boiling formalin in his workshop. His lungs were at the point of collapse.

When the doctor gave him the death sentence, Savitsky protested: "I can't die, doctor, I still owe the artists and their widows one and a half thousand roubles!" Doctor Efuni, who was an understanding doctor, sometimes gave Savitsky leave from hospital. He would use this time to visit studios in Moscow and collect even more art. His hospital room became an office, and the museum director continued to work here, dealing with correspondence, composing begging letters to the authorities, and receiving donors who came to him with paintings and drawings.

In June 1984, eight days before his sixty-eighth birthday, Savitsky died. In the eight months that he was ill and in hospital, he had managed to collect two shipping containers of art, rare books and antique furniture for his museum in Nukus.

Marinika Babanazarova, the granddaughter of Karakalpakstan's first president and a good friend of Savitsky, became the director of the museum, as was his wish. She was twenty-nine when she took over the museum.[15] Since 1991 the museum has slowly become known to art lovers all over the world. Today, it welcomes around four to five thousand visitors a year, which is not many compared with the Louvre, which on average has fifteen thousand visitors a day, but, given the museum's peripheral location, is impressive. Savitsky's dream was that people who were interested in art would fly from Paris to visit his museum. His friends laughed at him then, but now his dream has been realised.

After Savitsky's death, it took the museum years to pay off his debts to the widows and artists. Nor was there money to spare for humidifiers. Instead bowls of water were put out in the galleries. There was always great interest in the works, but Babanazarova was apparently never tempted to sell any of the art in order to ease the restrictive budgets. Savitsky believed that they had a moral duty to look after the pieces that had been entrusted to the museum by impoverished artists, and said that selling even a single painting would be paramount to betrayal. And, he warned, once you started to sell, it would be hard to stop. Babanazarova was loyal to this philosophy, even though it meant that she often did not have enough money to pay the staff a decent wage. Fortunately, the women of the museum (almost exclusively women work there) have been as dedicated as the director and see it as their moral duty to keep the museum in Nukus going.

Nor has it been easy to run a museum under the new political regime. A new museum building was begun in 1976 but not completed until 2003, and even though President Karimov opened the building, the authorities have an ambivalent attitude to the museum. While they are pleased that it attracts tourists to the region, any contact with foreigners arouses suspicion. When a documentary

15 Marinika Babanazarova was fired in 2015, after being accused of stealing treasures from the museum.

about the museum, "The Desert of Forbidden Art", had its first screenings in New York in 2011, Babanazarova was not permitted to travel and instead spent the day of the premiere being interrogated by the police.

The year before, the museum management had been given forty-eight hours' notice to evacuate the older of the two buildings, as the street outside was going to be refurbished. The weeping staff had to pack hundreds of paintings as rapidly as possible and stow them away in the overfull store. On the corner where the original museum stood, a spanking new bank has popped up. And on the opposite side of the road is an enormous, white parliament building. The new prestige buildings are part of the authorities' plan to give every city in the country a facelift.

But the plan also included two new buildings, which were opened to mark the museum's fiftieth anniversary in 2016. So now any art lovers who do make the long journey to Karakalpakstan to see the Russian avant-garde art can see some more of the eighty thousand artefacts and artworks that Igor Savitsky managed to collect in the eighteen years he was director of Nukus Museum of Art.

THE GOD OF COTTON

Shortly after we had driven out of Nukus, we came to a large bridge. Only when we were in the middle of the bridge could we see the river below: a narrow, silvery stripe of almost static water. This is all that is left of the Amu Darya, known by the Greeks as the Oxus, Central Asia's answer to the Nile, the very life blood of the desert. Some weeks earlier I had sat on its banks in the Wakhan Valley in Tajikistan and looked over to Afghanistan. It was still very much a river, wide and alive. From Pamir, it runs to Turkmenistan, and eventually to Uzbekistan, where it previously fed into the Aral Sea, via a network of rivers and watercourses. Even though it is now not so much as a shadow of its former self, the locals still speak of the Amu Darya with awe. The Amu Darya no longer runs into a sea or ocean, instead it just gets slowly narrower, tamer, dwindling until it eventually disappears into the sand.

In the desert, water is more valuable than gold. It was the Amu-Darya and its tributaries that made it possible for the nomads to live in old Khwarazm more than two thousand years ago. To the frustration of the settlers, the Amu Darya was a capricious river that often, without warning, changed course. And the people could do nothing but follow. Entire towns and cities uprooted and moved with the water. Eventually, people learned how to harness the water. They started to build water systems that could supply hundreds of thousands of people with clean, cold water. Thanks to these ingenious canals, oasis cities such as Merv, Khiva, Bukhara,

Samarkand and Kokand were able to flourish in the middle of the desert.

As is well known, the Soviet authorities were not satisfied with simply digging a few ditches; the bureaucrats in the Kremlin wanted to create a new world order. Nature would obey the Communists! The first bulldozers and excavators started to dig on the banks of the Amu Darya in the Fifties. Around the same time, thousands of men were ordered out into the fields. They were each given a spade. In the new world order, people no longer lived only for their families and themselves, they lived also for the Party, for the greater good and for the extended family. They were expected to give their lives, let alone their muscles, to the building of a new socialist empire.

When the Russians first came to Central Asia, cotton had been produced here for nearly two thousand years, but only on a small scale. In order to stimulate production, the Russians gave land to farmers who wanted to cultivate cotton. The Central Asian cotton plant was swapped for the American variety, which gave purer and stronger textiles. Gradually, cotton took over from other plants, which meant that the Central Asians, who had always been self-sufficient when it came to corn, fruit and vegetables, became dependent on food imported from Russia. In 1916 the locals protested against their colonial masters in the north: it was not fair that they were forced to grow cotton on their land, when they were starving. And to add insult to injury, they had to sell the cotton at artificially low prices ordained by the tsar!

When the Bolsheviks came to power, matters got worse. The Communists' dream was to make the Soviet Union the largest cotton producer in the world. Three-quarters of Soviet cotton was grown in Uzbekistan, which, owing to its climate and sizeable population, was best suited for this purpose. Cotton was grown on nearly all the collective farms. Fig and watermelon plantations, wheat fields, and flower beds were replaced with American cotton plantations. There was cotton as far as the eye could see, kilometre after kilometre of the short, brown stems that transformed into low cloud banks every autumn.

More than ninety per cent of the cotton grown in Central Asia was sent to Russia for processing. The price for cotton was still well below the market price, and, as a result, very few of the Uzbek collective farms managed to break even. For the entire Soviet era, Uzbekistan was therefore dependent on subsidies from the north, not only financial, but also meat, dairy products, wheat, fruit and vegetables.

The Communists had fantasies about also transforming the vast desert areas into cotton plantations, and under Brezhnev, who was not otherwise known for being a man of action, plans were accelerated. Several thousand kilometres of canal were dug with the help of bulldozers, excavators and raw muscle. Within a mere twenty years, from 1965 to 1985, the arable area of Uzbekistan nearly doubled. Rivers were diverted and forced out into the cotton plantations where the river water flooded the fields, soaking into the soil and ruining it, since there were big salt deposits under the poor soil. When the water penetrated far enough to reach them they started to push up to the surface. The soil was then covered in a fine layer of white crystals, the wind dispersed the crystals and people breathed in salt. To keep the cotton plantations going year after year in such impoverished soil, the use of artificial fertilisers and pesticides was widespread. Airplanes and helicopters flew over the villages and sprayed poison over the fields, gardens and playgrounds. An average of twenty to twenty-five kilos of pesticides was spread over each hectare, seven times the average for the rest of the Soviet Union. The use of artificial fertilisers was even worse: every cotton plant was given fifty times more than was strictly necessary.

As population growth in the Soviet Union outstripped Uzbekistan's cotton production, the market was never saturated. There was never enough cotton. The production requirements set by Moscow's planned economy were unrealistic, but instead of challenging the requirements, the Uzbek authorities started to fiddle the figures, allowing small and large producers to line their pockets with large amounts of fictitious cotton, while Uzbekistan more than met its quota on paper.

The whole of the Soviet Union was steeped in corruption and cronyism, but Central Asia was the worst affected: the central committee in each of the republics was really nothing more than the council of elders of the dominant clan, who were linked by family ties and mutual business interests. In Uzbekistan, Sharaf Rashidov was First Secretary – grand vizier may be a more apt title – for twenty-four years until he died, somewhat fortuitously, in 1983, shortly after the Politburo in Moscow had started to show an interest in the discrepancy between the number of tons reported and the actual amount of cotton delivered from Uzbekistan. The corruption case, which was simply known as the "cotton scandal", rumbled on through the Eighties until the end of the Soviet Union. Three thousand policemen lost their jobs as a result of the findings and four thousand party members were put on trial and sentenced. When Gorbachev came to power, he deemed it necessary to replace the greater part of the corrupt party leadership. Despite protests from the Uzbeks, the ousted leaders were, for the most part, replaced by Russians, and Gorbachev thereby dismantled the council of elders.

First Secretary Islam Karimov was from Samarkand, however. One of the first things he did when Uzbekistan became independent was to rehabilitate most of those sentenced in the cotton scandal. Many of them even got their old jobs back.

*

A sign with a large blue fish on it welcomes visitors to Moynaq, a reminder of its former heyday. Moynaq is three or four hours' drive from Nukus, and, until the 1970s, was Uzbekistan's only seaside town, with beaches, waves and a thriving fishing fleet. Now the sea is two hundred kilometres away. Uzbekistan is not only a country without a coast, it is surrounded by other countries that are themselves landlocked. So Uzbekistan has lost the only maritime connection it had.

In the Sixties, when Savitsky opened the Nukus Art Museum, Karakalpakstan was blooming, quite literally. Thanks to the new canals, there were cotton plants growing everywhere and no-one was unemployed. The local population was kept busy with sowing and harvesting the cotton, digging canals and fishing. Seven per cent of all fish consumed in the Soviet Union came from the Aral Sea, if Soviet statistics are to be believed. In Moynaq alone, thirty thousand people were employed in the fishing industry, either directly with the fleet or in the processing and canning factory. Even when the sea started to shrink and then disappeared completely, shift workers at the canning factory worked at full capacity. When the local fishers could no longer supply the conveyer belts with fish, the authorities arranged for frozen fish to be sent all the way from Murmansk for processing.

The remants of its former glory make Moynaq all the more depressing. In the centre, the Soviet-style official buildings are going to ruin. Just outside the centre, there is a cinema, built from mud bricks and clay and painted in what must once have been a bright colour. The film posters are no longer legible. There are no restaurants in Moynaq, and no shops to speak of. The town's only hotel is so dilapidated that very few tourist companies would risk sending people here. Goats graze in front of the concrete apartment blocks and sand drifts on the street. Close to the school, where half the classrooms are abandoned, some boys are playing football on an improvised pitch. Their hair and clothes are covered in dust, but they do not seem to mind. The old canning factory, once the heart of Moynaq, is like a haunted house. The windows are broken, the paint is peeling and the sign at the entrance hangs askew.

My driver, Boris, drove past slowly so that I could take a picture through the closed window.

"There are observers and police everywhere here," he explained. "For a short while after the end of the Soviet Union, there were the beginnings of an independence movement in Karakalpakstan, but it was quickly and bloodily quelled by Karimov's people. There hasn't been an organised independence movement here since then, but the authorities are terrified that they'll re-form, and are watching like hawks. There are informers everywhere. They warn the authorities in Tashkent about any vaguely suspicious or undesirable activities."

"And taking a photograph of a fish factory falls into the category of undesirable activities?"

"Exactly."

Boris had to be the only Russian who had stayed in Karakalpakstan. When the Soviet Union collapsed, his wife and children were on the first plane to Moscow. Boris found himself a Kazakh wife and stayed.

"I couldn't leave my old mother," he said. "And anyway, you should die where you were born. That's what I think."

Boris had not made the best first impression. He was wearing a pair of shabby joggers and a string vest which, despite being elasticated, did not hide his great girth. He had just turned fifty-seven, he said, but he looked at least twenty years older. He had been signed off for the past few years with chronic kidney failure, a common diagnosis in these parts. To supplement his social security money, he had specialised in driving disaster tourists to the shores of the

Aral Sea. Before we left Nukus, he stocked up on the local vodka, which he swore was the best in all Uzbekistan.

Despite my misgivings, Boris proved to be the best driver on the whole journey. Unlike his younger colleagues, who only used their brakes when they saw a police checkpoint in the distance, Boris drove at a relatively calm speed, seldom over one hundred kilometres an hour, depending on the road and surroundings. He saved the vodka bottle until we had parked up for the night.

Just outside the centre of Moynaq is the town's only tourist attraction: the ship graveyard. Eleven rusting hulks of various shapes and sizes lie stranded in a row on the sand, from small fishing boats to big trawlers. Countless couples have scratched their names and initials on the bows. I am obviously not the first Norwegian here: *Ole + Jørgen* is engraved in stubborn white letters on one of the fishing boats. Behind the boats, the brown desert sand stretches out to the horizon.

The boats are by a plateau that today functions as a parking place and viewpoint. Information boards about the Aral Sea have been put up behind the parking place. Satellite photographs are used to show how, from being the fourth largest inland sea in the world, it shrank until finally it split in two. Only a few years ago, two arms of the sea reached from Kazakhstan down to Uzbekistan; now only one remains, and it is steadily getting shorter and narrower. While the Kazakh authorities have managed to turn things around in the North Aral Sea, the South Aral is beyond recovery. The water is too saline for fish to survive, and the Amu Darya, which once supplied the sea with water, no longer even reaches its shores. Ninety per cent of the sea has disappeared in the past fifty years.

The plateau that is now a parking place used to be the main quay in Moynaq. Summer camps for young pioneers were held close to the quay. The local authorities had just started to build holiday homes here when the sea began disappearing. Day by day it receded, further and further, so slowly as to be almost imperceptible, until one day the sea had disappeared from Moynaq. Soon the first shipments of frozen fish arrived from Murmansk, and eventually the fishermen pulled their boats ashore for good.

"I used to come here and stay with my aunt in the school holidays," Boris said. "It was paradise in summer. We swam and played in the water, relaxed. But now all the Russians and Kazakhs have moved. Only the Karakalpaks are still here."

We stood for a while surveying in silence what had once been the seabed.

"Everything was better in the Soviet Union," Boris said, eventually. I looked at him in surprise.

"Cooking oil was cheap, bread cost nothing and an airplane ticket to Moscow didn't cost much either. Our wages were enough to pay for a whole family. Whereas now we never have enough money, and many of us are sick."

Anyone travelling in Russia and the former Soviet republics soon becomes accustomed to older people being overcome with nostalgia when they talk about the Soviet Union. "Everything was better before" is the usual refrain, and who can blame them? Not only were they young then, but the world was a simpler place, the social security system worked better and prices were indeed much lower. But here, of all places, in this town that had truly suffered the consequences of the Soviet leaders' megalomania, I had not expected to find Soviet nostalgia. My unkempt driver was not the only one, however. As in Kurchatov, where the Soviet Union carried out its nuclear tests, everyone I met in Moynaq longed for the good old days. Because everything was better before.

In a way, they are right. Life in Karakalpakstan was definitely better before. Today, it is one of the poorest and most underdeveloped regions in Uzbekistan. Unemployment is high, and most of the inhabitants are chronically ill. The incidence of cancer and tuberculosis is fifteen times higher than in the rest of Uzbekistan. Respiratory diseases and brucellosis, also known as undulant fever, are widespread, as are kidney and liver disease. Almost half the population suffers from jaundice. Child mortality is a record high: seventy-five of every thousand children born do not survive the first few years. Since the disappearance of the Aral Sea the climate has changed for the worse. The summers are hotter and drier and the winters are colder. What little groundwater is left is so full of salt, heavy metals and other toxic waste that it is not suitable for human consumption. And yet many people, for want of alternatives, are forced to drink the water.

For a short period, the Soviet authorities did succeed in transforming the desert into fertile cotton plantations, but, as a result, the sea is now permanently a desert, with all that that entails. Yet, seemingly, there was no bitterness in Moynaq.

The streets were still dark when we left at the crack of dawn the next day. Slowly, a dim light infused the sky and night became day in a play of pastel colours. The landscape was flat as a pancake, and the only things that seemed to thrive in the stony, salt-laden soil were a kind of thistle and some dry shrubs. The ground was covered by a white film of salt, and was dry and yet soft and giving at the same time. Other than the thistles and shrubs, the only plant that thrives here, ironically, is the cotton plant. So the Uzbek authorities started even more cotton plantations in the vicinity of Moynaq a few years ago, in the hope that the plant that had caused the town's downfall might also be its saving.

Even though investment in fruit, corn and other edible crops has increased in recent years, the Uzbek economy is still heavily dependent on cotton. Owing to the indiscriminate use of pesticides and fertilisers, and monocropping, production per hectare has fallen steadily over the past couple of decades and many of the cotton plants are diseased. However, the greater part of arable land is still dedicated to cotton, and Uzbekistan is currently the sixth largest exporter of cotton in the world. As most farms are still owned by the state and run as collectives, it is the authorities who decide what is to be grown, the quotas to be filled and the price of the product. In other words, they still follow the Soviet model. As a result, most Uzbek farmers are very poor. A handful manage to scrape together enough money to pay for a *propiska*, the document required if someone wants to move to another region. This is how the authorities prevent the mass movement of poor young people to the cities, and at the same time ensure cheap, stable labour on the farms.

For the first hour, the road over the seabed was surfaced. Had Boris not assured me that the road was only a couple of years old, I would have guessed it was another survivor from the Soviet Union. It was potholed and worn down by all the heavy Chinese lorries that shuttle to and from the gasworks. The environmental catastrophe has proved to have a silver lining for Uzbekistan: early this century, huge gas reserves were discovered under the former seabed, and Russia, China and Uzbekistan have cooperated on the construction of several major processing plants in the area. However, the local population has not benefited from this in any way, as the workers in these plants are almost all migrant workers from China and the east of Uzbekistan.

In the final stretch, we drove over a large canyon that was previously surrounded by water. The water had chiselled out smooth, red veins in the rock, which is now exposed to the pale morning sun, and an endless flat patchwork of thistles, sand and shrubs, sprinkled with sparkling salt crystals.

The struggle to secure what little water resources there were was complicated enough in the Soviet Union, when all the republics belonged to the same state. Today, it is possible to see the seeds of future conflict. The relationship between Uzbekistan and Tajikistan has already cooled, as a result of the latter's plans to build the Rogun Dam, which was first proposed in 1959. The idea is to exploit the full potential of the Vakhsh river, which has its source in Kyrgyzstan and runs through Tajikistan before eventually joining the Amu Darya. The planned dam is 334.98 metres tall, which will make it the highest in the world. Work on the dam started in 1976, but it has still not been completed, even though Tajikistan sorely needs the electricity that such a dam could provide. The Tajik authorities have tried several times to breathe new life into the project, but these attempts have been thwarted time and again by a lack of funding.[16] The Uzbek authorities, for their part, are very critical of the project, which they fear will steal water from the cotton plantations in the Fergana Valley. They are also worried about the consequences that an earthquake might have. President Karimov called it a "stupid project".

The construction of the Golden Age Lake in Turkmenistan is even more controversial. The lake, which lies in the middle of the Karakum Desert, will hold 132 billion cubic metres of water, cover two hundred square kilometres and be up to seventy metres deep. President Berdimuhamedov's great idea is that the lake will change the climate in the desert by generating more rain in the region,

16 The project was restarted by the Tajik government with help from the Chinese in 2017. The power plant's first unit was commissioned in 2018 and a second turbine is expected to be commissioned in 2019.

thereby making the desert more fertile. The excavation work is almost finished, thanks in part to the efforts of prisoners, whom the authorities have used for free labour. The old communist dream of making the desert green and profitable is still alive in Ashgabat.

Experts have objected that the water is most likely to evaporate in the hot desert air, and that what little water is left will be contaminated by fertilisers and chemicals. They have also questioned whether the ground under the desert is suited to supporting a lake, or if the water will slowly leak into the sand and transform the desert into mud. It is also unclear where Turkmenistan will get all the water. They claim that they will only use the run-off water from existing irrigation systems, but according to the experts most of this will evaporate from the canals before it reaches the Golden Age lake. As is to be expected, the Turkmen authorities have paid no heed to criticism of this megalomaniac project. In 2009, President Berdimuhamedov was flown into the desert to inaugurate the lake. "We have brought new life to these once lifeless sands," the president declared when he opened one of the canals that will supply the lake. He then went for a ride on a jewel-bedecked horse, raising great cheers from those present.

It will still take many years to fill the lake – assuming that it can be filled at all.

We had been driving for three hours when finally we glimpsed an unmoving, dark blue line in the distance. The South Aral Sea. There were fewer and fewer thistles and bushes; gradually the desert became a beach. A couple of simple yurts made from white plastic had been erected a few hundred metres from the water. A handful of Chinese people were driving about on the sand in four-wheel drives, and seemed to be very busy.

"What are you doing?" I asked the only one who spoke Russian.

"*Klevetki!*" He grinned. "We're collecting *klevetki*. Plawns!"

"Plawns?"

"Plawns!" He pointed to the big plastic bucket in front of him. It was full of grey mud. "Small, small, baby plawns!"

"They're collecting *krevetki*, small prawns, and prawn eggs," Boris explained. "They find them by the water's edge, collect them in big containers and send them to Thailand. And apparently they earn good money for it."

I turned my back on the Chinese prawn collectors and wandered down to the water. The sand was muddy by the waterline, and my feet sank in deep with every step. White foam rippled on the surface of the water. The smell reminded me of the fishing villages on the Lofoten Islands in spring, when there is cod drying everywhere. But there were no fish or seagull cries here. Only water and salt. And tiny *plawns*.

The sea was like a mirror. The water made bell-like sounds as little waves rippled and broke as they reached the shore.

The sky was so hazy that on the horizon it merged with the flat sea.

"Only a couple of years ago, the water was about a hundred metres further up the shore," Boris remarked when I got back to the car, ready for the long drive back. "Reckon I'll have to get another job soon." He gave a hoarse laugh. "Preferably one that can be combined with sick pay."

IN SEARCH OF LOST TIME

Going through the city gates into Ichan Kala, the old town in Khiva, is like stepping back hundreds of years. Blue domes and slender minarets decorated with mint-green tiles reach up to the heavens. In the khan's old palaces, you pass through narrow halls and dark, exquisitely decorated rooms – until suddenly you are standing out in the open, in a perfectly symmetrical square, in the middle of the building, protected from the noise of the streets outside. It is like walking onto a film set or into a museum. Everything is wonderfully preserved. There are no mounds of earth and ruins here; you do not need to guess or imagine what things looked like. The ten-metre high brick walls that surround the old town are intact, with battlements and smooth, elegant surfaces. Inside, the domes and madrasas, or Islamic colleges, are so tightly packed that it would be easy to miss the odd mausoleum or two.

If you go in through the West Gate, one of the first things you will see is the large, solid Kalta Minor minaret. The tower is decorated with wide bands of glazed tiles in different blue, green and red patterns. If things had gone according to plan, it would have been eighty metres high and the tallest minaret in Central Asia, but then in 1855, when the construction reached twenty-nine metres, the khan who had commissioned the building died and the work came to a halt. But it still stands like a thick, sawn-off trunk in the middle of the main street, a mute promise of a golden age that never came.

In the narrow side streets by the city wall, daily life carries on as it always has. All the dwellings are made from mud brick, and are low and light brown, with flat roofs. A flock of children in Nike trainers and Adidas tracksuits run laughing between the buildings. Two grey-haired men are repairing a window. A young mother is rocking a baby in her arms. But for the satellite dishes and cheap copies of western designer clothes, it would be easy to believe that life inside Khiva's old town had not changed in centuries.

Clearly first impressions are deceptive. Most of the buildings in the old town are not as old as they look; most of them are from the nineteenth century. The slim, elegant Islam Khodja minaret, Khiva's highest building, was not completed until 1910. The reason that the town feels so old and timeless is that the architects and builders continued to build in the same style over centuries and were not influenced by fashions and trends. The buildings rarely lasted very long, as they had poor foundations. Travellers here in the nineteenth century wrote about walls that did not meet, cracked corners and leaning minarets. Frequent fires also helped to keep the craftsmen busy. And the town was built from one of the least durable materials possible: baked mud and trampled earth.

After the Bolsheviks came to power, Khiva's old town was left to its fate. The Soviet authorities prioritised other types of building, constructed in concrete for a bright future, and they left the old brick buildings to fall into ruin. Some restoration projects were started after the Second World War, but work really only got underway at the end of the Sixties. The city wall was restored to its former glory, and the madrasas, palaces and minarets were given a sorely needed facelift. The old town was probably never more beautiful, sparkling clean and well maintained than it was in the final years of the Soviet Union. The Communists literally turned Khiva into a living museum. The mosques and madrasas' study cells were given new life as natural history museums. The cells are still full of dried cotton plants, stuffed lizards and dusty lemons and melons, a legacy of the Soviet authorities' penchant for filling religious buildings with science.

When I got to Khiva, it was November. The large tourist parties had long since left Uzbekistan: the streets were deserted and the museums were empty. Most of the hotels had closed their doors for the season. A handful of stallholders were still selling their knitted socks and jewellery, but otherwise the city appeared to have been taken over by wedding parties. On almost every corner there was a bride in mounds of white lace posing for a photographer.

Previous visitors to the city, from Ibn Battuta in the fourteenth century to Ella Christie at the start of the twentieth century, have all described Khiva as a bustling city. The narrow streets were so full of people and camels that it was barely possible to move. What made the greatest impression on travellers in the olden days was not the exquisite domes or blue minarets, but rather Khiva's lush gardens and many green trees. Having travelled for days and weeks through the barren desert under a relentless sun they arrived in a paradise of greenness and tropical fruit. Today, those green gardens, melon fields and vines have been replaced by cotton plantations. For a few short, hectic weeks in autumn, the scorched fields become a reflection of the sky and are full of white clouds.

When the Arabs invaded Central Asia in the eighth century, Khiva was just one of many small and large oasis towns in the rich Khwarazm region to the south of the Aral Sea. Merv, which was then one of the largest cities in the world, also belonged to Khwarazm. Only when the Uzbek tribes conquered the region in the sixteenth century did Khiva's star rise, and in 1624 it became the capital of the khanate of the same name. The Khiva khanate was never as big or powerful as Bukhara or Kokand, and when the Russians took control in 1873, Khiva had for many years been nothing more than an isolated outpost. The city was primarily known for its slave market, the second largest of its kind in Central Asia, surpassed only by Bukhara's.

In 1840, when the British envoys Abbott and Shakespear came to Khiva to persuade the khan to release the Russian slaves, they came to a poor, dirty city where most of the inhabitants were illiterate. It had not always been so. A thousand years ago, Central Asia was the intellectual centre of the world.

One of the best-known mathematicians in history, Ibn Musa al-Khwarizmi, came from Khwarazm, as his name indicates. He lived from 780 to 850 and is recognised as the father of algebra. In Greek, he was known as Algoritmi, a combination of al-Kwharizmi and *arithmós*, the Greek word for number. The word "algorithm" therefore stems from al-Khwarizmi. His famous textbook, *Algebr wal muqabala*, which in English is called *The Compendious Book on Calculation by Completion and Balancing*, describes al-Khwarizmi's two methods of simplifying equations. The word "algebra" derives from the title of this work. Al-Khwarizmi is also recognised as the father of spherical trigonometry. Furthermore, he wrote an extensive geographical reference work in which he listed 2,402 places in the world, alongside their precise coordinates.

One of the things that contributed to this flourishing intellectual life in Central Asia at the time was the availability of paper. Paper was invented in China about two thousand years ago, and the art quickly spread from there to Central Asia. The Chinese used fibres from the mulberry tree and bamboo to make paper, but craftsmen in Samarkand soon discovered that it was possible to make an even finer and thinner paper from cotton cellulose. And not only was their paper cheaper, it was also easier to come by, so Samarkand soon took over as the primary exporter of paper to the West.

The Silk Road could equally have been called the Paper Road.

For several hundred years, paper from Samarkand was one of the most important and lucrative goods to be loaded onto camels' backs and transported west along the caravan routes. Even when paper production was developed elsewhere such as in Damascus, Cairo and Muslim Córdoba, the demand for high-quality paper from Samarkand continued until the thirteenth century, when the Europeans started to produce paper themselves.

Whereas paper from Samarkand was deemed to be an expensive luxury in Europe, in Central Asia it was treated as a cheap consumer good. Even though printing had not yet been invented, handwritten books were produced in bulk, both in original and translation. There were so many handwritten books for sale at the market in Bukhara that booksellers had to compete for customers.

One day towards the end of the 990s, a young boy by the name of Ibn Sina encountered one such persistent bookseller at the market in Bukhara. He had not thought of buying the book, Aristotle's *Metaphysics*, as he had long since given up trying to understand Aristotle's thoughts on the subject. But the bookseller was so insistent and offered him such a good price that Ibn Sina eventually succumbed and bought it. The book proved to be a turning point in the boy's life and thinking.

At the time, the Greek philosophers were read and discussed widely in the Arabic world, including in Central Asia. The Arabs had discovered their work when they conquered parts of the former Roman empire, such as Egypt and Syria, in the eighth century. By the ninth century, several of the works had been translated into Arabic. Ibn Sina, otherwise known in Europe by his Latin name, Avicenna, was to become one of the most significant Aristotelian scholars of his age. Of the four hundred books and papers he wrote in his lifetime, two hundred and fifty have survived, of which a hundred and fifty are on philosophy, and forty on medicine. Even though he was primarily interested in metaphysical questions, he is remembered to this day for his contribution to medicine.

Ibn Sina was a qualified doctor by the tender age of sixteen. He himself remarked: "Medicine is not one of the difficult sciences." His best-known work is *The Canon of Medicine*, an encyclopaedia of medicine, anatomy and diseases. He discusses and describes the effects of various medicines based on his own experiments and clinical experience. He also explains how alcohol can be used as an antiseptic and advocates the boiling of water to prevent the spread of tuberculosis. The book discusses the importance of physical activity, cold baths, sleep and a healthy diet, as well as the positive influence a good marriage can have on health. *The Canon of Medicine* was translated into Latin in 1180, and for five hundred years was the standard work on medicine in both the Arab world and Europe.

Ibn Sina lived at the same time as another great thinker from Central Asia, Abu Rayhan al-Biruni. Biruni was born in 973, a decade before Ibn Sina, in Kath in Khwarazm. In 999, the two became locked in an intellectual debate. It started with a letter that Biruni sent to Ibn Sina listing ten philosophical questions. This gave rise to what was at times a heated exchange where the two philosophers discussed the teachings of Aristotle, the movement of heavenly bodies, life on other planets and the origins of the earth.

Were the movements of heavenly bodies linear or circular, or could they also move in an ellipse? Biruni believed the latter to be true, but only six hundred years later did Johannes Kepler prove it to be the case.

Was life on earth created at a given point in time, or had it developed gradually? The two philosophers agreed that the world had been created by God, to say otherwise would have been pure heresy, but they both believed that life must have developed gradually. This was almost as heretical. The fact that Biruni and Ibn Sina survived despite making such claims can be attributed to the open, intellectual climate at that particular time in the history of Central Asia and Islam.

It was Biruni who eventually won this philosophical duel, and there is much to indicate that it was he who ensured that their correspondence was published. Not many of his other books and papers have survived: of his one hundred and eight works, only twenty-two still exist. However, he is still recognised as perhaps the greatest scholar of the Islamic golden age. All his works demonstrate the same intellectual and scientific rigour that comes to the fore in his correspondence with Ibn Sina. He never wrote anything for which he did not have detailed evidence, and always tried to gather as many facts as possible about the subjects they discussed. And there were quite a few! Biruni was interested in such diverse disciplines as mathematics, astronomy, history and social sciences.

Biruni, the mathematician, is famous for having solved the classic wheat and chessboard problem: if you put one grain of wheat on the first square, two on the second, four on the third, eight on the fourth and then double the number of grains for each new square, until sixty-four squares are filled, how many grains of corn do you need in total? Biruni calculated that the answer was 18,446,744,073,709,551,615 grains of wheat. This would weigh more than 460 billion tons, and form a mountain taller than Mount Everest. It is more grains of wheat than exist in the world.

Biruni, the historian, set himself the task of writing an enormous work on world history, which is called *Chronology of Ancient Nations*. One of his greatest challenges was that nearly every culture and civilisation had their own calendar, so it was hard to give a definitive date to historical events. In addition to describing these calendars in detail, he spent a long time converting all the various systems into one system – the very first attempt to make a universal calendar system.

In his writings on the different religions, Biruni was careful to describe each religion in its own terms, in more or less the same way that he had approached the calendar systems. His purpose was not to find "fault", but to explain the logic behind each religion. Today, he is recognised as one of the leading pioneers in comparative religion. He is also deemed to be the founder of Indology as a separate discipline. Biruni spent his final years in India and wrote several important books on Indian culture and history. As always, he did his utmost to understand the logic underlying Indian society and Hinduism, and whenever he found something hard to understand, he dug a bit deeper until it made sense. Biruni believed that all cultures must share a number of features, as they are all human constructs no matter how alien and exotic they may seem. This thought is one of the cornerstones of modern social anthropology.

These are just a few illustrations of the intellectual life that prevailed in Central Asia a thousand years ago! People read voraciously and wrote prolifically, and the teahouses were places to discuss Aristotle and deep philosophical questions.

—⁂—

Ellik Kala, or the Fifty Forts, lie close to Khiva. There are in fact at least two hundred of them, but many are still hidden under the sand. It was here that Igor Savitsky spent eight years painting his landscapes under the scorching desert sun while his colleagues unearthed from the sand, centimetre by centimetre, forts and Zoroastrian temples that were two thousand years old.

The archaeological site is today divided by the border between Turkmenistan and Uzbekistan. Many of the most important towns in Khwarazm, such as Merv, Urgench and Kath, lie on the Turkmen side, several hundred kilometres from here.

One of the best-preserved forts on the Uzbek side is Toprak-Kala, which is more than 2,200 years old. The people who built it took into consideration the fact that the region was prone to earth-quakes, and made sure that they constructed buildings that were so solid they would withstand the occasional tremor. A couple of the watchtowers are still standing and some of the foundations remain intact. It is still possible to see how the rooms were divided, and in a few places the wall decorations are visible: large circles have been etched into the clay. Were the circles simply decorative, or did they have some other function? Were they supposed to symbol-ise the sun?

Rustam, my guide, bent down and picked up a piece of pottery decorated with a blue and orange pattern.

"There are still lots of treasures to be found here," he said and put the fragment in his pocket. "If you know any archaeologists, you should send them here."

The surrounding landscape was arid and flat. In a nearby field, a handful of farm workers were busy cutting down the season's cotton plants. Rustam and I drove on to the old Zoroastrian observatory, which lies on its own, deep in the desert, far from the forts. It was originally surrounded by three circular walls. Only fragments of the innermost wall have survived.

"The observatory is two thousand four hundred years old," Rustam said. "Tourists are sometimes disappointed by how small it is. It was originally much bigger, of course, but two thousand four hundred years is a long time, and clay is a perishable material. There was also a temple here, as well as the observatory, which was decorated with frescos. And do you know what they depicted?"

I shook my head.

"People drinking wine! Two thousand four hundred years ago! Isn't that amazing?" Rustam was beaming.

We clambered to the top of a low, circular mound. It was still possible to see some of the walls and the original floor plan; the rest could but be imagined.

"I think it's incredible that they had observatories here so long ago!" Rustam looked at me, full of enthusiasm. "Astronomy is the origin of all science. It led not only to a greater understanding of space and the movement of the stars, but also of time, which in turn led to the development of calendars, geography and, not least, maths."

"You mean that there were mathematicians and scholars here long before the Arab invasion in the eighth century?"

"Of course!" Rustam grinned. "The people of Khwarazm spoke a Persian dialect and eventually developed their own written language. They used the Aramaic alphabet before the Arabs came, which they learned from the Nestorian Christians who settled in the region very early on. Unfortunately, little has been preserved. The Arabs destroyed practically everything."

The Arab invasions of Central Asia began in around 650, but the region was not fully Islamified until hundreds of years later. This was in part because the Arab conquerors were soon divided into different factions which fought among themselves. So, for the first few decades, Islam existed alongside the many other religions that were practised there, including Christianity, Judaism, Buddhism and Zoroastrianism.

This tolerance ended in 705, when the Arab general Qutayba ibn Muslim was appointed governor in Central Asia. Qutayba immediately declared jihad, holy war, against all unbelievers in the region and put his words into action without delay. His forces met strong opposition from the local population, however, and only after

having held Samarkand under siege for four years did they manage
to enter the city gates. Qutayba gave orders that the Zoroastrian
temple should be destroyed and a mosque should be built in its
place. Initially, he forced the city's inhabitants to attend Friday
prayers in the new mosque, but soon realised that this was not a
wise strategy. Instead, he introduced a payment scheme: everyone
who came to Friday prayers was paid two dirham. Attendance soon
increased dramatically.

The infidels fared worse: several thousand Christians were
slaughtered by Qutayba's soldiers. He also ordered the soldiers to
destroy any books they came across. In Bukhara, one of the most
important libraries of the time was left in ruins, but it was the intellectual life in Khwarazm that suffered the most. In Kath, which was
the capital in those days, Qutayba's soldiers destroyed all Khwarazm's
books, including works on astronomy, history, genealogy, mathematics and literature. Not a single work survives.

Nine years after Qutayba was appointed governor, the caliph
died in Baghdad. Qutayba wanted to take the opportunity to gain
independence for his Central Asian domain, but his soldiers rebelled
and Qutayba was forced to flee. He was soon found and killed by
his own people. As no-one knows what was written in the works
that were destroyed in Kath, it is hard even to guess what treasures
were lost to future generations during Qutayba's fanatical jihad.

"Anything that was left by the Arabs was then destroyed by
Genghis Khan, and anything he had failed to destroy was then
destroyed by Timur Lenk," was Rustam's pithy summary. "We're not
supposed to say anything bad about Timur Lenk to tourists, because
the president has made him the national hero of Uzbekistan. But
the truth is that he killed just as many people as Genghis Khan.
And after Timur came the Uzbeks, then the Russians and then the
Bolsheviks!"

He looked around, as if to make sure that no-one else could hear. We were surrounded by nothing but sand.

"The current regime is no better. My dream is that Khwarazm, which is now divided between Uzbekistan and Turkmenistan, will one day be an independent nation again."

Rustam chuckled to himself.

"Of course, I know that will never happen," he said. "I'm not stupid."

PEARLS OF THE SILK ROAD

In November, the streets of Bukhara are virtually empty of tourists. Everywhere is empty and quiet; the air is raw and cold. I donned a down jacket, hat and scarf and went out to explore the old town. Bukhara is the fifth largest city in Uzbekistan, but the old town is so compact that all the sights can be reached on foot. For three days on end, I wander the labyrinthine back streets and spacious, open squares, I walk and walk and cannot get enough of this city. My wanderings take me past madrasas and caravanserai that are hundreds of years old, through narrow, windy streets and covered bazaars with domed roofs. The buildings in Bukhara, unlike those in Khiva, are made from brick. As most of the facades are bare and clean, the city is light brown, though occasionally it is as though it explodes with colour: emerald-green domes shine in the November sun, the tall, rectangular gates of the madrasas are bejewelled with blue mosaics and quotes from the Qur'an.

In the eleventh century, Bukhara was known as the Holy City and for a couple of hundred years it was one of the most important Islamic centres in the world. Unfortunately, only a few of the buildings from that time have survived. When Genghis Khan arrived outside the city walls in 1220, Bukhara's twenty thousand soldiers fled at the sight of his enormous Mongolian army. The few that remained in the city hid in the fort, where they believed the solid walls would protect them. The civilian population and priests, who in practice had been left to defend themselves, opened the city gates and surrendered to the Mongols. Since the inhabitants had given themselves up, Genghis Khan ordered that Bukhara should be plundered but not destroyed. In the ensuing battles with the few remaining soldiers, however, a fire broke out and the city was razed to the ground.

The old town, as it stands today, stems largely from the city's second golden age, from when the Uzbek tribes came to power in the sixteenth century. One of the few buildings that remains from the time before Genghis Khan is the slim, elegant Kalyan minaret, also known as the Tower of Death. As well as for the call to prayer, the minaret was used for public executions. The town crier first announced the crimes of the accused, then he or she was thrown from the top of the 45-metre high minaret. The executions often took place on market day, so that as many people as possible could attend. This practice continued under the Russians, who were pragmatic in their approach to their colonies: so long as the locals paid their taxes and did not rebel, they generally left them in peace. It was only when the more ideological Bolsheviks came to power in the 1920s that both the executions and the calls to prayer were halted.

—⁂—

One of the most important cities on the Silk Road lies only a short train journey from Bukhara. The name in itself conjures up adventure: Samarkand. It carries romantic associations with spices from distant lands, handwoven silk carpets, camel caravans, dusty market places and azure cupolas.

A Chinese traveller who visited the city in the seventh century noted that "all the inhabitants are educated to be merchants. When a boy turns five, they start to teach him to read and when he can read, they teach him about trade." [xiv] Samarkand was then the capital of Sogdia. The Sogdians were excellent merchants and for centuries controlled the trade between East and West. They established trading colonies all over Asia and administered a large number of routes from the Black Sea and Constantinople to as far afield as modern day Sri Lanka.

It is still possible to experience a hint of the old Silk Road atmosphere at the Siyab Market, one of the largest in Samarkand. Under the Karimov regime the market has been modernised and standardised, with a corrugated iron roof and rows of stalls, but the sellers who offer their carefully stacked wares with a big smile are as they always have been. Many are direct descendants of the Sogdian Silk Road merchants and have trading in their blood. Through the centuries, their grandmothers and great-great-great-grandfathers have sat here, in the same place, and haggled from behind their magnificent mounds of goods. Even the smallest deal, be it a single banana or an orange, has to be discussed and negotiated; it is like a ceremonial dance where everyone follows strict, unspoken rules. As was traditionally the case, the market is organised into various sections: apple sellers sit separately from bread sellers; the hat sellers sit side by side behind hillocks of white felt; in the corner by the exit the nut sellers display their nuts by colour and size. In the spice section, the stallholders peep out from behind colourful pyramids of cloves, pepper and saffron. I have seldom experienced such an intense smell as that of the cinnamon at Siyab Market in Samarkand.

From the spice mounds, it is just possible to see the blue dome of the Bibi Khanum mosque, which was once the largest in the world. The mosque is named after the favourite wife of Timur Lenk, the fifteenth-century conqueror. No-one has left a greater mark on Samarkand than he did. The Northern European sobriquet "Lenk", and other variants such as Tamerlan and Tamerlanes, are all derived from the Persian nickname Timur-i Lang, which means "Timur the Lame". When he was a young man, Timur fell from his horse and injured his right hip, hence the nickname that would stay with him for ever. Being lame did not stop Timur from becoming one of the greatest conquerors the world has ever known.

Timur was born in 1336 into a Turkic tribe in what is today southern Uzbekistan, more than a hundred years after the death of Genghis Khan, after his enormous kingdom was divided up between his descendants. The Mongol empire was already disintegrating, and when the Black Plague started to spread death and ruin in 1340, the empire's days were numbered.

Timur dreamed of re-establishing Genghis Khan's dominion. Before he was thirty-five, he had conquered Samarkand and the greater part of Central Asia. He spent the following thirty-five years subduing parts of what are today Turkey and Pakistan, the Caucasus, and the Middle East. He plundered and destroyed cities such as Damascus, Baghdad, Aleppo, Delhi and Ankara.

Thanks to Timur Lenk's victory over the Ottomans, he was hailed as a hero in Europe. Genghis Khan, on the other hand, was portrayed as a bloodthirsty monster in both literature and art. Timur was every bit as brutal as Genghis Khan. Historians believe that his army may have killed as many as seventeen million people, a figure it is impossible to verify. In Delhi alone, more than a hundred thousand were killed. Several thousand people were chased into the enormous Friday Mosque during the battle for Damascus. Timur's soldiers then set it alight. In Aleppo, Baghdad, Tikrit, Isfahan and Delhi, he ordered his soldiers to build what he called "minarets" from the skulls of the defeated populace.

In contrast to Genghis Khan, who left Central Asia in ruins, Timur Lenk restored several of the cities on the Silk Road to their former glory. During his campaigns in the Caucasus, the Middle East and India, he systematically spared the lives of skilled craftsmen and other professionals, and took them back to Samarkand. Here he set them to work on ambitious projects in which he himself was the chief architect and master builder.

Timur Lenk's buildings were impressive in both size and number. Because his craftsmen came from so many different countries, they included features and styles from Damascus as well as Baghdad. The great conqueror had no time to waste and prioritised speed over quality. Accordingly, only a handful of these buildings have survived to the present day. Bibi Khanum mosque had scarcely been opened before it started to fall apart. It collapsed altogether in the 1897 earth-quake. And in the city where Timur was born, Shahrisabz, about eighty kilometres south of Samarkand, only two pillars remain of Ak Serai, the White Palace, which was Timur's grandest and most expensive building. The two enormous pillars, which are visible from several kilometres away, give some impression of how big the palace must have been. In Timur's day, visitors were greeted with inscriptions such as "The Sultan is God's shadow," and "If you doubt our greatness, then look at our buildings."

Timur Lenk died in the winter of 1405, in Otrar in modern day Kazakhstan. He was sixty-nine, at the height of his power, but still hungry for more. When he died, he was on his way to China to vanquish the Ming Dynasty. His soldiers carried his body back to Samarkand; the journey must have taken several weeks. It was the coldest, snowiest winter in living memory. The remains of the great conqueror were laid to rest in the Gur Emir mausoleum in Samar-kand under an enormous green jade gravestone.

In June 1941, a group of Soviet archaeologists opened the grave to inspect Timur Lenk's remains. His coffin bore the following inscrip-tion: "When I rise from the dead, the world shall tremble." It is said that they found another inscription inside the coffin: "Whosoever opens my tomb shall unleash an enemy more terrible than I." Two days after the archaeologists opened the tomb, Hitler invaded the

Soviet Union. Timur Lenk was reburied in accordance with Muslim rituals in November 1942, just before the decisive phase of the battle for Stalingrad, in which the German forces suffered enormous losses.

Whereas Timur Lenk re-established the glory of Samarkand, it was the sense of aesthetics and detail of those who came after that made the city into the legend she is today. One of Timur's grandsons in particular, Mirza Muhammad Taraghay, left his mark. He is better known by the name Ulugh Beg, which means "The Great Ruler". Whether Ulugh Beg was in fact a great ruler is debatable – he was not so successful in his military campaigns and survived only two years on the throne after his father died – but he was without a doubt a great astronomer and mathematician. The observatory that he had built in Samarkand was recognised as the biggest, finest and most advanced observatory in the Islamic world at the time. It was here that Ulugh Beg and his students charted the stars with a preci-sion that was only surpassed by Tycho Brahe more than a century later. Ulugh Beg calculated the length of a year and he was wrong only by twenty-five seconds, making his estimate more precise than that of Nicolaus Copernicus a hundred years later.

Ulugh Beg was loved by the students of Samarkand. He often taught and gave financial support to the students. The mullahs, on the other hand, were less enthralled by the ruler's love of numbers, science and wine. They believed that Ulugh Beg was a danger to Islam and that he was leading people down the wrong path. When his father, Shah Rukh, died in 1447, Ulugh Beg was unable to main-tain a firm hold on power. After only two years as sultan, he was murdered by his own son in a carefully planned ambush. It did not take long for religious fanatics to destroy the observatory and ensure the closure of Ulugh Beg's school.

Even though the Uzbek dynasties that came to power in the

sixteenth century continued to make beautiful buildings, the intellectual golden age was over. While Europe entered the Renaissance and Age of Enlightenment, Central Asia lagged behind. China, which had always been so important to trade on the Silk Road, isolated itself more and more from the outside world. And the sea became the primary transport route between Europe and Asia. The Central Asians were partly to blame for this as Timur's empire had been divided up between rival clans. They imposed high tariffs on trade, but were unable to maintain security along the caravan routes.

All that remains today of Ulugh Beg's famous observatory is the large brass sextant. The school is still standing. Ulugh Beg's madrasa was erected on Registan, which means "Sand Square" and was the old market place. The building was completed in 1420 and Ulugh Beg himself taught mathematics here. As is the case for most Islamic colleges in Central Asia, the architect paid particular attention to symmetry, in the mosaic decorations as well as the building itself. The pointed arch in the otherwise flat, rectangular facade leads into a large, square courtyard. The building around it has two storeys with study cells, each formed like the entrance but on a smaller scale: a pointed arch in a flat rectangle, decorated with blue mosaics. In the middle of each wing of cells is a larger pointed arch that once again echoes the entrance arch. The overall effect is a striking balance between lightness and weight, symmetry and elegance.

In the seventeenth century, the Ulugh Beg madrasa got company. The Sher Dor madrasa, or Lion School, was built opposite and the Tilla Kari madrasa, the Gilded School, lies a bit further back between the two. Thus they make up a trinity. The Gilded School, as the name indicates, is richly decorated with gold, and even though it has a flat roof like the other two, the clever craftsmen managed to create the illusion of a shallow dome inside. It took seventeen years to complete the Lion School, and its unique feature are the two tigers that are depicted on either side of the facade. The Qur'an forbids the portrayal of living beings, but the artist managed to crack this particular nut by claiming that the tigers actually depicted lions and therefore were not tigers.

Of the three madrasas, which are among the oldest preserved Islamic schools in the world, Ulugh Beg's madrasa has best stood the test of time, despite the fact that it is the oldest and took only three years to build.

When the Russians absorbed the Bukhara emirate in the nineteenth century the three madrasas had clearly suffered centuries of neglect. The Soviet authorities later invested a considerable amount of time and money in restoring the Registan complex. Some scholars feel that they did too much, that some liberties were taken, but, on the whole, the restoration work was true to the original. In their eagerness to keep up with the times, the Uzbek authorities have installed loudspeakers on the lawn in front of the square, so that tourists can now enjoy modern Uzbek pop music while they visit these wonders from the past.

The first time I saw the Registan, the sun was going down. I sat by one of the fountains that had been turned off for the winter, taking it all in. Each of the madrasas, with its blue, blue facades and perfect arches, is a wonder in itself. But viewed together, with their perfect symmetry, the effect is sublime. It is as though the symmetry lifts the square into the air. The clouds behind the facades were light grey. And behind the grey, pink and orange streaks bled into one another. The sparrows in the trees behind me were singing as though their lives depended on it – there must have been at least a hundred of them. There and then, I felt that the purpose of my long journey, the culmination of these five months, was to sit right here, in front of the Registan, at sunset, listening to the sounds of modern Uzbek pop music and the twittering of a hundred sparrows.

THE END STATION

Tashkent is the end station on the Transcaspian railway, which stretches 1,864 kilometres from Turkmenbashi, through the Karakum Desert, all the way to the Uzbek capital. In the 1880s, the extension of the railway became a nerve-tingling factor in the Great Game between Russia and Great Britain. The British feared that the railway would give the Russians a military advantage, but the Russians, as it turned out, had no plans to invade India, and primarily used the trains to transport cotton. Today, the final stretch of the line has been upgraded to carry high-speed trains, and the carriages are full of tourists and businessmen.

Nurmat, who was sitting beside me, was going to Tashkent to meet his mistress. He was in his fifties, with the beginnings of a belly; his pockets were full of dollars, which he was more than happy to show off. His favourite topics were women and homosexuals.

"Is same-sex marriage allowed in Norway, like it is in the Netherlands?" was his first question when I told him where I was from. When I said that it was, he thundered: "Homosexuality is against nature. In my opinion, it's an abomination that must be eradicated. If a child is not exposed to homosexuality, he won't become a homosexual. Children see what their mother and father do in bed, and copy them, don't they?" He released a vile-smelling burp and apologised, saying that he had had a bit too much vodka the day before. "Women nowadays wear clothes that are far too fitting," he complained. "Nothing is left to the imagination any more. It was much more titillating before when we had to imagine what was under the long skirts." He yawned, burped again, and looked at me with curiosity. "Why don't you have children? Do you use the coil, like my wife?"

I sent my silent thanks to Uzbek railways when the train rolled into the station in Tashkent at precisely the time it had said on the timetable.

Tashkent snaps you back into the present. With more than two million inhabitants, the Uzbek capital is without question the largest city in Central Asia. There is nothing left of the idyllic city of the 1800s. Early in the morning of April 26, 1966, Tashkent was rocked by a powerful earthquake that within seconds more or less wiped out the old town. Several hundred thousand people were made homeless, but, by some miracle, only ten people were killed. The Soviet authorities took the opportunity to create a Soviet monster city with broad avenues, high-rise flats, enormous parks and plenty of open squares for parades and public events. The underground network that was opened only two years after the earthquake is comparable to the network in Moscow. The stations are adorned with marble pillars and chandeliers, and are an attraction in themselves.

As further proof that Uzbekistan, too, has substantial oil and gas reserves, if not as prodigious as those in Turkmenistan and Kazakhstan, a number of handsome buildings have sprung up in the centre of the city. The new library, with its blue glass facades and smooth white pillars, resembles a palace. The enormous parliament building, known as the White House, is several times larger than its namesake in Washington, and the new central bank looks like an oversized Greek temple. The main street is dominated by western luxury hotels, all with shiny facades and bellboys in smart uniforms. I spent an entire afternoon going from one five-star hotel to the next, as they are one of the few places in Tashkent where you may be lucky enough to find a cash machine. After going into eight hotels and trying six different A.T.M.s that were all "temporarily out of order", I gave up.

The shiny buildings and total absence of functioning cash machines were not the only things that reminded me of Turkmenistan. I was not watched over by a travel agency in Uzbekistan, which was something, but I had to behave like a tourist and could not interview anyone openly. Most people I met were afraid to talk about politics and other sensitive topics. When at one point I hinted to Nurmat, the unfaithful husband on the train, that the Uzbek president was a dictator, he clammed up and stared out of the window. And then resumed his monologue about women and homosexuals. The dictatorship in Uzbekistan is as extravagant as that in Turkmenistan – though there are surprisingly few posters of the president in public places, given that this is Central Asia – but the authorities have ears everywhere.

The only place where people would sometimes speak freely was in cars. As elsewhere in the former Soviet Union, every car in Uzbekistan is a potential taxi. There are policemen and video cameras on every street corner, as is often the case in a dictatorship, so hailing a taxi is seen as entirely safe, even for women on their own. For a few thousand som, I could get a lift wherever I wanted in the city. But how representative were these men who drove around in old, tired cars in the hope of earning fifty or sixty pence? And how truthful were they?

"Democracy?" one of these pirate drivers exclaimed. He was a tall, thin man in his forties and his Lada was so old that it was almost falling apart. "Of course we have democracy! In Kyrgyzstan, on the other hand, it's just chaos. And in Kazakhstan as well. War and violence and misery. Did you walk alone on the streets at night in Bishkek? No? Exactly! Here you can wander around until dawn if you like. Nothing would ever happen to you. You're safe here."

"I include President Karimov in my prayers every night!" another freelance driver claimed – a rather deaf pensioner in a threadbare but newly pressed suit. "I pray that he will stay in good health so that he can continue to rule the country for a long time to come. Thanks to the president we have peace. In Kyrgyzstan, there's just chaos, and in the Arab countries there's fighting and misery. Here, we have peace and stability."

The driver who took me to the airport, a stout man in his sixties, was the most critical: "The minimum wage here is less than a hundred thousand som," he said in a hushed voice. "That's less than fifty dollars. No-one can live on that. It's not even enough to pay for water, electricity and the rubbish collection. The people here have poor health, they get ill. The country is badly run. We can't even change our money to other currencies. You can in other countries, but not here. It's not normal, is it?"

While people spoke in almost inaudible voices whenever they said anything negative about the regime, even a harmless comment, for example, that the price of cooking oil had gone up, they would often shout in frustration when they spoke about Gulnara Kari-mova, the elder of the president's two daughters.

"She's stinking rich! She owns the whole of Uzbekistan, hotels, factories, cotton, gold, oil, gas, restaurants, you name it!" hissed the English student who drove me to the Timur Lenk museum. "She would sell her own grandmother to get what she wants. It's because of her that I want to move to the U.S.A. As long as she's her father's right hand, you won't be able to get anything done in this country. I wish they'd lock her up, but that's never going to happen . . ."

*

The student's wish has in fact been fulfilled: Gulnara Karimova,[17] who was deemed to be the most likely successor to the president, no longer sits at her father's right hand. She is being held under strict house arrest in Tashkent and has no contact with the outside world. The past year has been a mixture of a good, old-fashioned Shakespeare play and a modern soap opera for the Karimov family. Journalists and viewers have been able to follow it on Twitter and Instagram.

Gulnara Karimova's C.V. is unbelievable. The president's daughter has a Ph.D. in political science from the Tashkent University of World Economy and Diplomacy, where she also taught. And she seldom misses an opportunity to mention that she has a Masters degree from Harvard, but is rather less inclined to mention that it is not a normal Harvard Masters, but instead from an institute that courts rich applicants from developing countries. Her former lecturer at Harvard now teaches at the Nazarbayev Institute in Astana, Kazakhstan.

When it comes to work experience, Gulnara can boast, among other things, that she was ambassador to Spain and Uzbekistan's representative to the United Nations in Geneva. She has also been head of a number of humanitarian organisations and welfare initiatives to help women, children and young people in Uzbekistan, in the fields of sport and culture in particular.

She has more recently concentrated on developing her artistic side. In 2006, she released her first music video, "Don't Forget Me", under the stage name Googoosha, which was her father's pet name for her when she was little. When Julio Iglesias attended Fashion Week in Tashkent in 2008 (Gulnara was also one of the main architects of Fashion Week), the two sang the duet "Bésame mucho"

17 On March 6, 2019, Gulnara Karimova was sent to prison for allegedly violating the terms of her five-year house arrest.

together on stage. The song was subsequently banned from Uzbek radio when Iglesias refused to say, in an interview on Radio Liberty, who had invited him to Tashkent.

Another international star and friend of the dictator, Gérard Depardieu, visited Tashkent in 2012. One result of this visit was a duet with the evocative title "Nebo molchit", or "The Sky is Quiet". Gulnara sings in Russian, and Depardieu, dressed in a sleeveless white shirt, whispers hoarsely in French: "Forgive me. Forgive me everything I could not tell you. Forgive me for not being able to hold on to you . . . I forgive you." Depardieu also accepted the main role in the film "The Theft of the White Cocoon", the story of how cotton came to Central Asia more than 1,500 years ago, written by Gulnara Karimova herself, no less. But the film has still not been made, and given what has happened in the meantime, it is doubtful there will ever be a premiere.

Googoosha's best year was 2012. The dictator's daughter released her first album in the summer with extravagant launches in the U.S.A., Europe, Russia and Uzbekistan. The album was called simply "Googoosha". The music is heavily electronic and is apparently influenced by Massive Attack, Adele, Moby and Sade. On her website, Karimova describes herself as "a poet, mezzo soprano, designer and exotic Uzbek beauty". She wrote the lyrics to all the songs herself and in the dance-inspired "How Dare", she asks the very question that many Uzbeks have no doubt asked about her over the years: "You look fine, but what's going on in your mind? You look fine, but what do you hide in your soul?"

Despite all the expensive videos, Googoosha never made a breakthrough in the U.S.A. or Europe, but her songs were played night and day on Uzbek television and radio. Karimova's rather mediocre voice and long blonde hair were everywhere. She also launched herself as a fashion designer. Under yet another artist's name, this time Guli, she designed a pretty awful jewellery collection for the famous Swiss company Chophard, and had her own two perfumes: Victorious for men and Mystérieuse for women. Her collection was due to be shown on the catwalk during Fashion Week in New York in 2012, but the show had to be cancelled owing to protests by human rights activists, who objected to the fact that the dictator's daughter used cotton that had been picked by children.

Behind the glamorous, bimbo pop star image was an ambitious, and at times ruthless businesswoman. Karimova's former husband, Mansur Maqsudi, an American entrepreneur of Afghan descent, felt the force of his ex-wife's power following their divorce in 2001. As long as they were married, his Coca Cola bottling company in Uzbekistan did very well. However, when Karimova and Maqsudi got divorced, a battle ensued for the custody of their children. Karimova took the children back to Uzbekistan without her husband's permission, and an American court consequently found her guilty of kidnapping and issued an international arrest warrant. In response, a number of Maqsudi's business partners and relatives were arrested in Uzbekistan and deposited on the other side of the Afghan border. His bottling business floundered and then failed. And in 2008 Karimova was awarded custody of the children and the arrest warrant was withdrawn.

In her heyday, Karimova had lucrative deals with or substantial shares in all the main businesses in Uzbekistan. She was without a doubt the country's richest woman and owned everything from cotton plantations to gasworks, gold mines, hotels and restaurants. She and her business partners stopped at nothing to get their hands on new companies and businesses. The typical strategy was as follows: if Karimova was interested in taking over a company, she got the tax authorities to undertake a detailed investigation of the company, following which the company was closed down and had its assets confiscated, or was forced to sell them at well under the market value.

Foreign companies that wanted to establish themselves in Uzbekistan were pressured to pay bribes to the dictator's daughter. A Swiss-registered investment company called Zeromax was set up for this purpose. Zeromax had so much money that it bought its own football club, Bunyodkor. The former manager of Brazil and Portugal, Luiz Felipe Scolari, was taken on and given the task of leading ageing star players like Rivaldo to new heights in the Uzbek premier league.

In 2010, Zeromax was dissolved without warning. According to Kamollodin Rabbimov, a political commentator who used to work for the presidential administration but now lives in France, Zeromax caused so many problems that President Karimov decided to close it. "Gulnara monopolised entire sectors of the economy," he said in an interview with the BBC. "She started interfering in sales of natural gas, gold trade, logistics. She was sucking away so many resources that she single-handedly created a budget deficit."[xv]

Was the closure of Zeromax the start of Karimova's fall? In the autumn of 2013, things really started to fall to pieces. When she lost the diplomatic immunity afforded her as U.N. representative and ambassador to Spain, the Swiss, Dutch and American authorities opened an investigation into her financial shenanigans. To date, the Swiss authorities have frozen assets worth 800 million Swiss francs, which is a Swiss record. The dictator's daughter is formally accused of corruption and money laundering.

The investigation has also uncovered the biggest corruption scandal in the history of Sweden. TeliaSonera apparently paid 2.3 billion Swedish kronor to a company called Takilant Limited, registered in Gibraltar, to gain access to the 3G network in Uzbekistan. Takilant was owned by 25-year-old Gayane Avakyan, one of Karimova's personal assistants. The Norwegian company Telenor was also investigated in connection with the Uzbek telecommunications scandal. Telenor own thirty-three per cent of the Russian company Vimpelcom, which, like TeliaSonera, supposedly bought a licence for the Uzbek telecommunications network from Takilant Limited.

At the same time that Karimova's shady dealings were under the spotlight, her younger sister, Lola Karimova-Tillyaeva, gave her first ever interview to western media. Talking to the B.B.C., she disclosed that she had not spoken to her sister for twelve years. "Any good relationship requires a similarity of outlook or likeness of character," she said. "There is nothing like that in our relationship, has never been and is not now. We are completely different people. And these differences, as you know, only grow over the years."[xvi]

Lola is definitely less flamboyant than her elder sister, but there are still some similarities. She has a Ph.D. in psychology and lives in Geneva, where she is Uzbekistan's ambassador to U.N.E.S.C.O. She is married to an Uzbek, Timur Tillyaev, and they have three children. Her husband runs a large freight and import company in Uzbekistan, and the couple are reckoned to be among the richest people in Switzerland. Prior to the B.B.C. interview, she was best known for having sued a French website for calling her "the dictator's daughter". She lost the case.

In 2013, as autumn progressed, journalists and anyone else who was interested could follow the family feud from inside, via Gulnara Karimova's Twitter and Instagram accounts. She had previously only used social media to promote herself as an artist and to share photographs of herself in yoga poses. Now she used it to attack family members and people in power in the presidential administration. In cryptic posts, she accused her mother and sister of conspiring against her. "One part of the family (our father) provides, but the other destroys and is friends with sorcerers," she wrote on

Instagram in October 2013. Later, in a tweet that went viral, she asked if anyone knew about the practice of making star and triangle formations with candles, and said that she was worried about her mother, inferring that her mother was dabbling in black magic.

By late autumn, the net had started to close in on Gulnara. Her Twitter account was blocked on several occasions and then reopened. Her whole media empire, including several T.V. channels, was closed down and a number of charity organisations that she headed suffered the same fate. More than a dozen shops that sold western clothes in Tashkent and were owned by Gulnara had to close their doors, thanks to tax investigations – a tactic that Gulnara had used herself. Some of her friends and closest allies were arrested.

"The tension is growing everywhere, going home to my father, my path was blocked and they told me 'it's better not to'," Gulnara tweeted on November 30. But she caused an even bigger stir when she accused Rustam Innoyatov, the head of the S.N.B., of being behind all these actions against her, and said that he had his eye on the presidency. "He has!! He's already fighting for it!" she replied on Twitter when asked if she thought Innoyatov had ambitions to become the country's president. In interviews with western media, she started to express her concern about the S.N.B.'s breaches of human rights. She explained to the *Guardian* that "it took time to realise the reality we live in".

On February 17, 2014, the president's daughter fell silent. Her Twitter account had been closed for good, and Uzbek television and radio stopped playing Googoosha's songs. Soon there were rumours that Karimova and her fifteen-year-old daughter were living under house arrest. In March, the B.B.C. received an e-mail containing a handwritten letter that confirmed this. Handwriting experts believed that the letter was most probably written by Karimova herself. She said in a long, somewhat confused letter: "I am under severe psychological pressure, I have been beaten, you can count the bruises on my arms." Around this time, an unusual photograph of her appeared on the Internet. Dishevelled and without make-up, she is sitting on a bed in a white nightdress, drinking with a straw from a Nesquik carton.

At the time of writing, Gulnara Karimova, the once rich and powerful favourite of the president, is still under house arrest with her daughter. Several hundreds of her friends and allies have been arrested or threatened into silence. The interesting question is who is behind it?

There has been considerable speculation about the circumstances surrounding Karimova's house arrest. Some believe that that the 76-year-old president is no longer compos mentis and that in reality it is Innoyatov, the head of the S.N.B., who is standing in the wings and pulling the strings. And with Karimova under lock and key, the biggest obstacle to the presidency has been removed. Karimova gave credence to this idea herself in a letter smuggled out of the house where she is being held: "When God wants to punish a person, He takes away his mind. Otherwise no one stoops so low as to harass their own child, and the child of their child."

Others find it impossible to believe that Karimov, a powerful politician who has ruled the country with an iron fist for twenty-five years, is not behind his daughter's house arrest. She went too far, became too greedy and crossed too many lines, including those set by international law, so had to be taken out of the game.

Irrespective of who is behind it, the power struggle in the president's family has to be seen in the light of Islam Karimov's age. In the 2015 presidential election, he took ninety per cent of the votes, and when this term ends he will be eighty-four. He has not appointed a successor, and, given what has happened, it will not be his elder child who takes over, as is often the case with this kind of modern "president monarchy". Will it instead be the younger daughter, Lola, and her fabulously wealthy husband? Is there any truth to the rumours that the head of the S.N.B. has ambitions to be president? Or will Karimov do what he and his colleagues in the region have chosen to do until now: stand for another term? Still confused? Watch the next episode of "The Intrigues of the Karimov Dynasty"!

The power struggle that is going on in the wings is not dissimilar to the wars of succession in Genghis Khan and Ulugh Beg's day. With the exception of Kyrgyzstan, none of the other republics in Central Asia have become democracies, but seem instead to have gone back in time to the emirates and khanates. The presiding "khans" are all getting old, which is a cause of concern for both potential investors and political analysts. What will happen when Central Asia's "eternal presidents" die or become too ill to rule? What direction will the Stans take then? The only thing that seems certain is that it will not be up to the people to decide.

The Kazakh president, Nursultan Nazarbayev, is now seventy-four, and he has not yet appointed a successor. Kazakhstan's relationship with its neighbour, Russia, is relatively good these days and Nazarbayev has managed to balance and control the tensions between the Kazakh majority and the large Russian minority in the country. What will happen if the next president is not so Russian-friendly? How would an increasingly nationalistic and assertive Russia respond to that?

Tajikistan's president, Emomali Rahmon, is one of the youngest in the club at sixty-one. As expected, he was re-elected in November 2013. The turnout was a very respectable, if not record, 87 per cent and Rahmon took 83.6 per cent of the votes. The only real opposition candidate, the lawyer Oynihol Bobnazarova, did not manage to get the necessary 210,000 signatures, and was therefore not registered as a candidate; she was also threatened and pressured not to stand. Rahmon was re-elected until 2021, but it is in no way certain that he will sit that long. Tajikistan is a poor country with strongly divided clans and a long border with Afghanistan. As recently as 2012, scores of people were killed in violent clashes between the army, local smuggling gangs and civilians in Khorog, the capital of Pamir.

Turkmenistan has already experienced one shift in power when Turkmenbashi, who had been appointed president for life, died in 2006. After a brief battle behind closed doors, his dentist, Gurban-guly Berdimuhamedov, ascended the throne and flooded the country with colour portraits of himself. At fifty-seven, he is a mere youth. And to show off his vigour, he takes every opportunity to be photographed in sporting situations, not unlike the president of a big country further north. In other words, Berdimuhamedov may be president for a long time yet, unless he falls from his horse again.

But for now, he seems to be sitting firm in the saddle. According to the official Turkmen online newspaper, Turkmenistan.ru, Berdimuhamedov won "an impressive victory over the other jock-eys" in this year's horse race. The state news agency T.D.H. said: "The crowds rose to their feet and hailed the winner, the president of Turkmenistan, with jubilant and prolonged applause." And now, as I write, the same sources have announced plans to raise a monument to Berdimuhamedov, or the Protector, as he likes to be called, in central Ashgabat. "Our country's success, performance and, to a great extent, development are all inextricably linked with the name Gurbanguly Berdimuhamedov," the minister of foreign affairs and deputy prime minister Rashid Meredov stated by way of explanation. The plans have not, however, been approved by the president himself, because, as he explained: "I will listen to the opinion of the people and do as they choose."

The opinion of the people may be sacred, but they are never

asked. No-one listened to the Turkmens under Soviet rule, and their own politicians are more concerned about looking after themselves and their own nearest and dearest. But the new generation has grown up with satellite T.V. and the Internet, and many of them have studied abroad, so how long will the Turkmen people put up with the repression and the squandering of state funds by politicians?

In Kyrgyzstan, the only democracy in Central Asia, the political situation is fragile. Following the riots in South Kyrgyzstan in 2010, no convincing attempt has been made to punish the guilty parties. The ethnic conflict between the Uzbeks and Kyrgyz is dormant at present, but could flare up again at any point.

There are many such ethnic conflicts in Central Asia. In Tajikistan, the people in Pamir dream of independence, in Uzbekistan the Karakalpaks and Khwarazms do the same, whereas the people in the Fergana Valley are divided by national borders but share the same language and culture. It is not difficult to understand why the presidents in Central Asia have chosen to maintain Stalin's borders from the 1920s and '30s. If they started to redraw the lines on the map now, they would open the floodgates of suppressed nationalism.

In short, problems abound for the post-Soviet states of Central Asia. In addition to a lack of democracy, most of the countries' economies are struggling. The Soviet authorities did not invest in industry in the region, choosing instead to use the countries as sources of commodities. With a few exceptions, the current corrupt regimes have failed to pull their countries out of the quagmire, and many of them are still dependent on Russia. The economies in Kyrgyzstan and Tajikistan are heavily dependent on the contributions of migrant workers in Russian towns and cities. By joining the Eurasian Economic Union, Kazakhstan has tightened financial links with its big brother in the north. Uzbekistan has thus far maintained an isolationist stance, but rumour has it that Russia is working hard behind the scenes to ensure that the Kremlin-friendly head of S.N.B., Innoyatov, takes over from the ageing Karimov.

It is impossible to understand the five new countries of Central Asia without taking into consideration the way in which their past as Soviet republics has shaped them. During the seventy years of Soviet rule, Central Asia was forced to leave the Middle Ages and step into the twentieth century. It was a tumultuous leap. An entire inland sea disappeared, nomads were forced to give up their livestock and settle on collective farms, and more than one million people starved to death. Hundreds of mosques were closed, women were liberated from their headscarves, and polygamy was banned, at least in theory. Arabic calligraphy was replaced by the Cyrillic alphabet, but everyone learned to read, even the girls. Roads were built, and also libraries, opera houses, universities, hospitals and sanatoriums. Internal borders were drawn up, external borders were sealed with barbed wire fences, and five nations were born.

Nevertheless, Central Asia has managed to maintain some of its unique character.

The old clan culture survived the central committees and collectivisation. Autocracy never quite died, but found a new form. The hospitality, fascination with carpets, old market culture, and love of horses and camels are still alive and strong today, making any trip to the region unforgettable.

The Stans are at a crossroads. Should they forge closer links with Russia or China, or look to the West? Which interpretation of their own history should they trust? After nearly twenty-five years of independence, the five nations are still struggling to find their identity, bridging the span between east and west, old and new, in the middle of Asia, but surrounded by superpowers like Russia and China, and controversial or unstable neighbours such as Iran and

Afghanistan. Ninety per cent of the Russians who lived in Tajikistan, two-thirds of those who lived in Turkmenistan and half of those who lived in Uzbekistan have left. Central Asia has thus become "more itself" over the past twenty-five years, in terms of ethnicity. But as long as the economic and political heritage of the Soviet Union continues to shackle the Stans, there is little hope of change. As Murat, my guide in Turkmenistan, said as we crossed the desert from north to south: "The Soviet generation is what it is. They do everything in the same old way. I put my faith in the new generation. Many of them have travelled, seen the world. Only they can bring a breath of fresh air."

AFTERWORD –
THE DEATH OF A DICTATOR

On Monday, August 29, 2016, Islam Karimov's youngest daughter, Lola Karimova, posted a message on Instagram that made the headlines all over the world: "My father was hospitalised after suffering a cerebral haemorrhage on Saturday morning and is now receiving treatment in an intensive care unit. His condition is considered to be stable. At the moment it is too early to make any predictions about his future health. My only request to everyone is to refrain from any speculations and show respect to our family's right to privacy. I will be grateful to everyone who will support my father with prayers."

A few hours later, the renowned Moscow-based news agency Fergana published an article stating that Karimov had died at 3.35 p.m. local time, the same day. While foreign newspapers started to speculate about possible successors to the throne, the Uzbek authorities continued to insist that Karimov's condition was critical but stable.

Then, on August 31, Lola posted another message on Instagram. She expressed her gratitude for "your kind, sincere and encouraging words of support", and claimed that these sincere wishes had helped her father's recovery. The same evening at prime time, Karimov's speech to mark the twenty-fifth anniversary of Uzbekistan's independence was read out on Uzbek state television. Karimov, who, it transpired, had died two days earlier, sent his heartfelt congratulations to the people, via the news anchor.

The following day, on September 1, Fergana published photographs from Samarkand which showed that preparations for a state funeral were well under way. It was not until the evening of September 2, once the twenty-fifth anniversary celebrations were over, that the Uzbek authorities confirmed that Islam Karimov was dead. His death was officially recorded as 8.55 p.m. on Friday, September 2, 2016.

The dictator was laid to rest the next day, in keeping with Muslim tradition, following an elaborate funeral ceremony in Samarkand. There was keen interest in who would lead the funeral committee, as they were likely to be the next leader of Uzbekistan, according to the protocol of the former Soviet Union. Only one other president has died in office in Central Asia in the past twenty-five years, so it is perhaps too early to talk about traditions as such, but thus far the Soviet legacy has continued. When Turkmenistan's autocratic president, Turkmenbashi, died in 2006, the vice-president, Gurbanguly Berdimuhamedov, led the funeral committee. Shortly thereafter he was appointed interim president, even though it should have been the chairman of the assembly, Ovezgeldi Atayev, who led the country in the transition period. Atayev was instead imprisoned and charged with abuse of power and human rights violations.

Under the terms of the Uzbek constitution, the chairman of the senate, Nigmatilla Yuldashev, should have been appointed interim president. But it was the prime minister, Shavkat Mirziyoyev, who led the funeral committee. And sure enough: on September 8, Mirziyoyev was officially appointed interim president of Uzbekistan. The late president's infamous daughter, Gulnara Karimova, was not present at her father's funeral.

In December 2016, a few months after he was appointed interim president, Shavkat Mirziyoyev was elected president by the Uzbek people with a majority of 88.6 per cent.

So who is Shavkat Mirziyoyev? He was born in 1957, the same

year as his Turkmen colleague, President Berdimuhamedov. He is a qualified engineer and irrigation expert. He entered politics in the mid-1990s and has had a stellar career, starting out as governor of the Jizzakh region, and then of the Samarkand region. In 2003, President Karimov personally appointed him prime minister, a position he held until Karimov's death. Mirziyoyev is no novice in the corridors of power – the power may have shifted slightly, but essentially remains in the same hands.

There are, however, signs of some positive and very necessary changes. Mirziyoyev has worked hard to pull Uzbekistan out of isolation, making every effort to ease the inflamed relationship with its neighbours, Tajikistan and Kyrgyzstan. Border crossings that were closed have been opened again in several places, and direct flights between Tashkent and Dushanbe were reintroduced in 2017, following a 25-year hiatus. The strict visa regulations have been relaxed and steps have also been taken to simplify foreign investment in the country. In autumn 2017, the state adjusted the exchange rate for the Uzbek som from an artificially low 4,210 against the U.S. dollar to 8,100 som, thus doing away with the black market overnight. The central bank has also printed 50,000-som and 100,000-som banknotes, so it is no longer necessary to carry heavy bags of paper money with you wherever you go.

In 2017, Gulnara Karimova, who only a few years earlier had been the richest and most powerful woman in Uzbekistan, was given a ten-year prison sentence for corruption and money laundering, among other things. The sentence was later commuted to five years' house arrest, but as Karimova repeatedly violated the conditions of her house arrest, the dictator's daughter was sentenced again in 2019 to serve the remainder of her time in prison.

Rustam Innoyatov, the previously powerful head of the National Security Service, stepped down from his position at the start of

2018. Since becoming president, Mirziyoyev has systematically tried to reduce the power of the security service, and has among other things introduced a new law that forbids the use of torture to obtain confessions in criminal cases. Scores of journalists and political prisoners have been pardoned, and the unpopular practice of commandeering students, doctors, teachers and other civil servants to harvest cotton is now forbidden. In practice, however, many thousands of civil servants are still forced to pick cotton and often have to sign a document which states that they are doing so voluntarily. Thousands of political prisoners remain behind bars, and power is still centred on a single person. In other words, there is much that needs to be changed before Uzbekistan can be deemed to be good company, but in a region where developments tend to lead in the opposite direction, towards increasingly authoritarian regimes, any easing of restrictions gives grounds for optimism.

There can be no doubt that Karimov's death gave his Central Asian colleagues a fright. On September 14, twelve days after his death in Tashkent, the parliament and lawmakers in Turkmenistan raised the upper age limit for presidents, which until then had been seventy. There was never a need to raise the age limit for Turkmenbashi, who only lived to sixty-six, and who in any case had already been designated president for life. President Berdimuhamedov is currently sixty-one years old, but clearly has long-term plans. The presidential period was extended at the same time from five to seven years, as is the case in Russia.

The Turkmen economy has been in free fall in recent years. The sharp decline in oil and gas prices on the international market has led to a dramatic reduction in government income. The crisis has resulted in shortages of staple commodities such as flour, sugar and cooking oil, which in turn have caused long queues outside the state grocery shops. In autumn 2017, the authorities were forced to scrap the free provision of electricity, gas and water. Yet in the same year, Berdimuhamedov was re-elected as president with a majority of 97.69 per cent, despite the ongoing crisis.

There have also been several changes in Tajikistan, following Karimov's death. In 2016, the Tajik authorities voted to adopt a number of constitutional reforms, which included lowering the minimum age limit for presidents, from thirty-five to thirty. This was probably done to pave the way for President Rahmon's eldest son, Rustam Emomali, who first saw day in 1987. A resolution was also passed that allows President Rahmon, who the state media must now refer to as "The Founder of Peace and National Unity, Leader of the Nation, the President of Tajikistan, His Excellency Emomali Rahmon", to be re-elected any number of times. In other words, there is little to indicate that Rahmon has any immediate plans to hand over power to his son – but by lowering the minimum age, he has secured all bases. Even autocrats die, it turns out.

But it is almost unheard of for an autocrat to step down of his own volition, which is why it caused such a stir when Nursultan Nazarbayev, the then president of Kazakhstan, announced in a speech broadcast on television on March 19, 2019 that he was stepping down with immediate effect. In 2015 he had been re-elected for another five years, with a solid 97.7 per cent majority, but he was not going to complete the term.

Nazarbayev's departure was highly orchestrated. The first indications are perhaps a number of reforms that he implemented in 2017, which restrict the president's personal power. Among other things, the president can no longer issue decrees that have the power of law, or veto parliamentary votes of no confidence in cabinet members. At the same time, Nazarbayev extended the authority of the already powerful security council, and in 2018 he was appointed head of the security council for life. Thus, in reality, he continues to have full control over foreign policy and the military. Furthermore, as Elbasy, Leader of the Nation, Nazarbayev can still make important decisions on behalf of the country, even though he no longer has the title of president.

Another genuinely surprising aspect of Nazarbayev's announcement was the timing. Nazarbayev is now seventy-eight – the same age Karimov was when he died – and apparently in good health. Perhaps he felt that, after thirty years in power, the time had come to step down.

The day after Nazarbayev's unexpected resignation, the chairman of the senate, Kasym-Zhomart Tokayev, was sworn in as president, in line with the constitution. Tokayev, who is sixty-five and a career diplomat, did not waste time. On his first day in office, he proposed that Kazakhstan's capital, Astana, should be renamed Nursultan, after the first president. He also proposed that a monument be raised in the capital in honour of Nazarbayev, and that all major towns and cities have a street named after him. All these proposals were immediately approved by the parliament.

One month after Nazarbayev's resignation, Tokayev was nominated as presidential candidate by the powerful Nur Otan party. And the election was brought forward to June 9, 2019. Tokayev is therefore well placed to continue as president. However, if he were to withdraw or die, the former president's eldest daughter, Dariga Nazarbayeva, would automatically become the country's president, as she was elected chairman of the senate in March, after Tokayev had been sworn in.

Nursultan Nazarbayev has stepped down after three decades in power, but ingeniously continues to hold the reins. The advantage of a voluntary resignation is that he continues to control who his successors will be in both the short and long term, which naturally would not have been possible had he left the presidential palace in a coffin.

In a region where presidents have traditionally either been hounded out of office by a raging populace or died on the job, Nazarbayev's resignation is perhaps his most important legacy. Albeit without relinquishing power.

And what about Kyrgyzstan, the only democracy among the Stans? Dark clouds are gathering here. In 2014, the Kyrgyz parliament tabled motions to ban "gay propaganda" and "regulate foreign agents", following the example of Russia. Even though the law on gay propaganda has not yet been passed, there has been a significant increase in assaults on the LGBT community following the proposal, and the only gay bar in Bishkek was closed in 2017. Since joining the Eurasian Economic Union in 2015, Kyrgyzstan has developed even closer ties with Russia, and Kyrgyz nationalist groups are on the rise. On a brighter note, the 2015 parliamentary elections were more or less exemplary, and were described by the O.S.C.E. as "lively and competitive", and "unique in the region". The presidential election in 2017 also went smoothly. The former prime minister Sooronbay Zheenbekov won more than half the votes in the first round and took over the baton from Almazbek Atambayev, who had been in post for the maximum term of six years. For the first time in the history of Kyrgyzstan, one legally elected president was replaced by another, following a peaceful election.

When I travel around and give talks on Sovietistan, I am often asked what I think will happen to the countries of Central Asia. And that is a very good question. But, to paraphrase Peter Hopkirk, the author of The Great Game, I am neither bold enough nor foolish enough to attempt an answer.

Almost anything can happen there now.

ACKNOWLEDGMENTS

This book would never have been possible without all the help I received from near and far at every stage, when planning, travelling and writing. There are many people I would like to thank.

The Central Asian peoples are renowned for their hospitality and I experienced this generosity daily during my two extended stays in the region. My warmest thanks to everyone I met along the way, to all those who offered me tea and food, and shared their views and stories with me or helped me in any way. Wherever I went, I was met with a generosity, openness and helpfulness for which I am forever grateful. This book is the result of all those meetings. But some people deserve special thanks.

In Kazakhstan, I am particularly grateful to the following for taking the time to share their stories with me: Kirill Osin at Ekko Mangistau and the human rights activist Galym Ageleuov. I would also like to thank Aliya Tulateyeva, whose mother Roza is still in prison, accused of leading the oil workers' strike in Zhanaozen.

My former fellow student, Inga Lande, was kind enough to put me in touch with some of the people who helped her with her fieldwork in Tajikistan. Sayora Nazarova made my first days in Dushanbe less lonely. Saidamir Ashurov and Umed Mavlonov have no idea how much they helped me by putting me in touch with interesting people to interview. I am also indebted to Muqim Ergashboyev, who, for my week in the Yaghnob Valley, was not only my guide but also my research assistant and interpreter.

In Kyrgyzstan, I was given good advice and useful information by Gazbubu Babyarova at the Kyz Korgon Institute, Banur Abdiyeva from the organisation Leader in Karakol, Bubusasra Ryskulova at the Sezim Crisis Centre in Bishkek and Valentina Gritsenko from the human rights organisation Spravedlivost in Jalal-Abad. Nuraida

Abdykapar from the O.S.C.E. Academy, Jyldyz Modalieva from the U.N. office in Bishkek and Ruslan Rahimov from A.U.C.A., the American University in Bishkek, also helped me with contacts and information.

In addition to those mentioned above, Helge Blakkisrud from the Norwegian Institute of International Affairs helped me to get in touch with university people in Bishkek, and Steinar Dyrnes, *Aftenposten's* correspondent in Moscow, also gave me sound advice and good contacts in the region. The entomologist Lars Ove Hansen was kind enough to read through the chapter on silk production and help me with the facts.

Sadly, for their own safety, I cannot name any of my helpers in Uzbekistan or Turkmenistan. And for the same reason, many of the Turkmen and Uzbek people who appear in the book are not called by their real names.

Heartfelt thanks are also due to Free Word and the Norwegian Non-Fiction Writers and Translators Association for their financial support. Without it, this book could not have been written.

Ivar Dale, the Norwegian Helsinki Committee representative in Central Asia, gave me so much good advice that I eventually asked if he would be a consultant for the book. I am very glad that he said yes. His sharp eye and well-founded contributions have been of enormous help. Thank you so much!

And last but not least, my thanks to Erik, who was always there, when I was out travelling and when I was at home writing. As always, he has given me encouragement and good food along the way, as well as linguistic and literary advice.

NOTES

i   Quotation from Catherine A. Fitzpatrick's article WikiLeaks News Flash: "Turkmen Leader is a Micromanager", published on: www.eurasianet.org on 5 December 2010 (http://www.eurasiant.org/node/62507).

ii Jack Weatherford: *Genghis Khan and the Making of the Modern World*. New York: Broadway Books, 2004, p. 106.

iii Quoted in Dilip Hiro: *Inside Central Asia. A Political and Cultural History of Uzbekistan, Turkmenistan, Kazakhstan, Kyrgyzstan, Tajikistan, Turkey and Iran*. New York, Overlook Duckworth, 2009.

iv All quotations regarding Andrei Sakharov are taken from his *Memoirs*. London, Hutchinson, 1990.

v   Quotation is from p.13 of Christopher Robbins' book, *In Search of Kazakhstan. The Land that Disappeared*. London, Profile Books Ltd, 2008.

vi Peter Hopkirk's excellent book, *The Great Game. On Secret Service in High Asia*, 2006 [1990], has been the most important single source for this chapter.

vii Quotation taken from Kathleen Hopkirk's book, *Central Asia through Writers' Eyes*. London: Eland Publishing Ltd, 2013.

viii Kari Dickson's translation of Erika Fatland's translation from Walter G. Moss: *A History of Russia, Volume I: To 1917*. London: Anthem Press, 2002 (2nd edition).

ix Quotations taken from *The Travels of Marco Polo, Book 1*, translated by Henry Yule.

x   Quotation from Robert Middleton and Huw Thomas, *Tajikistan and the High Pamirs. A Companion and Guide*. New York: Odyssey Books & Guides, 2012.

xi Ryszard Kapuściński: *Imperium*, London: Granta Books, 1994.

xii The Norwegian Helsinki Committee: *A Chronicle of Violence. The Events in the South of Kyrgyzstan in June 2010 (Osh Region)*. Report 2/2012, p. 59.

xiii   Quotation from article by Alisher Sidkov and Deana Kjuka, "Karimov: Uzbek Migrants are 'Lazy', Beggars don't exist", published on Radio Free Europe Radio Liberty's website: www.rferl.org on 26 June 2013.

xiv   Dzhalilov, *Iz istorii kulturnoy zihzni tadzhikskogo naroda*, 38, quoted in S. Frederick Starr, "Lost Enlightenment. Central Asia's Golden Age from the Arab Conquest to Tamerlane". Princeton University Press, 2012.

xv   Quotation from article by Natalia Antelava, "Gulnara Karimova: How do you solve a problem like Googoosha?", BBC News Magazine, 16 January 2014.

xvi   Quotation from article, "Uzbekistan's Lola Karimova-Tillyaeva reveals rift in first family", on BBC News on 27 September 2013.

BIBLIOGRAPHY

To maintain the flow of the text, I have only given sources when I have used a direct quotation. The following is an overview of the books I found useful when working on my book.

Abazov, Rafis: *The Palgrave Concise Historical Atlas of Central Asia*. New York: Palgrave Macmillan, 2008.

Adams, Laura L.: *The Spectacular State. Culture and National Identity in Uzbekistan*. Durham, N.C.: Duke University Press, 2010.

Aitken, Jonathan: *Nazarbayev and the Making of Kazakhstan*. London: Continuum, 2009.

Alexander, Christopher Aslan: *A Carpet Ride to Khiva. Seven Years on the Silk Road*. London: Icon Books, 2010.

Applebaum, Anne: *Gulag. A History of the Soviet Camps*. New York: Doubleday, 2003.

Babanazarova, Marinika: *Igor Savitsky. Artist, Collector, Museum Founder*. London: Silk Road Publishing House, 2011.

Boyce, Mary: *Zoroastrians. Their Religious Beliefs and Practices*. London: Routledge, 2001 [1979].

Burnes, Alexander: *Travels into Bokhara. A Voyage up the Indus to Lahore and a Journey to Cabool, Tartary and Persia*. London: Eland Publishing, 2012 [1835].

Chambers, James: *Genghis Khan*. Stroud: Sutton Publishing, 1999.

Cooley, Alexander: *Great Games, Local Rules. The New Great Power Contest in Central Asia*. Oxford: Oxford University Press, 2012.

Cummings, Sally N.: *Understanding Central Asia. Politics and Contested Transformations*. London: Routledge, 2012.

Edgar, Adrienne Lynn: *Tribal Nation. The Making of Soviet Turkmenistan*. Princeton: Princeton University Press, 2004.

Golden, Peter B.: *Central Asia in World History*. Oxford: Oxford University Press, 2012.

Grousset, René: *L'empire des steppes*. Lausanne: Payot, 1970.

Hem, Mikal: *Kanskje kan jeg bli diktator. En håndbok.* Oslo: Pax Forlag, 2012.

Hiro, Dilip: *Inside Central Asia. A Political and Cultural History of Uzbekistan, Turkmenistan, Kazakhstan, Kyrgyzstan, Tajikistan, Turkey and Iran.* New York: Overlook Duckworth, 2009.

Hopkirk, Kathleen: *Central Asia through Writers' Eyes.* London: Eland Publishing, 1993.

Hopkirk, Peter: *Setting the East Ablaze. Lenin's Dream of an Empire in Asia.* London: John Murray, 1984.

Hopkirk, Peter: *The Great Game. On Secret Service in High Asia.* London: John Murray, 2006 [1990].

Kapuściński, Ryszard: *Imperium.* New York: Vintage International, 1994.

Khalid, Adeeb: *Islam after Communism. Religion and Politics in Central Asia.* Berkeley: University of California Press, 2007.

Kipling, Rudyard: *Kim.* New York: Dover Publications, 2005 [1901].

Kjetsaa, Geir: *Fjordor Dostojevskij – et dikterliv.* Oslo: Gyldendal, 1985.

Laurelle, Marlène and Peyrouse, Sébastien: *The Chinese Question in Central Asia. Domestic Order, Social Change and the Chinese Factor.* New York: Columbia University Press, 2012.

Lipovsky, Igor P.: *Central Asia. In Search of a New Identity.* Self-published, ISBN 978-1478303398, 2012.

Liu, Morgan Y.: *Under Solomon's Throne. Uzbek Visions of Renewal in Osh.* Pittsburgh: University of Pittsburgh Press, 2012.

Liu, Xinru: *The Silk Road in World History.* Oxford: Oxford University Press, 2010.

Malashenko, Alexey: *The Fight for Influence. Russia in Central Asia.* Washington D.C.: Carnegie Endowment for International Peace, 2013.

Markowitz, Lawrence P.: *State Erosion. Unlootable Resources and Unruly Elites in Central Asia.* Ithaca and London: Cornell University Press, 2013.

Middleton, Robert and Thomas, Huw: *Tajikistan and the High Pamirs. A Companion and Guide.* New York: Odyssey Books & Maps, 2012.

Moss, Walter G.: *A History of Russia. Volume I: To 1917.* London: Anthem Press, 2003 (2nd edition).

Moss, Walter G.: *A History of Russia. Volume II: Since 1855.* London: Anthem Press, 2004 (2nd edition).

Murray, Craig: *Murder in Samarkand. A British Ambassador's Controversial Defiance of Tyranny in the War on Terror.* Edinburgh: Mainstream Publishing, 2006.

O'Clery, Conor: *Moscow, December 25, 1991. The Last Day of the Soviet Union.* New York: Public Affairs, 2012.

Olcott, Martha Brill: *Tajikistan's Difficult Development Path.* Washington D.C.: Carnegie Endowment for International Peace, 2012.

Peyrouse, Sébastien: *Turkmenistan. Strategies of Power, Dilemmas of Development.* Armonk, N.Y.: M. E. Sharpe, 2012.

Pringle, Peter: *The Murder of Nikolai Vavilov. The Story of Stalin's Persecution of One of the Great Scientists of the Twentieth Century.* New York: Simon & Schuster, 2008.

Rall, Ted: *Silk Road to Ruin. Why Central Asia is the Next Middle East.* New York: NBM Publishing, 2004 (2nd edition).

Reeves, Madeleine: *Border Work. Spatial Lives of the State in Rural Central Asia.* Ithaca and London: Cornell University Press, 2014.

Robbins, Christopher: *In Search of Kazakhstan. The Land that Disappeared.* London: Profile Books, 2007.

Sakharov, Andrei: *Memoirs.* London: Hutchinson, 1990.

Shayakhmetov, Mukhamet: *The Silent Steppe. The Memoir of a Kazakh Nomad Under Stalin.* New York: Overlook/Rookery, 2006.

Shishkin, Philip: *Restless Valley. Revolution, Murder and Intrigue in the Heart of Central Asia.* New Haven: Yale University Press, 2013.

Solzhenitsyn, Aleksandr: *The Gulag Archipelago.* London: Collins and Harvill Press, 1974.

Starr, S. Frederick: *Lost Enlightenment. Central Asia's Golden Age from the Arab Conquest to Tamerlane.* Princeton: Princeton University Press, 2013.

Thubron, Colin: *Shadow of the Silk Road.* London: Chatto & Windus, 2006.

Turkmenbashy, Saparmyrat: *Rukhnama. Reflections on the Spiritual Values of Turkmenistan.* Ashgabat: Ashgabat State Publishing Service, 2005.

Weatherford, Jack: *Genghis Khan and the Making of the Modern World.* New York: Broadway Books, 2004.